Techniques of Archaeological Excavation

'We owe the dead nothing but the truth'
Voltaire, *Letters on Oedipus*

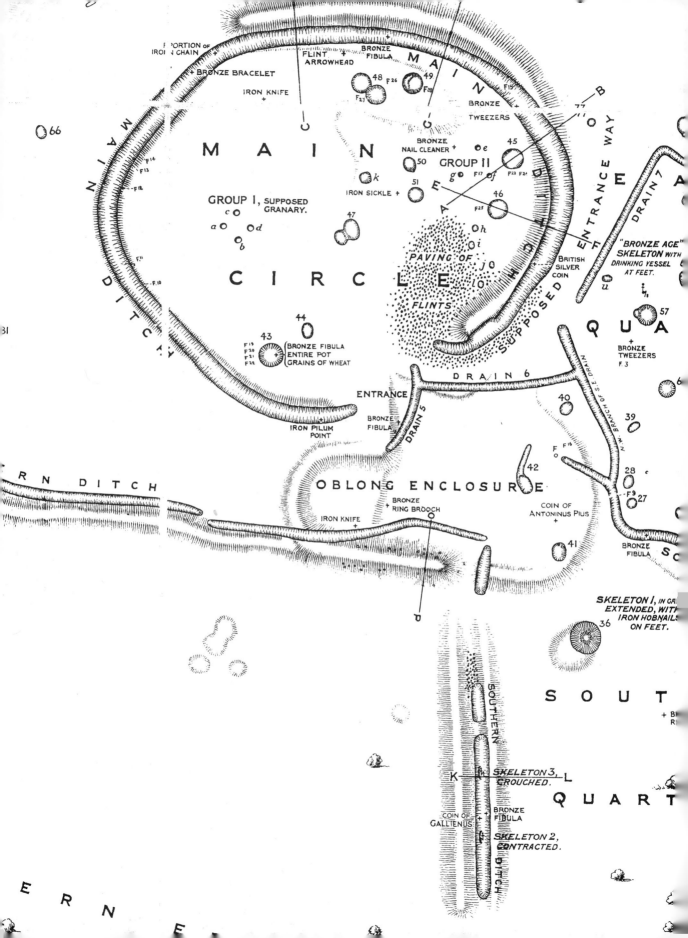

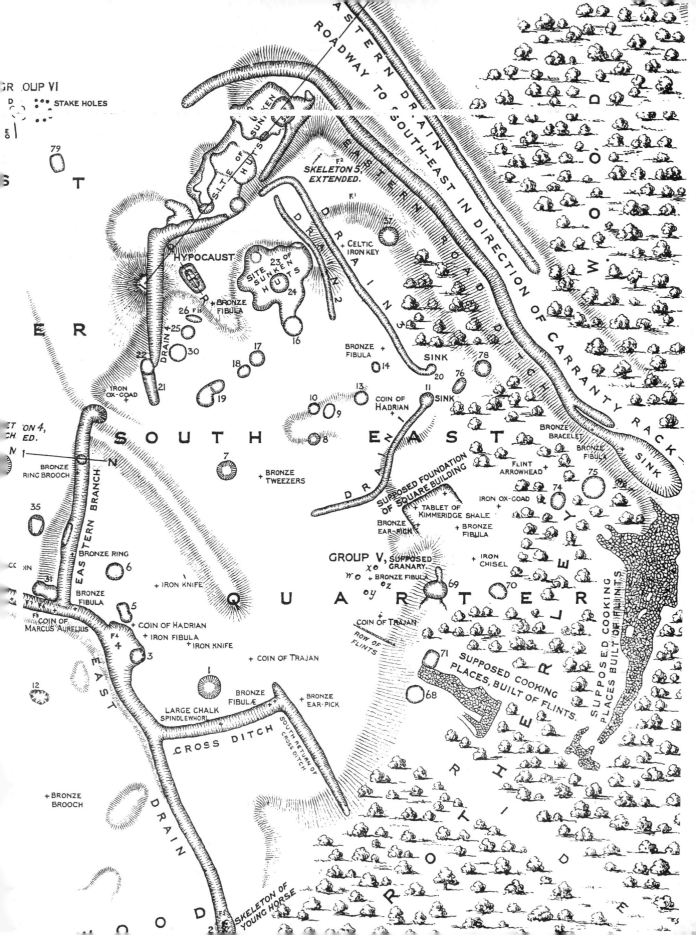

Techniques of
ARCHAEOLOGICAL EXCAVATION

Third edition

Philip Barker

B.T. Batsford Ltd • London

Acknowledgements

Thanks are still due to all those many colleagues and friends who contributed towards the first two editions of *Techniques of Archaeological Excavation* and to *Understanding Archaeological Excavation*, since these form the basis for this new book.

In addition, I must also thank Heather Bird for Figs 2, 3, 4 and 74; Philip Rahtz for Figs 15 and 30; Peter Barker of Stratascan for Figs 18, 21 and 28; GeoQuest Associates for Fig. 19; English Heritage for Fig. 23; Simon Buteux and the Birmingham University Field Archaeology Unit and Shropshire County Council for the section on the Wroxeter Hinterland Project; Dominic Powlesland for the section on the Heslerton Parish Project; Hereford and Worcester County Council Archaeology Section for Figs 62 and 82; Tony Wilmot for the section on the Birdoswald Excavation; Ed Harris for Fig. 80; Roger White for the section on the Bread Oven from Wroxeter; Richard Selby for the section on Geophysical Information Systems and Peter Scholefield for Fig. 84.

To all who have dug with me

First published 1977
Second impression 1979
New edition 1982
Reprinted 1987
New edition 1993
© Philip Barker 1977, 1982, 1993
Reprinted 1995

Produced for B.T. Batsford Ltd by
Chase Production Services, Chipping Norton
Printed in the EC by the Bath Press

Published by B.T. Batsford Ltd
4 Fitzhardinge Street, London W1H 0AH

A CIP catalogue record for this book is available from the British Library

ISBN 0 7134 7169 7

Contents

Illustrations

Preface to the First Edition

A number of good introductory books on the practicalities of excavation have been published in Britain since the war. Earliest of these was R.J.C. Atkinson's *Field Archaeology*, 1948, 2nd edition 1953, for long the standard primer. Sir Mortimer Wheeler's *Archaeology from the Earth*, 1954, while not setting out to be a handbook, contains much sound advice. Graham Webster's *Practical Archaeology* followed in 1963 (2nd revised edition 1970) and in its turn became the standard textbook. (Dame) Kathleen Kenyon's *Beginning in Archaeology*, 1964, is a useful guide to those wishing to take up the discipline, though job opportunities have changed a good deal in the last twenty years. John Alexander's *The Directing of Archaeological Excavations*, 1970, takes a world view and a specially problem-oriented stand. John Coles' *Field Archaeology in Britain*, 1972, is principally confined to prehistoric archaeology, but contains much that is relevant to all periods of excavation. David Browne's *Teach Yourself Archaeology*, 1975, is the most recent handbook and contains the fruits of the author's acquaintance with the 'New Archaeology'. In America, Heizer and Graham published *A Guide to Field Methods in Archaeology*, 1967, which, though somewhat old-fashioned, has sections which are relevant to European archaeology.

This book does not seek to repeat the advice and information given in these earlier publications and it is assumed that the reader will become acquainted with them. Today, no one book can embrace all the complexities of even a short excavation, and the would-be director or supervisor needs a small shelf-full of reference works. The most essential of these are noted throughout the text and in the bibliography.

The simpler pieces of advice given here may seem too obvious to be worth repeating. However, I believe that many excavators get into difficulties because they ignore some of the basic precepts, such as keeping excavated surfaces meticulously clean, or measuring always in the horizontal plane. Other practical hints are included because they help the excavation to run faster, or more smoothly and economically and thus increase its effectiveness in time and labour.

Inevitably, the book has a somewhat auto-biographical air, since I believe that it is more valuable to speak from first-hand experience when this is relevant than to try to preserve a colourless neutrality. I hope that readers will forgive the repetition of examples from sites which I have either dug or with which I have been involved.

1977

Preface to the Second Edition

In the five years since the first edition of this book was written field archaeology in Britain has changed perceptibly. Excavation has become concentrated more and more in the major units, both urban and regional, and it is from these that the principle advances in techniques have stemmed. The recent reductions, in real terms, of government and local authority finance have led to fewer excavations (often, however, on a larger scale) rather than a multiplicity of small ones. This lack of resources has led, beneficially, to a sharpening of the arguments for and against excavation, to the discussion of sampling strategies and to closer long-term co-operation between archaeologists and planning departments, in order that the most effective use shall be made of what money there is.

At the same time, the number of excavations directed by amateurs has declined, due principally to their recognition of the expense and complexity of effective excavation even on a small scale, and the inadequacy of excavation not backed up by laboratory facilities, the proper conservation and storage of finds, and the funds (and time) necessary for post-excavation analysis and publication. Increased professionalism results in higher standards of excavation, analysis and synthesis, but runs the risk that field archaeology, and particularly excavation, will become more and more remote from the experience of the interested layman (as it is already in most European countries).

Happily, many amateurs are willing to work under professional direction, and particularly to carry out or take part in field surveys, so that the link between the highly specialized major excavation and the historic base of British archaeology, the dedicated amateur, is still maintained.

A recent book central to the subject of excavation recording is Edward Harris' *Principles of Archaeological Stratigraphy*, 1979, while there is a number of important papers, among them, J.S. Jeffries, *Excavation Records, Techniques in use by the Central Excavation Unit*, 1977; *The Scientific Treatment of Material from Rescue Excavations*, D.O.E., 1978; P.J. Fasham, *et al.*, *Fieldwalking for Archaeologists*, 1980, and the essays in the section 'Strategies for sampling Infra-Site Variability' in J.F. Cherry *et al.*, *Sampling in Contemporary British Archaeology*, 1978.

The most important statement on excavation techniques made since the publication of the first edition of this book will be found in Chapter 2 of Brian Hope-Taylor's *Yeavering*, HMSO, 1977, pp. 31–45. If this report had not been delayed, but had been published ten years earlier, the art of excavation would have been immeasurably advanced and the present book scarcely needed.

This second edition has benefited from discussions of the first with many friends and colleagues. I am grateful to them all.

Worcester 1982

Preface to the Third Edition

In the ten years since the publication of the second edition of this book there have been rapid and profound changes in the organization and practice of archaeology in Britain. These include: the influence of Government policies on the way archaeology is seen by developers, leading to the publication of PPG16 and competitive tendering; the creation of the Institute of Field Archaeologists in response to increasing professionalism, coupled with the need for some form of regulation and the setting of standards, both ethical and practical; the increased emphasis on pre-excavation assessment and the use of more sophisticated computerized geophysical surveys; and the very rapid development and use in archaeological units of information technology, together with a continuing debate on the forms which archaeological publication should take, have led to many debates, formal and informal, about all aspects of our discipline.

This third edition does not pretend to have kept up with every development in the field, least of all the scientific and mathematical advances which assist in the interpretation of the results of excavation, partly because, in such a rapidly evolving situation, many views and techniques are quickly superseded and the book would become obsolescent before its time. It does incorporate elements of another book, *Understanding Archaeological Excavation* (1986; now out of print), particularly some sequences of illustrations which elucidate graphically themes common to both books.

Nevertheless, I believe that there are ways in which excavation has changed little in the last ten or twenty years – I mean in the strategies and the actual processes of excavation. In spite of highly sophisticated technologies, the trowel, the brush and the shovel are still the basic excavation tools, and the diggers, the draughtsmen and women, the supervisors, surveyors and photographers are still the most powerful and subtle recorders and interpreters that we have, and it is they who will produce the new evidence for the past which will modify our view of history and of ourselves. It is to them that this book is dedicated.

Worcester 1993

1
Introduction: the Unrepeatable Experiment

Excavation recovers from the earth arch-aeological evidence obtainable in no other way. The soil is an historical document which, like a written record, must be deciphered, translated and interpreted before it can be used. For the very long prehistoric periods of human history excavation is almost the only source of information and for the proto-historic and historic periods it provides evidence where the documents are silent or missing. The more, therefore, that we can refine our methods and techniques the more valid will be the interpretations which we derive from our results.

This book does not pretend to be the Compleat Excavator. It does not describe the way to dig every variety of site on every kind of subsoil. But it is written as the result of hard thinking, in the field and at the drawing-board, about the inadequacies of our excavation techniques and the possible ways in which we might refine them. However, each refinement will produce more complicated evidence, which, in its turn, will bring greater difficulties of observation and recording, more data to be sorted, more intricacies to be interpreted and more detailed plans and sections to be published. Yet, however complex and detailed ex-cavations become, we must always keep the wholeness of archaeology in mind. Excavation is only a method of producing evidence about the past, a means to an end, akin to

surgery in that it is drastic, unlike surgery in that it is always destructive.

The whole of our landscape, rural and urban, is a vast historical document. On its surface has accumulated a continuous accre-tion of hundreds of thousands of small acts of change, both natural and human. The purpose of excavation is to sample the se-quence and effect of these surface changes at a chosen point. Such samples will, inevit-ably, always be very small since even the largest excavation covers only a tiny fraction of the landscape it studies. The point chosen will ideally be one which promises to give the maximum information about the things in which we are interested: periods of occu-pation, types of structure, burial practices, a social unit, past environments or, happily, all of these and more on one site.

Every archaeological site is itself a docu-ment. It can be read by a skilled excavator, but it is destroyed by the very process which enables us to read it. Unlike the study of an ancient document, the study of a site by excavation is an unrepeatable experiment. In almost every other scientific discipline, with the exception of the study of the human individual and other animals, it is possible to test the validity of an experiment by setting up an identical experiment and noting the results. Since no two archaeological sites are the same, either in the whole or in detail, it is never possible to verify conclusively the results of one excavation by another, even on part of the same site, except in the broadest terms, and sometimes not even in these.

In the case of an urban excavation it may be feasible to confirm a defensive sequence or the broad stratigraphy revealed on one site, by excavation on another nearby, as equally it may be possible, on a site in which a sequence of stone buildings has been preserved after excavation, to re-examine the evidence as one would a written document. But generally excavation is destruction and often total destruction. Our responsibility therefore is very great. If we misread our documents as we destroy them, the primary evidence we offer to those interested in the past will be wrong and those following us will be misled but will have no way of knowing it.

The excavator's task is to produce new evidence that is as free as possible from subjective distortions and to make it quickly and widely available to other specialists in a form which they can use with confidence in their own research. This, however, is not enough. There is an increasing number of people who take a highly intelligent interest in the past. To these, the results of excavations and the integration of these results into local, national and continental history must be presented in different, but equally valid, forms, such as museum displays, synoptic books, lectures, television and radio programmes.

One of the tasks of the historian and the archaeologist is to modify our view of the past by continual reconsideration of the evidence and, in the case of the archaeologist particularly, the production of new evidence. For the many thousands of years before the invention of writing and the first surviving documents, whether in stone or clay or papyrus, archaeological evidence is all we have. Increasingly in later centuries, docu-

mentary evidence must be married to the archaeological evidence, which is continually expanding in scope and complexity. By contrast, it is unlikely that there are many ancient manuscripts left to be discovered. Inscriptions will be dug up from time to time, some more Dead Sea scrolls may be found, and, like the Haydn Mass recently discovered in Ireland, a precious manuscript may be waiting to be revealed, but there is little doubt that, in the future, new information about the past will derive chiefly from archaeology and from fieldwork, and excavation in particular. The purpose of excavation is therefore to solve, or at least to throw light on, problems which can be studied in no other way, since there is an absolute limit to the amount one can learn from an archaeological site by looking at it, walking over it, surveying it, or photographing it from the air, just as there is a limit to the inferences which can be drawn from documentary references (where they exist) to archaeological sites. Only excavation can uncover a sequence of structures or recover stratified and secure dating evidence, or the mass of environmental or economic evidence which most sites contain.

The multiplicity of disciplines which go to make up modern archaeology combine to study every aspect of the lives of early peoples — their environment, their trade, their diet, the rise and fall of individual settlements and groups of settlements, their cultural affinities, the influences which shaped their buildings and their art — to look beyond the objects and the debris of everyday life to the thoughts that lay behind them, and the intentions that produced them. The chief function of the excavator is, therefore, to produce primary evidence of as high a quality as possible for the use of other archaeologists, historians, and all those whose interest lies in understanding the past.

This evidence, and the reasoned deductions

which can be drawn from it, using all the parallel evidence from other sources, documentary, linguistic, scientific, epigraphic or whatever, enables us by acts of sober imagination to recover fragmentary glimpses of the past, like clips from an old silent film, badly projected.

Slowly we are building up a fuller and more accurate edition of the film. It will never be complete, and like any film will always be subject to the distortions of cutting and editing, and the viewpoint not only of the director but of the audience. Our task is to minimize the distortions, to bring into focus the unclear images and to discern the converging patterns which over the last fifty millennia have brought us to the point where I write, and you read, this book.

2

How Archaeological Sites are Formed

It is much easier to understand the evidence recovered from excavations if we appreciate the ways in which archaeological sites are formed: how a castle becomes an earthwork, or a Roman town a field of corn; how a prehistoric village becomes a series of dark green lines seen only in the spring – though not every year; and how a modern city's past can be buried under tons of concrete yet still be recovered.

The surface of the earth is almost entirely covered by soil which derives from the underlying bedrock, be it sand, gravel, chalk, granite, clay or any other rock, hard or soft. The nature of the soil cover is determined, therefore, by the rock on which it lies, and this, combined with the drainage of the subsoil, will in turn determine the fertility of the soil, which, in its turn will influence the patterns of vegetation, of farming and of settlement.

Archaeological sites are merely the residues of settlements and structures, reduced to rubble and earthworks by decay, erosion, stone-robbing and the invasions of plant and animal life. Even in temperate Britain the 'jungle' returns with astonishing speed to an abandoned garden or neglected copse. Bombed sites in city centres were colonized within a few months, and there are places known to the writer where almost impenetrable woodland cloaks ruined cottages inhabited only half a century ago. Stone buildings, even deeply robbed ones, leave more evidence of their presence than wooden ones, which may be reduced to no more than a line of dark pits, or barely discernible discolorations of the soil, or concentrations of stones.

In order to interpret the evidence which we uncover, we need to understand as fully as possible what happens to a building when it is abandoned or is pulled down, and what happens to rubbish when it is thrown into a pit or spread as manure on the fields. We need to know how ditches and pits silt up and how banks and mounds erode, as well as something of the action of the soil on organic materials from leather and cloth to human bodies.

It is illuminating to observe what happens to a derelict building over a period of years, or the way in which plants invade an unused path, or a disused railway. Sometimes it is possible to find a recently abandoned settlement which is on its way to becoming an archaeological site and to observe the processes of regression at work. Because of the more intensive agriculture and redevelopment of the lowlands, such sites are more often found in hill country. One such is illustrated in Fig.1. The processes of destruction and decay which transform structures into the archaeological features which we excavate are perhaps best illustrated by simple examples which can, as it were, be multiplied up into

1a

1 a–e The way archaeological sites are formed.
At Blakemoorgate on the northern end of the ridge
known as the Stiper Stones in Shropshire, lies a
deserted settlement. The remains of houses and
outbuildings are contained within paddocks whose
layered hedges have grown into trees, and the drove
roads on each side of the site are overgrown with grass
and gorse.

Since the site was deserted gradually, eventually
leaving only one occupied farm, which was abandoned
in the 1950s, the whole process of collapse and decay
can be seen, from the empty farmhouse still with its
roof, *1a*, to a mound of stones and earth, *1e*, the site
of a desertion of perhaps a century ago. Such a site
deserves detailed survey repeated at intervals to chart
the processes of decay, and the recording of the
memories of people, still alive, who knew it, before it
goes back into the hillside.

1b

1c   1d

1e

the highly complex series of interrelated components which make up most archaeological sites. Some of the commonest features found on excavations are illustrated later in this chapter.

The other factor of major importance in the understanding of the formation of archaeological sites and their unravelling by excavation is the theory of stratification. This derives originally from the realization by geologists that those rock strata which lay uppermost were later in date than those which lay below them. In its simplest form it is easy to see that layers deposited on the bed of the sea are formed later than the rocks beneath or that a sheet of lava is later than the moutainside on which it lies. But the earth's surface is not static – rocks are thrust up through overlying layers; erosion removes upper layers, exposing the rocks beneath; sometimes gigantic folds seem to reverse the proper order. Yet in all these cases the sequence of events can be under-

stood – the intrusive rocks can be seen to be earlier, though the upheaval which caused them to become visible is later; the process of erosion is later than the rock it exposes and the folding which turns the layers upside down presents a stratification which might be misleading if it were not realized that folding had occurred.

It is the same with archaeological sites. This is most easily demonstrated by a series of superimposed floors, where it is obvious that the lower ones must be earlier. Similarly, if a roof collapses on to the uppermost floor, and the walls then fall in on top of the fallen roof, the sequence of events is again obvious and will be revealed when the layers are excavated in the reverse order to the sequence of events. The construction, abandonment and decay of a simple stone building are shown in Fig. 2, 1–9.

2 1–9 illustrates in simplified form the construction and decay of a small stone building.

In *1* a trench is dug to take the foundations. *1a* is a plan of the trench.

2 shows the completed building in the foundation. *2a* is a plan of this trench, which has been backfilled on the outside of the wall foundations.

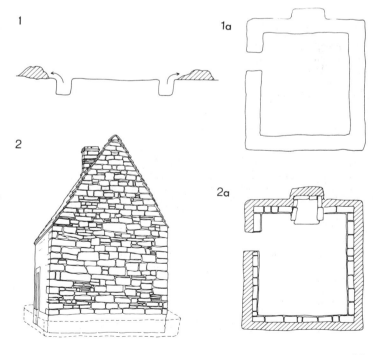

3 shows the building abandoned and losing its roof,
the tiles becoming scattered at the back of the building.
In *3a* the floor can be seen to be beginning to break up.

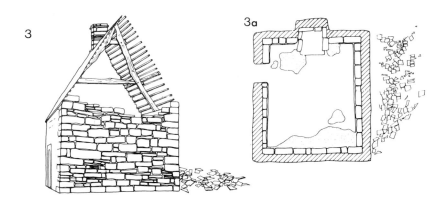

In *4* the process has accelerated, and in *5* stone robbers
have removed most of the stone and usable timber and
are burning the rest. The two plans *4a* and *5a* show
the development of what will eventually become
buried archaeology.

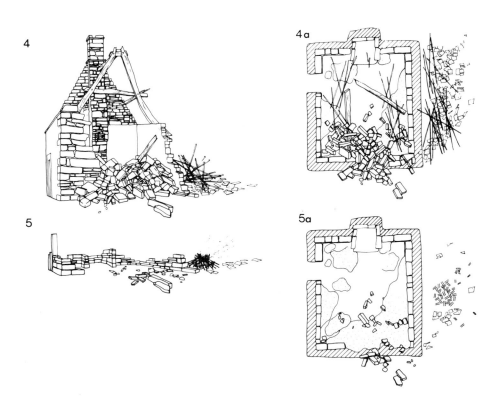

6

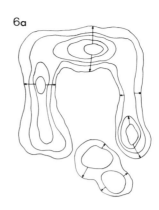

6 shows the site when the walls have become covered with soil and grass.
6a is a conjectured contour survey of this phase.

7 is a section through this phase, showing the buried walls; 8 is a section after the walls have been dug out for their stone.

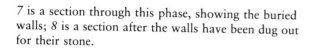

7

8

9 is a section when the robber trenches have become filled up and the site is barely visible on the surface.
9a shows the plan of what would be found if the site were then excavated.

9

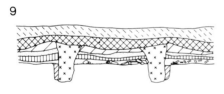

9a

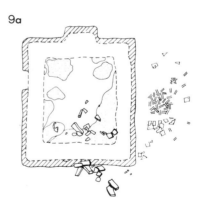

These examples could be extended to cover every possible situation met with on an archaeological site. Stratification can be defined, therefore, as any number of relatable deposits of archaeological strata (from a stake-hole to the floor of a cathedral) which are the result of 'successive operations of either nature or mankind' (Harris 1975, 100). Stratigraphy, on the other hand 'is the study of archaeological strata . . . with a view to arranging them in a chronological sequence' (Harris, *ibid.*).

How post-holes are formed

Many timber buildings are based on posts set into the ground (rather than standing on the surface – see Figs 3–6). In the majority of cases, a pit is dug to the required depth and the post inserted (Fig. 3); the post is sometimes set against the side wall of the pit, sometimes centrally. In either case the remaining space in the pit is backfilled with the earth taken out of it, or with stones or rocks. When the building is abandoned the post can disappear in a number of different ways:

1 It can be removed. In this case it may be possible to see that it has been rocked backwards and forwards in order to loosen it to make removal easier. The hole thus left may be deliberately backfilled with earth in order, perhaps, to remove a hazard, or it may simply be left to fill up naturally. It should be possible for the excavator to tell the difference. The deliberate filling is likely to be coarser and contain stones, and perhaps pottery or other artefacts, rather than fine silty material which has been carried by rain or wind or worm action. However, as with all the examples given here, each case will depend on factors which must be assessed on site. For example, post-holes cut in sand will have a filling which is likely itself to be sandy, whether it is deliberately or naturally filled, and in addition, very difficult to distinguish – as the excavator of the Anglo-Saxon halls at Yeavering said: 'The general distinction (between the post-hole and its filling) may best be made by calling the colour of the subsoil a very pale greyish-yellow and that of the fillings a pale yellowish-grey' (Hope-Taylor 1977, 29).

2 It may be sawn off at ground level or simply left to rot. It may be difficult to distinguish between these two, since in both cases the stump will be left in the ground.

This will gradually be invaded by insects, moulds and bacteria, and will eventually be replaced by humic soil. This will normally be easily distinguished from the surrounding layers, since it tends to be darker and damper (as the humus retains moisture). Because the wood tends to rot from the top the post-hole filling often becomes darker with depth, as the humus sinks and the upper part fills with earth. This is important since post-holes may not always be seen at the original ground surface, but only picked up as the excavation proceeds downward. This, in turn, may lead to the post-hole being assumed to belong to a lower layer than it really does, so that it will then mistakenly be assigned to an earlier period in the site's history.

3 and 4 show some of the ways in which post-holes, as found on excavations, are formed. 3 shows the post structures in section and 4 (overleaf) shows the same features in plan.

3.1

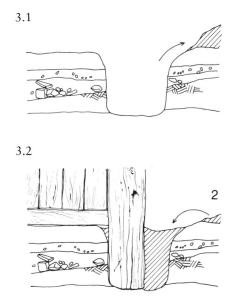

3.2

In *3.1* a pit has been dug to take the post, and in *3.2* the post has been inserted as part of the building and the remainder of the pit backfilled. This is the way in which countless washing-line posts and telegraph poles have been erected.

3 It may be burnt. In this case, the rim of the post-hole will often be charred or burnt red. The stump of the post may have burnt freely in the open air, but below ground, where there is less air, it will tend to be turned to charcoal. This charcoal may well be datable by radiocarbon analysis.

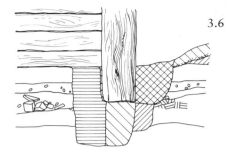

3.6

In *3.3* it has been assumed that the post has rotted *in situ*. This rotting usually occurs at ground level, for the reasons outlined on p. 22.

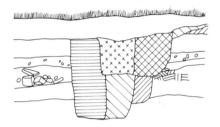

3.7

3.3

3.4

4 The post may have been set in water-logged ground, as in a marsh, or may have become waterlogged due to a rising water table. Sometimes only the bottom of the post, if it is set in stiff clay, for example, will be waterlogged. In all these cases, the timber will tend to be preserved due to the fact that decay is inhibited by the lack of air. Clearly, waterlogged sites provide tangible evidence of timber structures and help to interpret those sites where only ghosts of timbers, in the form of post-holes are left. (For an excellent example, see Der Hüsterknupp in Higham and Barker 1992, p. 271.)

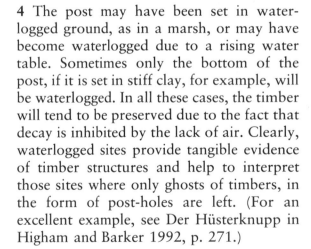

A distinction must be made between the post-hole (or post-pipe) and the pit in which it is set – the post-pit. This is sometimes very difficult to distinguish in the ground, since the post-pit is often backfilled immediately with the material which has just been dug out of it. One of the skills which the excavator needs is to be able to distinguish

3.5

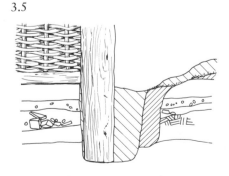

4.3 shows the pit with the remains of the post in plan. This is one of the commonest features on sites which contained timber buildings. In *4.4* it is supposed that the building burnt down. In this case the top of the post-hole is full of charcoal; in other cases there will be only a trace around the edge of the post-hole which may be reddened or charred. The remains of the post which are left in the ground may be dug out so that the post can be replaced, or the post may simply be left to rot. In the latter case, the wood is eventually replaced by soil, due to the actions of micro-organisms, fungi and other agents of decay, and of earthworms and insects, which transport soil into the vacant spaces left by the rotting timber. If the ground is waterlogged, however, the remains of the post may be preserved, due to the fact that, under these conditions (which are known as anaerobic, because of the lack of air) micro-organisms and other agents of decay cannot exist, and so the decaying process is stopped or considerably retarded.

If the post-stub is dug out it usually happens that the new hole is not the same size as the first, and it then becomes clear, on excavation, that the hole has been re-dug (*4.5* and *4.7*). The process of renewing posts in the same place can be repeated many times – some hillfort gateways have had as many as fifteen replaced posts, detectable to the excavator because they have been replaced in slightly different positions each time.

3.7 shows a notional section of a series of post-holes and pits which might be found if a post had been replaced twice. The plan view is seen in *4.7*. It will be seen that, if the posts have been replaced many more times than this, a very complicated situation will be created in the ground – one which requires a great deal of skill in digging and interpretation.

4.1

4.2

4.3

4.4

4.5

4.6

4.7

5 A vertical stereoscopic view of a post-hole. The post-pit, which is oval, can be seen packed with stones placed to support the round post which was placed in one corner of the pit. The post-pit is 70cm (28in) across its greatest width and the post-hole (and therefore the post) is 20cm (8in) in diameter. This pair of pictures has been placed so that they can be viewed stereoscopically with a hand viewer. (Photo: Sidney Renow.)

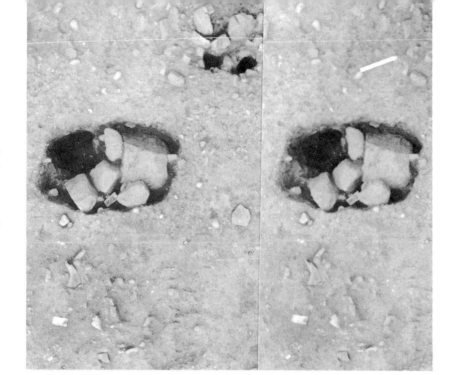

6 Most post-holes are formed by the posts rotting in their holes. *6a*, *b* and *c* show two spectacular posts and the beginnings of their decline into nothing more than vegetable mould filling two large holes in the ground. It will be appreciated how impossible it would be to imagine what the totems were like simply on the basis of their post-holes – a good exampe of the limitations of archaeological evidence.

6a was taken in 1901, when the poles were probably only 30 or 40 years old. The carving on the nearest pole represents a killer whale and the protruding plank of wood is its dorsal fin. It can be seen that plants are already growing on the ledge of the mortuary niche.

between disturbed and undisturbed soil – to notice the way in which the stones in it lie, or the very slight changes in colour and texture brought about by the fact that disturbance loosens the structure of the soil and often makes it slightly darker, perhaps because it becomes mixed with small amounts of humus, perhaps because it is slightly more aerated, and the iron salts in it become oxidized. At Hen Domen, Montgomery, the undisturbed boulder clay is slightly paler and yellower, rather than ochrous, compared with the disturbed clay of post-pits (Barker and Higham 1982). Sometimes the distinction between the post-pit and the subsoil can only be felt with the trowel, where, though the difference is not visible, the texture changes and can be detected.

Sometimes it is possible to distinguish between two or more groups of post-holes on the basis of their filling. To take a simple example – the post-pits belonging to the first buildings put up on the site will be filled with clean earth; subsequent buildings will contain a proportion of recognizable debris from the occupation which preceded their digging. (See a good example from the excavation at Yeavering – Hope Taylor 1977, Fig. 1 and pp. 42–5.)

6b was taken in 1948. The dorsal fin has been lost. Sitka spruce are growing in both mortuary niches.

The photographs of the totem poles were taken in 1901, 1948 and 1971 respectively. The poles belong to the Kunghit Haida people of Ninstits Village on Anthony Island in British Columbia. This is the largest and best preserved collection of *in situ* totem poles in the world. The two illustrated here are mortuary poles, with a niche for the remains of the deceased at the top. The village was abandoned in the 1880s and the age of the poles is thought to be between 130 and 140 years. They are situated on the shoreline, with a dense Sitka spruce forest behind them. Because of photographs taken from time to time by visitors (often on the removal of some of the remaining poles to museums) the deterioration and eventual collapse of these fine wooden monuments can be monitored.

In the course of the years the forest has moved forward to engulf the poles. In the niches of the graveposts, on the exposed ledges of the sculptured surface and at the base of the poles, seeds, leaves and bird droppings accumulated and retained enough moisture to support the growth of plants and other organisms, including seedling spruces, fungi and bacteria. Eventually, it was the weight of the spruce trees growing in the mortuary niches which caused the poles to snap at ground level and to become uprooted, rather than decay at the base, though the humus and moisture on the poles has accelerated the decay of the wood by micro-organisms (fungi and bacteria). Shrubs and grasses growing at the bases of the poles produced optimal conditions (moist and shade) for bacteria and soft rot fungi on the wood. Once a pole falls to the ground it rots very quickly.

6c was taken in 1971. Both poles have fallen. Eventually all that will be left will be two large postholes. (Photos courtesy of the British Columbia Provincial Museum, Victoria, British Columbia).

Ditches

Defensive ditches and drainage ditches are very common on sites of all kinds and periods, and some general rules apply to their understanding. To take defensive ditches first – the spoil from the ditch digging is usually thrown up on the inside to form a rampart if the ditch surrounds the site, or on the side to be defended if the ditch is linear, like Wansdyke or Offa's Dyke. Most dry ditches are V-shaped, though ditches which are intended to be waterfilled, such as those around moated sites, are usually flat-bottomed. The ditch starts to silt up almost as soon as it is dug. The first shower of rain will erode the sides and bring down fine runnels of soil to the bottom, and, more importantly, the loose earth and stones on the edge of the new rampart will fall back into the ditch. This earliest filling is known as the 'primary silt'. Thereafter, the silting of the ditch will depend on a number of factors: the soil in which the ditch has been cut (there will clearly be a great difference between the speed of silting of a ditch cut in sand and one cut in boulder clay or rock); the steepness of the original sides; the rapidity with which the surfaces are consolidated with vegetation and whether the ditch is dry or waterfilled.

If the ditch is accompanied by a bank or rampart, it follows that there will be more silting on the rampart side than on the open side (see Fig. 7). Even in cases where the rampart has been completely ploughed away it is nevertheless often possible to postulate its former existence by the greater quantity of silting on that side (Fig. 7.7).

7 1–7 illustrate the digging and redigging of a typical bank and ditch. In *7.1* the ditch d1 has been cut through five layers, the topsoil (vertically shaded) and four underlying layers of undisturbed subsoil. Part of the topsoil has been thrown up on the outside (the undefended side) of the ditch to form a small counterscarp bank c-s b. Turf and topsoil have also been thrown up on the inside to form a marking-out bank, m-o b. These two slight banks mark out the size of the ditch to be dug by the ditch-digging labourers, who then throw the material up to form the bank. Though shown rather simplistically in the drawing, the layers will tend to be deposited on the bank in the reverse order from that in which they lay in the ground (reversed stratigraphy).

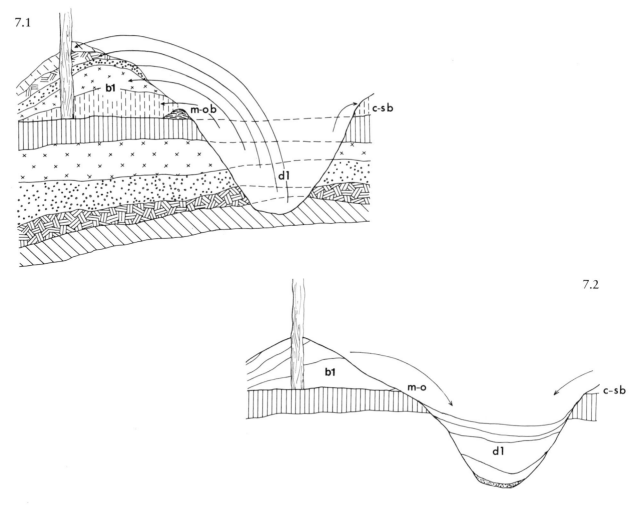

7.1

7.2

7.3

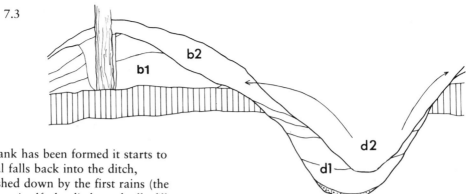

Immediately the bank has been formed it starts to erode. Loose material falls back into the ditch, followed by silts washed down by the first rains (the primary silting). Left to itself, the ditch gradually fills up, while the bank is denuded, and becomes lower and less steep-sided. The point may come where the bank and ditch have lost their defensive capability, and the ditch is then recut to deepen it while using the material to heighten or reinforce the bank (7.3). It very often happens that the recut is shallower than the original ditch. If this happens, the layers forming the earliest silting of the first ditch are preserved (d1 in 7.3).

Bank 2 erodes in its turn, and fills the bottom of ditch 2 (7.4). This in turn, may be recut, forming ditch and bank b3 (7.5). Bank 3 erodes in its turn and fills ditch d3 (7.6). Eventually when the site is abandoned, the whole may be ploughed, but, nevertheless, under the ploughsoil the evidence remains of the three

ditches and, at least by inference, their banks (3 having been completely ploughed away) (7.7). Of course, it is possible that the last recutting of the ditch might be deeper than all the others, removing the whole of the evidence we have been discussing. If the banks have all been ploughed away as well, there is no way that the real sequence of events can be reconstructed. This applies to all excavations – if the evidence is simply not there we shall be unaware of whole periods or phases in the life of the site.

7.4

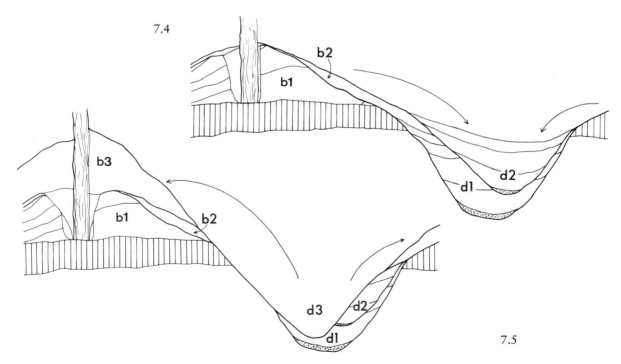

7.5

29

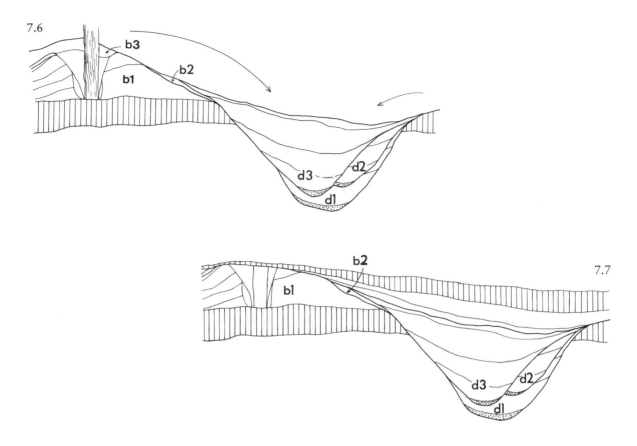

To the natural erosion of the banks and the silting of the ditch must be added the accidental filling which will occur if the defensive site is slighted or destroyed, when rampart material is likely to collapse into the ditch. Sometimes, also, ditches are filled deliberately, either to deny their use to an enemy (a common practice in Roman times) or to bring an abandoned site back into agricultural use. It is usually, though not always, possible to tell whether a layer has been thrown into the ditch deliberately or has silted naturally due to weathering – the deliberate filling is likely to be in the form of clods or unsorted stones, though here again, if the ditch is filled in dry weather, the stones contained in the soil will sort themselves naturally on the way down, as any one who has ever backfilled a hole will know.

The reading of ditch sections is, however, complicated by the fact that ditches are very often recut, sometimes almost to their original depth, at other times quite shallowly, in order to maintain their defensive effectiveness. When this has happenend, the recuts can usually be distinguished by the fact that they cut across the lines of the normal silting and filling. Fig. 8 1–5 illustrates this.

Drainage ditches are, by definition, meant to carry water, and so they will silt up due to material carried down after rain, both from their sides and along their length. One effect of this is that small objects may be carried a considerable distance down the drain, far from the place in which they were dropped, so that deductions about the buildings or settlements near the ditch may be mistaken.

8 1–5 Three sections of the motte ditch at Hen Domen cut within a length of 20m (66ft). As will be seen, each section is different so that only correlation of all the sections produces a reliable picture.

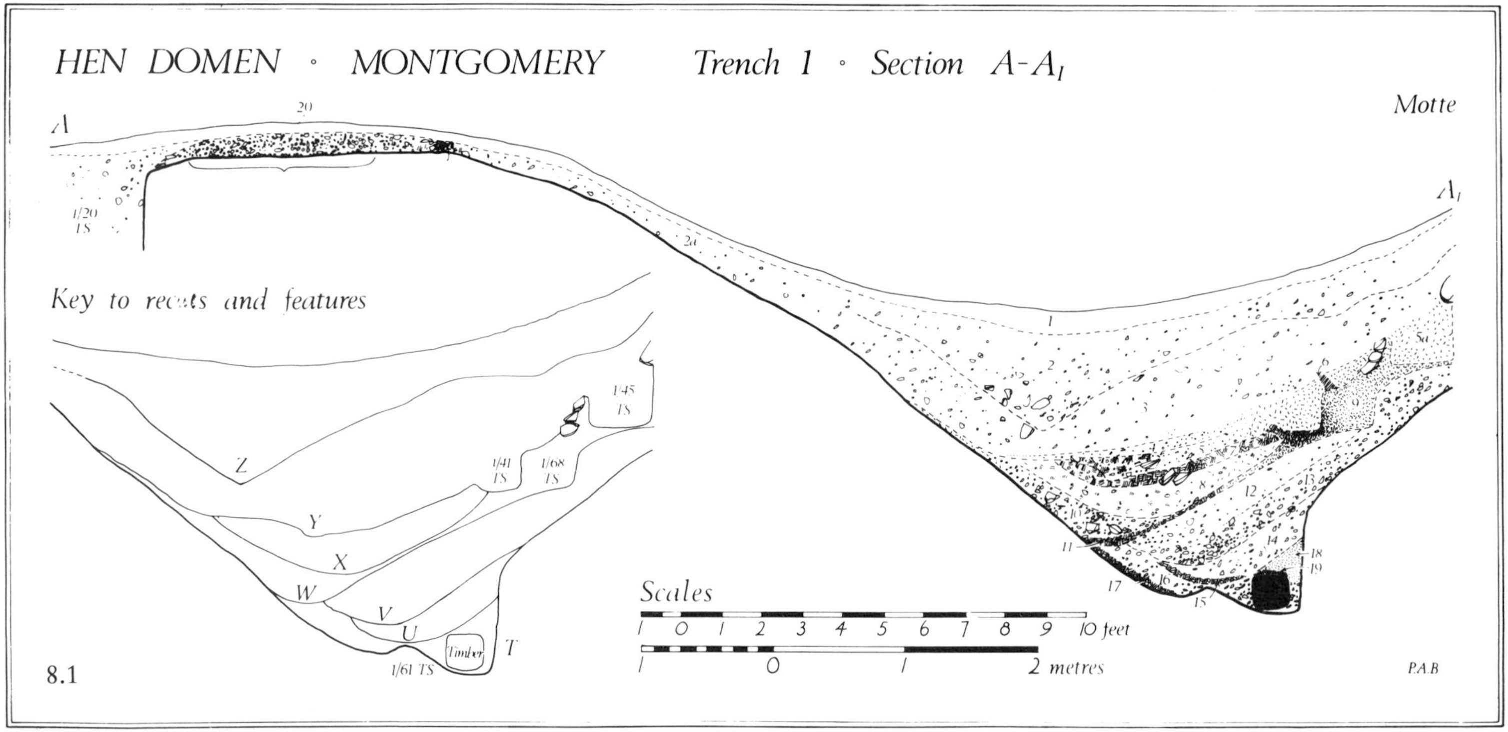

HEN DOMEN · MONTGOMERY   Trench 1 · Section A-A₁

Key to recuts and features

Scales

Motte

8.1

PAB

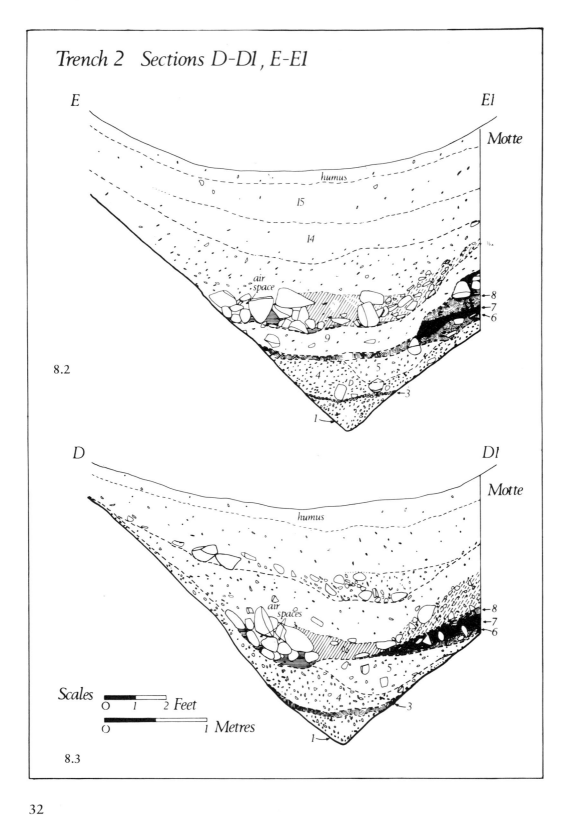

Trench 2 Sections D-D1, E-E1

E ... E1
Motte
humus
15
14
air space
8
7
6
9
4 5
3
1
8.2

D ... D1
Motte
humus
8
air spaces
7
6
5
4
3
1
Scales
0 1 2 Feet
0 1 Metres
8.3

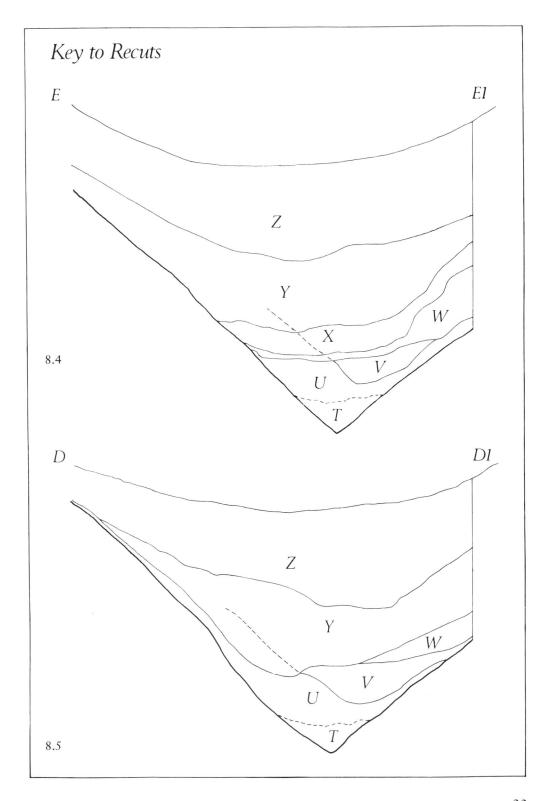

Ramparts

Ramparts are usually formed from the spoil upcast from the ditch which goes with them. In many cases, therefore, the size of the rampart is determined by the size of the ditch. Since, except in the case of linear earthworks, such as Offa's Dyke, defensive ditches are usually used to form enclosures, the circumference of the rampart inside the ditch will be a good deal less than that of the ditch itself, so that the rampart can be correspondingly higher than the depth of the ditch.

From the archaeological point of view, the layers within a rampart will tend to be inverted from those that the ditch has been dug through. Often, the topsoil or plough-soil will have been stripped off and placed on the surface of the topsoil along the line of the intended rampart, to form a marking-out bank. As the ditch-diggers dig through the layers of subsoil they will throw them up on top of one another (see Fig. 7). Things are rarely as simple as that, of course; for example, the sequence may be complicated by the fact that the palisade and rampart are built simultaneously, the rampart material being piled round the palisade post from the ground up.

Sometimes it is possible to detect gang-work in the building of ramparts, where different lengths are built separately, as Sir Cyril Fox suggested in the construction of Offa's Dyke (Fox 1955, 89, 121–2, 153, etc). At Hen Domen, Montgomery it was possible to see that the rampart had been piled from west to east in overlapping mounds of clay (Barker and Higham, 1982, Fig. 17, section g–e).

Mounds

The construction of mounds may vary from a motte or barrow of simple dump construction to a highly complex series of superimposed occupation deposits, as were found, for instance, in the terpen of Holland and north Germany (see Higham and Barker 1992) or, at the far end of the scale, the tells of the Middle East, which contain the remains of whole cities. Generalizations are not, therefore, very helpful. Yet more mounds of various kinds have been excavated, and excavated badly, than perhaps any other sort of monument, since they are not only obvious, but they seem to be self-contained, to have edges, and therefore to be suitable for limited excavation. It is not surprising that one of the earliest published archaeological sections (in colour!) is that which Thomas Jefferson cut across an Indian burial mound in 1784 (Sheratt, ed., 1980, 15).

Stone robbing and robber trenches

The quarrying of stone is very laborious and costly, especially if it entails transporting, the stone over long distances. As a result, stone is reused whenever possible, often many times. A late Roman tombstone from Wroxeter, for instance, had started life as a tombstone probably in the first century, had subsequently been cut down and used as building stone, when it had been exposed to considerable wear on one of its faces, and was then, perhaps as late as the mid-fifth century, again used as a tombstone (Barker *et al.* 1994). Churches, either in part or entire, were constantly being knocked down and their stone reused, often simply as rubble.

The two well-attested Anglo-Saxon minsters at Worcester, one dating from the seventh century and the other from the tenth and both still in existence just before the Norman Conquest, have disappeared completely, presumably incorporated into the fabric of the cathedral begun by St Wulstan in 1084. The parish churches of Wroxeter, Atcham and Upton Magna, all near the Roman town of *Virconium Cornoviorum*, are built very largely of stone from the Roman buildings as are farm buildings and walls for miles around. These examples can, of course, be paralleled all over the world where stone is the principle building material.

Not only do masons demolish buildings to reuse the stone, but they dig out the foundations of demolished buildings to reuse them, though they may only be of rubble. The trenches thus left, usually backfilled with unusable mortar and stone debris, are termed robber trenches (see the glossary) and are very often the only evidence for former building (Fig. 9).

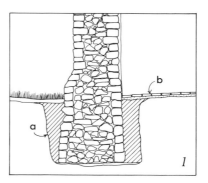

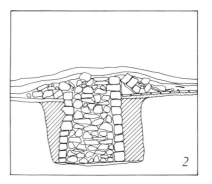

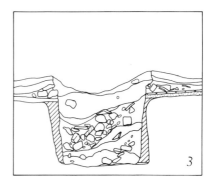

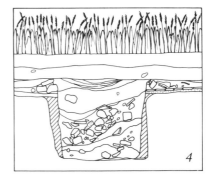

9 1–4 shows the stages by which a wall may first be robbed of its visible stone and then the wall base and its foundations dug-out leaving a rubble-filled trench which, when ploughed over, cannot be seen on the surface.

3

The Development of Excavation Techniques

The growth of archaeology, and with it the techniques of excavation, has been outlined, with many contemporary quotations and a bibliography, by Professor Glyn Daniel (1950 and 1967) and its more recent aberrations castigated by Sir Mortimer Wheeler (1954). Our modern techniques stem from the fifteen years between 1881 and 1896 during which Lieutenant-General Pitt Rivers carried out a series of masterly excavations on Cranborne Chase (Pitt Rivers 1887–98), where he had inherited estates and was therefore able to work with unhurried care, with adequate finances and labour, but, above all, to publish with a lavishness which we can now rarely hope to emulate. As he tells us (vol. 1, 1887, xix), his first lessons as an excavator were derived from Canon Greenwell, the opener of Yorkshire barrows, but he far transcended his tutor, and dug with a breadth of vision and a grasp of detail which were quite unprecedented. It was this meticulous attention to detail that was, and is, important, together with his realization that all the observed evidence should be recorded, even if its meaning is not understood at the time. Two short quotations will put his point of view:

> Excavators, as a rule, record only those things which appear to them important at the time, but fresh problems in Archaeology and Anthropology are constantly arising, and it can hardly fail to escape the notice of anthropologists . . . that on turning back to old accounts in search of evidence, the points which would have been most valuable have been passed over from being thought uninteresting at the time. Every detail should, therefore, be recorded in the manner most conducive to facility of reference, and it ought at all times to be the chief object of an excavator to reduce his own personal equation to a minimum (Pitt Rivers, vol. 1, 1887, xvii).

> I have endeavoured to keep up in the present volume the minute attention to detail with which the excavation commenced. Much of what is recorded may never prove of further use, but even in the case of such matter, superfluous precision may be regarded as a fault on the right side where the arrangement is such as to facilitate reference and enable a selection to be made. A good deal of the rash and hasty generalization of our time arises from the unreliability of the evidence on which it is based. It is next to impossible to give a continuous narrative of an archaeological investigation that is entirely free from bias; undue stress will be laid upon facts that seem to have an important bearing upon theories current at the time, whilst others that might come to be considered of greater value afterwards are put in the background or not recorded, and posterity is endowed with a legacy of error that can never be rectified. But when fulness and accuracy are made the chief subject of study, this evil is in a great measure avoided . . . (Pitt Rivers, preface to vol. II, 1888)

As a result of his 'fulness and accuracy', the General's excavations can be reinterpreted in the light of our much more extensive background knowledge (see for instance Hawkes 1948, and Barrett *et al.* 1991). Similarly, a large-scale excavation of his assistant, Harold St George Gray, has recently been fully published for the first time by Richard Bradley (Bradley 1976). This was only possible because Gray kept detailed records in the manner of Pitt Rivers. The General also realized that area excavation was the only way to understand the structures and the sequences of settlement sites (see the front endpapers). His chief weakness was his summary treatment of layers above the natural chalk. They tended to be ignored except in ramparts, ditches and pits, so that only major features cut into the subsoil were seen and recorded. It may be a platitude to say that the General was in advance of his time but it is true that the lessons implicit in his work were not fully appreciated for many years.

Sir Leonard Woolley modestly describes his first experience of digging when, in 1907, the great Haverfield agreed to supervise an excavation at Corbridge on behalf of the authors of the Northumberland County History. It was considered that 'a small-scale dig' would 'settle the character of the site', and Woolley with an assistant, some volunteers and labourers, taught himself by trial and error: '. . . we were all', he says, 'happily unconscious of our low performance, nor did anyone from outside suggest that it might have been better . . .' British field archaeology was at a low ebb (quoted in Daniel 1967, 246).

In the years leading up to the First World War Harold St George Gray modelled his own excavations on the General's. In fact, as Richard Bradley says 'His actual digging was cleaner and more orderly than his mentor's and some of his photographs must rank

among the best of all time' (Bradley, 1976). But the publication of Maumbury Rings had to wait until 1976, and as a result Gray's work did not have the influence on British excavation that it deserved.

Since the late nineteenth century there have been significant shifts of emphasis in excavation techniques, first towards horizontal, then to vertical, and now again towards horizontal methods. The earliest excavators of Roman towns, such as Caerwent, Silchester and Wroxeter, excavated horizontally in large areas, attempting to see the sites as a whole, but failing to observe the subtleties of stratification which are necessary not only for the understanding of the chronology of the site but even for the recognition of more tenuous evidence (see Figs 65–7 below). One result was that these sites, among many others, appeared to contain only stone buildings whereas we now know that almost all have long sequences of timber buildings, some earlier, some contemporary with and some later than the stone buildings. Thus the chronological and structural sequences were distorted by this summary digging, which, though fundamentally the right method, was crudely applied. The plan was dominant. For example, in both the Silchester and the earlier Wroxeter reports there are large diagrammatic plans but very few sections (Fox and Hope 1891; Fox 1892; Fox and Hope 1893; Bushe-Fox 1913, 1914, 1916).

In Britain, reaction came in the 1930s, mainly under the powerful influence of Sir Mortimer Wheeler, when the section, the grid system and three-dimensional recording became paramount, and as a result the importance of the plan decreased.

Sir Mortimer, like many innovators, transcended the limitations of his innovations. This is perhaps because he worked on the grand scale, and because he was aware of the need to see the evidence horizontally as well as vertically (Wheeler 1956, 149, 246), so

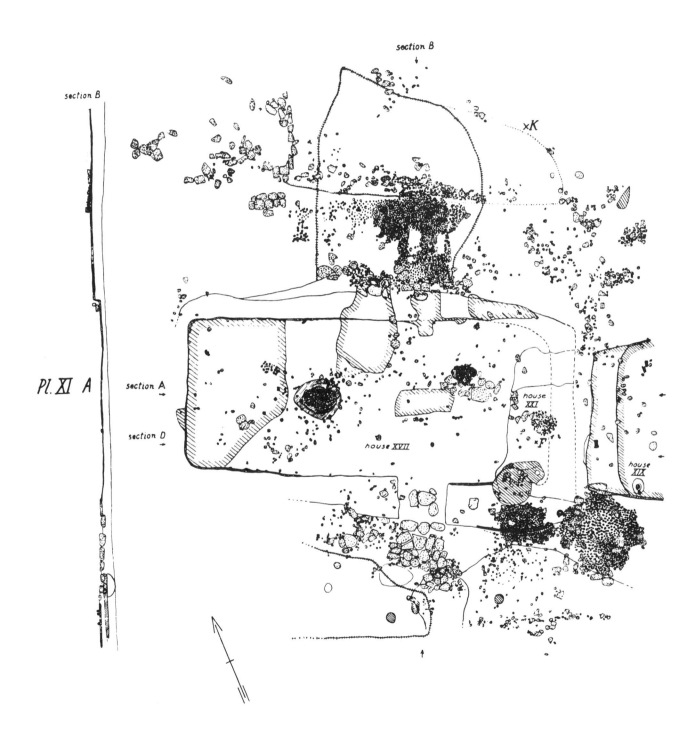

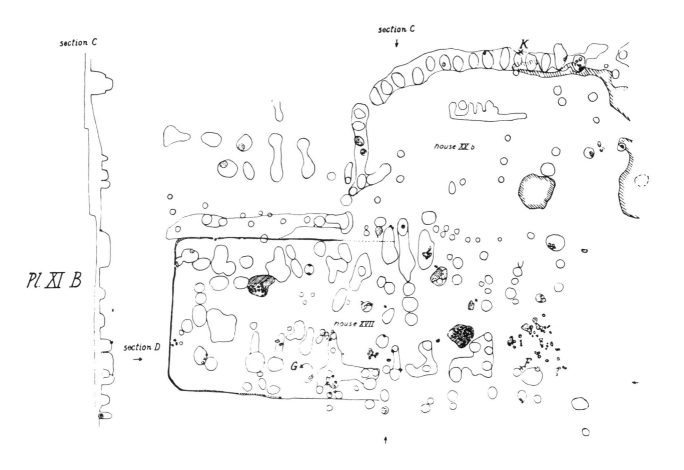

10–11 Nørre Fjand: these drawings show the plan of a series of houses, XVII, XXI, XIX, as first discovered (left), and, above, the pattern of underlying post-holes revealed when the uppermost layers were removed. At this point house XXb was revealed.

that he usually finished up with a large open area. His followers – that is, nearly all excavators working in Britain between the 1930s and the 1960s – usually worked on a much smaller scale. As a result the sample was too small, often no more than one or two trenches or a small grid of boxes, even, on occasions, tiny trenches leap-frogging in a line across large and complex sites (but see Fig. 15 below).

Sections were now drawn in the greatest detail, whereas plans, even of totally excavated features, were recorded much more summarily and where structures disappeared under the frequent balks, they were completed with conjectured dotted lines. The section seemed to offer an economical, swiftly obtained microcosm of the site's development and this led to the trial trenching of hundreds of sites, with the results being used as the basis for generalized statements about the whole site, and often also other, unsampled sites.

These techniques were used particularly on Romano-British sites. Because it is possible to separate the four centuries of Roman rule from the rest of British history there have been, and are, a considerable number of 'Romano-British archaeologists' both professional and amateur, whose interest waxes c. AD 43 and wanes c. AD 410. Archaeologists in the countries of north-west Europe outside the Roman Empire are fortunate in that they are much freer of these period divisions, so that their archaeology is seen as a continuum to be studied naturally as a whole.

The Roman occupation was a period of building in stone and timber sandwiched between periods of timber building in the prehistoric period and the immediate post-Conquest years, and again in the so called sub-Roman period. Since stone buildings can more easily be dug in trenches and boxes, it can reasonably be argued that the isolation of the Roman period by scholars, coupled with the widespread use of stone buildings in Roman times, led to the general adoption of the grid system, even on sites where it was unsuitable.

Prehistorians were the first to become aware of the limitations of this method (for instance Case 1952), chiefly because they were more often dealing with structures which simply cannot be understood in trenches or boxes, if they are seen at all. Pioneer work, notably by Dr van Giffen in Holland (van Giffen 1958), Professors Gudmund Hatt and Axel Steensberg in Denmark (Hatt 1957; Steensberg 1952, 1974) and Professor Gerhard Bersu in Britain (Bersu 1940, 1949) showed that the only way to elucidate the intricate patterns of the timber buildings found on by far the majority of ancient sites is to combine highly detailed observation of the layers in plan with a study of their composition in depth; a fully three-dimensional approach in which every cubic centimetre of soil is made to yield the maximum information.

Professor Hatt's last excavation, that of the Iron Age village of Nørre Fjand in Jutland, carried out between 1938 and 1940 (Hatt 1957) was his most highly developed and influential (Figs 10 and 11).

Professor Steensberg has described, in a letter to me, the evolution of Hatt's technique in the 1920's. He writes:

However, Hatt realised – being a geographer – that in the case of indistinct sites it would be necessary to uncover bigger areas in order to follow the edge of the houses. The break came in 1927 when he had to excavate a house site in Tolstrup, Himmerland (south of Ålborg). The local archaeologist, S. Vestergaard Nielsen, who had found the site, could not be present all the time, because he was a school teacher. He told me later on, that the following day he came out to the site and found that Hatt made use of wheelbarrows and uncovered a considerable area before he started the real digging. This amused Vestergaard Nielsen, and he threatened Hatt saying: 'I am going to write a letter to the National Museum's First Department telling C. Neergaard, that you are excavating like a peasant's servant!' The method proved, however, to be very profitable. But as can be seen from Hatt's publications in *Aarboger for nordisk Oldkyndighed*, 1928 and 1930, he still made use of the traditional measuring tapes from two main points A and B. Therefore the features had a rather awkward outline which irritated Hatt. He wished to uncover the features according to their real shape, and what is very important he wished to remove layers just as they had been deposited, not taking away a layer of 5 or 10cm everywhere. This must have been due to his geological training. And he did not use sections where it was not necessary, though in his investigations of prehistoric fields he dug through the low division walls and analysed them as other geologists would have done.

Hatt realized that sections cut across the very flimsy and discontinuous floors and superimposed hearths of Iron Age houses would destroy them unseen, so in order to keep vertical records he levelled-in layers, features and finds on the assumption that a notional section could subsequently be drawn across the site wherever required. This method was adopted and refined by Steensberg who had assisted Hatt at Nørre Fjand, in a series of excavations on farm sites in Denmark (Steensberg 1952) and reached its fullest development at Store Valby (Steensberg 1974). Fig. 12 shows the successive buildings of Farms 3 and 4 at Store Valby.

The internment of Professor Gerhard Bersu on the Isle of Man during the Second World War was an ill wind which blew good for British archaeology, for while there Bersu dug a number of sites (in spite of being under armed guard, with fixed bayonets) (Bersu 1949 and 1977). Outstanding among them, technically, was the excavation of a Viking camp at Vowlan (Bersu 1949) where it is clear from the plan alone (Figs 13 and 14) that a system of grids with intervening balks would seriously have hampered the understanding of the site (op. cit. 67). Though Bersu's section drawing has sometimes been criticized for its excessive naturalism and over elaboration, the naturalistic technique of the plan of Vowlan is most appropriate, showing, as it does, the soil changes which were the sole evidence for the buildings.

The lessons implicit in excavations such as Vowlan were slow to be understood but are now the basis for the very large investigations of sand and gravel sites which form a great proportion of the rescue excavations in the lowlands of Britain.

Two crucial excavations of this type were carried out by Brian Hope-Taylor from 1953 to 1958 at Yeavering (Hope-Taylor 1977), and by Philip Rahtz in 1960–62 at Cheddar (Rahtz 1964). Both, as it happens, were on the sites of Anglo-Saxon palaces. The excavation of Yeavering, though only recently published, has had a profound influence on the standards of excavation in Britain due to the exceptional acuteness of the observation, the precision of the recordings and the beauty of the draughtsmanship, which led to a depth of interpretation beyond the capacity of most previous excavators. Rahtz, working on the grand scale at Cheddar, demonstrated conclusively that very large sites cannot be understood unless they are excavated totally.

There is, of course, a fundamental difference between those excavations in which the sole evidence consists of horizontal changes in the colour and texture of the soil and those where there are superimposed levels, complicated by the presence of vestigial stone walls, pebble surfaces and other fragments of structures. The latter type of site is

12 Store Valby: part of the highly detailed plan of farms 3 and 4 at the medieval Danish site. The position of each find with its number is included. Schematic sections are printed at the side of the plan.

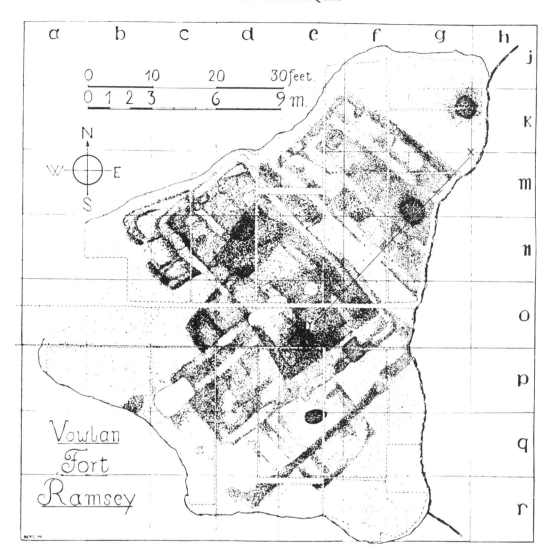

13 Vowlan, Isle of Man: excavated area inside the promontory fort at the level of the untouched soil. The drawing indicates, by means of differential shading, the varying colours and shades of the surface of the sand revealed when the turf and topsoil were removed.

immeasurably more complicated to dig, especially if the superimposed layers are very thin, and if subsequent structures have removed parts of even these thin layers, their discontinuity making them yet more difficult to trace and interpret.

In England, research in the 1950s on the peasant houses of deserted medieval villages faced just this sort of problem. The excavation of the now classic site of Wharram Percy, begun by Professor Maurice Beresford, was continued in 1955 by J.G. Hurst and J. Golson, using techniques derived from those of Steensberg. The account of the development of the excavation (Hurst 1956, 271–3 and 1979), with its cautious beginnings, using balks which were abandoned when

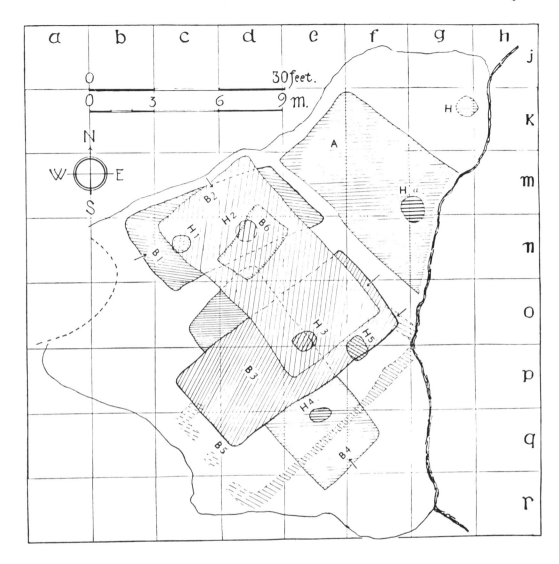

14 Vowlan: diagram of houses inside the promontory fort. This drawing is a simplification and interpretation of the plan shown in Fig. 13. It is clear from both plans that a system of trenches or grids cut across the site would not have uncovered an understandable pattern. If the reader doubts this, a salutory game can be played by taking a piece of cardboard and cutting in it holes to represent any desired system of trenches or grids (to scale), laying it over the plan, and then attempting an interpretation from the visible areas. A similar game can be played with any of the other area excavations here reproduced, for example both endpapers.

they proved to mask vital evidence, records a turning point in British archaeology. The methods used at Wharram have since been further modified, the levelling of all finds being discarded in favour of the recording of finds within their layers. This continuous modification of techniques during the course of long-term excavations is one of the principal ways in which the science, or art, of excavation advances. In addition, techniques developed on one type of site have been tested on other sites of quite different character. It is now clear that the methods used at Wharram Percy are equally valid on sites containing major stone buildings and that if such sites, which once might have been thought to contain only stone buildings, are excavated horizontally and in great detail, the plans of unsuspected timber buildings may well emerge.

During the 1950s and 1960s urban excavation was developing in parallel with the rural excavations of prehistoric and medieval sites. Professor Sheppard Frere's excavations at Verulamium in 1955–61 (Frere 1959 and 1971) pointed the way towards Martin Biddle's rapidly expanding excavations at Winchester in the early 1960s. It is very instructive to follow the development of Biddle's techniques through the series of interim reports which began in 1962 and continued until 1975 (Biddle 1962–1975).

On many sites timber and stone buildings were intermixed or followed one another in varying sequences. It is in those areas and periods in which timber buildings follow stone that the elusive evidence of wooden structures is most vulnerable either to later disturbance, or to the excavator's desire to get at the underlying stone buildings. How many Roman villas have been dug with the possibility in mind that later occupants of the site might have used the destruction rubble as foundation rafts for timber buildings? Similarly, the final phases of Roman towns and the 'Dark Age' layers of cities have been neglected in the past partly because they require the uncovering of large areas if they are to be understood, but partly also because they require a different attitude of mind, one that is open to any form of structural evidence which presents itself, and does not look simply for preconceived features, such as walls and post-holes, and ignores the unexpected.

We are only just beginning to realize the potential of excavated evidence, especially the wealth of information which might be revealed by a really detailed analysis of every aspect of the soil removed in the dissection of the structures we are excavating.

Techniques in the past have often been too panoramic, too clumsy to reveal more than the broadest outlines of the more obvious structures. The excavation of the Roman town of Silchester is an often-quoted example, where it is suspected that the published plan, showing, as it does, only a scatter of stone buildings in a sort of garden city, may be quite misleading, the gaps being filled by undiscovered timber buildings. This is an old and obvious example; what is much more worrying is that it is at least possible that the majority of all published (or, for that matter, unpublished) excavations may be misleading in that, either by taking too small a sample of the site or by digging too insensitively, especially in the upper levels, whole periods of the site's occupation have been lost, ignored or distorted. The consequences for the history and prehistory of Britain are far reaching. If I am right, the syntheses made from these excavation reports and integrated with other forms of evidence will be falsified because the distortions and missing phases, being unknown, cannot be taken into account.

In the earlier editions of this book I said:

> It is sometimes argued that if an excavation is published as fully as possible, the evidence should be sufficient for reinterpretation by future workers in the light of their greater background experience. However, if the evidence from the original excavation was mistakenly observed or inadequately recorded in the field, the inadequacies will lie further back than the published drawings and lists of finds, however plausible they may seem; and the more

skilful the drawings, the more convincing they will be. There is no absolute safeguard against this since excavation can never be completely objective, but we must be constantly aware that all interpretation is, in a sense, a personal opinion, or a consensus of opinions, and be careful, as far as possible, to keep the interpretation separate from the evidence on which it is based. Naturally, the more detail there is in the publication, the more confidence the reader will have that the losses of evidence are minimal; although this in its turn brings further difficulties. In an age of larger and more complex excavations drawings must now be published at a much greater scale if the mass of significant detail is not to be lost, and here the problems of ever increasing printing costs become a major factor in the adequate publication of excavations [but see below p. 190].

Yet it may well be that greatly increased attention to detail is the key to all improvements in excavation techniques.

The archaeological dilemma of our age is that just as it is becoming necessary for us to excavate more slowly, and in much greater detail, we are beginning to realize the full extent and speed of destruction of sites and whole settlement areas which is going on around us. How can we justify months spent on the minutiae of part of a small site when the hearts of great cities are being torn out in a matter of weeks and when square miles of prehistoric settlement are being totally removed in a matter of months? There is no single, simple answer, but the dilemma must be faced and a solution attempted.

4

Pre-Excavation Research

Non-destructive examination

Until comparatively recently, digging on site began with the minimum of pre-excavation research. If earthworks were being dug, the obvious targets were entrances with a section or two across the ramparts of defended sites. Cropmark sites were dug at selected points where the cropmarks were clearest, or looked most interesting. Often, the reasons for digging a particular site were non-archaeological – the fact that the site belonged to the excavator or his neighbour, or that it was the local landmark or a newly discovered cropmark of special interest to the excavator. There was little sense of an overall national or even regional strategy of research, though individuals from Pitt Rivers to Wheeler had their own strategic projects. Now the situation is changing, partly because of the increased realization of the fact that each site is unique, and partly because the speed of destruction of sites and whole landscapes means that there are less sites every day, that we are dealing with a rapidly diminishing asset, and that those sites which are dug, whether for 'rescue' or 'research' must therefore not be dug without adequate pre-excavation preparation.

The more that non-destructive examination of sites can be developed the more effective will be the subsequent excavation, and the better the use of money and

resources and particularly of skilled people – the most valuable resource we have. The principal ways of examining monuments by non-destructive methods are outlined below.

1 *The study of relevant documents.* Documentary references to archaeological sites may simply be a passing reference to a prehistoric monument in an early manuscript such as John Leland's 1542 reference to the hillfort at South Cadbury, which he called Camallate (Camelot) (quoted in full in Alcock 1975, p. 11), or William Stukeley's drawing of the same site in 1723 (*ibid* Plate 2). A useful piece of evidence from Leland's description is that 'Much gold, sylver and coper of the Roman coynes hath been found ther in plouing . . .', suggesting at least Roman, if not later, occupation in an Iron Age fort, and Stukeley's drawing shows that in his day the ramparts were free of trees and undergrowth. His profile of the defences is more elaborate than at present and it may simply be that he did not count the ramparts correctly, but he was a good observer and it is worth considering that the lowest rampart that he shows has been lost to ploughing on the lower slopes.

At the other extreme, references to sites in towns may be very full, enabling an almost complete record to be built up of landlords and tenants, with their occupations. In this case, excavation may help to flesh out the documentary story by revealing the form and development of the successive buildings on the site and in so doing use the documents to help in their interpretation. In the choice of sites to be dug in a town, the site with the most complete documentation would always be given preference if all other factors were equal.

Castles are another class of monument often very well documented, but sometimes for only one or two periods of their occupation. The earliest structures have often been replaced long ago, and their excavation not only extends the history of the site backwards, but puts these structures into context by reference to the documentary description. Here again, given a number of similar sites, it is those with firm documentation which will take precedence. Even one documentary mention may be of crucial importance in the choice of site. The motte and bailey castle now called Hen Domen, Montgomery, was chosen for excavation because of two entries in the Domesday Book for Shropshire, which mention it by name, one saying that 'the earl [Roger de Montgomery] himself has here constructed a castle, which he calls Montgomery' (after his birthplace in Normandy) (Domesday Book, I, f245a, i). Roger was made Earl of Shrewsbury in 1070 or 1071, so the castle must have been built between then and 1086, the date of Domesday Book. Since almost no other motte and bailey castles on the Welsh border are referred to in contemporary documents, the opportunity to excavate a castle whose date of building was very soon after the Conquest and is known within 15 years, coupled with the fact that it was built by one of William the Conqueror's chief lieutenants, made it the obvious choice for long term excavation (see Barker and Higham 1982, esp. Chap. 3). There were, however, problems. We had taken it for granted as had everyone before us, that Hen Domen

was the first Mongomery Castle, but this view was challenged by a local archaeologist, and we had to do a good deal of further research before being able (we believe) to prove that they were one and the same (*ibid.*). So it is very important to be sure that the documentary references actually refer to the site that is about to be dug and not to a quite different one down the road (see also Chapter 4, The Documentary Contribution, in Higham and Barker 1992).

2 *The study of old maps and drawings.* All archaeological sites are part of the landscape which surrounds them, and the best excavators study the site's context as well as the site itself. Invaluable sources of information about the landscape of the last two centuries can be found in estate maps and terriers, in the tithe maps with their Apportionment (which gives the names of fields and their owners), and in the early editions of Ordnance Survey maps. From these and from fieldwork in the neighbourhood, a picture of the landscape of which the site is part can be built up. This is important, since no site is isolated from the fields, woods or hamlets which surround it, and on which, in varying degrees, it depends.

The maps may have crucial information about the site itself, showing changes which have occurred since the map was drawn or showing that features which were thought to have been modern are at least as old as the map.

Sometimes engravings or watercolour drawings of the site exist in local, or even national collections. The views of castles made by the brothers Buck in the eighteenth century are well known sources of information about the state of the castles then, and churches and abbeys were favourite subjects for artists. Here again, however, there are pitfalls. Dr Warwick Rodwell has drawn attention to two illustrations of the tower of the church of St Peter, Barton-on-Humber, where one illustration, made partly to prove the writer's theories, can be shown to have a number of fundamental inaccuracies when compared with the other (he has not even managed to count the arches in a blind arcade correctly) (Rodwell 1981, fig. 8, p. 22).

The seventeenth-century town maps of Speed and Roque are invaluable sources of information, particularly about street patterns, but often giving details of buildings now lost, or the lines of town defences. In most towns there are maps of many dates, scattered through the last three centuries, and from them can be built up a picture of the town's development, or the development of a street frontage or tenement, to be supplemented by the excavation, which will take the story back beyond the days when maps were made. The older editions of the Ordnance Survey maps, beginning with the first edition of 1801–5 are invaluable, and many public libraries have sets of the 1:2500 sheets published in the nineteenth century, which show a great deal of information that has since been lost. The 1:500 sheets of towns are a unique record which is a necessary tool for the urban archaeologist, and the early town maps in the British Library are also invaluable. The Public Record Office and most libraries and county archive collections have estate maps, terriers and tythe maps which may contain a scrap of information about a long vanished site, trapped like an insect in amber. Field names from early sources may lead to the discovery of lost sites or to sites peripheral to the one under excavation. Many collections of documents in libraries and museums include topographical drawings of the sort popular in the eighteenth and nineteenth centuries. These are often the only record of pre-historic monuments, castles, churches and other subjects suitable for the Romantic

15 Wharram Roman villas. These are on the chalk wolds in eastern Yorkshire, 2km (1¼ miles) each side of the well-known medieval village site of Wharram Percy. Each villa was explored by four techniques: aerial photography; geophysical survey; fieldwalking of the ploughed soil; and excavation. The first three provided in each case an excellent framework, showing the broad outline plan of the site, and a spread of Roman pottery and building materials.

Excavation elucidated this general picture, providing useful data on pre-Roman activity (back to the Mesolithic); the depth and nature of the subsoil; the range of building material used in the villas; many coins and other finds to show the standard of living and date range of the occupation; and details of infant burial, tessellated floors, ditches and roads.

The method used was to dig rows of 1m square boxes, and record these meticulously (A-A on lower diagram). The excavations were of only 25sq.m (270sq.ft) on each site, were done in four days with about ten people on each site, and cost about £400. Together with the other three methods of investigation, they provided a very useful sample of the history of each site, assisting materially in current planning and protection schemes, and providing a useful picture for later more extensive excavations.

The work of these two digs has resulted in a publication of monograph size.

pencil, showing them in less weathered or damaged condition than they are today.

3 *Previous work on site.* Many archaeological sites have been dug into in the past two centuries. Only too often there is no record of the excavation, and the evidence for this has to be found when digging begins, but in other cases there may be a report in a national journal or in the local archaeological society's Transactions, or the local paper, or in the local history collections of the relevant library or record office. Unfortunately, few early excavators, professional or amateur, left plans of the exact positions of their trenches, and their interpretations of their excavations often prove to be wildly inaccurate. Nevertheless, much can be gleaned from even the most inadequate

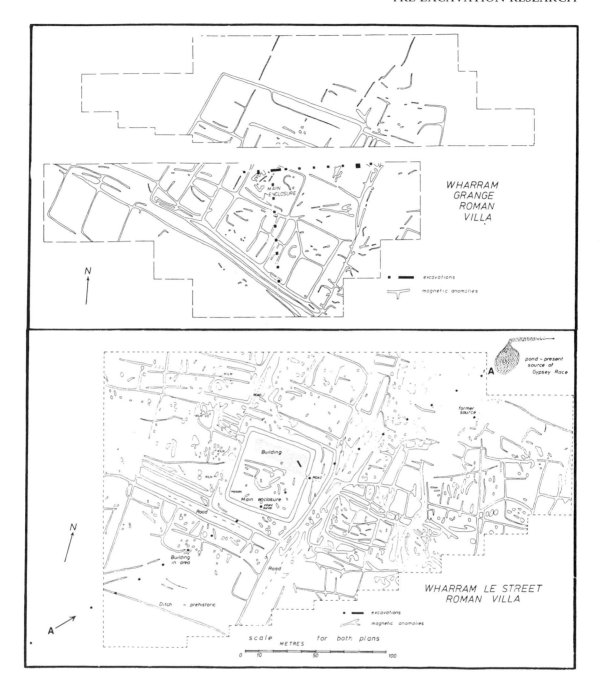

report, especially if it is accompanied by measured drawings. Positive evidence – the inclusion of a layer, or a wall, or a pit – is more to be trusted than an omission, which may have occurred because the excavator did not notice or understand the evidence.

All the previous trenches dug on the site of the Baths Basilica at Wroxeter, have had be be found by trowelling, yet the reports of these early excavations, from Thomas Wright to Kathleen Kenyon, have been informative when used with care, and their trenches, when emptied in advance of the present excavation, have given very valuable information about what is to come (see Barker *et al.* forthcoming, 1994).

4 *Aerial photographs.* Archaeological aerial photography has made some of the most spectacular advances of the past half century in our knowledge of the number and variety of archaeological sites in many countries. Hundreds of sites have been dug because their potential was discovered from aerial photographs, and in many other cases, aerial photography has helped to decide where, on a large site, digging would be most productive. Aerial photographs often indicate the potential of a site, but almost always

16 a–d These illustrate the examination of a small field, C, next to the motte and bailey castle at Hen Domen, Montgomery. Excavations under the rampart of the castle bailey at B had shown that the ridge and furrow cultivation of the northern field, A, continued under the rampart, proving that the ploughing was pre-Norman in date. Further evidence suggests that it was probably of the tenth century. This, and other aerial photographs, taken in glancing light (at 2.30p.m. on Boxing Day 1984, to be precise), showed that field C also was full of ridge and furrow. However, this ridging was not nearly so obvious from the ground – what appeared more clearly was a group of three small platforms at D (in the photograph in the long shadows of the tree on the other side of the road). It was first considered that these platforms might be the site of the small settlement whose inhabitants ploughed the pre-Conquest fields.

16a

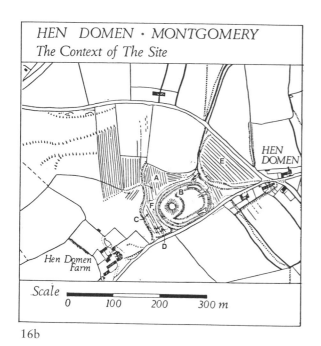

HEN DOMEN · MONTGOMERY
The Context of The Site

HEN DOMEN

Hen Domen Farm

Scale
0   100   200   300 m

16b

However, the aerial photograph shows clearly that the ridging runs right across the platforms, so that these must be earlier. They may, nevertheless, belong to a settlement relating to an earlier form of the field system.

A contour survey of field C was made in 1973 and plotted (by Susan Laflin) with the aid of the computer at the University of Birmingham, and the results are shown graphically in a three-dimensional display from each of the field's four sides in turn (*c*). (The contours are at 10cm vertical intervals above the temporary benchmark.) These plots show the ridging, but not so clearly as on the aerial photograph. One of them, but only one (no.2), shows the small platforms at D. Yet these were more obvious to the eye than the ridging.

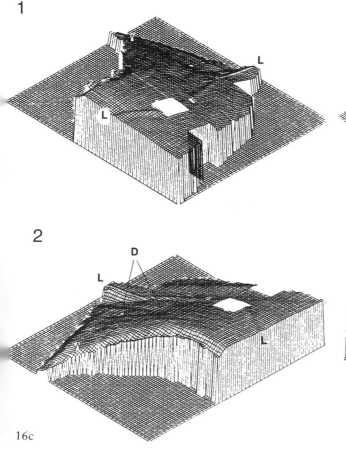

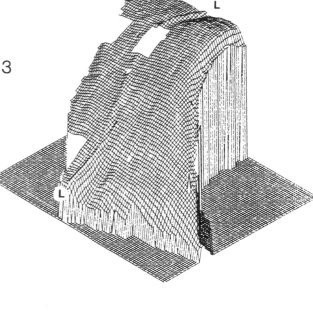

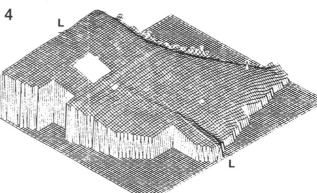

1

2

3

4

16c

In 1972 a fluxgate magnetometer survey was carried out to try to detect magnetic anomalies, such as hearths, pits or ditches. The results are shown in *d* and it can be seen that they bear no relation to the visible earthworks, except that the apparent ditch, G, runs roughly parallel to the outer ditch and counterscarp rampart of the motte, F. It is possible, therefore, that it is a previously undetected marking-out ditch dug to indicate the line of the defences to the ditch-diggers. It may, on the other hand, be a slot in which an outer palisade stood. The other anomalies, at H, I, J and K, do not seem to have any obvious connection with the castle and may be connected with the slight hollows close to them; or they may, of course, be part of another, altogether different, phase of occupation here. In fact, the hollow way, L–L, which at its southern end rises up on to a small causeway, seems to be sited deliberately between the two obliterated ditches, I and J. Whether this is simply coincidental can be solved only by excavation. It is perhaps also significant that the 'pits' grouped together at K are all south of ditch J which suggests that they are outside (or perhaps inside) whatever is bounded by ditches I and J.

HEN DOMEN · MONTGOMERY   Field C

Contour and magnetometer surveys 1972/3

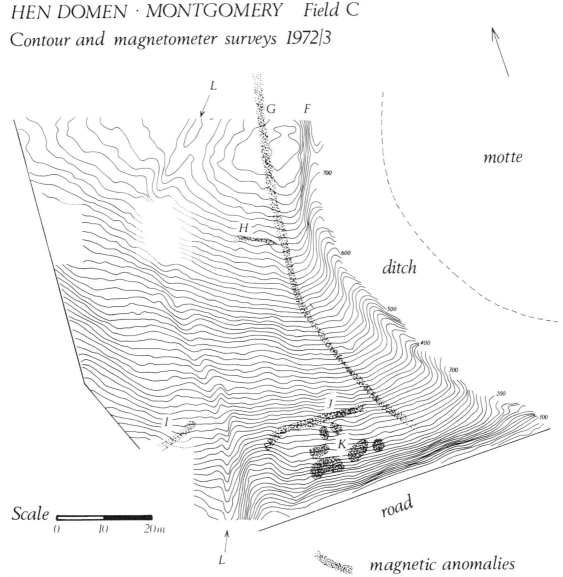

Scale
0   10   20m

L

magnetic anomalies

16d

The lesson we have learned from this quite intensive study of what is really a very small field is that no one method of investigation tells all – the field was photographed from the air for many years before the slight ridging showed up; studying the surface from the ground and from the air gave no hint of the ditches and pits revealed by the magnetic survey. And there is no doubt at all that excavation would, in an attempt to solve these problems, reveal new ones. A further complication is that excavation here would be inhibited by the fact that this is one of the very few areas of provable pre-Norman ridge and furrow in Britain, so that there is every reason to leave these problems permanently unsolved, since the proper excavation of the field would destroy its chief asset. It would, of course, be possible to pin-point the ditches and pits and excavate them in isolation, but, though this might produce some finds and some dating evidence, it would not be likely to tell us anything about the circumstances in which they were dug, or to what nearby occupation they related. All experience shows that the evidence produced by the magnetometer survey (like that produced by aerial photography) is likely to be only the tip of the iceberg. (Photo: C.R. Musson.)

sites prove to be far more complex and difficult than they look from the air, so that aerial photography only shows the minimal potential of a site; its real potential is almost always much greater

The major collections of archaeological aerial photographs are held by the National Monuments Record and the Committee for Aerial Photography at Cambridge, though large collections are also held by some of the major museums and universities, by the archaeological trusts and by a number of private flyers. Not all of these collections are easily available for inspection, even by scholars, and there is no doubt that an immense amount of information much of it unique and unprecedented, awaits assessment. Unfortunately, one might almost say disastrously, many of the sites newly revealed from the air will have been destroyed before their existence is known to more than a very few. The problem, which is primarily one of manpower and money, is in storing, cataloguing, interpreting and making available the prints. This is beyond the scope of this book, but is under active consideration by a Committee of the Council for British Archaeology. The papers read at a symposium entitled 'Aerial Reconnaissance for Archaeology' have been published by the CBA under that title (Wilson (ed.) 1975). This volume forms an excellent summary of recent developments while the realization of the importance of aerial photography has led to the founding, in 1971, of the *Journal of Aerial Photography*.

The early Royal Air Force cover is an invaluable source of high level photographs though not, of course, taken with archaeology in mind. Sometimes it happens, however, that the circumstances are favourable. For instance, part of the Second World War Royal Air Force cover for Shropshire was taken when light snow covered the ground – the conditions could not have been better for the definition of earthworks and the series has produced much new evidence. Many development corporations and road construction units have commissioned photogrammetric surveys made from vertical mosaics of photographs. Both the surveys and the photographs are usually available if a proper approach is made.

Aerial photographs, vertical, oblique or stereoscopic may reveal earthworks or cropmarks related to the site to be excavated. The site itself, if it has been, or can be, photographed from the air before excavation may reveal details of earthworks or cropmarks within it not otherwise visible. If aerial photography can be arranged during or immediately after the excavation, the resulting photographs will greatly enhance the published report. By giving a panoramic view, they may also reveal patterns in the excavated surface not readily seen from the ground.

17a

17 a–c In the mid-second century AD the city of Wroxeter was almost doubled in size with a new defensive line, a–a, being drawn north of the Bell Brook. The very large area thus added does not seem to have included any metalled streets or stone buildings north of the valley in which the little Bell Brook runs. However, a series of very fine aerial photographs by Arnold Baker, of which a and b are two, shows what appears to be a grid of ditches or gullies within the defences, together with a multiplicity of pits of all sizes, many of them rectilinear (and therefore not, for example, tree root holes). There appears to have been intensive occupation here, but in timber buildings rather than stone. However, the immediate impression of a grid of streets has a misleading element, since it is overlain by ridge and furrow (which can be seen clearly outside the defences). Nevertheless, when the ridge and furrow has, as it were, been subtracted from the total picture, the pattern of pits, ditches and gullies which is left is still rectilinear and argues for a planned extension of the city into this northern sector.

Outside the defences, converging trackways, enclosures and, in particular, enclosed cemeteries (b–b) can be seen. What is remarkable is that the outer pattern of cropmarks bears no relation to that inside and since the spread of the counterscarp rampart obliterates the outer cropmarks, these must be earlier. The trackways disappear under the defences at c and do not reappear inside (there is no trace of a gate), so it is clear that the enlargement of the city not only erased the earlier landscape but denied access at this point to the cemeteries. These must, therefore, themselves be early and perhaps even disused and forgotten by the time of the enlargements. It is apparent also that the trackways cut across some of the enclosure cropmarks which may, of course, be pre-Roman.

The intensively occupied area shown in c covers some 360,000 sq.m or 36ha – nearly 90 acres. It is very probable that, as with all cropmark sites, the complexity of the evidence and the depth of stratification would prove to be many times greater than appears on the photograph.

17b

The recent excavation of the Baths Basilica site in the city centre covers some 5600 sq.m, or a little over half a hectare – about 1⅓ acres – and it took some 29 seasons' work with an average labour force of 90 people working for five weeks each year (8550 worker-weeks) to excavate the upper levels only, those layers which represent the period from *c.* AD 300 to *c.* AD 500+. On the assumption that it would take as long again to reach the beginnings of the city's occupation, it would then take 17,000 worker-weeks to excavate the whole site. Simple arithmetic suggests that it would take in the order of 1,224,000 worker-weeks to excavate the area in the photograph. Even if this estimate is wrong by a factor of ten, it is clear that the excavation of even this part of the city, about a third of the total would be an immense task. The defences alone have proved, in recent excavations, to need digging on a scale commensurate with their size, if they are not simply to pose more questions than they solve.

There has been an understandable tendency in the past to concentrate on Roman city centres, their baths and fora, their shops, theatres and amphitheatres (if they had them). But a complete picture of town life in Roman Britain should include much more.

WROXETER ROMAN CITY

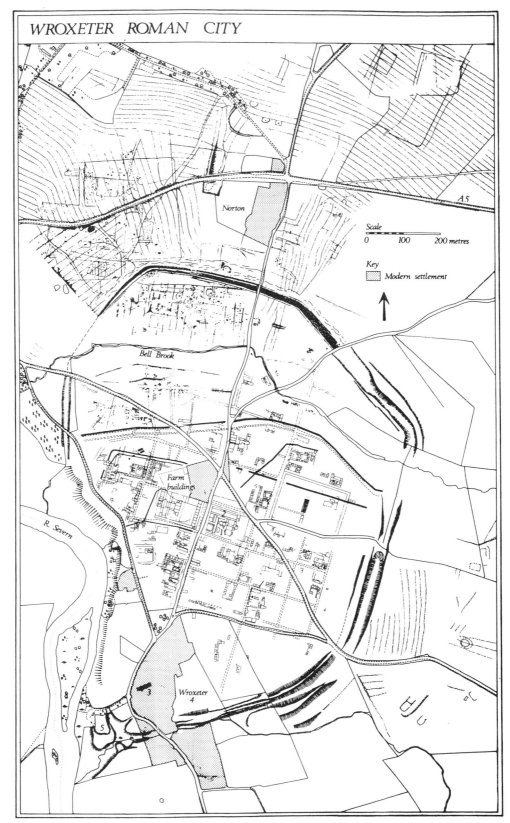

Norton

A5

Scale
0   100   200 metres

Key
Modern settlement

Bell Brook

Farm buildings

R. Severn

Wroxeter
4

3

5

17c

The suburbs and cemeteries, and the surrounding farms, for instance, which provided much of the city's food and the raw materials for its workshops, since a city such as Wroxeter (*see opposite*) comprised a vast range of trades and industries, as well as commerce from most parts of the Empire, even from as far away as the eastern Mediterranean.

Large sample excavations, perhaps amounting to a total of a quarter of the whole, might be sufficient to establish the nature of the occupation within and outside of the defences, and solve outstanding problems of the defences themselves. But the cemeteries would have to be completely excavated if they were to provide a full and unequivocal picture of their occupants. Smaller, carefully devised sampling strategies would provide viable environmental evidence in the form of seeds, pollen, insects, snails and so on over a larger range than the area excavations. The question which must be asked is whether all this very considerable expenditure of labour and money would be worthwhile. There is no doubt that such a programme, allied to similar excavations in the rest of the city, would provide a vivid and highly detailed picture of life in Roman Britain. If this were displayed to the public in simple graphic terms, using all the resources of modern technology, the result could be dramatic.

This is not the place to discuss either the techniques of aerial photography or its specialized interpretation. The best introductions to the subject are J.K.S. St Joseph, *The Uses of Aerial Photography* (1966), Wilson, op.cit, and *Air Photo Interpretation for Archaeologists* (1982), together with M.W. Beresford and J.K.S. St Joseph *Medeival England, An Aerial Survey* (2nd ed. 1979) and J. Bradford, *Ancient Landscapes* (1957).

5 *Fieldwalking.* The interpretation of artefact scatters from fieldwalking has undergone intensive study within the last ten years, moving a long way from the assumption that a concentration of flints or pottery in the ploughsoil marked the site of a building or settlement, when it might, in fact, represent quite the opposite, since, as an aboriginal informant told an excavator '. . . them old-timers never put their houses on the garbage dump . . . they don't like to live in their garbage any more than you would' (Gould 1966, 43, quoted in Schofield (ed.) 1991, 6). Much pottery is spread on the fields in the course of manuring, and a concentration of flints may be the debris from mining or off-site working. On the other hand, a dense scatter of roof-tiles, plaster, tesserae, pottery, coins and other finds is likely to mark the site of a Roman building, though conversely, the site of a timber building in an area where little or no pottery was used, is likely to escape detection completely.

The recovery of potsherds may be distorted by the same factors which distort recovery from excavations – red pottery is more easily seen than black; more pottery is recovered in dry weather than in wet (though heavy rain may wash exposed sherds clean) and more pottery and artefacts of all kinds will be recovered from sandy or chalky soils than from heavy clays. In addition, agriculture, for example deep ploughing, of one field contrasted with shallow ploughing of an adjacent one, or the natural processes of soil movement or erosion may distort the picture in other ways.

In all cases, fieldwalking shares with geophysical surveying and other forms of fieldwork the characteristic that positive results have positive implications for activity of some sort, whereas negative results – the absence of positive evidence – may be due to a variety of extrinsic factors that conceal the archaeological evidence which, nevertheless, exists in another less detectable form.

Techniques of fieldwalking and recording, and their interpretation, are discussed in a number of papers which have been published within the last few years or so. The essays in Schofield (ed. 1991) gather together much of recent thinking, and include extensive bibliographies. Clearly, from the point of view of this book, there is still much scope for experimental excavation of the sites of artefact scatters of all kinds to determine what they represent.

18 a–c In Ireland a number of geophysical surveys were carried out in connection with the 'Discovery Programme'. At Ballyrobin, Co. Tipperary a sub-rectangular earthwork and an adjacent circular earthwork to the east were surveyed. Both can be readily seen on the ground as they are raised by some 1m above the average level, and each contains a small barrow, again visible on the ground. In addition, aerial photography had revealed several cropmarks in the immediate vicinity (a).

The geophysical survey was carried out in the summer of 1992 to establish the site's likely date and potential for investigation. The area illustrated covers 1 hectare and was surveyed with both resistance meter (b) and fluxgate gradiometer (a type of magnetometer) (c). Both techniques revealed many features in addition to the earthworks.

The magnetometer survey (c) shows a series of parallel features (in the south) which may be field drains with a collector drain at their ends. However, within this area are sub-circular and linear features which are not associated with the drainage. Both techniques show an annexe to the subrectangular earthwork and other linear features tangential or radial to the main features.

6 *Contour surveying.* A close contour survey of the site to be excavated is a necessity for a number of reasons. First, it is the best way to present an accurate plan of the site in the eventual report; second, it may well reveal features of the site which might otherwise be missed; and third, if the site has to be reinstated when the excavation is finished, it provides the best record on which the reinstatement can be based. It also provides data for the building of a model for museum display.

7 *Geophysical methods of site survey.* These are methods which detect underground anomalies such as wells, pits, gullies, ditches, walls, floors, hearths, kilns and roads. Resistivity meters measure the differences in electrical resistivity between terminals driven into the ground at intervals – pits, ditches and gullies, which are normally filled with damp humic soil offer less resistance to the current than walls, roads and floors. If the readings are taken on a grid covering the whole site, the varying

18a

resistances can be plotted as a series of contours, or simply as anomalies or features. Similarly, the same anomalies or features tend to carry a detectably different magnetic field from that of the earth. Hearths and kilns (or burnt down buildings), in particular, have a strong local magnetic effect, though pits, ditches and roads etc can also be detected. The magnetic anomalies can be plotted in a number of ways to reveal their pattern. Examples will be found in Figs 18 and 19.

While magnetometer surveys can produce detailed plots of silted-up ditches, pits and post-holes, as well as hearths, kilns and the sites of burnt buildings, magnetic suscept-ibility uses a broader brush, detecting evidence of occupation and defining its limits in the topsoil itself, so that shallow sites which may only have survived in the topsoil can be detected, sometimes in quite fine detail. (This ability to detect occupation in the topsoil is paralleled by the evidence of cropmarks which have been found to derive only from the topsoil and so are difficult, if not impossible, to excavate. See p.146.)

Magnetic susceptibility can also be used where the topsoil has been eroded and redeposited, in situations such as valleys, lakes and estuaries. The displaced soil retains its magnetism and can be detected in cores or sections, even if the landscape from which it derives has long ago been destroyed. Where stratified deposits exist, it is possible, using relative magnetic susceptibilities, to identify phases of clearance and exploitation.

Magnetic susceptibility surveys, being swifter than magnetometer surveys, can also be used for covering large areas to identify areas of magnetic anomaly where a targeted magnetometer survey might be more effect-ively and economically concentrated. Clark (1990, Chap. 4), describes the technique in detail with many examples.

18b

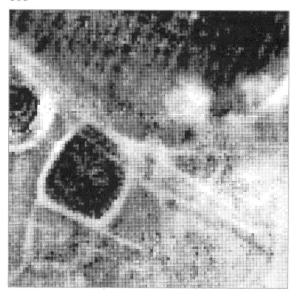

18c

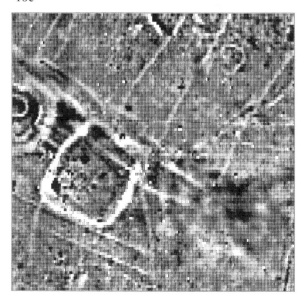

19 a–b Geophysical survey of the Roman auxiliary fort of *Longovicium*, near Lanchester, Co. Durham. This image represents a total of 93,552 measurements made using a fluxgate gradiometer on a 0.5 × 0.5m grid. Most of the features typical of a Roman fort can be identified including eight barracks, the *principia*, a pair of buttressed granaries and the road system. A is perhaps the site of a pair of granaries; stables; an internal bath-house or the Commandant's house, B a building of uncertain use, though perhaps a store, or an alternative location for the Commandant's house, C perhaps an internal battlehouse. *Longovicium* is evidently well preserved and undisturbed by excavation or ploughing. This result illustrates the potential of modern geophysical excavation. (Image courtesy of GeoQuest Associates.)

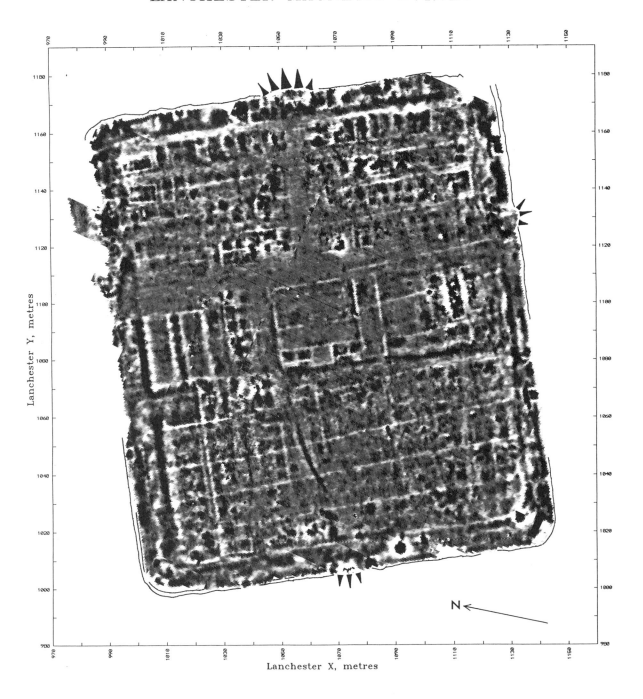

LANCHESTER MAGNETIC SURVEY

LANCHESTER MAGNETIC SURVEY

ARCHAEOLOGICAL INTERPRETATION

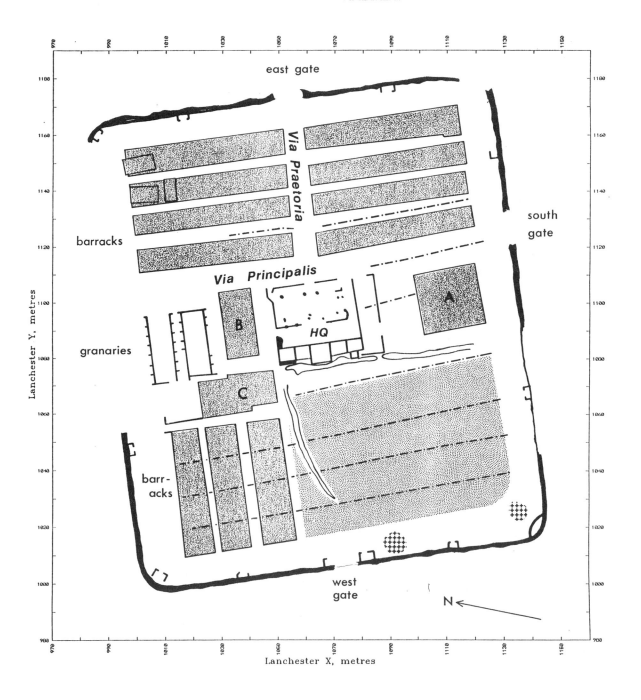

20 Caersws – a radar survey. The illustration shows the plan and section of a trench dug across a group of cropmarks at Caersws, Powys, together with a radar profile along the edge of the trench. As can be seen, the radar trace clearly parallels the features revealed in the trench section, particularly the ditches. It is thus that radar can provide a non-destructive third dimension in geophysical prospection. (Illustration by courtesy of Stratascan Ltd.)

More recently, ground-probing radar has been developed. With this technique an antenna transmits electromagnetic impulses into the ground. Reflections are received back by the antenna and are displayed at the surface on a colour monitor (Figs 20–1). Varying materials and voids transmit the impulses of energy at different speeds and

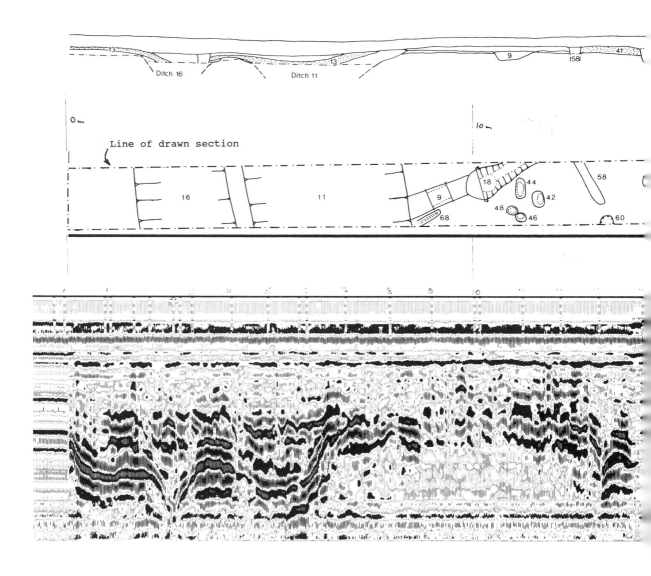

when the varying patterns are interpreted areas of interest can be identified and their depths calculated. The radar antenna is normally hand-towed over the site. Simultaneous recordings of the signals are made both graphically and on magnetic tape enabling an immediate on-site assessment to be made as well as preserving data for later analysis and more detailed interpretation.

Ground-probing radar surveys add depth to features, producing a trace analagous to an excavated section and enabling three-dimensional plots to be made. The technique is still being evaluated, and some of its results are not yet understood, but it clearly has immense potential.

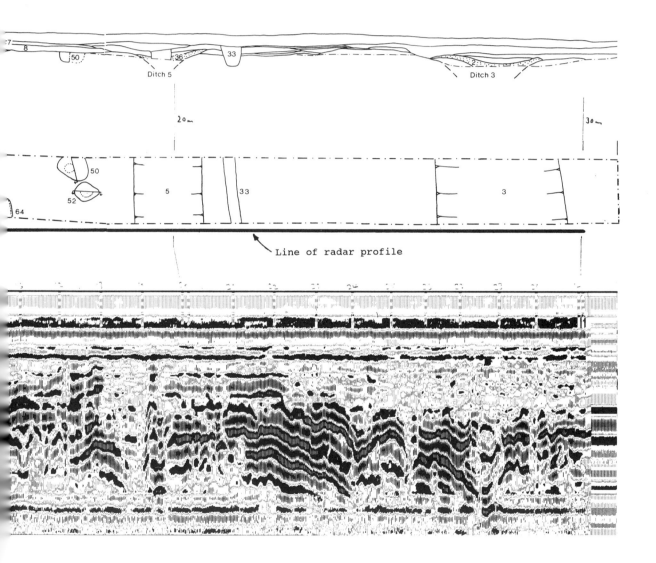

21 a–d The Charnel Chapel Crypt, Worcester Cathedral. In the early thirteenth century, the clearance of part of the monastic cemetery at the east end of the Norman Cathedral led to the building of a Charnel Chapel with a Crypt to house the retained bones outside the North Porch of the Cathedral. This Chapel was demolished in the seventeenth century and the Crypt vault was partly demolished and replaced by a lower, brick vault in the mid-nineteenth century.

21a

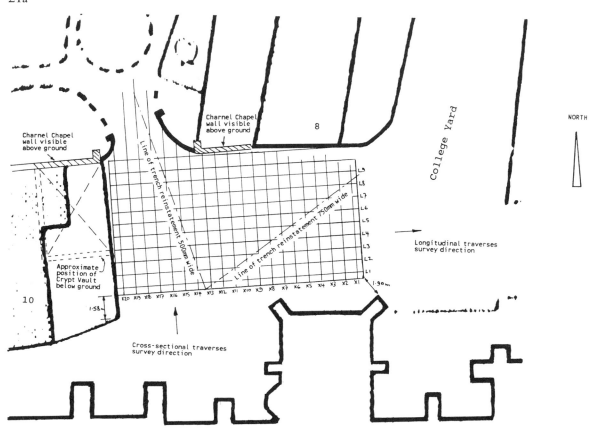

21b

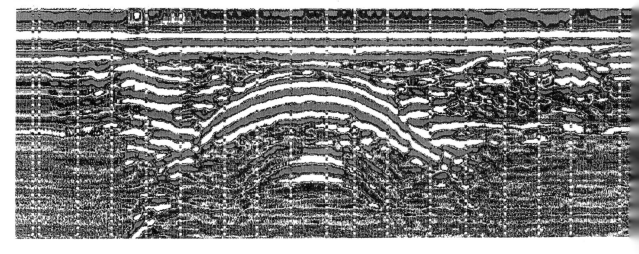

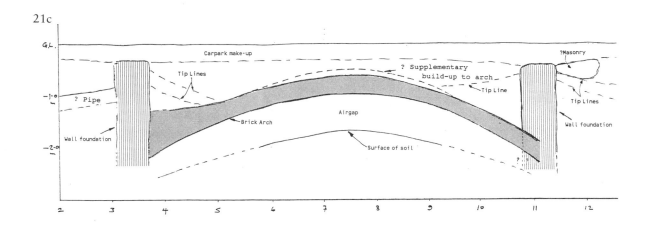

21c

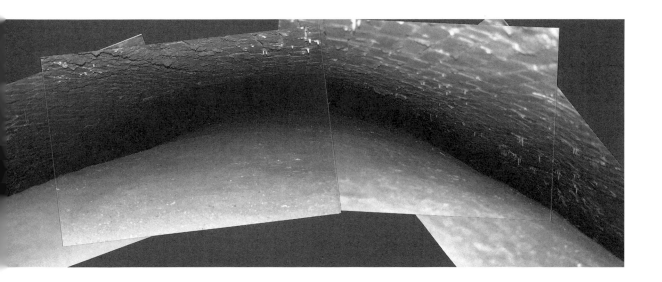

The exact extent of the Crypt was unknown, but a radar survey not only revealed its plan clearly but also showed the brick vault constructed between the original walls. A mound of earth had been formed to act as centring for the construction of the vault and this mound of earth and bones had settled with time leaving a gap below the vault. This showed clearly on the trace, **b** and was wide enough for a person to crawl along it. As can be seen, the radar profile (of which this is only one of a sequence) reflects with remarkable accuracy the actual situation below ground. (Illustrations by courtesy of Stratascan Ltd.)

8 *Phosphate and other chemical analyses*. Animal excreta and other organic remains contain quantities of detectable phosphates, and there have been a number of experiments in sampling the quantities of phosphates in the soil of suspected occupation sites in the hope of showing the intensity of occupation or isolating those areas occupied by animals either in pens or in the byre ends of long-houses (see Gurney 1986). There have been

some successes with chemical detection methods, though they are by no means uniform, and will, of course, be dependent to a great extent on the subsoil and the climate, since there is much more leaching of chemicals through the soil in, say, a wet climate on a sandy subsoil than in a dry climate on rock. Another experiment which has been tried with mixed success is to attempt to detect oak beams which have simply lain on the ground as foundations, by testing for traces of tannin in the soil. There is no doubt that chemical methods of detection are in their infancy, and that the next few decades are likely to see rapid advances in this field.

9 *Metal detectors and treasure hunting.* Metal detectors (or more particularly, those who use them to rob sites of their metal objects) have rightly been condemned by archaeologists and others interested in recovering the whole picture of a site, and not just its more desirable (and saleable) objects. Metal detectors are, however, akin to magnetometers and can be used in conjunction with them. At Sutton Hoo, they have been used to screen out stray metal objects, leaving the larger anomalies found by the magnetometers, while radar resolves the deep and shallow anomalies (Carver 1984).

Some archaeologists have set their faces firmly against those who use metal detectors, others have attempted to join with them, to explain what archaeology really is, and to enlist their help. Unfortunately, there is a hard core of professional treasure-hunters who loot sites systematically. These, not surprisingly, give all metal detecting a bad name, and make it harder for those who wish to help in site prospection to be accepted.

The sale of metal detectors for treasure hunting is now widespread and its defenders claim the right to pursue what they see as a harmless hobby and invoke the freedom of the individual as an argument. Many claim that since they obtain the prior permission of the landowner, and give or sell any objects they find to a museum, complaints by archaeologists are unjustified and are prompted chiefly by sour grapes and professional jealousy.

I do not intend here to discuss the legal or moral issues which often confuse the purely archaeological arguments, but to show that any treasure hunting on an archaeological site is indefensible on purely archaeological grounds. I have demonstrated elsewhere in this book that the digging of holes (even quite large holes) in archaeological sites produces fragmented, often distorted, evidence which can rarely be understood (Chapter 5). The same arguments have even more force when applied to the tiny holes dug at the prompting of a metal detector. Many of these holes may produce nothing more significant than a modern horseshoe, a fragment of farm machinery or a nail. But the purpose of treasure hunting is primarily to find archaeological objects which have market or intrinsic value. It is hard to think of any such object of metal which is not also potentially valuable as a piece of archaeological evidence. A coin, or a group of coins, an object such as a brooch, an arrow or spearhead, a fragment of harness or a finger-ring are all likely to be datable and to yield a great deal of information about the people who lost them, but only if they can be closely related to their position in the site and to all the other objects used and lost in the settlement, farm, temple, fort or whatever the site was that was being searched. An object of any kind divorced from its context loses almost all its value as evidence. To say that a coin came from a certain depth and a particular point in a field is simply not good enough. If the coin is to yield its full potential information about the dating and economy of the site we need to know precisely its relationship to the stratigraphy, the layers in or under which it was found – its archaeological context. It follows that we need to know a great deal about the stratigraphy of the whole site, or at least a large part of it, before we can understand what the coins or other objects mean and that there is no chance whatever of recovering that information in a hole six inches square, or even three feet square. Only the most meticulous trowelling and accurate recording of the occupation layers in which the objects were embedded will provide the necessary contexts, and, as the rest of this book attempts to show, excavation has to be extensive if it is to be properly understood. Thus there can never be an archaeological justification for treasure hunting, or the use of a metal detector to find and dig out objects from archaeological sites.

If it is argued that the objects dug up were not from an archaeological site, the onus of proof of this must lie with the treasure hunter, since there is no way that a field can be shown not to contain, or be part of, an archaeological site, without very extensive geophysical survey and excavation. In other words, the treasure hunter either knows beforehand that an archaeological site is there, or he is digging blind, in which case he cannot know that it is not there.

10 *Dowsing.* Dowsing with hazel twigs or copper rods has been used from time immemorial to find water, wells, pipes and drains and it certainly works. Whether it is a sound basis on which to plan an excavation is another matter. The writer has no first-hand experience of an excavation with a successful strategy based on dowsing; however, three people, including the author, working independently with copper rods, found the same west-facing apsidal shape in the nave of Worcester Cathedral. This was promising because somewhere under the cathedral are two Anglo-Saxon minsters, no traces of which have ever been seen. Unfortunately, when we came to dig where the apsidal structure should have been, there was nothing resembling it. One of our number, having more faith in the rods than the rest, said that the apse had been dug away in antiquity and that we had traced the place where it had been, its 'ghost'.

The most rigorous testing of the method yet carried out was undertaken in and around a number of churches by Richard Bailey, Eric Cambridge and H. Denis Briggs and the results published in *Dowsing in Church Archaeology*, 1988 leaving no doubt about the potential of the technique, though it has yet to be accepted by a majority of archaeologists as a basis for research design.

Bore holes

Many contractors bore test holes in sites before development in order to examine the underlying strata, since they need to know as much as possible before designing buildings, especially multi-storey ones. Archaeologists can often use these borings to obtain a preview of the nature and depth of the occupation layers and the nature of the undisturbed subsoil. There may be snags, however – one bore hole in the centre of Worcester went through 9.7m (32ft) of black earth (it had probably gone straight down a well). And during the examination of the foundations of the central tower of Worcester Cathedral excavations had shown that the piers were founded on massive blocks of beautifully built masonry surrounded by packed gravel (see Fig. 27). But a bore hole drilled exactly in the centre part between the tower piers found nothing like

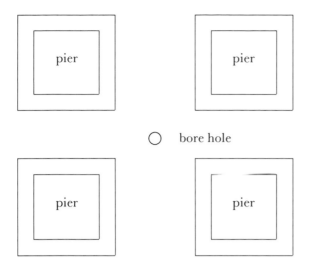

○ bore hole

this — simply layers of rubble and then the subsoil. From this it is clear that the builders of the tower dug not one but four enormous holes, constructed the masonry foundations and packed them with gravel before building the tower. Bore holes can, then, be very informative but suffer from the same limitations as trenches and test pits — it is dangerous to extrapolate far beyond the point which is tested.

Trial trenches and test pits

Trial trenches have for decades been the standard method of sampling a site; of seeing whether it was what it appeared to be; of testing the depth of stratification; of obtaining a sample of the pottery and finds so as to be be able to decide whether or not to continue with a larger excavation.

Trenches and pits have many limitations — one is illustrated in Fig. 24a–d — but at the same time they do provide much information very quickly. In advance of a rescue excavation where time is limited a machine-dug trench may be necessary to prove, not only to the archaeologist, but to a town council, a landowner or even the Inspectorate of

Ancient Monuments, that there really is something there that should either be dug before destruction or preserved for ever.

Inevitably, machine-dug trenches or pits destroy almost everything within the trench and the excavator has to rely chiefly on looking at the two sides of the trench or the four sides of the pit. Because pits have four sides some excavators prefer to dig a series of pits in line, a sort of discontinuous trench. In this way less damage is done to the site in the event of a full-scale excavation being carried out later. If time permits, trenches and pits can be dug slowly and by hand, in which case far more evidence can be recorded (see the examples from Wharram, Fig. 15 above), and therefore, in the event of a larger excavation which encompasses the test holes, these can be incorporated in the stratigraphic record.

The siting of trial trenches and pits is also a matter for considerable thought. They can be taken deliberately across the major features of the site in order to sample them, though if these are, for example, the sort of buildings which it might be desirable to display later, it might be better to avoid the buildings and rely on sufficient evidence on which to make judgements being obtained from the spaces between. It would, after all, cause some embarrassment if, when sampling a Roman villa, the head of Christ in mosaic came up in the bulldozer bucket. One major problem is that it is difficult to predict the spaces — what seems to be a space often contains a mass of features. The 'hollow way' at Wharram shown in Fig. 30a might have been thought to be a fairly straight-forward sunken road with few complications; Fig. 30b shows how mistaken this assumption would have been.

Sometimes it is possible to obtain a preview of the site without destroying it. For example, in a town there may well be cellars under demolished eighteenth-century or

Victorian buildings. These cellars can be emptied of their rubble filling and the walls removed, when four sections through the site, each 1.8m (6 ft) or more deep, can be seen without any more damage than had been caused a century before. In the same way, if it is known that disused sewers or drains or other services cross the site, the trenches in which they lie can be emptied providing two long sections.

The problem with all trial trenches and pits is that they not only destroy areas of the site without them being understood but they also cut the stratification, divorcing one part of the site from another. If these cuts exist on the site already, in the form of old trenches or cellars or pits, the damage has been done and the maximum information should be gleaned from them without any further losses of evidence.

In many cases the potential of the site can be at least partially assessed by a trench or trenches dug down only to the surface of the uppermost archaeological layers and features. This was a technique used in designing the extensive new workshops needed for the fifteen-year restoration for the Cathedral at Worcester. A long trench trowelled down to the first archaeological layers revealed considerable evidence of timber buildings some 20cm (8in) below the topsoil. As a result the buildings were designed to stand on a raft laid above the present ground level, thus preserving the archaeology intact.

5

Problems and Strategies

There is a continuing debate on the strategies to be adopted when designing an excavation. English Heritage's *Management of Archaeological Projects* 1991, is required reading for all archaeologists who have responsibility for fieldwork and excavation projects. It is an aid to clear thinking at each stage of a projected piece of work, proposing five stages through which a large archaeological project would normally pass (though there seems to be every reason for applying the same reasoning to small projects also).

The five phases are:

1 Project planning
2 Fieldwork
3 Assessment of potential for analysis
4 Analysis and report preparation
5 Dissemination

As the document says, these phases are familiar components of archaeological projects, with the possible exception of phase 3, discussed below in Chapter 10, p. 238. Nevertheless, the adjoining table, reproduced here as Fig. 23 (overleaf), does aid clear thinking and a logical procedure which should be the model for all projects.

Some archaeologists, using the parallel of scientific experiments set up to prove hypotheses, would advocate specifically problem-orientated excavations designed to throw light mainly, or sometimes only, on the questions which are uppermost in their minds at the time. The danger of this procedure is that, by investigating one period or aspect of a site single-mindedly, other periods or aspects might be ignored, or given scant treatment, and any remains belonging to them may well be destroyed in the course of the excavation. The grossest examples of this approach were the unconsidered bulldozing or summary digging of the medieval and post-medieval levels of towns in order to get at the underlying Roman levels.

Apart from the problems of the size of the excavated samples of a site (discussed below on p. 89), archaeological excavation differs from other scientific research in that postulated theories cannot be proved by the setting up of duplicate experiments, as already mentioned. Each part of every site is unique, so that the results obtained on one part of a site cannot, except in the broadest sense, be demonstrated to be correct by reference to work on another part of the same, let alone a different, site. Moreover, archaeological experiments cannot be set up to investigate isolated problems, since every site is not only unique but complicated and above all unpredictable. An excavation designed to answer a specific question will almost certainly run into completely unexpected evidence, in all probability tangential to, or even entirely unconnected with, the problem to be solved, evidence which is likely to raise more questions than it answers and which should certainly not be ignored.

It may be useful to cite some examples of mistakenly conceived problem-orientated digs. A long trench was dug, under my direction, across the ditch and part of the inner bailey of a castle not otherwise threatened (Barker 1961). This excavation was specifically planned to recover a pottery sequence dating from between 1115 and 1225, dates suggested by the documentary evidence.

It not only produced a plausible and entirely misleading pottery sequence (Barker 1961, 76, 77) but, though care was taken to do as little damage as possible, the trench destroyed parts of timber and stone buildings of the inner bailey without producing enough evidence to understand them. When eventually the castle is properly excavated the missing evidence may prove to have been vital and I shall rightly be castigated.

I also directed a limited excavation on the castle mound at Hastings (Barker and Barton 1977). The work was initiated principally to prove whether or not the mound was that built by William I and which appears in a famous scene on the Bayeux Tapestry. The excavation, showed, among other things, that the primary mound was probably of near-Conquest date (it contained a large unabraded sherd of c. 1050–1100, which strictly only gives a *terminus post quem* of that date), but it is now clear that it is impossible to prove by excavation that this is the mound depicted in the Tapestry. Even if coins of William I were found in the mound, or its make-up proved to be banded like that shown on the Tapestry, it could still be the castle said to have been built at Hastings by the Count of Eu a year or so after the Conquest. It is extremely improbable that any dating methods capable of a precision of ± one year will be evolved, methods moreover which would date the

construction of a mound and not simply the objects or other material found in it.

There is some reason to believe that William's castle was sited on the beach to protect his ships, in which case the present mound on the cliff-top cannot be the one shown on the Tapestry. But there is now no way of establishing this, especially as the coastline on which William landed has long been eroded away. In retrospect this was a piece of problem-orientated excavation, which, although producing interesting results did not, and I believe could not, have satisfactorily answered the question posed.

Trenching the ramparts and ditches of a series of individual classes of earthworks, such as Roman forts or medieval moats, in order to obtain a sequence of dated periods of occupation, will almost certainly fail to produce reliable information, either because the whole sequence is not present at the point or points chosen, or, if it is, it cannot be shown to be so without very much more extensive excavation. Such trenches are also notoriously liable to destroy other unsought for and unexpected evidence.

A dig which aims to shed light on a particular problem or period in a town's history is also liable to run into similar difficulties since towns are probably the most complicated and unpredictable of all archaeological sites. A long-buried castle ditch, of great interest to the student of the Norman period, may be overlain by a series of seventeenth-century industrial buildings, unique in the region and of vital importance to the industrial archaeologist. The Roman and medieval town nuclei may sandwich between them the much more elusive evidence of the immediate post-Roman centuries. In the past, holes carefully sited to determine the extent of the forum or the *principia* or other monuments of Roman towns or forts have been dug oblivious of a host of over-

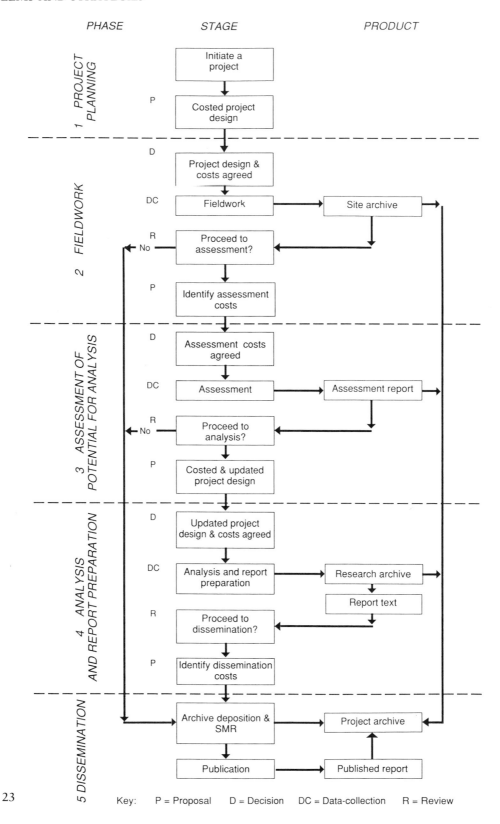

PHASE   STAGE   PRODUCT

1 PROJECT PLANNING

Initiate a project

P   Costed project design

2 FIELDWORK

D   Project design & costs agreed

DC   Fieldwork → Site archive

R / No   Proceed to assessment?

P   Identify assessment costs

3 ASSESSMENT OF POTENTIAL FOR ANALYSIS

D   Assessment costs agreed

DC   Assessment → Assessment report

R / No   Proceed to analysis?

P   Costed & updated project design

4 ANALYSIS AND REPORT PREPARATION

D   Updated project design & costs agreed

DC   Analysis and report preparation → Research archive → Report text

R   Proceed to dissemination?

P   Identify dissemination costs

5 DISSEMINATION

Archive deposition & SMR → Project archive

Publication → Published report

Key: P = Proposal   D = Decision   DC = Data-collection   R = Review

23

lying problems. (See Barker *et al.*, forthcoming, 1994).

What questions can be asked about a deserted medieval village which do not require virtually the total excavation of the village? Sampling trenches will certainly not give answers relevant to dates or structures except in a purely general sense. Such trenches may show that occupation extended beyond the period suggested by the documentary evidence, or that the village overlay an earlier sequence of settlements, that the houses were of wood, or clay or stone; but the price paid for this information may be the mutilation of the site to the extent that the structures trenched may never be subsequently understood. Even the total excavation of one or two house sites will only give answers which relate to those houses, which may be, for some reason, anomalies in the village, either in date or function, and cannot, in any case, be proved to be typical without further excavation. For example, at Abdon in Shropshire, R.T. Rowley excavated two house sites at opposite ends of the complex of earthworks which filled the large field in which stood an isolated church. One house proved to date from the thirteenth century, the other from the late eighteenth. Without extensive excavation it would be hazardous to assign a date to any of the other houses which appear to be there.

Such examples could be multiplied tenfold. What questions therefore should we ask of our sites and what sampling units might be considered valid? No one, presumably, plans an excavation without some inkling of what is likely to be found and some reason for digging this, rather than another site. Even under emergency conditions, or perhaps especially under emergency conditions, excavation is selective, dependent on the predicted richness of the site in structural or material evidence, or its importance in the area, or its rarity, its availability, its degree of preservation or the particular interests of the excavator or a controlling academic committee. In the absence, as yet, of any planned and co-ordinated strategy of investigation of sites on a national scale all these factors may, or may not, be considered before digging but usually some of them are.

M.O.H. Carver has admirably expounded the problem and suggested solutions in 'Sampling Towns: an optimistic strategy' in Clack and Haselgrove (1981). He argues that one should concentrate on those areas of a town where the archaeological deposits are deeper or more intact, and preferably waterlogged, especially if these coincide with good documentary and architectural evidence. Thus, the effectiveness of the excavation will be at its maximum at these points. This strategy is in contrast to that which advocates either digging wherever opportunity occurs within a town, or digging only in those places where specific, often isolated problems, might be expected to be solved.

Such an approach can, of course, be extended into the countryside. If it is, it follows that untouched earthworks will take precedence over cropmark sites, that, by definition, have been damaged by the plough, which, in many cases, will have churned up or removed all the superficial layers. Again, Hen Domen, Montgomery, illustrates this point. One nine-inch ploughing of that site would have destroyed the last two periods of occupation, leaving only the deeper, post-hole structures (which may well have appeared as marks in a subsequent crop). Clearly, therefore, if there is a choice between a ploughed and an unploughed site of the same type, excavation of the second will be likely to be more productive. It follows that, in general, intact earthworks deserve more protection than cropmark sites, as they are likely to embody more (and more reliable) evidence.

Any excavation strategy should therefore include intensive site evaluation by all the non-destructive methods available. The decision to excavate one rather than another site can then be made on more strictly archaeological grounds than has often been the case in the past. Such site evaluation may, of course, result in the site's preservation rather than its excavation, since the best and richest of our sites (in terms of surviving evidence) should be protected from destruction by archaeologists and should be conserved as part of a rapidly diminishing resource.

Nevertheless, we seem to be moving towards a more coherent research/rescue policy, in which non-archaeological factors, such as individual interests, local availability of funds or manpower, as well as the patterns of destruction are minimized. The question has been discussed in relation to the Anglo-Saxon period (Wade 1974), where, after the very great practical difficulties of statistically random sampling of sites are acknowledged, cogent arguments are put forward for a mixed strategy of large-scale excavation together with small-scale sampling based on extensive fieldwork. It is an open question whether fieldwork on the scale needed, particularly the assessment of the vast back-log of aerial photographs, can be made before a large proportion of the sites has disappeared or been deeply damaged. It is also open to question whether one should pursue the study of settlements of a particular period, since unless they happen to be founded on virgin territory, and to have had no successors, other periods of occupation will be drawn into the enquiry, and may receive less than their due from the single-minded worker. So we are brought back to the relationships of sites to their setting and the concept of landscape archaeology, in which it is the landscape which is sampled, rather than a series of sites; Wade's discussion of sampling criteria and strategies is therefore as applicable to the landscape as to Anglo-Saxon settlement research (*ibid.* p. 88)

There are two levels of sampling: since all known or suspected sites cannot be sampled, some must be selected for large-scale work, some for small-scale sampling, and others left either to be eroded by natural processes or destroyed by development or ploughing, or preserved intact for future investigation. The difficulties of making such a selection are formidable and liable to the grossest errors of judgement, especially if the only criteria are cropmark photographs, field names, scatters of pottery (with their bias toward ceramic periods in regions which have long aceramic periods) and other imponderables. To this must be added the complication that many village, town and city sites overlie sites of the period or period under consideration. The Deserted Medieval Village Research Group changed its name and its objectives to the Medieval Village Research Group because by definition it had been studying failed settlements. The successful villages had flourished and are now under expanded settlements. The village of Beornmund-ingaham (Birmingham) is a notable example.

To all the difficulties of statistical sampling of the population of sites must be added the continuing distortions due to the fact that they are not a static, fossilized entity but a rapidly changing and diminishing asset, disappearing, like the expanding universe, at a rate faster than we can overtake.

If we can envisage an Ideal Excavation, in which every scrap of the surviving evidence is recovered, from complete plans of major buildings to the total pollen count (and if it is remembered that all of this will only be a small fraction of what existed during the site's occupation), then it will be clear that this level of recovery would give us the best chance of interpreting the site most fully and that anything less than this ideal situation will give us progressively less information down to the point where much of the structural and stratigraphic evidence cannot be understood. Since the Ideal Excavation is unattainable we have to decide what the acceptable levels of recovery are. In the case of structures and buildings I believe that total recovery should be the aim. Only in a very few special cases, where the structures are known beforehand to be repetitive and the stratification simple (as, for example, at Trelleborg or Fyrkat) can sampling provide valid and satisfying evidence. The case of Chalton may here be cited. Champion (1978) has shown that a 20 per cent random sample using 8m quadrants covering no more than 30 per cent of the site gave a fair estimate of the total number of buildings (60 against an observed total of 57) and some information about the nature of the structures. However, Chalton is an exceptional site consisting of many buildings of roughly similar size, and with little, if any, superimposed stratification. In addition, this exercise was retrospective and sampled an excavation rather than an untouched field. The difficulty is to know beforehand what the size and variety of the structures present are likely to be, so that a sampling strategy can be devised. Aerial photographs and geophysical surveys are notoriously deceptive, detecting the major structural features such as walls, floors and large post-holes, but failing to detect those more tenuous sorts of evidence such as pebble spreads, lines of stones, shallow post-sockets and discolorations of the soil which may, nevertheless, indicate the presence of major buildings. In addition, a large proportion of sites are vertically stratified with the sizes and distribution of structures changing through time and the nature of the occupation. The writer knows of no sampling strategies which would be adequate sampling for the structures in the excavations illustrated in Figs 24a-d and the end papers of this book.

Nevertheless, it would be patently ludicrous to take a total sample of every type of evidence. A total soil sample would mean keeping the whole spoil heap, while the labour involved in recording a total seed or pollen sample can be demonstrated statistically to be pointless. The problem then resolves itself into a determination of the size of sample of each type of evidence which is valid.

R. Lee Lyman in *Prehistory of the Oregon Coast: the Effects of Excavation Strategies and Assemblage Size on Archaeological Sampling* (1991), considers in detail and analyses mathematically the relationship between the sizes of excavations and recovered artefact assemblages. Not surprisingly, he and his colleagues conclude that the larger the samples the more reliable the results and recommends the 'excavation of 100m per thousand radiocarbon years per site as a minimum . . . which will produce a rich data base much more quickly [and reliably] than an accumulation of small excavations'.

The case is different if the site is to be destroyed and a rescue excavation is mounted. Here, a whole range of sampling techniques may be deployed, aimed at the site's subsistence, economy, diet and industry, technology, trading links as evidenced by pottery and other artefacts, animal bones and other faunal remains, together with the evidence for the natural and man-made environment. Such sampling is, however, less likely to answer questions of the site's structures and their interrelationships or to relate the sampled evidence to the structures.

Faced with the destruction of a large and complex site a number of interrelated decisions have to be made. These will be based on the expected survival (or not) of the structural remains and their nature, the likely survival of organic material, the expected density of artefacts such as potsherds (a Roman site as opposed to a Bronze Age site, for example), and the amount of information already available about this type of site in the region – an early Anglo-Saxon site is proportionately more important in the West Midlands than in East Anglia (see Ellison 1981, p. 1, for a suggested rank order of sites in Wessex). Intensive and extensive sampling should be preceded by site evaluation which uses all means of archaeological prospection. (See Carver 1981, for a discussion of the problem in the context of a town, and Cherry, Gamble and Shennan (eds.) 1978, for a comprehensive discussion of sampling methods and strategies, and see pp. 79–88 below.) Nevertheless when a site has been selected for excavation, whether total or partial, I believe that the questions should be widened as far as possible to include all those aspects of the site which might be recovered.

I am becoming more and more convinced that ultimately the only valid questions to ask of a site are 'What is there?' and 'What is the whole sequence of events on this site from the beginnings of human activity to the present day?' Any other question must only be a part of this all-embracing one. (See Collingwood 1939, Chapter V and particularly the example of the non-starting car and the spark-plug.) If the question is asked, 'Was there prehistoric occupation here?', an excavation designed merely to answer this question will probably do so fairly quickly but perhaps at the expense of later occupation levels. Or if it is asked 'What is the date range of the occupation of the site?' then a series of cuttings through the whole sequence of deposits may answer this but only for those parts of the site tested; there may be other periods of occupation in the untested areas. Again the questions might be asked 'Does this site contain a sequence of imported pottery?' or 'Is it a deserted medieval village?' or 'Was it a ring-work before it achieved a motte?' or 'What is the extent of the suspected Mesolithic occupation area?'; in obtaining answers to all these perfectly reasonable questions, other aspects of the site may, and probably will, be ignored and perhaps irretrievably damaged. If, however, while keeping firmly in mind the questions which prompted the excavation in the first place, together with all the myriad subsidiary questions which are posed by the emerging evidence, we are alert to the possibility of the unexpected – the medieval cottage built into the Roman fort, the motte encapsulating a Bronze Age barrow – we shall avoid finding only what we set out to find rather than what is there. On this point Collingwood's advice is less than sound (*ibid.* p. 124) and runs counter to the considerations which prompted this book.

If a trial excavation is required for some overriding reason, to produce evidence of dating of the structures rather than simply the fact that they are there and something of their nature, it will be necessary to empty features, and remove floors, foundations and other structural remains in the hope of recovering stratified datable material. In such a case, the recording must be especially rigorous. Only if each surface, layer or feature is precisely levelled and drawn with an accuracy of ± 1cm will it be possible for a subsequent excavator to be certain of correlating his results with those from the trial trench.

However, no excavation can be totally neutral in its approach. We inevitably enter a site with some preconceptions as to what we hope to find and we constantly formulate questions and as constantly abandon them. The evidence as it emerges will pose new questions of tactics, and may even alter the course or strategy of the whole excavation. Whatever major problems are uppermost in our minds we must always be prepared to encounter entirely unexpected (perhaps unwanted) evidence, which must be treated comprehensively, and not given scant attention or even be swept away as irrelevant. What is more important is that the unexpected evidence may present itself in an unexpected form, one with which we are not familiar or which does not fit in with our preconceptions of what might or should be there.

The scale and complexity of all but the smallest sites may deter us from total excavation, especially when the increasing refinement of excavation techniques can turn the study of one quite small site into a lifetime's work. Almost always in the past, research by means of excavation has been aimed at solving the problems of a site as quickly as possible, within a year or two, or at least within the lifetime of the excavator. Now, however, complete excavation is necessarily such a slow process that we shall not know within our own lifetimes the answers to many of the questions asked about single sites, let alone complexes of related sites. Research excavations, therefore, must be planned for posterity, eschewing the quick answer and setting up a framework of excavation and recording which can be handed over, extended, modified and improved over decades, and in some cases, centuries.

I have in mind particularly the case of the Roman City at Wroxeter, where some 60ha (150 acres) are being preserved for the nation. Total excavation of the city, spreading out from the central area which has been the focus of most previous excavation, would occupy at least two centuries even if the present rate of progress were to be doubled. Since all previous work has shown that each area of the city is radically different from its neighbour, the results of the work at present being carried out there cannot be extrapolated to any other part of the site.

The whole will have to be dug in the greatest detail if the rise, heyday and decline of the city are to be fully understood, and the city itself lies within a complex hinterland many square miles in extent. The same argument applies to many other complicated and comparatively unthreatened sites, such as deserted medieval villages, hillforts, and motte and bailey castles. We must be patient and work for the future so that we do not leave our prospective colleagues a legacy of mutilated indecipherable monuments. Some would, of course, argue that such major unthreatened sites should remain untouched, presumably in perpetuity. While this will certainly achieve the maximum protection for these sites, such a policy paralyses research, simply because it confines it to rescue and salvage excavations, carried out under less than ideal conditions, and usually limited to those parts of the site threatened by destruction unrelated to the archaeology.

Sample trenching and gridding

To dig holes, however well recorded, in an ancient site is like cutting pieces out of a hitherto unexamined manuscript, transcribing the fragments, and then destroying them, a practice which would reduce historians to an uncomprehending stupor, but whose counterpart is accepted by the majority of archaeologists as valid research. A single section, even of a ditch, can be grossly misleading, as anyone who has cut multiple sections will know. Many layers are discontinuous, appearing in one side of the section only or changing in composition across the cutting to reappear in a different form on the opposite face. Clearly it is not sufficient to dig a section either by hand or with a machine and attempt an interpretation on the basis of the observed vertical surfaces. The old archaeological maxim 'it will all come out in the section' is simply not true.

79

Extensive excavations on sites previously trenched (such as Dorestad, van Es 1969, 183ff.) have so often shown that the earlier conclusions have been completely misleading, that it is now clear that only total, or near-total, excavation will yield results which are not deceptive. One possible exception is the more formalized, stereotyped Roman building which may be dug in small areas, the plan then being extrapolated from them with some confidence, but this presupposes that there are no anomalous or unexpected buildings above or below the stereotype. Even Roman forts are now seen to contain so many unconventional, even eccentric features, that argument from the part to the whole is becoming increasingly hazardous in an area of investigation once thought to be comparatively simple (for instance The Lunt Roman Fort, Hobley 1973).

Too often a trench cut across the defences of a site has been held to reveal, in concise form, the whole sequence of events on the site. Subsequent area excavation usually shows that the facts are more complex. One section of the ditch of the outer bailey at Hen Domen, Montgomery, showed the ditch there to have been dry, V-shaped and once recut. Another section, 15m (50ft) away, showed that there the ditch was of at least three periods, flat bottomed and wet. It might have been assumed from these cuttings that there were three phases in the life of the castle, but five sections of the motte ditch, all different in their evidence, showed a minimum of seven phases. In some of these sections, drawn within a few metres of each other, varying depths of recutting had removed almost all traces of two or three of the earlier ditches; and careful collation of all the sections was needed to produce a solution which total excavation of the whole ditch system might yet modify (see Fig. 8, 1–5).

24 a–d The easiest way to explain the uses and limitations of trenching and gridding is by a series of illustrations.

24a is a plan of an area of the bailey or courtyard of the timber castle at Hen Domen, Montgomery. About a quarter of the bailey was stripped of its topsoil and the visible features planned. These were then removed and the underlying layers were cleaned and planned. This was the surface shown in 24a (phase Y). They consisted mostly of pebbles with a few post-settings which are shown in black. As can be seen, the concentrations of pebbles of various sizes are not random, but have clearly been laid purposefully. d shows the excavator's interpretation of this surface. Building IV was a polygonal tower sited on the bulbous end of the bailey rampart – it had burnt down and imprinted itself on the surface by reddening the clay of which the rampart was built. Building VIII was a small rectangular building behind the rampart, approached by a pebble path, while IX has been interpreted as a three-cell chapel, with a polygonal apsidal end, close to a double-post-hole palisade, V, which ran parallel to the motte ditch. The functions of the other, subsidiary, structures are less clear. A full account of this interpretation will be found in Barker and Higham 1982, pp. 41–8. It will be seen, though, that it would have been very difficult to make any sense at all out of the partial evidence provided by trenching or gridding. In the past, the trench has been the most popular and common way of exploring archaeological sites. In b it is imagined that a trench 3m (10ft) wide has been laid out at right angles to the bailey rampart to explore the interior of the bailey. It will be seen that, although the patterns of pebbles and post-holes would suggest structures, there would be no hope of understanding them.

When the excavation at Hen Domen began, the area was laid out in a series of grids, of 10 sq.ft separated by balks 2ft wide. This was soon abandoned, as it was realized that it was producing distorted results (Barker and Higham 1982, p. 23), but in c it is imagined that the grid system was continued into Phase Y. It will be seen immediately that it is virtually impossible to make sense of the features which are visible. In particular, Building IX could hardly be postulated from the evidence seen here. It would be clear that there was a series of structures of some sort – in particular the band of heavier stones running parallel to the rampart would be obvious, and the presence of buildings IV and VIII assumed, though their form would be impossible to describe.

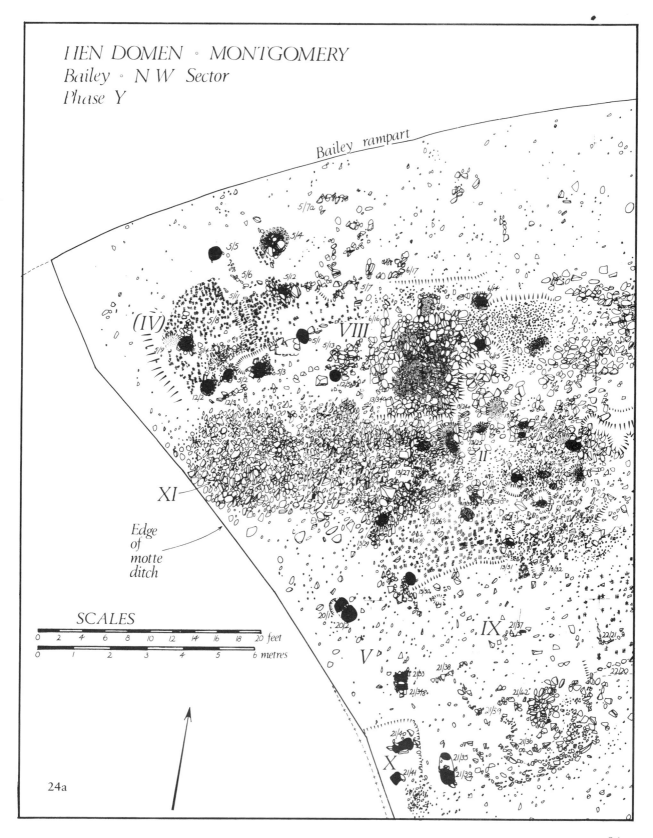

HEN DOMEN · MONTGOMERY
Bailey · N W Sector
Phase Y

Bailey rampart

(IV)

VIII

XI

Edge
of
motte
ditch

II

IX

V

X

SCALES

0 2 4 6 8 10 12 14 16 18 20 feet
0   1   2   3   4   5   6 metres

24a

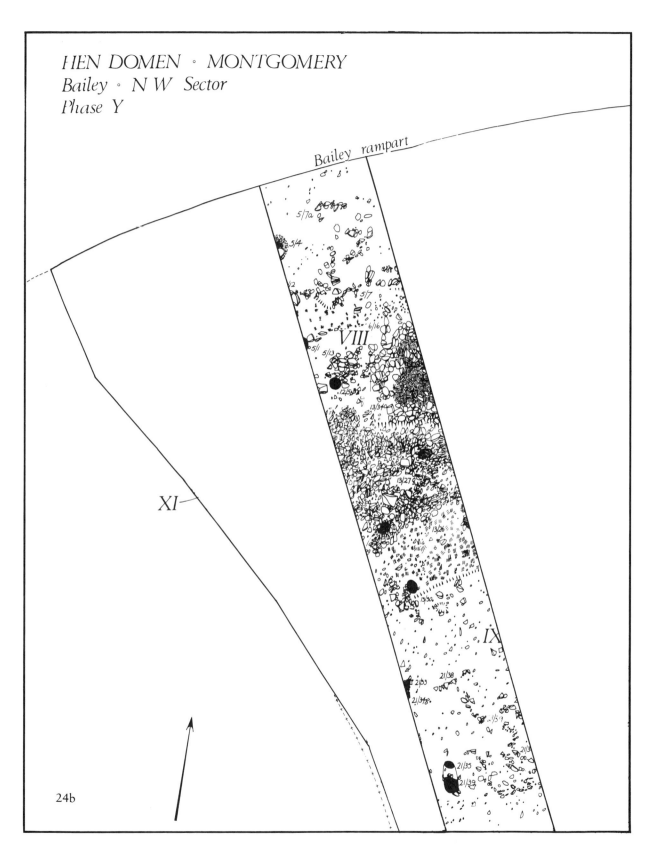

HEN DOMEN · MONTGOMERY
Bailey · N W Sector
Phase Y

Bailey rampart

XI

VIII

IX

24b

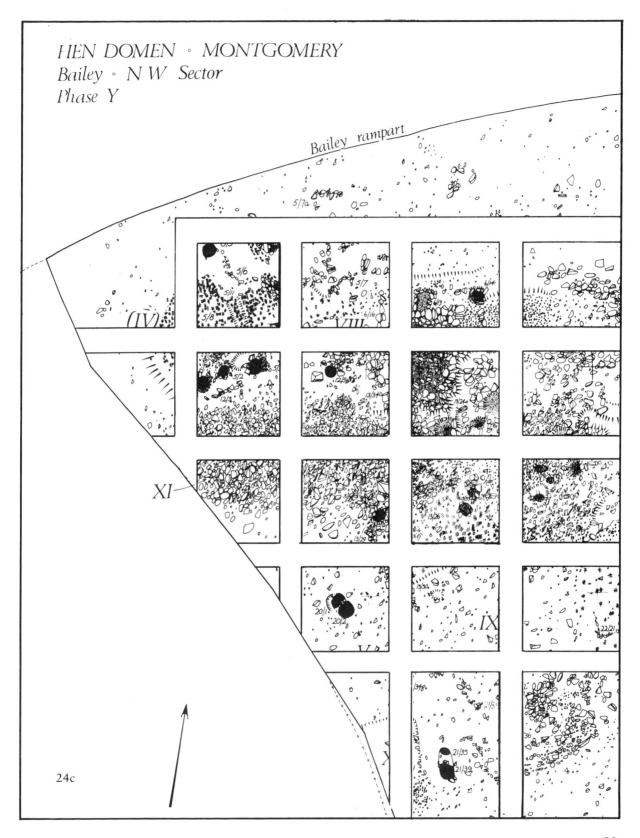

HEN DOMEN · MONTGOMERY
Bailey · N W Sector
Phase Y

Bailey rampart

(IV)

VIII

XI

IX

24c

83

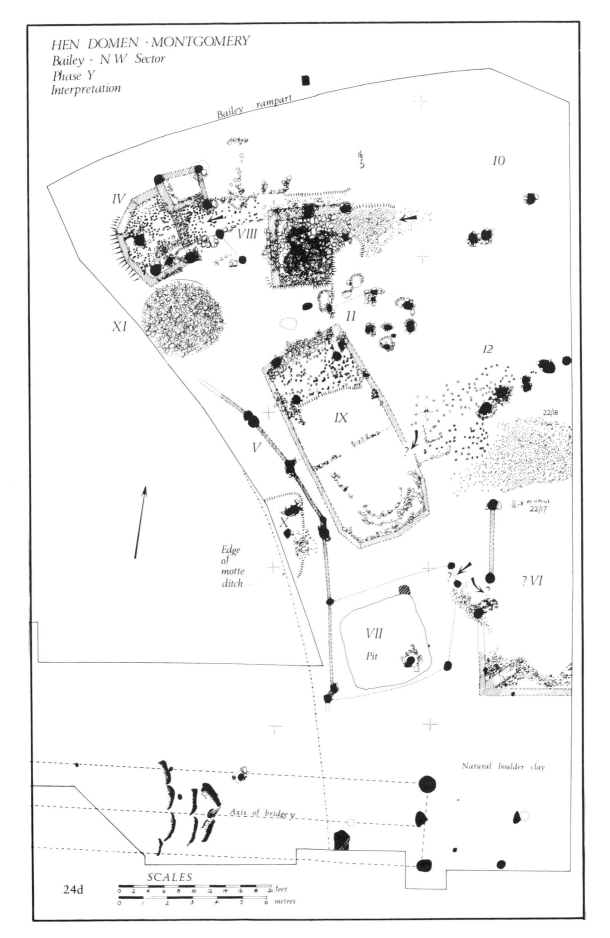

HEN DOMEN · MONTGOMERY
Bailey · N W Sector
Phase Y
Interpretation

Bailey rampart

10

IV

VIII

XI

11

12

22/18

IX

V

22/17

X

Edge
of
motte
ditch

? VI

VII
Pit

Natural boulder clay

Axis of bridge y

SCALES

0 2 4 6 8 10 12 14 16 18 20 feet
0   1   2   3   4   5   6 metres

24d

It is astonishing how close a trench can be dug to stone or brick structures without revealing their existence. Take, for example, two short emergency excavations on moated sites in Shropshire (Barker 1958 and 1964). In both, trenches passed within a metre or two of the foundations of brick or stone buildings, in one case the foundations of the Manor House at Shifnal, without encountering any evidence such as fragments of tile, brick, stone or mortar which would have suggested the imminent presence of a major building. At Shifnal, a subsequent trench cut at right angles to the first encountered the massive sandstone foundations of the house. In both these cases, geophysical prospecting would probably have discovered the structures in advance, in which case the trenches would not have been needed or could have been sited more usefully. The problem for the prehistorian interested in the earliest periods of man's activities is a very difficult one, since structures are less likely to be discovered, partly because they were flimsy and partly because they will have suffered far more from weathering than later structures (see Atkinson 1957, 219–33).

A further form of sampling excavation may seek to obtain environmental evidence from a sequence of waterlogged ditches or drainage channels. I have in mind the investigation of, for instance, a system of medieval fishponds. Total excavation would be impossible, even ludicrous, but a series of trenches across the ditches, leats and pools might produce very valuable and valid environmental samples. Even here, however, any structures on the islands surrounded by these pools and ditches will have to be given the full treatment (see reports on excavations on a fishpond site at Washford, Worcestershire, M. Gray, forthcoming, and at Bordesley Abbey, S. Hirst and P.A. Rahtz 1976).

Nevertheless, trenches often give immedi-

ate and apparently satisfactory results. The broad dates of the site, the nature of its occupation, whether it had timber or stone buildings; the richness of its deposits and the wealth of its preserved finds may quickly become apparent. Thereafter the law of diminishing returns rapidly begins to operate. Six trenches will not give three times as much information as two, and the second, third and fourth weeks' work will not quadruple the information of the first.

What, then, is the value of the trench? It can test the site's potential for future exploration and it can check the results of geophysical surveys, or establish the depths of deposits and the nature of the subsoil. Although this information may be of considerable value, and although trial trenching may be unavoidable in the planning of some emergency excavations, I believe that if possible trenches should not be dug below the surface of the first archaeological layer encountered, that is, the latest occupation layer. Only an excavator who has dug on a site already riddled with trial trenches from previous excavations will know how almost inevitably these trenches destroy areas of vital evidence, sometimes in the only places where relationships between structures can be tested. On other occasions they will have removed parts of timber buildings, unrecognized because the trench was too small in area.

It may be useful here to use an analogy. Imagine a room, the floor of which is covered to some depth by an assortment of carpets, rugs, blankets, newspapers, magazines and sheets of cardboard, the whole covered with wall-to-wall carpet. A person wishing to understand fully the layers covering the floor will naturally begin by rolling back the uppermost carpet and then recording the surface revealed beneath. They will then remove one by one each overlying rug, newspaper or blanket, recording its removal and

85

the layers revealed beneath, until they reached the floor. Surely no one faced with this problem would take a knife and cut a rectangular hole in the carpet and then continue this hole downwards to the floor removing the partial layers of paper and cloth as they went. How could they in this way know that, though they have recovered a portion of yesterday's *Times*, a whole Persian rug may lie a little to the right?

This seems a fair parallel to the archaeological situation, even down to the fact that, on most sites with timber buildings, the layers will be as difficult to see and interpret in section as the layers in my analogy

There are some occasions, of course, when for sheer practical reasons a trench is all that is possible. This is particularly likely to be the case in towns, where the work has to be confined to the space between two buildings, or along a sewer trench, or to the hole dug for a manhole or so forth. Classic examples of such trenches on the grand scale are those dug by Dame Kathleen Kenyon in Jericho and Jerusalem where, short of a great disaster, it will never be possible to dig very large areas. The restrictions here are extra-archaeological, so to speak, and they are not trial trenches dug into sites which could, and might in the future, be dug more extensively.

It is argued also that there is some value in knowing the depth of the deposits before work starts. This is necessary if an estimate of the length, and therefore the cost, of the excavation is to be made, for example, to a developer who is expected to fund the excavation in advance of the development. Though the correlation between depth and time seems eminently reasonable, in that the deeper the stratified deposits, the longer the excavation will take and the more it will cost, there is an important *caveat*, because, conversely, a shallow site, with a multiplicity of thin layers, may take many months to dig. The depth of the stratification at Hen Domen between the bottom of the topsoil and the top of the subsoil averaged between 20 and 30cm (8 and 12 in), yet this thin layer contained the evidence for five phases of buildings (none of which, incidentally, could be identified in the section) (see Barker and Higham 1982, Fig. 5).

Still less should holes be dug into the site to determine the nature of the subsoil. If the subsoil is homogeneous over the whole area it can be examined at a point away from the site; but if this is not the case, in drift deposits, for instance, there is no point in taking samples at one or two points within the site; it will have to be recognized afresh everywhere it is eventually encountered. In many areas of Britian the subsoil changes so rapidly that it is pointless to examine it except within the area of the excavation.

In a recent excavation, directed by the writer, on the floor of an occupied thirteenth-century timber-framed hall, there was some doubt as to the nature of the subsoil on which the yellow clay floor was based. The subsoil under the garden immediately outside the house, and no more than 20m (66ft) from the excavation was dark red marl. This marl was therefore expected under the floor. The excavation showed, however, that the house was built on an outcrop of grey-green lower lias – a fact which caused some confusion at first. In this case examination of the surrounding subsoil had not been helpful but the reverse.

A way of examining the depth and nature of deposits on town sites, particularly large ones, without damaging intact archaeological layers, is to remove recognizable modern surfaces, such as concrete platforms, rubble foundations, floors and so forth, and then identify recent wells, pits and other intrusions into the underlying layers. If these are emptied it will be possible to observe the stratification in section at a number of places around the site. Cellar walls can also be selectively removed and the stratification behind them examined. In this way assessments of the depth and nature of deposits can be made, and costings estimated without damage to the site. Since, in towns particularly, vital evidence often survives only in small 'islands' or 'peaks' left between pits and other disturbances, it is vital that these should not be lost in blind trial trenching or their understanding jeopardized by digging them in trial holes where their context cannot be appreciated. Only if such methods of prior examination fail should one resort to trial trenching, and especially to trial trenching by machine.

This approach is more difficult in the countryside, where recent holes are likely to be fewer, or non-existent. It may be possible to trace field drains (by magnetometer, resistivity meter, ground-probing radar or even dowsing) and empty them as a first stage. Where stratified sites do survive they are so precious that all non-destructive methods of examination should be exhausted before we begin to destroy them.

However, all these methods will only give a broad picture of the depth and nature of the thicker deposits at the places examined – they will not reveal the existence of the thin or discontinuous layers which are often of crucial importance and may even represent whole periods of occupation. It is, perhaps, safe to say that any site is likely to be at least three or four times more complex in plan than it appears in section, so that when estimates of time and money are being calculated a multiplier of at least three may be necessary.

A stronger case can be made out for trenching linear features, such as ramparts, dykes and roads. Obviously it would be impossible to excavate Offa's Dyke or the Antonine Wall completely, so a series of carefully selected sections across such monuments will give a great deal of information about their construction; and if circumstances are fortunate, about their date. However, the same limitations which apply to all excavations do still apply here. A trench cut across an undated dyke may recover Iron Age pottery from the old ground surface beneath it, and if no other sections are cut a post-Iron Age date can correctly be assumed for the dyke. But for how much of it? It may not all be of one build; centuries may separate two periods of its construction, or two short portions of pre-Roman dyke may have been joined together in Saxon times. The evidence from the section only relates to the sectioned part of the dyke, and cannot be projected to a point two or three kilometres away unless very careful fieldwork makes it virtually certain that the dyke is all of one build (for a good example which illustrates this point see Hill 1974).

Moreover, a section cut only a few metres away from the original section may recover a medieval sherd from the lower layers of the dyke's make-up. Are we then justified in putting the whole earthwork into the medieval period? Is it perhaps a park boundary? Or is this section a late infill? Only more extensive work can hope to provide a satisfactory conclusion. Furthermore, sections cut across ramparts and dykes will not provide answers to important questions such as the existence, or not, of a palisade. Even Sir Cyril Fox, in his great work, did not advocate the stripping of a length of Offa's Dyke to see if it was palisaded, although this would be the only way to find out. (See Barker, in Everson 1992.)

In the case of Roman (or any other) roads the limitations of sectioning can be reduced by cutting wide trenches which enable each road surface to be seen in plan before it is removed. In this way a great deal more will be learned about the road than from a narrow vertical trench. The existence of buildings on its latest surface, or the traces of cart ruts, will be much easier to discover in a wide section, dug layer by layer.

The choice of site to be dug and methods used

With limited time and resources all excavations cannot be total, so that partial investigation of many sites must be planned to give optimum results. To that end, they must be problem-orientated and the limitations of such excavations must be realized and accepted. The factors which govern the choice of sites to be dug vary enormously. They will include purely practical considerations such as the availability of money, and, more important, of competent directors and site supervisors, the length of time the site is available (which will determine the strategy of the digging) and its size and probable complexity. If the dig is to be financed by public funds then the site's relative national importance vis-a-vis sites not only of the same type and period but also of a totally different kind must be assessed. To make a decision on the importance of a small but complex and apparently unique cropmark site in rural Shropshire relative to a development in the centre of a well-known Roman town in Lincolnshire is difficult almost to impossibility, but is the kind of choice which is constantly being forced upon us. If neither can be dug completely, the amount of information likely to be achieved by a partial excavation of one or both must be estimated (perhaps incorrectly), and a strategy for each devised. This strategy will itself depend on a number of factors. It may be agreed, however reluctantly, that some aspects of the site must be abandoned if light is to be shed on those aspects which are considered the most important. In the case of the cropmark site these aspects may be its dates, and its length of occupation rather than the

details of its structures. In the case of the town site it may be suspected that an earlier defensive line runs through the available site and therefore that this, rather than any overlying or underlying buildings, should deserve the highest priority. Note that in both these cases, and in many others which could be postulated, it is the buildings that take the most time to elucidate, and thus tend to be abandoned first. Broad dating ranges and defensive works (together with massive stone buildings) can be more rapidly dealt with.

Other factors which may affect the decision to dig entirely or to sample, or abandon, perhaps with a watching-brief, are the uniqueness or conversely the ubiquity of the type of site in the region – whether it is representative of a common, generally recognized type, or an anomaly; the paucity in the region of previous studies of the period thought to be represented by the site; its degree of preservation or its apparent relationship with structures of other periods which seem to overlie or underlie it, promising relative stratigraphy. These are the considerations which will affect problem-orientated strategy. Problem-orientated tactics will depend on the practicalities outlined above, such as time, and the availability of finance and skilled labour. If these are not sufficient for a full-scale excavation yet the site is irrevocably to be destroyed, painful decisions will have to be made as to what will be sacrificed and what, if possible, recovered. All such decisions, made before the start of the excavation, are liable to drastic modification within hours of the commencement of the dig, since the immediate results may be quite unexpected. It is, therefore, necessary to maintain a flexible approach and not to plough on, determined to solve only the problems discussed round the committee table. New, more important, problems may be revealed by the emerging evidence or it may transpire that the evidence for the solution of the original problems is simply not there.

Sometimes we are faced with the situation, such as the construction of a motorway, where many sites will be destroyed or damaged, and only one or two can be dug. Here the decision may well be based on gaps in the knowledge of a particular kind of earthwork or cropmark site, rather than on other more practical considerations such as the longer availability of another site or its clearer indications on the ground, or its state of preservation. The decision to dig one site rather than another having been made, the question of techniques will then depend on the time, money and other resources available. If there is only time for a short excavation it will be necessary to decide whether to dig a number of trenches across the site in the hope of establishing a chronological sequence, to strip off the topsoil over a large area in order to recover a broad plan of the structures; or whether to use geophysical methods, basing the decision as to the method of excavation on magnetic anomalies or other similar evidence. If, in the latter case, magnetic or resistivity or radar anomalies indicate the existence of a building in one area of the complex of earthworks, the decision to recover the plan of this building rather than attempt, in the time available, to sample the whole site for other equally interesting information will be a conscious decision based on what is currently needed in the archaeology of the region, or of that class of earthwork. If the opposite decision is taken, to strip the site summarily in order to recover the broad picture, losses of detail and perhaps some confusion of chronology must be expected.

To summarize: it seems to me that where ten sites are to be destroyed it is far better to dig two of them totally and salvage excavate the others than trench or partially excavate all ten. Of course, the choice will be a difficult one and mistakes are inevitable; but the principle should stand in spite of this.

Total excavation of a non-threatened site, which inevitably means its destruction, must not be undertaken lightly. Trenching will mutilate it, and extensive trenching will make it virtually impossible to excavate the site properly in the future. Total excavation of half a site, leaving the other half for future more refined excavation is a solution that has been suggested, although the two halves of even a small site may be very different from one another in the length, intensity and nature of their occupation.

This my colleagues and I have found to our cost at Hen Domen (Barker 1969a), where one quarter of the bailey has presented quite different problems and a different sequence of events from the immediately adjacent area, excavated earlier. Another team of excavators, digging the new area independently some years after the end of the first stage of the excavation would have been baffled (as we were) by the results, and would probably have concluded that our earlier conclusions were totally mistaken. It is only because we have much the same personnel digging the site in exactly the same way as in the first stage that we know that it is the site which is changing across the width of the bailey (a mere 30 or 40m (100 or 130ft)) and not the result of different techniques.

The problem of sampling resolves itself ultimately into the question of the size of the sample. Ideally the smallest valid sample is a complete site, or better still a whole area of ancient landscape, but since we do not live in an ideal world, we have to compromise and accept all the external constraints which leave us with far smaller samples than we would wish for; and we must be wary of projecting into the surrounding undug areas those aspects of the excavated evidence which cannot justifiably be extended on whatever scale we may be digging.

Only full, highly-detailed excavation will yield all the available evidence, itself only a fraction of what was originally there. Anything less than total excavation must be problem-orientated if it is to give the maximum results, and, in my view, is only justified if the site, or part of it, is to be destroyed or if it is too vast to be dug completely, when the excavation must be planned on the assumption that the rest of the site may one day be dug.

If a site is inevitably going to be destroyed and time, finances, or other considerations forbid excavation on a large scale, then it may be decided to sample for particular aspects of the total evidence which is assumed to be present. For example, it might be considered that the most important aspects of a large multi-period prehistoric site are not the structural sequences but the environmental changes which have occurred since before the site's occupation up to the present day. A sampling strategy based on extensive bore holes and test-pits may answer these questions in a very economical way, though other questions which may be asked will evade such a strategy.

Other strategies may be devised to sample pottery scatters over a large site, to determine the lengths of phases of occupation or shifts in their nuclei. A difficulty here is that aceramic phases some of which, in western Britain, are very long, will escape this net and the picture thus become distorted.

Do sites of different periods require different methods?

So far it has been implied that all sites should be excavated in the same way, regardless of date and type of structure or function, that is, whether they are military, religious, secular, domestic or palatial.

To take first the question of period. It has often been maintained that excavations should only be carried out by specialists in the particular period of the site concerned, and there is some force in this argument. It is reasonable to expect specialists to concentrate on their chosen periods, and to dig those sites of particular interest to them. Only thus, it is argued, will the peculiar features of a barrow or iron smelting furnace be discovered since the specialist will know what to look for. Here we have, however, the teleological argument that people may find what they wish, albeit subconsciously, to find.

The opposite point of view sees the excavator as a technician producing evidence from the ground regardless of its date or function. In an ideal archaeological situation in which excavation was a scientific discipline with the excavator able to choose precisely the material on which to conduct experiments, specialization would perhaps be automatic. But this is not the case. With few exceptions British sites consist of a multiplicity of periods, and, more often than not, prove to be entirely different from what is expected. What is the motte digger to do if the motte being dug is found to be based on a barrow? Or the medievalist if an Iron Age settlement underlies the deserted village? The situation is even more complex in towns. The urban archaeologist must be prepared to find evidence of any date from the palaeolithic onwards immediately under the pavement. It would obviously be ludicrous for a medieval archaeologist to abandon the site and call in a Romanist because a Roman building had been encountered, the Romanist in turn passing on the excavation to a prehistorian when an Iron Age hut circle appears. Under these circumstances, which cannot be avoided, excavators must be all-period technicians, recording in meticulous detail evidence which they do not necessarily fully understand at the time, but which they can discuss, preferably while the excavation is open, with specialist colleagues. If this is not possible, the discussion will have to be based on the recorded evidence, which must therefore be of the highest quality if it is to be properly understood.

I do not believe that sites or monuments of different periods require differing excavation techniques. A Bronze Age hut should be dug with precisely the same techniques as a medieval longhouse, a Roman villa with the same methods as a medieval manor house.

The excavation of timber and stone buildings – are different methods required?

The fundamental principle of all excavations should be to remove and record each layer, feature or context in the reverse order from which it was deposited, over as extensive an area as possible. There will be some occasions on which this ideal must be modified. One of them is the presence of standing walls which may introduce complicating factors into the day-to-day planning and direction of the excavation.

To take a typical example: a large and complicated stone building may lie under continuous or intermittent layers of plough soil, rubble and debris, including the deposits of later timber buildings. These layers should be dug horizontally in the way described in Chapter 6. When the tops of the walls of the underlying building are reached the layers on each side become separated by the walls and the site divides itself into smaller areas which can (in fact, must) be dug separately, in some cases room by room. This introduces a complication, since the site grid is unlikely to coincide with the shape and size of the building's divisions or rooms (see Barker *et al.* forthcoming, 1994). If the walls are standing to an appreciable height measuring over them from an external grid point may become tedious and inaccurate. In this case a subsidiary datum point can be established within the walls, or when the walls themselves are accurately plotted they themselves, or points on them, may be used. Excavation within the walls can then proceed like any small-scale area excavation, with cumulative sections taken wherever desired. This excavation of the levels associated with the building should ideally continue downwards until the pre-building layers are reached. However, the situation is unlikely to be as simple as that. If the walls have been built in construction trenches (Fig. 25) these trenches should, in theory, be emptied before the layers into which they cut. But the walls themselves are by definition later than the construction trenches and therefore should be removed first. Usually, at this point, non-excavational factors enter. Walls, unlike post-holes, are tangible, emotive fragments of the past, capable of being preserved and displayed to the public. Unless the site is irrevocably to be destroyed, it may well be desirable to keep the walls intact. Under these circumstances it will not be possible to excavate those layers which run under the walls, and the site will have to be dug in smaller areas. This may make interpretation of underlying timber structures exceedingly difficult if not impossible.

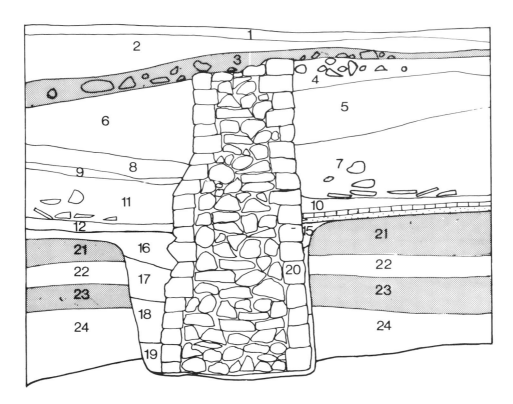

25 (*Above*) Diagrammatic section of a wall built in construction trench layers 15–19, cut through earlier layers, 21–24.

26 (*Below*) This figure shows diagrammatically a section through a robber trench in which it is possible to distinguish: the ground level at the time of the building; the construction trench for the wall – a; the accumulations of material with debris during the life of the wall – b; and the robber trench with unwanted debris thrown back into the trench – c; d represents the mortar raft on which the wall originally stood.

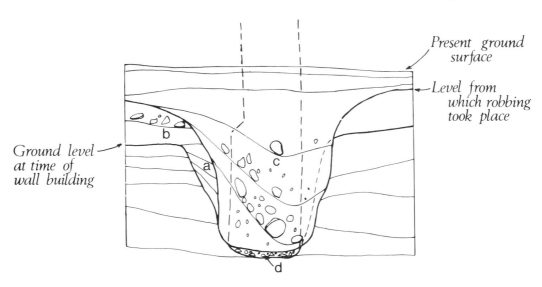

At this point also safety factors must be considered. Foundation trenches, emptied along the lines of the walls, may seriously weaken their stability, and any attempt to dig pre-building layers may leave the walls standing on highly unstable balks. If the walls are to be preserved for eventual display, they must be shored professionally. This further reduces the area archaeologically available.

The situation is even more complicated if the stone walls have been robbed out in antiquity, so that robber trenches as well as foundation trenches have to be dealt with (Fig. 26 shows a typical situation in section). Ideally the robber trenches should be emptied in sequence before any earlier layers are removed, but this is not always practicable. If the robber and foundation trenches have been cut through soft or friable layers the risk of collapse will be considerable. In this case it may be necessary to lower the filling of the robber/foundation trenches a little ahead of the main excavation. This requires strict control of the digging and recording but guards against the loss of evidence which collapse would make inevitable. If resources are available the robber trenches may be emptied completely and then backfilled with sand or sifted earth in order to preserve them intact while the excavation proceeds from the upper levels. This was the strategy used on the excavation of the Baths Basilica at Wroxeter (Barker *et al.* forthcoming, 1994).

One temptation, which all excavators of stone buildings must have felt, is that when a stone wall or floor is encountered it is very easy to become careless of the strict sequences of stratified excavation and to follow the wall or expose the floor in a sudden flush of enthusiasm. A subtle form of this aberration shows itself in the outlining of stones or walls by slight over-digging. Establishing the presence of the tops of walls

or foundations is almost irresistible but may destroy important stratigraphical relationships and therefore should be resisted.

The recording and interpretation of standing buildings is, strictly speaking, beyond the scope of this book. Nevertheless, underground archaeology cannot be separated from that which is visible above ground. The excavation and interpretation of churches, cathedrals and castles cannot be divorced from the evidence of the standing buildings, whether they are intact or ruined any more than urban archaeology can be divorced from the surrounding fabric of the town or city. The publications of the large urban units, such as those of London, York or Lincoln, demonstrate this conclusively, while Warwick Rodwell's *Church Archaeology* (new ed. 1989) illustrates graphically the intimate relationships between church buildings and their excavation.

The excavation and interpretation of buried walls and foundations appear at first sight to be easier than that of timber buildings. If anything they are more difficult. This is perhaps because the excavated masonry presents more evidence in tangible form than the elusive post-hole or fragment of pebble floor. Post-holes or stake-holes which are not understood or which do not fit a pattern can be (and often are) conveniently overlooked in the final interpretation. (If this statement is not believed compare almost any field drawing of the excavation of a complex of timber buildings with the final publication.) They can after all be dismissed as the remains of ephemeral structures such as scaffolding, or peat stacks, temporary enclosures or whatever the fertile imagination can create. It is not so easy to ignore fragments of masonry, brickwork or concrete foundation, which must represent something large and solid, even if short-lived.

One of the best ways to learn about or to

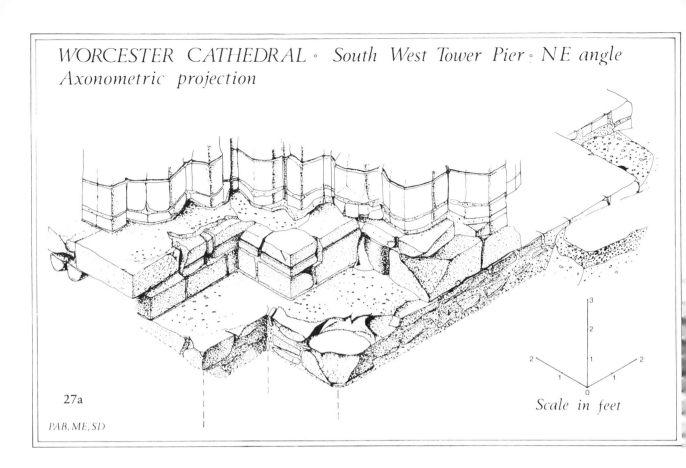

WORCESTER CATHEDRAL · South West Tower Pier · NE angle
Axonometric projection

3
2
2   1   2
1   1
0
Scale in feet

27a

PAB, ME, SD

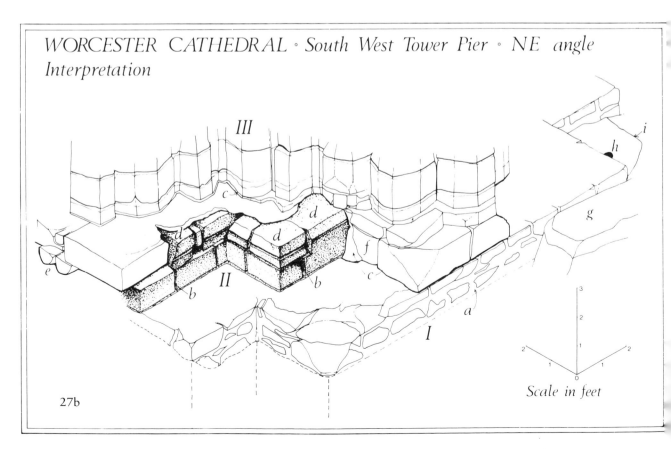

WORCESTER CATHEDRAL · South West Tower Pier · NE angle
Interpretation

III

i

h

c

d

d

g

d

d

e

f

b

c

II

b

a

I

3
2
2   1   2
1   1
0
Scale in feet

27b

27 a–b An example of the excavation of a stone building. In 1981 a small excavation was carried out to examine the foundations of one of the piers of the central tower of Worcester Cathedral. The present tower dates from the mid-fourteenth century but it was known that it stood on the foundations of the tower of the Norman cathedral begun by Bishop Wulstan in 1084. However, there is a record in the annals of Worcester that the new tower of Worcester collapsed in 1175 (*nova turris Wignorniae corruit*). Victorian writers were sure that this was the central tower but more recent opinion asserted that it was one of the western towers. The excavation at the base of the pier showed conclusively that there were three phases of construction: first, a massive base of uncoursed rubble, clearly, for reasons which there is not space to detail here, the Norman foundations of c.1084. On this stood a foundation which, at first sight, appeared to have a chamfered plinth of Norman date and to be contemporary with the base below. However, closer examination showed that the stones of which it was constructed (*d*) were, in fact, reused abaci from capitals or string-courses paralleled exactly in the nearby crypt of 1084, but here reused upsidedown.

Mortar samples were taken from joints *a* and *b*, examined and compared and shown to be different from one another. Mortar samples from joints in the fourteenth-century pier at *c* were also examined again. Clearly there were three phases of construction. However, it was also seen that the fourteenth-century pier, which was a different shape from the underlying bases, had itself been packed with reused Norman architectural fragments, including a column drum, *f*, and a double capital *e*. A floor, *g*, probably of the first period, had sunk and tilted, while *h* is a post-hole, perhaps for a scaffold pole, set in a pit, *i*. The probable sequence of events is thus:

The building of the first Norman tower, *I*, after 1084 and perhaps as late as 1150; the collapse of this tower and the building, after 1175 of a second tower, *II* on foundations derived from the collapsed masonry; the building of the third tower, *III*, in the late fourteenth century, again reusing Norman masonry, but this time probably from the destruction of the ambulatory of the crypt when the east end of the cathedral was rebuilt in the thirteenth century.

teach the complications and unravelling of the development of a masonry structure is to study a church with a long history, or simply to examine one wall of such a church (Fig. 28). Even without a detailed knowledge of ecclesiastical architecture it is usually possible by a logical dissection of the evidence to determine the sequence of building periods, alterations and repairs. Add to this an acquaintance with the styles of church architecture and the relative periods of building can be given dating brackets. As in excavated buildings and their foundations, the interpretation of standing buildings is very often complicated by repairs, later renovations in earlier styles or reused fragments of earlier stonework or sculpture (Fig. 27).

Differences in types of masonry, of stone, of mortars, of stone dressing, and the existence of butt or bonded joints must all be looked for and recorded with the same meticulous detail that is given by the excavator to the recording of a series of thinly stratified floors or groups of stake-holes. The only satisfactory way to record and study masonry is by a stone-by-stone drawing annotated with the types of stone, mortar samples and other relevant detail. In the case of large expanses of standing masonry or brickwork, photogrammetry or rectified photographs is a fast and accurate method of recording the elevations.

If all that is left of a complex of masonry buildings is a series of robber trenches, these must be excavated with the same attention to detail which is given to the rest of the site. It is not enough merely to empty them along their length in order to obtain the outlines of the former buildings. Close study of the backfilled material and its stratification will give information about the mortar used in the robbed wall, about the direction from which the backfilling was made, about the level and therefore perhaps the date from which the robbing was carried out, and

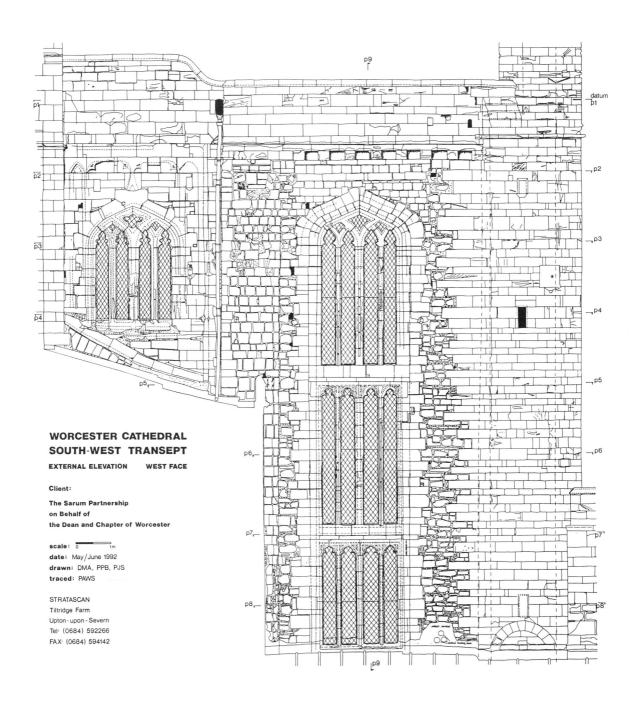

WORCESTER CATHEDRAL
SOUTH-WEST TRANSEPT

EXTERNAL ELEVATION   WEST FACE

Client:

The Sarum Partnership
on Behalf of
the Dean and Chapter of Worcester

scale: 0   1m
date: May/June 1992
drawn: DMA, PPB, PJS
traced: PAWS

STRATASCAN
Tiltridge Farm
Upton - upon - Severn
Tel· (0684) 592266
FAX· (0684) 594142

28 a–b (*Left and right*) Worcester Cathedral: the
west elevation of the south-west transept.

As part of the progressive recording of the whole
Cathedral the west face of the south-west transept,
which is badly weathered and due for renovation, was
recorded by drawn survey from scaffolding, backed up
by detailed photography.

Close examination of the fabric and analysis of the
mortars revealed four building phases. The wall was
shown to be part of the original transept of Wulstan's
Cathedral of 1084, with two large inserted
Perpendicular windows of the fifteenth century, and a
parapet of the eighteenth century. In the major
restoration of the mid-nineteenth century large areas
were refaced.

Such detailed recording and analysis together with
the evidence from excavations are enabling the earlier
phases of the building to be reconstructed.

29 (*Below*) An axonometric drawing of the great hall
at Okehampton Castle, in Devon. In this form of
drawing, the measurements can be scaled off correctly
along three axes – those shown on the bottom left-
hand corner of the figure. The viewpoint from which
the drawing is made is chosen to give the maximum
information, and the result is a little like an aerial
view, except that it is not, of course, in perspective.

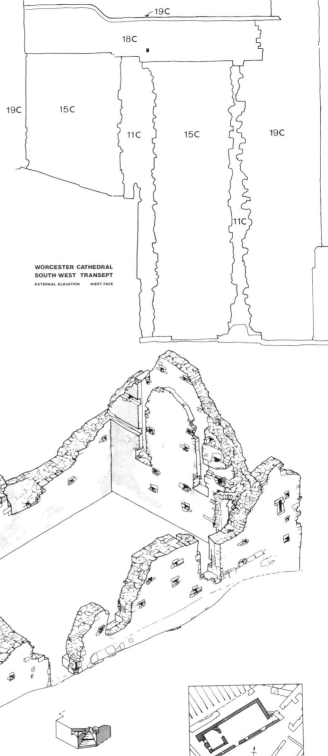

WORCESTER CATHEDRAL
SOUTH-WEST TRANSEPT
EXTERNAL ELEVATION   WEST FACE

97

whether the robbing was carried out in two or more stages. It may also yield dating evidence in the form of coins or pottery. Careful trowelling of the bottom of the robber trench may reveal the imprints of the stones, bricks or tiles which formed the structure.

The excavation of the Old and New Minsters at Winchester was a brilliant example of the way in which robber trenches can be made to yield the maximum information (see Biddle and Kjolbye-Biddle 1969, and interim reports in *The Antiquaries Journal*, 1964–75 and full report forthcoming).

Competitive tendering

The increasing professionalism of archaeology and its relationship with developers has led to the demand for competitive tendering for all forms of archaeological work, especially that in advance of development. This puts archaeology on a commercial footing, a transformation which would have been anathema (and probably still is) to an earlier generation of archaeologists. While competive tendering is possible, and perhaps even desirable, in site evaluation, geophysical survey, building survey, post-excavation analysis, publication and other forms of non-destructive archaeology, there are real problems with competitive tendering for excavation simply because of the non-predictability of the results. While every form of non-destructive survey and prediction is valuable, all experience shows that the results of highly detailed excavation are likely to be many times more complex than the predictions. Even trial trenching, which may give information about the depths of deposits and something of their nature, cannot do more than suggest the complications which may be revealed by horizontal detailed excavation over a large area. For example, there is no way that either geophysical survey or trial trenching could have predicted the complexities of Hen Domen or Wroxeter, the two excavations most often quoted here. In the case of Hen Domen, the two last phases of occupation were contained within 4cm (1½in) immediately under the topsoil and a trial trench would have made nothing of them – see Fig. 000 – and recent geophysical survey has shown the presence of the larger anomalies, but not the mass of small features on which the interpretation has depended. In the case of Wroxeter, there had been extensive earlier excavations based on trenches, which had drawn completely erroneous conclusions from them. In both cases, if the sites were to have been threatened with development and competitive tenders invited, the tenders would either have had to have been realistic, amounting to hundreds of thousands of pounds and years of continuous work or, in the hope of obtaining the contracts, would have been geared to what the developer might have been assumed to be willing to pay, a procedure not unlike offering to do a quick, cut-price heart transplant, because in both cases – of excavations and surgical operations – the scale and complexity of the operations should be dictated not by expediency but by the irreducible needs of the patient or the site.

Another example of the inherent difficulties of site prediction, quite different in scale and type from those cited above has been revealed in the course of writing this chapter. The basement of a house near the Cathedral at Worcester was to be refloored by removing the existing floor to a depth of 300mm (approx. 1ft) and replacing it. The workmen taking up the floor revealed a number of human bones immediately beneath. Subsequent archaeological excavation revealed some 55 skeletons and fragments of many more within a relatively small area, in a layer no more than 200mm (8in) thick.

The burials were coffinless and had been cut one into another, clearly over a long period of time. This necessitated very careful and meticulous excavation and recording and a protracted post-excavation programme of skeletal analysis and radiocarbon dating of sample burials together with conservation and analysis of the finds (one of the skeletons having, for example, an arrow buried in its rib-cage).

The writer can think of no technique by which a pre-excavation assessment could have been made of this site – geophysical survey might have shown anomalies but not their nature, especially as the burials were coffinless, and the most careful excavation and observation failed to discern the grave cuts. A trial trench might have revealed a skeleton or two but could not, by definition, have shown all that was there.

The writer does not know the answer to the problem of competitive tendering for excavation because the parameters will always be largely unknown, and in many cases unknowable before the work is well advanced. The temptation to put in the lowest tender could lead to the use of 'broad brush' techniques which would certainly tend to distort the evidence, while on the other hand a tender which took a more realistic view based on the sort of examples quoted here would probably be met with amused disbelief and rejection.

6

The Processes of Excavation

The principle of all excavation, large or small, is to remove the superimposed contexts one by one in the reverse order from that in which they were deposited, recording each in as much detail as is necessary to reconstruct, in theory at least, the site context by context, complete with its features and finds, long after the actual process of excavation has destroyed it. Only by doing this can we obtain sufficient evidence to begin to understand the evolution of the stratification of the site, let alone interpret its periods and structures.

Under present circumstances, when a great proportion of all excavations are carried out under rescue conditions, few of us are fortunate enough to have at our disposal the time and resources to dig at the pace dictated by the nature and complexity of the site, but unless we keep the ideal situation firmly in mind during even the most rushed salvage dig we will lose more information than is necessary.

Methods of excavation

The ideal excavation would extract from the site everything that could possibly be known about it — everything that has survived the physical and chemical changes of centuries of burial. So little is now left of the original house or village, cemetery or fort, that the methods of excavation used have to be increasingly refined — crude digging will only recover a tiny percentage of what is already reduced to a fraction. Only too often, excavations are hurried or partial, or carried out with a JCB instead of a teaspoon, because of factors which are quite outside the control of the archaeologist — an imminent development, a chance discovery or simply lack of resources.

There is an unresolvable conflict between proper excavation and the need for speed, since there is an optimum speed at which the excavation can be carried out — the site, of whatever sort, should dictate the speed of the excavation. To try to go two or three times as fast without serious loss is like asking a surgeon to carry out a heart operation in half an hour with a knife and fork. This is because archaeological sites are immensely complicated, and those that appear simple have usually been made so by inadequate excavation.

On the other hand, the total excavation and recording of every facet of the site, from the documentation of the size, shape, weight and geology of every pebble to the recovery of every seed and every grain of pollen, is clearly unnecessary, even ludicrous, and certainly not cost-effective in either cash or the time of skilled personnel. So a balance has to be struck between the sweeping butchery of many earlier excavations and the necessary recovery of a minimum of highly detailed information. It might, for example, be decided, after discussion with the various specialists concerned, to recover every possible animal bone, but to sample the seeds and pollen, the snails and oyster shells.

In earlier days pottery was 'sampled' by throwing away all but the rim and base sherds. This is now unacceptable, because of the considerable losses of information which result, but it is now realized that wet sieving produces a large number of sherds which have been missed even by experienced trowellers and dry sieving. Furthermore, experiments have shown that, understandably, far more red sherds, even tiny ones, are recovered with the trowel and in the dry sieve than black or grey ones, and that far more sherds of all kinds are missed in wet weather than in dry, because of the thin film of mud that obscures them. It will be appreciated therefore, that even in this small area of research the ideal excavation is very difficult to achieve.

I believe that the larger the continuous area of excavation can be, the more complete and undistorted the results will be. For example, there is no doubt that if we could have excavated the bailey of the small motte and bailey castle at Hen Domen, Montgomery, as a whole we should have understood it more easily, and not lost evidence along the balk between the two quadrants which have been excavated (Barker and Higham 1982, p. 23). All experience shows that wherever there is an edge or a balk there is some loss of evidence, either because of simple erosion or because of the great difficulty of matching the two parts together, even if they have been dug with great care and meticulously recorded. However, few archaeological sites have natural edges. Even apparently self-contained monuments, such as burial mounds, motte and bailey castles or churches, extend, archaeologically, beyond their obvious limits, as many excavations have shown.

What for instance, are the limits of a Roman town? Not the defences – there are almost certainly suburbs beyond, and the defences themselves very probably overlie earlier occupation which spreads beyond them. Nor can a single *insula* or block within the town be considered an isolatable unit. It might be thought that an excavation which had edges down the middles of the streets dividing the *insulae* would be self-contained but at Wroxeter we should never have understood the remarkable late development of the east–west street if the excavation had not included it complete, though in doing so, it sliced off the fronts of the buildings facing the street, so that a subsequent excavator may have great difficulty joining his excavation to ours along this edge (Barker *et al.* forthcoming, 1994).

On the other hand, some sites have edges because the surrounding area has been destroyed, or because it is not available, nor is ever likely to be. Such a case may be a site in a town, with the houses on both sides occupied and likely to remain so. The excavation has, therefore, to be confined within that area, though it is very likely that underlying Roman or prehistoric occupation will not respect those limits. Because I believe that the larger the horizontal area which can be excavated, the more the evidence will be understood, so I believe that trenches will almost always give partial and probably misleading answers. Compare an excavation with the dissection of a human body. A trench across the chest will give a certain amount of information about the heart and lungs and part of the spine, but nothing at all about the brain or the kidneys, or, for that matter, the kneecaps. The only logical way to 'excavate' a body is to dissect it layer by layer, taking the skin from the muscles, the muscles from the skeleton and so on, eventually dissecting each organ down to the nerves and tiny blood vessels which make it up. So it is with an archae-ological site. It should be dissected logically from the surface down, in the way that the site dictates, layer by layer, feature by feature, down to the smallest visible unit, and sometimes beyond (for example, the mechanical or chemical analysis of deposits in order to understand their structure or their contents). However, this is not to say that sections are not useful and sometimes essential. At one extreme, the total stripping of a great linear earthwork, such as Offa's Dyke, or the ramparts of Maiden Castle, would be out of the question logistically, politically unacceptable and hardly cost effective. In such cases, a series of sections at critical points will provide the maximum practicable obtainable information, while, at the other end of the scale, it is helpful to section features of many sorts in order to reveal and record their structures. Some

30 a–b shows how successful a wide trench, sited in the right place, can be. The medieval village of Wharram lies on the chalk Wolds of Eastern Yorkshire. The site is a large one, now under permanent guardianship, and being developed for visitors to see the medieval village earthworks and ruined church and churchyard. It is the scene of one of the best-known excavations in Britain, which has been going on for over thirty years, for three weeks each year, with up to 100 people working at one time. Even with this massive input of research, time and labour, less than five per cent of the site has been dug. Certain areas have, however, been very rich in archaeological evidence. Between 1980 and 1984 in the North Manor area, a wide trench was cut by Philip Rahtz across a hollow-way, or sunken road (a). A sequence was recovered of: *1* a major defended late Iron Age settlement lying under the manor; *2* extensive Roman levels including a road and corn-dryer (there is probably a villa close by); *3* Early Saxon huts of the sixth century, cutting through the Roman road; *4* Late Saxon wooden buildings and pottery; and *5* the medieval manor itself, b. The dig was only *c.* 400sq.m (4305 sq.ft), a tiny fragment of Wharram, but a remarkable sample of its long history.

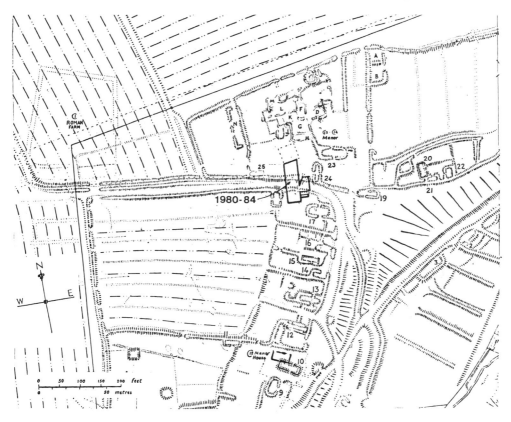

30a

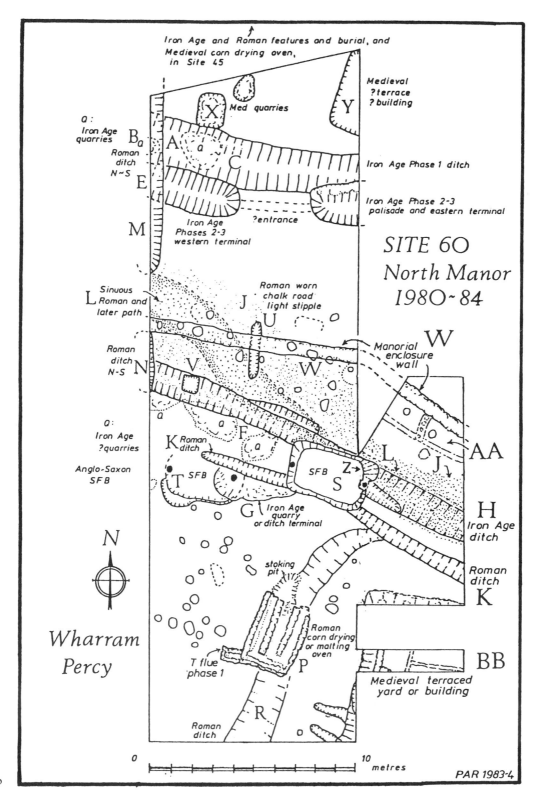

Iron Age and Roman features and burial, and Medieval corn drying oven, in Site 45

Med quarries

Medieval ?terrace ?building

Q: Iron Age quarries

Roman ditch N~S

Iron Age Phase 1 ditch

Iron Age Phase 2-3 palisade and eastern terminal

Iron Age Phases 2-3 western terminal

?entrance

SITE 60
North Manor
1980~84

Sinuous Roman and later path

Roman worn chalk road light stipple

Manorial enclosure wall

Roman ditch N-S

Q: Iron Age ?quarries

Anglo-Saxon SFB

Roman ditch

SFB

SFB

Iron Age ditch

Iron Age quarry or ditch terminal

Roman ditch

N

Wharram Percy

stoking pit

Roman corn drying or malting oven

T flue phase 1

Medieval terraced yard or building

Roman ditch

0   10 metres

PAR 1983-4

30b

excavators attempt to get the best of both worlds by excavating in extensive areas, but leaving thin balks, or undug strips, across the site, drawing the visible faces of the balks as they proceed. The balks can be removed at any time to reveal the whole surface plan. Others, of whom I am one, prefer the cumulative section, i.e. to excavate up to a predetermined line, draw the visible section, and proceed to excavate the rest of the layer or feature (see Fig. 32); obtaining a plan of each feature together with a section through either the whole site, or any part of it.

A method used by Scandinavian archaeologists is to level-in every surface and every find, so that, theoretically, a section could be drawn anywhere across the site. This is meant to overcome the problem of the siting of sections before it is known what to section. For example, in the excavation of a deserted village site, a section line might be set up across a visible house platform. When the building has been excavated and removed, it may well happen that there is a series of underlying buildings all on different alignments. Under these circumstances, using the method described above, it is possible to publish sections wherever they are desired, in order to show particular features (Fig. 12). The method is, however, very time consuming and the cumulative section, described below, which can be equally flexible is more commonly used.

The excavation of timber buildings poses somewhat different problems from that of stone buildings, since in most cases the timber has rotted long ago, so that, although the methods of excavation are similar, in that there is no special way to dig timber buildings as opposed to that used to dig stone buildings, the evidence for timber buildings usually presents itself in different ways: as negative features if the timbers have been embedded in the ground or as very slight traces if they have simply rested on the ground. The case of waterlogged, and therefore preserved, timbers is different again, since, while the preserved timbers can hardly be missed, their recording presents special problems as the timbers very often lie in many separate planes, needing three-dimensional recording of a different kind from that used for stone buildings where plans and a series of elevations may be sufficient, since their planes tend to lie at right angles to one another. Stereoscopic photography, or even small-scale models, may be the most accurate way of recording such waterlogged remains in a way which can be immediately 'read' and understood. Those interested in the problems of excavation of waterlogged wood should read the

31a Tenuous evidence. The photograph shows the north portico of the Baths Basilica at Wroxeter after the removal of an overlying rubble platform which had supported a timber-framed building. From the angle at which the photograph is taken four equidistant parallel lines defined by pebbles, tiles, mortar, slight hollows and ridges are visible. The most likely interpretation of these traces is that they mark the lines of parallel joists supporting a board-walk which had replaced an earlier portico floor of tiles or pebbles. This view is reinforced by the fact that a number of uncrushed ox skulls were found between the putative joists, suggesting that they lay in the spaces under the floorboards. It will be obvious that only area stripping would have revealed this phase in the site's development. (Photo: Sidney Renow.)

31 b–c These photographs of the northern portico of the Baths Basilica at Wroxeter, show the same area as in 31a after further excavation. The ranging rods are laid along the lines of the joists which held the boardwalk running the length of the portico. The faint traces of the joists are due to their weight (and the weight of the people who walked on the joists above) compressing the underlying layers. Subsequently the trowellers sensed the harder material and left it, removing the softer material on either side (c).

31a

◀ 31b

reports of the excavations of the Somerset Levels (Coles and Coles 1986) the Fens (Pryor 1991) or the Coppergate site in York (e.g. Hall 1984).

By far the majority of all the buildings ever built were in wood, though because stone buildings leave impressive remains they have, in the past, received most of the attention; another factor is that sites with timber buildings are difficult to dig, and have often eluded crude and summary excavation. Moreover, many sites contain both stone and timber buildings, often inextricably mixed at all periods of occupation, so that the concentration in the past on a site's stone buildings often led to the evidence for the timber buildings being dug away unnoticed. The whole site must be dug in the same sensitive way if more than the bare outlines of its development are to be recovered. Even buildings which were principally of stone may have incorporated timber partitions (see Fig. 67) or outhouses or alterations (see, for example, Chapter 6 in Higham and Barker 1992).

Excavation techniques are not dependent, therefore, on the date of the site or the nature of the occupation but more on the nature of the subsoil, the depth of the deposits, and the length of time and the amount of resources available. For example, an excavation on a stone-free site, that is, on sand or loess or some clays, can use methods impossible on one in which the evidence for structures consists chiefly of pebbles or rubble spreads, or, in hill country, solid rock.

On a site composed of pebble or rubble, only meticulous hand cleaning of the surfaces will reveal their patterns and structure (see, for example, Fig. 31a–c). On stone-free soils, horizontal cleaning with machinery or hand shovels is possible. This technique, known as the planum method, lowers the whole site progressively, recording it at each stage as a series of horizontal sections. This method is particularly useful on sand, where, because there are no vertical sections, there are no sides to collapse, with the consequent loss of evidence, even of workers. The planum method has been used with spectacular success in north-west Europe, for example, at Dorestad and Wijster in Holland (back endpapers and van Es 1967 and 1969, and see also Farrugia, Kuper, Luning and Stehli 1973). It has also been used in East Anglia on clay, and by Guy Beresford at Goltho and Barton Blount, in the excavation of these deserted village sites (Beresford, 1987). Clearly, waterlogged sites, such as the Somerset Levels or the Fens, will require their own adaptations of the basic techniques. Other excavations may demand a combination of many different approaches; Hen Domen, Montgomery, is one of those where horizontal excavation has been combined with cumulative or running sections cut across linear features, such as the defensive ditches. Sometimes it has been possible to dig features entire, on other occasions they have been sectioned in quadrants or subjected to miniature planum excavations. In other words, although the ideal of extensive horizontal excavation has been kept in view, it has been modified to cope with particular problems. For a more extended discussion of the methods used at Hen Domen, and the reasons for using them, see Barker and Higham (1982).

The key to all good excavation is the scrupulous cleanliness of the excavated surface. Soil is, regrettably, opaque. A layer of dust or mud only a few millimetres thick will obscure all but the grossest differences in colour and texture. This is why most surfaces are at their best when newly trowelled and why it is useless to use a brush in wet weather. The cleanliness of the surface is so important that site supervisors should require the trowellers to go over the surface time and again if necessary until, colloquially, they could eat off it. Sometimes, though, stony or rubble layers 'improve with keeping', as they are washed by rain. The improvement in the cleanliness of the extensive rubble layers on the Baths Basilica Site at Wroxeter, Fig. 31a–c, was very marked after a winter's rain, though the individual stones were cleaned as thoroughly as possible during the excavation. Trial hosing of stony surfaces will show if they may be cleaned in this way without damage.

As little spoil as possible should accumulate on the site. It should be the rule, followed wherever possible, that each troweller only accumulates as much spoil as will fill a hand shovel before it is removed to the bucket, sieve or barrow. In this way the site is kept clean, and the spoil does not get trodden or knelt into the surface.

It is sensible to use kneeling mats when trowelling, as they save the knees from becoming sore after long periods of work and, more important, protect them from damp. Rheumatism and arthritis are the occupational diseases of the long-term digger and every precaution should be taken to avoid them.

Tools

The trowel is the fundamental excavation tool. Whatever supplementary tools such as knives, teaspoons, ladles and the like may be used, the small (3–4in long) trowel is the most versatile implement in the hands of the competent digger. The art of trowelling can only be taught in the field, so that if newcomers to archaeology are employed it is a very good idea to use the monitorial system whereby inexperienced trowellers are set to work next to or between experienced ones who will be specifically told to teach them by example. This process considerably lightens the teaching burden of the site supervisors who, nevertheless, keep overall control. The beginner should be taught to use the trowel delicately or strongly, as circumstances dictate, to use the point, either with a scraping motion, or a chopping, digging one, or to clean a horizontal surface with the straight edge with millimetre accuracy.

The basic advantage of the small trowel is that it allows much greater pressure to be put on its point than on that of the 5 or 6 inch trowel, which should be used when, for instance the layer to be removed is silt or sand.

The hand-brush is an essential adjunct to the trowel. When it should be used is a matter of constant judgement. In dry weather it is easy to brush a soft or dusty surface and produce something that looks like a new layer, or even a floor, especially if the brush removes fine soil or stones from between other stones which are in fact an integral part of the layer. Equally a stiff brush used on a dry clayey surface will often polish it, producing a surface resembling a floor. On the other hand, the brush, whether hard or soft, used at the right time can be a most delicate and subtle instrument. Churn brushes with very stiff bristles which project forward from a wooden handle, softer bristle and plastic brushes of varying degrees of stiffness, and paint brushes, varying in width, all have their uses.

Like many apparently simple operations, brushing is not so easy as it looks and usually has to be taught. The stiff brushes should be used with a motion which rotates them about their long axis, so that the springiness of the bristles flicks the spoil from the surface rather than spreading it across it. It is remarkable how effective this technique is. The brush should be kept clean and once the surface becomes damp enough to clog the bristles with dirt, brushing should be abandoned and the surface cleaned by scraping alone.

In addition to trowels and brushes any implement which will do a job properly may be employed. Teaspoons, dental probes, scalpels and spatulas, all have their uses. Ladles of all sizes and a variety of spoons with the bowls bent at an angle are very efficient post- and stake-hole emptiers. A blunt penknife will excavate delicately without damage and for really fragile objects a wooden toothpick might be the most suitable tool, while wooden implements are the normal tools for excavating waterlogged sites.

Picks of various sizes are sometimes necessary, but heavy picks can only dig 'blind', simply removing soil or clay or shale or whatever in bulk, whereas small hand picks, either of the types used by tilers or those adapted by a blacksmith from coal hammers or other small hand tools, are a necessity when it comes to dissecting a rampart of boulder clay or a mound of chalk. Such small picks are ideally made with one end pointed and the other end flattened, for chopping, and, used properly, they can be delicate tools. The choice of tool for each job is a matter for decisions made on site, for while there are undoubtedly great excavators who could dig anything with a 6in trowel, the majority of us only achieve the optimum results with the right tools. Coles (1972, 166–75), contains many useful hints on tools and their uses.

Trowelling

It is often difficult to know how best to instruct trowellers in the removal of the uppermost context. It is impossible to say 'take this layer down to the clay/pebbles/sand below', since there is no way of knowing in advance what underlies the uppermost layer at any point even if a visibly underlying layer runs under its edge. This layer may peter out, or an intervening layer may start

a little way further on. It must be impressed on the beginner that one layer only is to be removed at a time. The only general and golden rule which one can give trowellers is to remove the uppermost layer until a change of any kind is encountered, or in other words, 'until you find something different, even if this is only millimetres below'.

It is probably unnecessary to stress that trowellers should move backward across the site, so that they do not kneel on the freshly trowelled surface and can look at the newly revealed surface at the optimum time for the distinguishing of soil colour and texture changes. It should be the rule, in fact, that no one may walk on an excavated surface unless they have imperative reasons for doing so. Few archaeological surfaces will stand repeated treading and many will not survive the pressure of even one pair of feet. The necessary encroachments of draughtsmen, finds plotters and photographers should be kept to the minimum and in some cases paths on to the site can be indicated by, for instance, using large stones as stepping stones and avoiding fragile pebble surfaces. Backfilled robber trenches (or earlier excavations) are often useful means of traversing the site. If planks or Summerfield tracking are available, pathways supported on sandbags (or fertilizer bags filled with earth) will keep traffic off the site. Control of movement around and over the site is part of the essential site discipline which must be instilled from the beginning.

So far it has been assumed that layers are neat, homogeneous slices that can be peeled off the surface of the site, but even on more or less level surfaces the situation usually becomes much more complicated and one is often confronted with discontinuous layers interleaved in bewildering variety and, worse, merging imperceptibly into one another so that their edges are impossible to define. In this situation one can only do one's best to determine which layers overlie others, and to do this one may have to explore the junctions of the layers in question, without damaging the site, by miniature trenching. If mistakes are made, and a layer thought to be uppermost is trowelled away and proves to run under one or more adjacent layers, the best action to take is to record the situation by means of a drawing and a detailed note and then proceed to remove the uppermost layers.

It should be a golden rule that every excavational problem should be tackled horizontally, from above. In other words, do not dig in from the side of a feature to determine its limits, but lower the whole surface, if necessary a few millimetres at a time, until the soil differences can be seen. In this way much less damage will be done and far fewer mistakes made.

Natural processes of weathering and leaching, of soil formation and worm action, coupled with the effect of, say, the original occupants of the site treading on the newly cleared surface around buildings under erection, all tend to make the junction between the lowest layers and some subsoils, such as clay and sand, difficult to determine. As a result most excavators probably over-dig quite considerably in the determination to 'establish the natural'.

On some subsoils, particularly on sands and gravels, and permeable rocks such as chalk and sandstone, confusion is often caused by natural formations which simulate archaeological features. Solution holes look like post-holes, fissures resemble ditches, palisade trenches, or timber slots and ponded hollows can be deceptively like man-made pits (Limbrey 1975, 281ff.). On sites where the archaeological features themselves are filled with clean material and where there are few finds, the help of the geologist or soil scientist is invaluable. Ultimately, experience may be the only guide,

and it will almost certainly be necessary to grade the features into all degrees of archaeological validity from positively man-made to positively natural. When the report comes to be written care must be taken not to use too many 'uncertain' features in the interpretation, unless this fact is clearly stated so that the report can be treated with caution.

Care must also be taken in the use of the word 'natural' as a synonym for the undisturbed subsoil, since many layers on archaeological sites are natural in origin. Some may be so thick and free from artefacts that they may be deceptively like the subsoil. Gravel redeposited by flood water, for example, may seal occupation layers under many metres of entirely clean material. Even down-wash from a nearby hillside can cover archaeological features with 'natural' silt. And, of course, the earlier the periods being excavated the more likely it is that the remains of human occupation will be embedded in natural strata, so that much palaeolithic archaeology is carried out in what specialists in later periods would call 'the natural'.

On difficult sites, where the layers are varied in composition and thickness, where, for instance, a very thin floor may lie on a layer of make up 5–10cm (2–4in) thick, composed of rubble in earth, it may be necessary to excavate the underlying layer a centimetre or so at a time – to explore it by means of a miniature planum excavation in order not to miss interleaved layers which may be structural. The strictest control must be exercised over this operation as it is only too easy to invent new surfaces (and even new buildings!) halfway down a thick layer.

If timber buildings are founded on rafts of rubble or other material, or their post-holes and slots are packed with stones or tiles and other debris, this substructure must be dissected and not merely stripped off until the next putative building layer is reached. It goes without saying that this is a slow process but it is often within these sub-structures that evidence of changes in plan or repairs are to be found.

Sieving

However competent the trowelling on an excavation is some small objects such as tiny coins, gems, intaglios, fragments of metal objects and other potentially important finds may be missed. In addition there is no doubt that some excavators, however reliable in other ways, are less sharp-eyed than others. It has been found that dry sieving with ordinary garden sieves with a mesh of c. 10mm recovers a sufficiently large number of otherwise lost finds to make the extra work and time worthwhile. At the excavation directed by the writer at Wroxeter, in spite of very careful trowelling, some 10 per cent of all small finds came from sieving. The sieved earth should be kept in a separate spoil heap for winter backfilling or other similar purposes, or even for sale as topsoil, for which there is a considerable demand in some districts. Finds from the sieve will not be closely stratified, though if each bucketful of soil is sieved individually, its general context will be known and as far as possible the spoil should be sieved from each layer or feature independently. Finds from sieving should be marked as such so that the degree of their reliability of stratification is made quite clear. A coin or other datable object found during sieving of a layer from above which a number of layers have been removed can be rightly held to provide a *terminus post quem* for the layers above since it must derive from the underlying layer, even though its precise horizontal position may not be known. Such an assumption depends of course, on the care-ful and complete excavation of the upper layers. (For wet sieving see p. 244.)

Sections

Vertical sections

Vertical sections, just as much as horizontal surfaces, must be meticulously clean if they are to yield the maximum information. They should be cleaned from the top downwards (an apparently obvious rule not always observed), with the tip of the trowel and/or with the tip of a stiff brush. With a very loose section a paint brush may be sufficient. It is important to reveal the textures of the various layers by cleaning round stones, tiles and other fragments protruding from the surface. It is not sufficient simply to cut the section vertically with a spade or trowel, when protruding stones will be knocked out of the surface leaving holes, and perhaps causing miniature landslides. As Limbrey (1975, 271) has pointed out, the nature of the soils which make up a vertical section will best be revealed by using the tip of a sharp trowel in a chopping motion, rather than by scraping, which always tends to smear the junctions of layers. Under some special circumstances, in hard-packed gravel or where there are concrete floors, roads, layers of tile and other rubble in the section, the section can be cleaned with a thin high pressure jet of water, which washes out small particles and leaves a clean section with its textures enhanced. This method should only be used after careful tests on a small area. A soft brush and an air line, if available, can also be used on some loose and dusty surfaces.

Too much insistence has been made in the past on the vertical cutting of sections. If there is any doubt about the stability of the soil there is no reason why the section should not slope at an angle sufficient to reduce the risk of collapse and the resulting loss of evidence. Needless to say, if the cutting is more than 1.5m (5ft) deep it should be shored and the *Health and Safety at Work Act, 1974*, observed (see also Fowler 1972). A side-effect of sloping sections is that in narrow trenches more light is reflected from the surfaces, making them easier to draw and photograph. Equally there is no reason why, under some circumstances, sections should not be stepped. Whether they are sloped or stepped it is important to record them in exactly the way they are cut, and not to make them appear more vertical than they really are, as if in shame at a transgression of one of the cardinal laws of archaeology.

As will be clear from the earlier parts of this chapter, it is my opinion that the cutting of vertical sections should be kept to the minimum. Nevertheless, all sites, however large, have edges, which may ultimately reach considerable depths and provide long sections encircling the excavated area, and on other occasions trenches and sections may be archaeologically unavoidable. A flexible approach is needed, in which no appropriate technique is outlawed on doctrinaire grounds.

The cumulative section
One of the greatest difficulties with horizontal excavation is to reconcile the need for a constant overall view of the excavated surfaces with the need for sections. One of the principal values of drawn sections is for publication, for the visual demonstration of relationships which are otherwise difficult to describe though they may be fully appreciated while the excavation is in progress. (It will be noticed, for instance, that most of the diagrams in this book are sections, though illustrating situations which are often encountered horizontally.) My belief is that if sections are cut, and they reveal relationships not detectable in horizontal exca-

vation, then the excavation is a bad one. The assertion that many layers, easily observed in plan, cannot be seen in section has become a commonplace. It follows therefore that horizontal excavation, so long as it is sensitive enough, is always likely to recover more information than can be seen in a section. The reservation which must be added to this statement is that the section demonstrates the vertical relationships of soils and their development in a way in which is not possible by horizontal excavation and the soil scientist will always prefer to see the whole intact stratified sequence from top to bottom (see p. 133).

How, therefore, to reconcile these two requirements – to see the site in plan and in section? The best solution, I believe, is a compromise, using the cumulative section. In this method, the excavation is carried up to a pre-determined line and the section drawn. The excavation then proceeds beyond this line. Each time the excavation reaches that line in the future the section will be drawn (Figs 32, 33). Needless to say, with this method, accuracy of levelling and surveying are necessary if mistakes are to be avoided; but it has one very considerable advantage over the section cut on a notional line, say along a grid line or at 45 degrees to the grid, in that it can be sited to section particular large-scale features, such as a building, or a rampart, invisible at an earlier stage of the excavation. There is no reason at all why a cumulative section should be not started at any stage of the excavation, based on a line chosen to give the maximum information about an emerging structure. The cumulative section is also very useful for the excavation of large pits or similar structures (Fig. 33a and b), especially if they themselves contain floors or other subsidiary structures.

A slightly different solution, used at Winchester and described in Biddle and Kjolbye

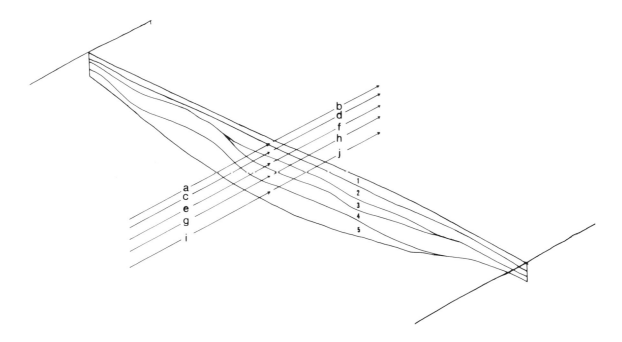

32 The cumulative section. *Above*: a diagrammatically simple situation, in which a cumulative section is drawn by removing Layer 1 up to the proposed line of the section (operation a). The section is then measured and drawn visually and the remainder of it removed (operation b). This process is repeated, pausing each time after operations c, e, g, and i, to draw the section before proceeding.

Below shows a slightly more complex situation where, again, the operations are carried out in alphabetical order. Since the upper layers will have been removed before the section of each exposed layer is drawn it is easier to use a level and staff than a horizontal string to determine the upper surface of the new layer. Needless to say, the plan of each layer is drawn before it is removed.

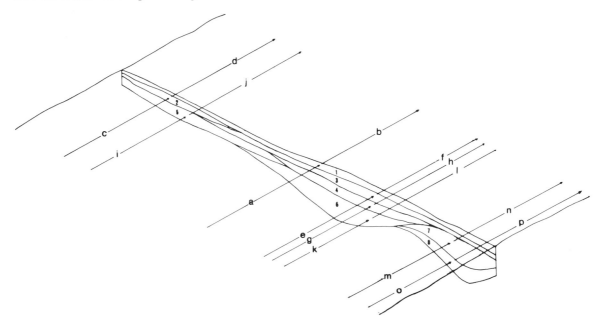

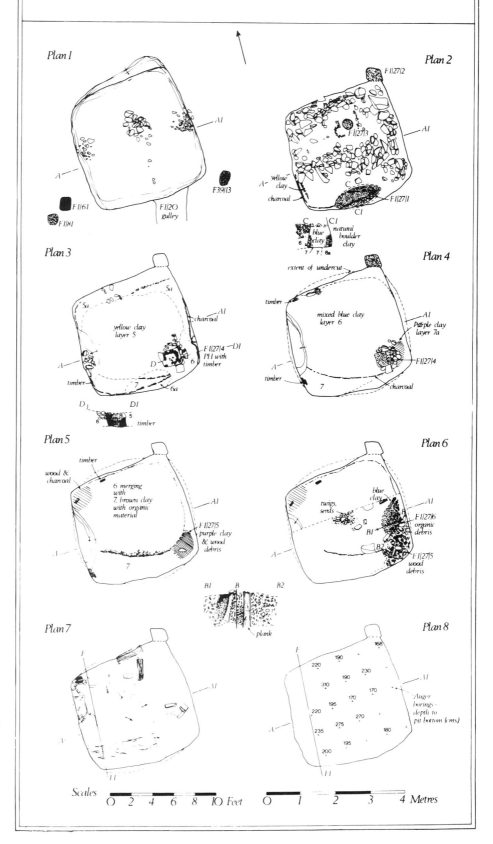

HEN DOMEN · MONTGOMERY
Feature I/27 Pit

Plan 1

A1

A

F1/61

F1/81

F39/13

F1/20 gulley

Plan 2

F1/27/2

A1

F1/27/3

A

yellow clay

charcoal

C

C

C1

F1/27/1

C1

C

C1

natural boulder clay

blue clay

6

7   7   6a

Plan 3

5a

5a

A1

charcoal

yellow clay layer 5

F1/27/4 PIT with timber

D1

A

D

6

timber

7

6a

D

D1

5

6

timber

Plan 4

extent of undercut

timber

mixed blue clay layer 6

A1

Purple clay layer 7a

A

F1/27/4

timber

7

charcoal

Plan 5

timber

wood & charcoal

6 merging with 7, brown clay with organic material

A1

F1/27/5 purple clay & wood debris

A

7

Plan 6

blue clay

twigs, seeds

A1

F1/27/6 organic debris

B1

B2

A

F1/27/5 wood debris

B1   B   B2

plank

Plan 7

I

A1

A

II

Plan 8

I

168

220   190

230

190

A1

310

170   170

Auger borings – depth to pit bottom (cms)

220   195

A

270

235   275

180

200   195

II

Scales

0 2 4 6 8 10 Feet   0   1   2   3   4 Metres

33a Hen Domen, Montgomery, feature 1/27, pit. Plans at successive levels.

Feature I/27 Pit · Cumulative Sections

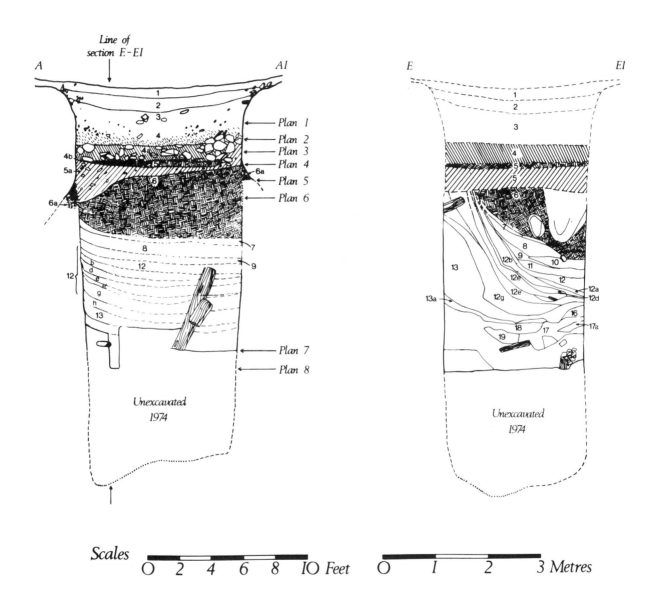

33b Hen Domen, Montgomery, feature 1/27, pit.
Cumulative sections on two axes: A–A1, E–E1.

Biddle (1969, 212–13), is to leave narrow balks which are continuously drawn and removed. This involves working on both sides of a 20cm balk rather than up to a section line and beyond it, and has the advantage that the whole site can be worked all the time. The height to which a 20cm balk can be left – the depth of the excavation on either side – will depend on the nature and stability of the deposits, and on the complexity of the features. For instance, where there is a complicated mass of stake-holes in each layer, the balks will have to be removed at each level if the stake-holes within the balks are to be seen and understood in relation to those around them. On the other hand, in heavy rubble it may be necessary to leave a wider balk. A flexible approach, which takes into consideration all the special problems posed by the site, must be adopted.

In most cases the edges of the excavation will ultimately form a section round the whole site, and one moreover that can be seen at once and drawn from the vertical face. It should be noted how many layers drawn in plan and cut by the edge of the excavation are not visible in the section and have not been seen in plan! Here an inquest should be held.

Special problems

The excavation of structural features
Post-holes and pits normally appear as shapes differentiated from the surrounding area by colour or texture or both. However, not every dark patch is a post-hole, and the features must be dissected in order to establish their character. There are a number of ways of doing this. One is to section them, either on one or two axes, thus removing either half or two quadrants of the fill to the bottom of the hole, when it is possible to draw sections A-B and C-D (Fig. 34).

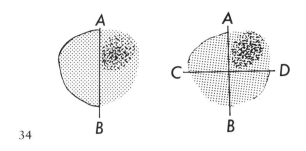

34

Unfortunately it may be that the feature is a post-pit (as the drawings indicate) and that the post-hole may lie completely in either the excavated or the unexcavated portion. In either case no vertical section of the post-hole is seen, which is a disadvantage in rescue excavation, since although removing only half the fill may halve the work, it might recover less than half of the evidence. If the post-hole can be seen in the post-pit at the surface it may then be sectioned across an axis which cuts both (Fig. 35).

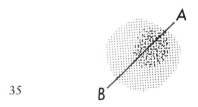

35

Another method, much used in some rescue excavations because it can be applied more mechanically, is to reduce the filling of the feature 5cm or so at a time, drawing the series of resultant plans (Fig. 36 overleaf).

The advantage of this method is that the feature can be reconstructed three dimensionally with some accuracy, especially if the excavated levels are close together. But it requires considerable skill and vigilance on the part of the troweller to ensure that finds from the post-hole are not confused with finds from the post-pit since they may be crucial in dating, and there may be as much

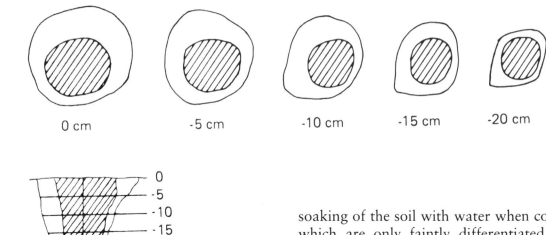

36

as half a century between the digging of the post-pit and the eventual filling of the post-hole. If the post-hole or pit is large enough the methods can be combined and cumulative sections drawn along any required axes. This method has the added advantage that the line of the section can be changed if circumstances require it; for example, if the post-pit proves to contain two post-holes of different periods. The same principles may be used to excavate other features cut into the subsoil or into earlier levels. Gullies may be sectioned lengthwise as well as transversely, and cumulative sections drawn at all stages (Fig. 37, opposite).

Large pits should certainly be excavated in great detail if the maximum evidence is to be extracted from them; and here, presuming that the filling is in detectable layers it is better to excavate them separately, using cumulative sections rather than the planum method (see Fig. 33a–b).

Methods of enhancing soil colour differences
Every excavator of timber structures is aware of the considerable changes in soil colours brought about by the dampening or soaking of the soil with water when colours which are only faintly differentiated in a dry state become much stronger, making features such as post-holes or pits easier to distinguish. This is a different effect from that of the drying out of the surface after rain or artificial soaking, when pits, post-holes and the like may retain the moisture longer and thus appear as damp marks in the drying ground. This is an ephemeral effect which can sometimes, though not always, be repeated by a new shower of rain or a second spraying, followed by a period of drying.

Methods of enhancing the soil differences, which are the only means of detecting post-holes and other structural anomalies, have been tried with varying success. Olsen (1968) describes some of the methods used in the re-excavation of the Viking fortress at Trelleborg, first excavated between 1934 and 1943 (Norland 1948). Doubt had been cast on the validity of the evidence obtained from the earlier excavation and the site was therefore in part re-excavated using a number of methods to enhance differences in the colour of the soil. Use of a blue filter brought one of the post-holes up as a darker stain (Olsen, op. cit., plate f) and another post-hole was treated after sectioning with hydrochloric acid and potassium sulphocyanate, which take a strong red colour when in contact with traces of iron in the soil. Olsen found that the use of coloured spectacles was not very satisfactory, nor did infra-red photography give very decisive results.

Clearly there is still scope for considerable experiment in the detection of decayed timber structures and related soil disturbances. One of the values of long-term research

excavation is that such experiments can be mounted at these sites under something approaching laboratory conditions, usually impossible on an emergency dig. Moreover, the results of such experiments might ultimately speed up the excavation of threatened sites.

37 Cumulative sections showing a stylized gulley with post-holes. It is decided to excavate it so that one longitudinal and two transverse sections can be drawn. Segments 1, 2 and 3 are removed first and the exposed faces of layer 1 are drawn. Segments 4, 5 and 6, are then removed, and the plan is drawn (this stage is not illustrated). Segments 7, 8 and 9 are removed and the process is repeated. When 10, 11, and 12 are removed dark patches, possibly indicative of post-holes, are

seen and drawn in plan. The post-holes are themselves quadranted, and drawn in section and plan before 13, 14, 15, 16, and 17 are removed. The process is repeated until the feature is cleared either down to the undisturbed subsoil or until the layers into which it was originally cut have been fully exposed.

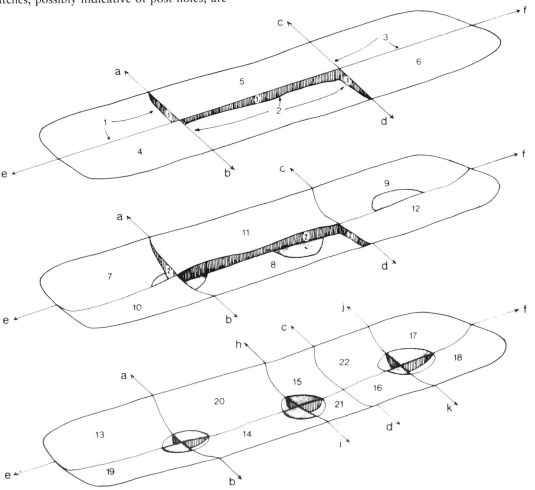

The excavation of small finds

The generic term 'small find' tends to be given to almost anything that can be lifted out of the ground, from a Roman minimissimus, 2mm in diameter, to an architectural fragment, so that it is difficult to lay down rules to cover all eventualities.

It has been well said by Coles (1972, 185) that every find is important and 'never more so than at the moment of its recognition when its precise relationship with other finds and with its containing deposit can be seen'. Ideally finds should not be removed from their surrounding material by levering or pulling, but should be taken out with the layer itself. Unfortunately this is often impracticable. As a feature or layer is removed finds may be seen protruding from the layer beneath. If these finds are not in any way fragile or vulnerable to exposure they can be left until the layer in which they are embedded is removed; but this might be days, months or even a year or more later, according to the size and nature of the excavation, so that a decision will have to be made on the basis of the lesser of two evils.

If the exposed features/layers are given identifying numbers as soon as they are exposed (as they should be) then the finds can be removed from them and labelled as coming from these underlying features. If a find is deeply embedded and yet vulnerable it may be best to cover it with sand, or polythene and sand, or re-bury it in its own soil until the excavation again reaches that point and the object can be removed with the feature/layer.

Only in the last resort should a miniature trench be cut round the find in order to release it from the ground. Doing this destroys its relationship with unseen layers and may well obscure its real function, origin or derivation.

Often a find will first be seen in the loose earth just trowelled from the surface. If the excavation is being kept scrupulously clean, and one layer only removed at a time there should be little doubt from which layer, and, within a few centimetres, from which spot the find came. If, however, finds appear during the demolition of a rampart or the shovelling up of a hastily removed deposit, their provenance should be regarded with considerable suspicion. Sometimes characteristic soils such as clay or sand still clinging to the find may make its provenance more certain, but it would still be unwise to use the discovery of such finds as important interpretative evidence.

Again, finds often appear at the junctions or interfaces between two layers. While it is usual under these circumstances to assign such finds to the upper, later layer rather than the one below, a more subtle approach may be necessary. Imagine a pebble surface in use for a century. When it was laid, pottery and small finds contemporary with it and earlier than it become incorporated in it by accident. During its lifetime, pottery and small objects and perhaps coins were dropped on it, some of them becoming embedded in its upper surface. When it was abandoned, another layer accumulated or was laid over it. This layer incorporated slightly later material (together, no doubt, with some residual material from earlier deposits). It is useful therefore to distinguish the finds (both pottery and objects) from layer A and layer B and from the interface of the two layers A/B. In practice, it has proved possible in this way to separate out pottery of the medieval period, spanning only a century or so, more critically than if the material from A/B had been labelled simply A. Nevertheless it must also be borne in mind that potsherds and objects tend to sink through the soil, due to worm action, until they reach a more solid layer (see pp. 137ff. below), so that some of the material labelled A/B may have moved downwards. Thus the activity of earthworms on the site should be taken into account.

All finds, however indestructible they may seem, should be treated with the greatest respect, and their removal undertaken, as far as possible, without touching them with any tool likely to mark or damage them. Finds which may look most unprepossessing in the ground may prove to be of major importance when they have been cleaned and conserved. Every find, then, should be given equal care in its removal, recording, immediate treatment and storage.

Finds that have been lying in the earth for centuries will have reached a more or less stable chemical and physical state until they are disturbed by the excavator. Immediately they are exposed to the air, to drying, or moisture or any other change of environment, processes which have been halted or slowed to an imperceptible rate will begin to affect them, sometimes so rapidly and irreversibly that within minutes irreparable damage may be done to them. In the case of any find which is considered to be vulnerable the golden rule is to keep it in the environment in which it was found. This may mean leaving it embedded in its matrix of earth or lifting it as a block to be dissected under laboratory conditions. If this is impracticable, the find should be kept in conditions approximating in moisture or dryness to its recent environment. For this purpose sealed polythene boxes or bags used in conjunction with dessicators or wet wrappings are invaluable. For some exceptionally fragile or vulnerable finds immediate field treatment will be necessary.

An essential handbook, *First Aid for Finds*, has been published by RESCUE (Watkinson and others, 1987). This gives short but explicit instructions on the immediate treatment and packing of objects made of all the materials likely to be found during an excavation, emphasizing that 'with the majority of metal and organic remains deterioration of some kind is inevitable unless positive steps are taken in the field to arrest it'.

The materials and methods of first-aid treatment described in *First Aid for Finds* should be within the budget and competence of even the smallest excavation. (If they are not, the excavation should not be taking place.) It must be emphasized, however, that only immediate and essential procedures for arresting deterioration in finds are described. Ideally a trained conservator should be attached to every excavation, but since there are comparatively few conservators in Britain (and probably in the world) and since the annual output of trained conservators does not begin to meet the need, directors have to fall back on their own resources and stabilize their finds at least until they can be drawn, photographed, studied and handed to a museum or other institution for conservation.

The excavation of fragile finds

An excellent maxim is to treat all finds as fragile until they are proved not to be so, although proving that a find is not fragile may damage it irrevocably! This is a problem to which there is no straightforward answer. One can only urge trowellers to be vigilant and to ask for help if there is any doubt about the robustness of a find, preferably at the moment at which it is first seen.

The excavation of finds of potential importance (which will vary according to the site and the circumstances) should be photographed at every stage, and they should be carefully drawn before lifting. Such a record may be crucial to the eventual understanding of their significance, or their relationship with adjacent finds. If a find is almost completely rotted away and is little more than a stain in the ground, the only way to lift it is to cut out the whole block of soil in which it lies. There are difficulties, however. It is seldom easy to see how large the object is, or was; the stain may simply be the tip of the iceberg. Investigation round the object will destroy its relationship with its environment and isolate it from its contiguous layers. Above all it is essential not to become so excited by the presence of an unusual find that the fundamental principles of excavation are temporarily forgotten. Later, when the object comes to be interpreted and its relationship to the site assessed every scrap of evidence will be needed.

Whenever a block of soil has to be taken from the site every effort should be made to record its stratification as it is cut out, and every stage of the operation should be photographed. Here the polaroid camera is most useful. The block may be firm enough to be lifted out on its own, though more often it will need to be supported on all sides with sheets of plywood or hardboard until a sheet of ply, hardboard or metal can be slid underneath it. In extreme cases the block may have to be encased in plaster of paris or polyurethane foam and then in a wooden box in order to get it out intact. If, to all intents and purposes, the object has disappeared, leaving only an impression of its shape in the ground, a plaster cast can be made of this impression. A notable large scale example of the use of plaster was in the re-excavation of the Sutton Hoo ship burial mound (Bruce Mitford 1974, 170ff.) and later, on the same site, Martin Carver used moulds to record burials which had themselves become sand. On other occasions the object may be consolidated in the ground before its removal. Ideally, this should be done by a conservator, who will choose the materials to be used with due regard to the nature of the object, since the consolidating

agents may have to be removed in the laboratory before the object can be studied. In general, a 5 per cent polyvinyl acetate solution in toluene for dry objects, and a polyvinyl acetate emulsion for damp or wet objects is recommended. The emulsion can be thinned with water, when it penetrates the object more easily and can be painted on in a number of operations rather than one thick layer. This enables the excavator to judge the effect of the treatment and to use the minimum amount of emulsion necessary to consolidate the object sufficiently to hold it together while it is lifted. It is useful to note that the emulsion hardens without drying so that the object can be kept damp during the operation. If a fairly large find, such as a shattered pot or a mass of metalwork, is to be held together, a crepe bandage may be useful as it has strength combined with gentle elasticity. Needless to say, any fragile object should be taken to the conservation laboratory as soon as possible after lifting so that it can be given skilled treatment. Comprehensive packing instructions for all kinds of objects are given in Watkinson (op. cit.).

The excavation of waterlogged finds

In waterlogged deposits organic materials such as wood, leather and fabrics are preserved to a greater or lesser degree due to the fact that their environment is anaerobic, and so does not provide sufficient oxygen for the support of fungi and the bacteria of decay, or for the oxidation of metals. Immediately preserved organic materials (or metallic objects) are exposed to the air they begin to deteriorate, partly due to oxidation but, more quickly, due to drying. This deterioration begins even while they are being uncovered and removed from their layer of deposition; while, for instance, they are being photographed or drawn *in situ*.

Excavation and the subsequent packing of waterlogged finds should therefore be swift and delicate. Sometimes objects such as preserved shoes, or fragments of wood can easily be detached from their matrix, but very often, in cess-pit fillings or the bottoms of moats, the layers may consist almost entirely of preserved organic material: reeds, bracken, twigs, branches, leaves and seeds, together with the remnants of human occupation. If the amount of this solid organic fill is only small it can be saved complete, but in the case of large deposits the logistic problems of lifting and storage and the impossibility of working on tons of preserved material make sampling of the matrix essential. The preserved artefacts then have to be removed from the matrix, an operation which may be quite distinct from environmental sampling. As it is often impossible or highly undesirable to walk on the surface of the deposit, a system of planked cat-walks or inflatable beds should be arranged so that they do as little damage as possible to the deposit. The excavators can then lie on the cat-walks in order to dissect and remove the layers. If the deposit is in a deep cutting, such as a ditch section, or in a cess-pit or well, it should not be difficult to erect scaffolding from which a cradle can be suspended. The excavator or excavators can then lie on this cradle (preferably on an air bed if they are to work for long periods).

Where the waterlogged deposit includes extremely fragile objects preserved in quantity, the problem of excavating them on the spot becomes almost insuperable, but equally the removal of blocks of the matrix involves the grave risk of damaging unseen objects while the block is being cut out. Obviously under these circumstances the larger the mass of matrix that can be lifted the less damage will be done, and if the deposit is of major importance a civil engineering contractor should be brought in to deal with the problem on a large scale. If sufficient funds are not available, the deposit should be left where it is until it can be dealt with properly. Only under salvage conditions should the matrix be dug out wholesale.

When waterlogged finds have been lifted they should immediately be packed in an environment as close as possible to that from which they came. Polythene bags and polystyrene boxes are the most convenient and efficient means of doing this, and both can be obtained in forms which are self-sealing and watertight. Self-sealing bags are made with white panels on which details of the find can be written in Pentel or similar pens, but they cannot be opened and resealed more than once or twice without losing their watertight property. Polythene boxes with airtight lids can be obtained in many sizes and are useful for more bulky finds.

Large objects can be made into parcels with heavy duty polythene sheet. A waterlogged bridge timber from Hen Domen, Montgomery, 30cm (1 ft) square and 4.25m (14 ft) long, was fed into a large diameter polythene tube and the ends firmly tied, so that it looked rather like an oversize Christmas cracker. It has remained in this tube since 1962 and, when last examined, was still in excellent condition, since the lack of air had inhibited fungal growth and the timber had dried out very slowly.

The lifting and preservation of large timber structures, such as dug-out canoes or complete bridge foundations, is not easy but does not always require elaborate museum facilities if treated with patience. Timber will begin to deteriorate immediately it is exposed. Although the core may be extremely hard, the surface, to a depth of a centimetre or so, is likely to be very soft, and to be bruised even by the pressure of the fingers. While the timber must obviously be handled if it is to be removed from the ground and studied, this handling should be kept to the minimum, and the exposed surfaces kept wet by constant spraying, and covered with saturated sacking or similar materials at night. In the case of especially important remains 24-hour spraying should be maintained if possible. Good accounts of the large-scale excavation of preserved timber are contained in the Skuldelev Ship's report (Olsen and Crumlin Pedersen, 1968) and in the account of Flag Fen (Pryor 1991). Except in the most unexpected emergencies, the excavation of large waterlogged finds should be made with the active co-operation of the museum in which they are ultimately to be housed or, in the case of English Heritage sponsored excavations, with the aid of the Inspectorate's Laboratory. Only thus will the finds be guaranteed professional treatment.

The storage and safe keeping of portable finds

This is one of the most difficult problems facing the excavator. The rescue excavation explosion of the last twenty years has added a vast quantity of archaeological material to the crowded and sometimes neglected storerooms of our museums. As a result, a high proportion of all excavated objects are rotting away, most of them unpublished. The training of conservators, the provision of museum or other suitable storage space, and the availability of laboratories are all woefully inadequate. A contributory factor in this crisis in conservation is the apparent reluctance of excavation directors to take an interest in their finds once the more important among them have been drawn and photographed. There is a largely unspoken feeling that from then on they are someone else's responsibility, probably that of a museum, although which one is often not specified. The days are over when excavations could be lightly undertaken, without a great deal of thought

about the publication of results or where the finds were to be stabilized and stored. Excavation must be seen as a long and complex process ending only with the publication and storage of the data, and its interpretation and proper treatment, and the storage and display of the finds. It follows that arrangements for all these should be made before the excavation begins. If a total lack of facilities in the area prevents this it is the director's responsibility to make adequate temporary arrangements. If necessary a conservator must be trained in the immediate treatment of the material, and access to a store room obtained for the finds so that they can be kept under the optimum conditions until disposal arrangements can be made.

Museum directors in general are acutely aware of this hiatus in archaeological provision but lack of funds, space and trained staff make the prospect of an early solution improbable. In the interim, excavators and museums must work closer together to make temporary arrangements, and to agree on their areas of responsibility. It is easy to sympathize with the hard-pressed museum director who blanches at the thought of storing hundredweights of undisplayable pottery, bone and formless lumps of iron. But it is no solution to keep only selected objects, rim sherds and the like and get rid of the rest, since we do not know what questions we shall be asking of our material in the future. For example, tons of Roman pottery, particularly body sherds, have been dumped from earlier excavations on major sites in the belief that they had told us all we needed to know. However, the study of Roman pottery is constantly changing our views on dates and places of manufacture. Here quantitative analysis may be as important as qualitative. In addition, it is only comparatively recently that it has been realized that a very considerable quantity of pottery was imported into Britain from Gaul, North Africa and the eastern Mediterranean in the late- and post-Roman periods. Very probably a great many sherds from these pots have been dumped unrecognized and as of little interest. Storage of all the finds from very prolific Roman, medieval and post-medieval sites is a daunting task, but inescapable if we are ultimately to extract the maximum information from the material.

Excavating graves and cemeteries

Brothwell (1963) has written the standard text book on the excavation of human remains and the reader is referred to this. However, he does not pay much attention to the recording of skeletons (and their possible accompanying grave-goods) beyond advocating photography *in situ* before lifting. Vertical photography is preferable to oblique if there is only time for one photograph of each grave in the cemetery and ideally a stereoscopic colour pair should be taken of each burial. Very tall tripods with reversible heads enabling the camera to be attached pointing vertically downwards can be obtained and are more convenient to use than the larger structures described in Chapter 8. Overlapping stereo-pairs or a mosaic are the ideal photographs, giving the maximum information about the burial. Since the orientation of graves is crucial in the interpretation of cemeteries it is most important that a north point should be included. Scales should be laid with the skeleton, not on the side of the grave. If grave-goods are present the whole complex should be photographed in black and white, and in colour (to show, for example, verdigris staining on bones where bronze ornaments have been). Here oblique and detail photographs of the positions of ornaments, weapons, dress attachments and so on will be necessary, if the full

implications of the grave-goods are to be understood, or if it is intended to reconstruct the burial for museum display.

Detailed drawing of all the skeletons in a large cemetery may be an impossibly long task, especially if the work is being done under rescue conditions. A most useful form, including a diagrammatic skeleton, has been designed for use by the DUA (Archaeological Site Manual 1990, and see Fig. 46a) and this is intended to be used in conjunction with photographs, the extant bones being indicated on the diagram by means of coloured pencils. Needless to say, if this method is used it is absolutely necessary to be sure that the photography is satisfactory before lifting the bones. If a dark-room is not available on the site, a polaroid camera will ensure that a photographic record is obtained, though at present polaroid prints are no substitute for large, detailed photographs.

A carefully surveyed plan of the whole cemetery is vital if its growth, use and abandonment are to be fully understood. Changes of orientation or the size and shape of the graves, or their grouping, can only be studied from a full and accurate plan. This plan will also be the basis for overlays, demonstrating in coloured diagrammatic form, the types and distribution of grave-goods, on which much of the interpretation of the cemetery may depend. Further overlays containing details of the skeletal material, such as age, sex, height and other characteristics can eventually be constructed from the anatomist's reports.

In some cases, where the soil is unsuitable for the preservation of bone, the skeleton may only be revealed as a soil mark, a series of discolourations in the bottom of the grave (see Jones 1968, plate Lb). Here filters of various colours may be needed to give the clearest black-and-white photographs, or methods of soil colour enhancement may be tried. If possible, an environmentalist or soil scientist should be present during the excavation in order to sample the soils around and within the skeletons for organic remains, such as clothing or food. If this is impossible, samples whose origins in relation to the skeletons are carefully noted, should be taken for laboratory examination.

More information will be obtained from inhumations if an anatomist can be present on the excavation since he will be able to examine the disposition of the bones *in situ* and will also be able to draw attention to the possibility of finding gall stones or the remains of food, etc. Chemical analysis of the soils which have replaced the various organs may under some circumstances also yield vital information. The evidence to be obtained from human burials will include not only demographic statistics, details of ritual and in some cases a corpus of grave-goods, but when closely studied they may also produce data on family groups and other relationships and evidence of disease or skeletal distortions resulting from patterns of work (Wells 1964). More recently it has even proved possible to recover DNA from bones, with extraordinary potential for the establishment of relationships between individuals and family groups.

Berthe Kjolbye Biddle has published a frank and illuminating account of the excavation of the deeply stratified cemetery north of the Cathedral at Winchester (1975). Because this cemetery overlay the foundations of the Old Minster, its excavation was accelerated by more summary digging than would be normal on a research excavation. Nevertheless the carefully considered compromise strategy employed recovered a mass of detailed information regarding the medieval population, medieval grave types and graveyard topography 'probably at present unequalled in Britain' (*ibid.* p. 92). The whole article is required reading for excavators of cemeteries whether under research or rescue conditions.

Vertical stereoscopic colour photography combined with recording on pre-printed forms would speed up the mechanics of planning considerably and thus leave more time for excavation. The outline plans of the graves must, of course, be plotted on to a master-plan as the work proceeds, with the double-check of carefully recorded co-ordinates. This is Kjolbye Biddle's 'approach 2' (*ibid.* p. 97) with the addition of stereoscopic photography to offset the disadvantage of drawing skeletons at the rather small scale of 1:20.

Site organization

Providing an optimum micro-climate
For most of its existence British archaeology has shared a serious drawback with other major sports in that rain stops play, sometimes for days on end. Even when the rain clears, the pitch is seldom fit for hours or even days, and then, in excavation as in cricket, a day's rain can produce a drastically different result from that predicted when the sun was shining.

Apart from the loss of time and temper, relying on the vagaries of the weather is extremely inefficient. We must, especially in these days of increasing emergencies and decreasing resources, use our time and skilled manpower as intensively as possible. I do not believe that the best way to do this is simply to press on regardless through all weather. Saturated ground is rarely fit for efficient trowelling and often becomes so sticky that it is impossible to work properly. I no longer believe either that 'any information is better than none'. If the information produced under bad weather conditions is only partial, with great loss of detail and possible loss of whole periods of occupation, the evidence is so distorted that it might have been better not to have dug the site at all. As far as resources permit we must attempt to create over our excavations a micro-climate which will enable us to extract the maximum information from the soil.

Anyone who has dug in a temperate, variable climate will know that the changes of humidity in the soil, rain followed by a drying wind for instance, will reveal soil differences quite invisible when the ground is either dry or soaking wet. What we have to do therefore is not simply to keep the site dry so that we can work in comfort, but vary the humidity (and, if possible, the temperature), thus giving the optimum soil conditions for the area being excavated.

The first necessity is shelter. Ideally a shelter should be waterproof, stable (that is, not so light that it will be blown away by strong winds), and large enough to cover not only the area immediately being excavated, but also to leave room for the removal of spoil behind the excavators. For a comparatively small site, such as a barrow, an inflatable tent of the kind used for temporary exhibitions would be perfectly adequate. These shelters are kept up by a small difference in the interior air pressure and since this is maintained by a pump (either electric or petrol driven) it has the advantage that either cold or warm air can be circulated. Air conditioning would be necessary here, as shelters of all kinds become very hot in sunshine, and the type under discussion is, in fact, completely enclosed. Marquees of all sizes can be hired, and the best are constructed on rigid frames. These would provide almost ideal conditions for excavation and especially on long-term excavations would probably be cost effective in that no working time need be lost to bad weather.

A less expensive form of shelter is provided by large horticultural tunnels which can be obtained in bays up to 10m (30ft) wide and 5m (16ft) long. Each bay can be joined to the next forming a tunnel of any required length. Heavy-duty polythene sheeting is attached to the supports by means of spring clips. The polythene must be drawn very tightly over the framework so that rain water does not collect in pockets in the roof, and to prevent the wind from turning the whole thing into a highly inefficient sail plane. In practice it has been found advisable to anchor the shelter along the sides with sandbags, or fertilizer bags filled with spoil. The 'skirt' of polythene on which the sandbags rest also stops water running off the roof from cutting channels in the excavation. The metal framework has proved to be sufficiently flexible to adapt itself to the undulations of the site, as long as these are not too extreme.

The surface of the site can be protected from damage by sandbags placed under the edges of the shelter. These shelters, though heavy, can be carried about by six people per unit. They do have a number of disadvantages, however. They produce a feeling of claustrophobia in some workers, they are noisy in rain and in wind, and because they reduce the visible area of the site it may become difficult for trowellers and supervisors alike to see the context of the part being excavated, so that a sense of perspective is lost, and the site cannot be viewed as a whole.

These disadvantages can to some extent be overcome by rolling back the polythene sheeting when the weather clears rather than leaving it on permanently. It is an advantage too if the shelter can be erected so that its back is to the prevailing wind, when the front can be rolled up, lessening the claustrophobic feeling and giving the trowellers a view of the area that has been completed. Shelters, of whatever kind, will keep the site dry, but it is also necessary, in almost all cases, to keep it damp. For this, hoses with variable jets or lawn sprinkler attachments are most convenient. The rotating sprinkler should make the droplets as fine as possible so that an evenly soaking 'Scotch mist' falls on the area. On very large sites agricultural sprays of the sort used to water market gardens and race courses would be more appropriate. If mains water or water carriers are not available, hand-pumps, such as stirrup-pumps or those used for portable showers or for spraying insecticide, are ideal for giving a spray varying from a fine mist to a downpour. For small sites these are preferable to the more indiscriminate lawn sprinkler.

It is important to spray finely and evenly, soaking the site gradually and thoroughly so that false damp marks are not created by the sprayer. Merely dampening the surface is of little use. Great care should also be taken not to flood the site so that hollows become filled with a fine layer of silt, and do not dry out for several days. Spraying is useful, if not essential, on a very dusty site where working conditions can become highly unpleasant, and thus counterproductive. Now that the cost effectiveness of excavations in both time and money is being more and more studied, it is an economy to spend money on hoses, sprays, pumps and, if necessary, water tanks, in order to provide optimum conditions, where the site can be kept working at maximum capacity. A pleasant aspect of spraying on very hot days is the cooling not only of the surface but of the surrounding air, so that working conditions are improved. The days when it was a test of stamina to dig under the most atrocious conditions are surely on the way out. Efficiency, both in digging and recording, falls off markedly in extreme weather conditions: in rain, ancilliary services, such as drawing and photography, become difficult if not impossible and on a sun-baked surface both the person drawing and the camera will see less.

If an excavation has to be left open for long periods it is important to protect it from damage by weathering. The surface should, of course, first be recorded as thoroughly as possible. Any vertical face which is left open will be liable to erosion or collapse, taking with it unrecorded evidence. One useful by-product of area excavation is that, with few balks, there is less risk of this kind of loss.

Nevertheless every excavation has edges, and excavated pits, post-holes, gullies and the like will need protection. One way that has proved successful is to fill, or better overfill, the pits, post-holes etc with clean sand, and in the case of especially important or vulnerable features, cover them with polythene sheet, preferably black to exclude the light and inhibit plant growth. The features can then be emptied accurately and swiftly on the resumption of the excavation of that part of the site. If they cut through a number of surrounding layers, these layers can be removed progressively, while lowering the backfilling of the features in parallel. If sand is not readily available sifted earth (derived from the sifted spoil of the site) may be used. If there is any reason to suspect that it might be difficult subsequently to distinguish the backfill, the features can be lined with polythene sheet before they are filled. This is in some ways less satisfactory as the free movement of water is impeded and, in the more extensive features, worms are liable to die under the sheet in considerable numbers leaving an unpleasant layer to be cleaned off. The edges of shallow excavations can be protected by packing sand or sifted earth along them; and horizontal features, such as floors or hearths, can be protected in the same way. Additional protection from frost may also be required, and here straw bales packed on top of the polythene sheet will give adequate insulation. If a ready source is available, expanded polystyrene chips will give excellent insulation, are easily removed, and can be reused. Polythene sheets will need to be anchored against strong winds, by means of large stones, bricks, planks or straw bales.

So long as holes and other features with vertical surfaces are protected in the ways outlined above, extensive areas of varied soils, from soft sands to boulder clays, can be left open for long periods. An area of sandy clay at Wroxeter had to be left open for two years. At the end of this time it was trowelled, and an average depth of some 1–3cm was removed. The underlying surface was in good condition and the features of the immediately preceding period of the site's occupation were intact. The same encouraging results have been experienced on boulder clay and on rubble surfaces. Naturally, some soils weather less well, and all will erode if the site has an appreciable degree of slope.

A site that has to be left for more than a few months will need to be sprayed with weed killer to prevent weed growth, particularly of deep-rooted weeds, as their removal is not only tedious but, more important, will damage the stratification. It is unlikely that a weedkiller such as paraquat will alter the chemical balance of the soil for any subsequent soil analysis.

Site logistics
The siting of spoil heaps and the removal of spoil should be given a good deal of thought before the excavation starts. Only too often, spoil heaps prove to lie over crucial areas of the site and have to be moved before the excavation can expand, and if this has to be done by hand it can be very dispiriting.

If the site eventually has to be backfilled and the spoil kept for this purpose, the heaps should be as neat as possible with a clear 2m (6½ft) between the spoil and the excavation, and if necessary they should be revetted along their bottom edges with sandbags or

stones or with planks held upright with pegs. If the excavation is expected to achieve any depth, it must be remembered that spoil is very heavy, especially if it becomes waterlogged, and should therefore be kept as far away from deep excavations as possible; this considerably reduces the risk of collapse.

If the excavation has to be backfilled and re-turfed, the turf should be cut carefully and stacked, grass face to grass face, well away from the rest of the spoil, and should be kept damp. Topsoil should also be reserved in a separate heap so that it can be replaced on the surface before re-turfing. If the excavation does not have to be backfilled, skips can be used to remove spoil, and if necessary a number of them can be stood end to end in a line and joined across the top by a plank runway, the furthest away being filled first. Lorries standing waiting are pointlessly expensive, so that if skips are not available it is more economical to employ an earth-moving machine to fill lorries from a spoil heap in one operation, as required.

For barrowing, either on the level or up on to spoil heaps, Summerfield tracking, developed for emergency runways in wartime, is preferable to planks, which become slippery and potentially dangerous on steep slopes. This tracking, supported on sandbags, also makes excellent barrow runs across the site, especially as the separate sections can be wired together to form continuous runs.

Anything that can be done to shorten barrow runs will save time and labour. It may be more economical of skilled labour to make spoil heaps near the excavated face and employ mechanical or unskilled hand labour to move them rather than to have trowellers barrowing hundreds of yards to a major dump.

Any way of reducing unnecessary work should be used. For instance, it takes less energy to turn an empty barrow to face the way it will be pushed when full, than to turn it after it is full, a simple precept not always observed. Mechanical means of removing spoil include conveyor belts and small cranes driven by electric motors or petrol/diesel engines. Even if such aids are not available it is a simple matter to rig up a system of pulleys over a deep excavation rather than to haul up buckets at their dead weight. The removal of spoil from the surface of the excavation has always been a tedious and time-consuming task and the author has often wished for a series of large vacuum cleaners to do the job quickly and easily. Industrial vacuum cleaners capable of sucking up dirt and stones up to 5cm (2in) diameter are available and may be hired. Though it is obviously impracticable to equip each troweller with a vacuum cleaner there are occasions when it might be invaluable, such as in the emptying of a large group of stake-holes or in the cleaning of a pebble surface.

Obviously this would only be feasible in dry weather. On the other hand, excavation inside standing buildings is often a very dry and dusty process which can be made much more efficient and less unpleasant with the aid of a vacuum cleaner.

Site logistics are ultimately a matter of practical common sense, of constantly seeing ways in which work can be made easier and more efficient.

Safety precautions
The Council for British Archaeology has produced an essential pamphlet, *Responsibility and Safeguards in Archaeological Excavation*, 1972, edited by P.J. Fowler. This outlines the law regarding excavation current at the time, and describes the CBA insurance scheme for third-party and personal accident cover for archaeological societies and groups affiliated to the CBA. It has a section on precautions against soil collapse and another on working with

machinery. One of its most cogent sections is that on personal safety and medical precautions. The pamphlet as a whole is required reading for all field archaeologists, and as it is cheap and readily available there is no need to reproduce it here.

A facility not mentioned in the pamphlet is the Post Office telephone number Freefone 111 which can be reached via the operator. Through this, information on the position of Post Office telephone cables can be obtained before excavation begins, and expensive accidents avoided. The positions of all other services such as sewers, electricity cables and gas and water pipes should also be accurately ascertained before work begins. This is obviously important in towns and cities, but it must also be remembered that many stretches of open countryside are now criss-crossed with gas or water pipes, electricity cables and drains, the lines of which may only be vaguely known. If in doubt, a geophysical survey should pick them up. In the absence of geophysical equipment, dowsing might be tried. Though this technique is regarded by many as suspect, it has been proved to work, in the right hands and given the right conditions (see p. 69).

In 1974 Parliament passed the *Health and Safety at Work Act, 1974*. This Act considerably tightens up regulations concerned with duties of employers to their employees in regard to health and safety, and to the general public who may be affected by activities of which they are not part, such as falling masonry from a demolition close to public highway, or subsidence of a footpath due to excavation. The Act also includes the self-employed and other persons (not employed by them) who may be affected by their activities. The Act defines an 'employee' and 'an individual who works under a contract of employment' (Chapter 37 Part I, 53, (1)). There is no doubt, therefore, that archaeologists working under contract to units or other excavating bodies are employees within the meaning of the Act, as are self-employed archaeologists, such as some conservators or other specialists, who will be liable, for example, for the effect of any toxic chemicals they may use.

The position of volunteers of all grades is less clear. An Inspector of Factories consulted on this point thought that the Act was meant to cover anyone at work and at risk, and that it would be reckless to assume that persons called volunteers and paid subsistence would not be covered by the Act if an accident occurred. He felt that it would need a test case to prove the point. Since the maximum penalties for those convicted under the Act are a fine not exceeding £400 and a term of imprisonment not exceeding two years, it would seem advisable to avoid such a test case!

The parts of the Act particularly relevant to archaeology appear to be Chapter 37, Part I, Sections 1, 2, 3, 4, 7, 8, 9, 33, 36, 37, 40, 52 and 53. Other important regulations include the Construction (General Provisions) Regulations, 1961, (Statutory Instruments 1961 No. 1580); The Construction (Working Places) Regulations, 1966 (Statutory Instrument, 1966 No. 94); and the Construction (Health and Welfare) Regulations 1966 (Statutory Instrument 1966 No. 95). These are all obtainable very cheaply from H.M. Stationery Office and should be used as guidelines even by those directors who do not believe that their fieldwork and excavations are covered by the Act, since it should always be borne in mind that a volunteer, even a totally unpaid one, might bring a civil action for damages against a director in the case of serious accident. Under these circumstances, it would be a powerful defence if the director could show that all the relevant aspects of the excavation conformed with the standards laid down in these regulations, and that every other

reasonable precaution had been taken. In spite of a few serious incidents within the last few years, British archaeology has been very fortunate in its accident rate, although safety precautions on some sites are frighteningly non-existent. Now that excavations are larger, and archaeology in general more public, it would not only be potentially tragic for individuals but damaging for the discipline as a whole if it were seen to be amateurish and negligent in its safety precautions.

Cost-effectiveness
In these times of economic stress, tight public expenditure and the wholesale destruction of sites, cost-effectiveness, that is 'getting' as Philip Rahtz has put it, 'as much history as possible per £', is crucially important. At first sight it seems obvious that the bigger the area you cover and the faster you dig the more you are likely to get for your money, but I believe that this is a fallacy, like driving faster to get to the filling station before your petrol runs out. These thoughts arose from discussions with friends who maintained that very slow, detailed excavations while admittedly producing interesting, even unexpected results, were not appropriate to rescue archaeology where time was of the essence, and the maximum results had to be obtained for the money spent.

It is difficult, if not impossible, to quantify the results from excavations on any agreed scale of values, but it is self-evident that some excavations are very fruitful, while others are a waste of time and money, and that many fall somewhere between these two extremes.

It may be argued that on some deeply ploughed sites there is little to find beyond the features dug into the undisturbed subsoil and that therefore the fastest methods of recovering these features will be appropriate and that there will be little chance of recovering a great deal more evidence even if the work is carried out much more slowly and carefully. On stratified sites I do not believe this to be the case. Experience has shown that highly detailed (and therefore necessarily slow) digging can produce a markedly greater quantity of evidence, in the form of buildings and other structures, many of them unsuspected, than fast digging could possibly have recovered.

It is apparent, for example, that the bailey of the timber castle at Hen Domen was packed with timber buildings of which the plans or partial plans of almost 50, spanning 250 years, have been discovered in one quarter of the bailey's interior. This has taken about 50 weeks' work (spread over 10 years, though under other circumstances the work could have been carried out continuously over one year). However, faster digging would have recovered only the plans of the more obvious structures, of which there are only about a dozen. The recovery rate would have fallen off very sharply as the work was accelerated beyond the point where every thin layer and every pebble surface was cleaned and dissected. It need hardly be added that the recovery rate for finds of all kinds is likely to be higher if the digging is more careful and that the finds will be more securely stratified in closer contexts so that the results adduced from them will be correspondingly more reliable.

Equally, at Wroxeter, on a site which had been dug in more summary fashion by a number of previous excavators, the recovery of over 70 unsuspected buildings has only been made possible by slow excavation over a large area. At the same time, the recovery rate of finds of all kinds, including pottery and bones, has been high and should provide information at a level unprecedented for the site. I maintain that more information, and more reliable information, is obtained pound for pound by slow, detailed digging than by digging which is faster than the site demands and which produces a 'broad picture' but one that may be grossly distorted.

This, therefore, is another argument for planning a long-term rescue strategy which permits excavation at the optimum speed and not at speeds dictated by the quarryman or developer.

The soil

Timber buildings are by far the most common structures to be found on the majority of our archaeological sites. These sites now consist almost entirely of superimposed layers of soil, or soil and stones, containing the ghosts of structures which themselves have undergone an earth-change into soil. Those of us who excavate these sites often have to interpret soil layers with little more than our intuition and experience to guide us. We say that this feature is a hearth (might it not be a small dump of burnt clay?); this layer was washed down (could it have been wind blown?); this post-hole filling looks and feels the same as that one (are they therefore contemporary?); does this micropodsol, itself a natural event, reflect a man-made disturbance?; what is the source of this vivianite and what archaeological significance has it? – and so on. An archaeologist who uncovers the substantial remains of stone buildings must have a working knowledge of architecture in order to be able to interpret them. Equally an excavator digging timber structures will need at least a basic understanding of the soils he will encounter if he is to understand fully the medium into which his buildings have been transformed (therefore see Cornwall 1958; L. Biek and I.W. Cornwall in Brothwell and Higgs 1963, 108–22; and Limbrey 1975).

In the process of understanding our excavated structures and their surroundings we must not only be able to recognize and explain structural features such as floors, post-holes, hearths, drains, fences and the rest, but we must also attempt to understand the derivation of every layer that we encounter.

From geological times to the present day the surface of the earth, this very thin series of layers which so preoccupies us, has been subjected to continuous change. Some of these alterations have occurred slowly: the development of the soil, the establishment of vegetation, and centuries of cultivation; some have been much faster. From the moment a site is occupied by man its surface undergoes rapid and drastic changes; and it is principally these changes which we have to excavate and attempt to understand. But the process of change does not stop when the last occupants leave the site and it reverts to pasture or is ploughed or adapted as a car-park. Natural agencies continue to transform it, frost and ice break up exposed surfaces, rain and wind fill its hollows with mud, dust, soil and stones. Water seeps through the underlying layers, leaching out chemicals, and redepositing them in new forms. The roots of bushes and trees grow along and into organically rich layers, post-holes and pits, or create their own root holes. Animals and insects traverse the site with burrows; micro-organisms feed on debris and the remains of timbers, and worms move up and down through the soil, passing, if we are to believe Darwin, millions of tons of our sites through their bodies in the course of a century or so (Darwin 1881). It is a wonder that we have any understandable archaeology left . . .

Clearly we must learn to recognize all the changes that have occurred on the sites we are digging and not merely those which are structural and man-made, attempting, as we do so, to explain or account for every piece of detectable evidence. We shall make mistakes, but these can be minimized by the intensive study of natural, as well as human, factors. We should like to know the subtle but real differences between a number of what we gliby call 'occupation layers'; for example, whether a floor has been used by cattle or for corn storage. Experiments in determining comparative amounts of phosphates, lignite and other residual traces have not been uniformly successful; but a comprehensive analysis of soil composition, presented visually and laid over plans of the excavated area, may prove to be more valuable.

Ultimately, it should be possible to sort apparently undifferentiated post-holes into groups by comparative analysis of their filling. However, observation of the contents of post-holes known to belong to one building often shows that they contain different materials; and it may be that dating techniques such as thermoluminescence will eventually prove to be of more use than physical or chemical analysis. Again, the bottoms of post-holes may contain pollen spectra that will differentiate them into widely separated periods, for instance Neolithic and Saxon, when superficially they are similar.

At the moment the sampling methods used by soil scientists are often at odds with the excavation techniques advocated here. Soil scientists quite reasonably require to see the whole soil profile, from the surface to the subsoil, in vertical section. Not only is this patently impossible all over the site, unless it was dug by means of a series of thin vertical slices, a sort of planum technique (see p. 146–7) tilted through 90 degrees (a method which might be tried on a selected site just to see what happened) but the excavator often does not know that he will require crucial soil information until a layer or feature has been uncovered; by which time, of course, the superimposed layers will have gone; and the very last thing he wants is a column dug through a floor or a buried soil into the underlying layers (about which he knows nothing). It is sometimes possible to reserve columns of soil, leaving them standing until the soil scientist can sample them *in situ*. Again, it would have to be known in advance, or predicted, what layers lay below the point where the column was to be left.

The only possible solution to this problem is for a soil scientist to work continually on the site, alongside the excavators, taking samples where necessary, and observing the vertical relationships as they are revealed by horizontal methods. This may not be entirely satisfactory for the soil scientist, but test holes or trenches, except on the smallest scale, are unacceptable on an area excavation, especially as they will inevitably be dug into *terra incognita*, and therefore of little value to the excavator who cannot have any idea what the underlying layers may represent when the samples are taken. More important, a dialogue between an excavator and a soil scientist is likely to raise questions that would not have occurred to either individually.

On an excavation where a soil scientist cannot be present, samples may be taken from layers and features. They must be labelled in sufficient detail for a person who has not seen the site to identify them, with the aid of plans, sections and photographs, preferably in colour; and they must be accompanied by specific questions, of a kind which might reasonably be solved by soil analysis. No soil scientist will thank an excavator who sends 200 polythene bags full of samples divorced from their context and without comment, and the excavator must not expect miraculous solutions to all the problems simply because spoonfuls of each layer removed have been collected.

Soil analysis falls into two main categories: the physical and the chemical examinations of the profile or sample. The physical examination will give information about the parent geology of the sample (which may not be that of the underlying subsoil), the particle size, the proportion of humus, the presence of mortar or other building materials, whether the material is wind blown or water sorted, and so on. This will not only throw light on the derivation of the material, but may also give information about aspects of the site which would be obtainable in no other way. For example, post-holes filled with earth containing flecks of painted plaster may be the only evidence for the former existence of a timber building with rendered or painted walls. Analysis of the backfilling of robber trenches which appear to be the same superficially, may show that the robbed walls were of different materials and therefore perhaps of different dates, or it may be possible to show that a gulley has been filled in its early stages with wind-sorted rather than water-borne silt.

Layers or fillings of features which seem at first to resemble each other may prove, on detailed examination, to be very different. Quite often layers occurring on different parts of a site have been said to be identical simply because they look alike. This in turn led to generalizations about 'destruction levels' and 'building levels' which may well not be justified.

The chemical analysis of soil provides information of another kind. Sometimes it will go hand in hand with the physical examination to prove the existence or composition of mortars and plasters, or it may be a purely chemical examination which attempts to show, for example, that floors have been occupied by animals; or determine the existence of industrial processes otherwise undetectable.

At the long-term and very meticulous excavation of the deserted medieval village at Wharram Percy, Yorkshire, it has usually been possible from the house plans to determine their internal sub-divisions and also to

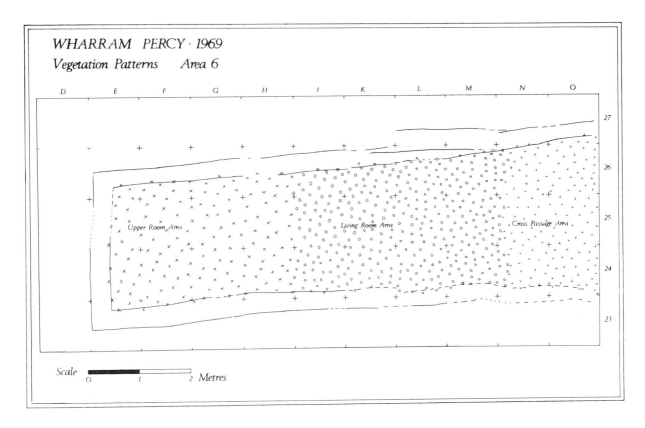

WHARRAM PERCY · 1969
Vegetation Patterns   Area 6

Upper Room Area   *Living Room Area*   *Cross Passage Area*

Scale 0   1   2 *Metres*

38 This illustration shows the excavation of a house at Wharram Percy, Yorkshire, under the direction of J.G. Hurst and Professor Maurice Beresford. Analysis of this phenomenon is not yet completed and I am grateful to Mr Hurst for permission to mention it in advance of publication.

distinguish the living end from that used for cattle or storage. However, in one area, 6, a house was excavated without any trace of sub-division. The site was left open until the following year, when it was noticed that the vegetation growing within the house was sharply differentiated between the 'upper end', the 'living room area' and the 'cross passage' area (Fig. 38). This clearly indicated that soil differences, hitherto undetected, had operated to provide a different environment in each of the three areas. A highly detailed analysis of the soil would presumably have detected the unseen elements that were responsible for these differences.

While it is not feasible to undertake a total analysis of each layer of sites it is obvious from this example that much significant information might be obtained from overall examinations, even from one in which specific questions were not asked. Mr Norman Bridgwater has been working on the theory that oak beams lying on the ground will leave a deposit of tannin that will show where they have been. While the value of this technique has yet to be verified it is a good example of the type of experimental approach that may reveal hitherto unsuspected buildings.

For obvious reasons it is vitally important that the soil scientist and the archaeologist should speak the same language. The terms of each should be used not only in the field, but also in publication. At the moment archaeological colloquialisms like 'the natural' (meaning the undisturbed rock or subsoil) have no meaning for soil scientists who rightly point out that a lot of archaeological layers are 'natural' while the word 'silt' used loosely by archaeologists to describe the soil that has filled a hollow has a much more precise meaning for the soil scientist. A textbook by one of the country's leading authorities on soil science in archaeology (Limbrey 1975), is essential reading, and it is very much to be hoped that the stimulus this book gives to the archaeological study of soils will convince all directors and would-be directors of excavations to train themselves in soil science; and that this study will be given a greater prominence in all future archaeological training.

There is little point in attempting to summarize Dr Limbrey's book here. It is required reading for all excavators, but it may be useful to re-emphasize some of the points she makes. Soil descriptions should be a normal entry on context record cards, and the terminology used should be that standardized by soil scientists. Limbrey makes the good point that it is the trowellers themselves, closest to the soils in an excavation, who should be responsible for the soil descriptions, since they will be most sensitive to the soil variations as they are the first to encounter and identify them.

The two chief characteristics of soils are colour and texture. Colours are described using a Munsell Soil Colour Chart, or its cheaper Japanese equivalent. Colour determinations should ideally be made on the soils in both moist and dry conditions. However, the labour, in a damp season, involved in drying a sample of each layer or feature filling encountered on a large site would be enormous and it is probably more reasonable under these circumstances to record all the soil colours when they are damp, since it is obviously much easier to moisten a sample than to dry it. In practice,

on large and complex sites where the colour changes run into thousands, it may be necessary to record only those which seem to be significant or anomalous, or different in some way from the general matrix of soil which often covers large areas of a site. These alone may run into many hundreds.

Soil texture, structure and consistency can best be taught in the field, though Limbrey (op.cit. 259–70), is a concise introduction. She makes the point also that the traditional method of using the trowel, by scraping, is not the best way of revealing the nature of the soil since it tends to smear clay soils and obscures the structure of all other soils except sands. Rather, the soil should be 'made to part along its structural planes'. This is best achieved by 'a levering or flicking action' with a sharp trowel. In this way also the nature of the boundaries between the layers, often a most difficult problem of identification, is made clearer.

Limbrey's chapter on 'Soils associated with archaeological features' is an essential discussion of the development and composition of soils in pits, post-holes, tree-holes, ditches, mounds and other man-made features. There is little to add to it except to point out that the filling of ditches particularly, but also of pits and post-holes may be partly deliberate and partly natural. The slighting of defences or a rampart may lead to a tumble of stones into the adjacent ditch. This may be followed over the next few days or weeks by washed down soil and small pebbles, which may partly fill the spaces between the stones. If the defences are refurbished, the builders may redig the ditch, though not deeply enough to remove all the recent tumble and wash down. The new ditch will immediately begin to silt naturally in the manner described by Limbrey (290ff.), but may again be recut or filled with debris. This process may be repeated a number of times (see Fig. 7, 1–7).

Worms and weathering

This is the title of a crucial paper by Professor R.J.C. Atkinson (Atkinson 1957) in which he discusses the role played by earthworms in the modification of archaeological sites, and the weathering of the natural subsoils which lie below the archaeological layers, and which are often considered by archaeologists to have remained sealed and unchanged from time immemorial. It is not my intention to repeat Atkinson's paper here but simply to stress one or two of his most important conclusions.

In favourable soils, the worm population is commonly as much as half a million per acre, and may even be as much as six times this number. Worms passing up and down through the soil and the subsoil below it, transport fine soil, in the form of worm casts, from lower levels and deposited on the surface.

> Amounts from 2 to 24 tons per acre per annum have been recorded from Britain and amounts up to 36 tons on the Continent. This represents the formation of a surface-layer of fine mould varying in thickness (in Britain) from $\frac{1}{50}$ to $\frac{1}{4}$ in (0.5mm to 5mm) per annum or from $\frac{1}{5}$ to $2\frac{1}{2}$ in (4mm to 65mm) in ten years.

However, this process clearly cannot go on without modification since at 65mm (2½in) every ten years, there would theoretically be a mould layer 10cm (25in) thick in a century or 6.5m (21ft) in a thousand years. Even at the lowest figure of 4mm (⅕in) in ten years the mould layer would be 50cm (20in) thick in a thousand years. Observation of worm-rich sites that have remained untouched by the plough since they were abandoned shows that they frequently have only a thin soil cover above the uppermost archaeological levels. At Hen Domen, Montgomery, which is built on boulder clay, and has lain untouched for 750 years, worms have burrowed to a considerable depth, and the layer of fine stone-free humic soil lying on the uppermost archaeological layer is only an average of 70mm (3in) in depth. It is possible that the chief activity of the worms was confined to this thin layer of topsoil, except in winter when they burrowed deeper to escape the colder weather and when casting on the surface would be at its minimum. On deeply stratified sites where movement up and down through the layers is easier, the movement of fine earth to the surface is likely to be greater. A very important side effect of this movement of fine soil by earthworms is stressed by Atkinson. This is the burial of small objects, which are continually undermined by the worms' burrows and the deposition of casts on the surface. For example small objects left on the surface of a lawn will gradually disappear, moving downwards until they reach a more solid layer. It is a matter of common observation on many archaeological sites that modern objects such as coins, bottle tops, fragments of Victorian teapot and so on lie on the uppermost archaeological surfaces together with the objects deposited on those surfaces by the last occupants. This can lead to considerable confusion if the cause, earthworm activity, is not appreciated. As Atkinson summarizes:

> in many cases significant archaeological finds have been displaced downwards from the position in which they were originally deposited; in some cases at least the amount of displacement may have been sufficient materially to alter the apparent stratigraphic relationships of the objects concerned (op. cit. 222).

He goes on to cite two examples of the way in which the burying activities of worms may affect the interpretation of stratified finds. They are so important that it is worth repeating them here (in slightly shortened form):

In many Romano-British and medieval excavations, for instance, floors are uncovered consisting of *opus signinum* (cement), *tesserae* or tiles. The surface of these floors is often sealed by a layer of fine soil containing sherds, coins and other debris of occupation which is itself covered by a thicker layer of rubble derived from the decay and collapse of the surrounding walls. Such 'occupation layers' are usually referred to as a reoccupation of the building by squatters, after it has been abandoned by the original inhabitants and has perhaps already become partially ruined.

The exact processes by which such 'occupation layers' have been formed is seldom if ever discussed in excavation reports. In fact, such 'occupation earth' is almost certainly the product of earthworms, which penetrate cracks in apparently solid floors and gradually build up a layer of castings on their surface. Meanwhile this layer will itself have been colonized by worms, whose activity will bury coins and other objects dropped on it, and some of these will be displaced downwards so that they eventually come to rest immediately on the surface of the original floor.

Now finds discovered in this latter position will usually be interpreted as belonging either to the very latest stage or the original occupation, or to the intial stages of 'squatting'; in either case they will be held to date approximately to the period at which the building was initially abandoned. But in fact, as a result of the processes outlined above, the objects found on the floor may be of widely differing dates, and will include not only those dropped just after the abandonment of the building, but also those of much later date which have been displaced from above. Consequently, if the normal practice is adopted of dating a horizon by the latest objects contained in it, the date assigned to the initial abandonment of the building may be significantly later than it should be.

Another common case in which the activity of worms may lead to serious misinterpretation of the evidence occurs in the silting of pits and ditches. Such silting usually exhibits four basic divisions. On the bottom and up to half the depth of the ditch, there is coarse or rapid silting, formed chiefly from the weathering of the sides. Above this is a thin deposit of earthy streaks, due to the undermining and collapse of the surface soil on the lips of the ditch. Both these stages are normally completed within a few years at the most. Thereafter, silt forms much more slowly, and usually contains a far higher proportion of earth, particularly in structures of the second millennium BC, such as barrow ditches which collect considerable quantities of wind-blown surface-soil. Finally at the top there is a turf layer of virtually stone-free soil which supports the surface vegetation.

Since the first two stages of silting take place rapidly, the formation of the lowest levels of the third stage may be regarded as virtually contemporary with the original excavation, and in the absence of finds from the primary silt (those in the secondary silt, being derived possibly from the adjacent surface-soil, are unreliable), objects occurring at the base of the tertiary silt may often be used to date the original excavation. But it is clear that such finds may have been displaced vertically through considerable depths of silt particularly where a high proportion of wind-blown or other soil encourages the activity of worms. Since such vertical displacements may take centuries to achieve, the date ascribed to the structure on such evidence may be grossly in error.

The classic case of the probability of an error of this kind is afforded by the Y and Z Holes at Stonehenge, in which the main part of the silt consists of earth, apparently wind-blown and almost free from stones and rubble. This silt contained Iron Age and Romano-British sherds at quite low depths, which have in the past been held to date the holes to not earlier than the last few centuries BC. But once the possibility of vertical displacement is recognized, it becomes clear that this pottery must have been deposited on the surface of the silting many centuries after the digging of the holes, and in fact other evidence suggests a date for the holes as much as a thousand years earlier than that of the pottery they contain.

These examples, and particularly the last, may perhaps be regarded as extreme cases: and certainly it would be foolish to deny that in many instances the vertical movement of objects, though it has undoubtedly taken place, has no significant effect on their interpretation. None the less, one may justly say that the excavator who ignores the capacity of worms to displace small objects downwards does so at his peril.

Although there is no doubt that objects can travel downwards through considerable depths of comparatively friable soil they tend to stop when they reach a harder layer, one that is either resistant to penetration by worms, or at least does not collapse internally if there are worm burrows in it.*

Two things should be noted. First of all it is most unlikely that the vertical stratigraphic relationship of objects will be reversed by earthworm action; that is, objects will rarely overtake one another so that a later object finishes up below an earlier one in the same series of layers. Secondly, objects will never travel upwards due to the action of the earthworms. Though it may seem ludicrous to point this out, it should be stressed that the worm cannot be held responsible for every anomalous find in the recorded stratigraphy.

Another effect, not noted by Atkinson is that one often finds a layer of dark humic soil surrounding buried stones or large architectural fragments. It is easy to assume this to be a pit into which the stone has been set, though it is more likely to be caused by worms coming up underneath the stone and being forced round its sides (Fig. 39):

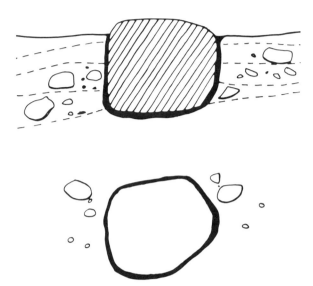

39 Diagrammatic plan and section of a large stone showing enveloping layer of fine soil (in black) deposited by worms travelling round stone.

As Atkinson explains, the familiar thin and irregular deposits of pea-sized pebbles, free from admixed soil, found at the bottom of pits, etc and on the buried surfaces of floors, arise from the long accumulation of the small stones used by worms to line the terminal chambers of their burrows. These layers of tiny pebbles tend to be concentrated at the lowest levels to which worms can penetrate locally (op. cit. 225).

The second part of Atkinson's article concerns weathering and its misleading effects particularly on permeable and partially soluble subsoils. The section is too long to summarize satisfactorily here, but, together with the section on worms, is required reading for excavation directors.

* At Wroxeter a considerable accumulation of eighteenth- and nineteenth-century sherds was found on the surface of a Roman Street on the Baths Basilica site (excavated from 1966 onwards). These sherds had probably been brought onto the site from the mid-eighteenth century when the field was first ploughed. They had travelled between 60cm and 1m (2–3ft) downwards through deep layers of top soil before they reached the gravelly surface of the street where they remained. Since the excavation has proved by horizontal stratigraphy that the street is unquestionably late Roman, the eighteenth/nineteenth century sherds have no dating significance for the street or the layers immediately above it. (see Barker *et. al*, forthcoming, 1994)

7

Rescue and Salvage Excavation

Archaeology everywhere has faced a crisis situation for many years. Over the whole developing world sites are being destroyed or eroded at an unknown rate. The implantation of new towns and the enlargement of existing conurbations together with the proliferation of motorways; the extraction of sands and gravels for aggregates; open-cast mining; the exploitation of peat bogs containing preserved timber structures and the afforestation of hitherto untouched marginal land, all represent threats to archaeological sites on an unprecedented scale. But the most extensive and insidious threat of all is ploughing, particularly deep ploughing, which, though justified on the grounds of increased agricultural yield, levels earthworks and cuts into the underlying structural evidence.

The statistics of damage and destruction in Britain have been collated and are published elsewhere (Rahtz (ed.) 1974) and they have forced a fundamental debate here on archaeological policy. Is there any excuse, in the face of this widespread and inevitable devastation, for the archaeological destruction, in the name of research, of otherwise unthreatened sites; or should field archaeologists devote all their time and energy to rescue and salvage excavation? The crux of the debate is whether sites which are in no danger should be left untouched for future examination and the whole of our archae-ological resources, both amateur and professional, used to rescue whatever information can be extracted from those sites that are imminently threatened.

It is often argued that any information rescued from a site about to be destroyed is better than none. But if the documentary analogy, begun in Chapter 1, is allowed to continue, one must imagine a newly discovered manuscript available only for a minute or two before destruction. Under good conditions a few sentences or even a whole paragraph might be rescued before the document vanishes for ever. Some of these sentences might contain information which could revolutionize ideas; other phrases or sentences, perhaps the majority, may be highly ambiguous or positively misleading. A single paragraph, torn from its context, could lead to misconceptions on which a whole series of false assumptions might be based. This is certainly the case with some rescue excavation, which at its worst is done hurriedly and incompletely, often under tremendous pressure, against a background of thunderous machinery or collapsing masonry, when all discussion must be shouted, and when there is no time for the deliberate thought, amounting to contemplation, which is necessary if fundamental errors of interpretation are to be avoided.

Too often we have been led to believe that

a sample of a site provides a microcosm of its development; but further work, perhaps undertaken many years later, all too often reveals that the earlier interpretation was entirely wrong (see, for example, Barker *et al.* forthcoming, 1994 and Van Es 1969). If the site had been destroyed during the initial excavation these revisions could never have been made, and the earlier evidence would have been accepted as part of the corpus of archaeological data which is used to build up a picture of the past. If sampling excavations, carefully planned to answer specific questions, can be misleading, how much more so will be those whose course is dictated by the progress of a building schedule or the availability of a bulldozer? There is also a tendency to believe that a hurriedly carried out total excavation will give a précis or abstract of the site, recovering all its essential information and merely leaving the details to be filled in by further work, if this were possible. Nothing could be more mistaken. Swift excavation by machine or coarse hand digging is not so much like a photographic negative, which, as it develops, progressively reveals the broad outlines and important masses of light and shade of the subject, but is more like an X-ray which shows many important elements of the structure but fails to reveal others which are of equal importance in its function. Here is the core of the dilemma. If total excavation of most sites is patently impossible and partial excavation is known to be potentially misleading, what are we to do? We must, I think, be acutely and continually aware of the situation and its limitations, and attempt as far as possible to reduce these limitations to a minimum. Those sites which are to be completely destroyed by other agencies must claim priority for total excavation if only they can be dealt with in time. This will require planning, perhaps years in advance of their destruction, if we are to be able to

conduct rescue work in the manner of a research excavation, with the tactics and pace dictated by the archaeologist rather than the developer or gravel extractor.

This desirable situation has already been achieved on a number of sites, and is a policy which is gradually being implemented by English Heritage as the limitations of hurried and partial excavation become more generally recognized. One of the greatest difficulties in assessing the viability and strategy of a rescue excavation is the difficulty of knowing beforehand how complex the site may be and therefore how much time should be spent on each phase of the occupation. This is particularly the case with urban sites. A machine-cut trench may show that there is a complex of Roman and sub-Roman banks and ditches 3m (10ft) below the surface, with prehistoric occupation beneath, and many undatable layers above, heavily mutilated by post-medieval pits. It would be easy to strip off the first metre or so by machine and then to deal with the comparatively undisturbed major features below. But by doing so a whole sequence of medieval and post-medieval tenements might be lost.

Alternatively, there is a strong argument for the detailed area stripping of the upper layers on the grounds that it would never be known what would be lost if they were bulldozed away. Such slow and detailed work might produce plans of ten successive backyards and leave us oblivious of the Roman and Dark Age defences below. If there is not time to do everything (and we must work strenuously towards making sure that there is time for everything) then painful decisions must be made. These decisions should be based on an assessment of the nationally considered academic priorities, and not on personal research interests or the ease with which the more obvious features might be excavated. The strategy of any

141

large-scale excavation, whether urban or rural, should be a matter for discussion so that a balanced view can be considered and a consensus of opinion achieved. It is true that a great number of the most spectacular excavations of the past have been the result of individual flair, but the centres of historic cities and major rural sites are too precious to be left to arbitrary decisions or personal whims.

Before decisions are taken to sacrifice the uppermost structures, late and comparatively unimportant though they may prove to be, it must be remembered that the attitudes of developers, sand and gravel extractors, farmers and national and local government agencies can be changed in the light of what is discovered. The meticulous demonstration of a group of post-medieval buildings combined with suitable propaganda may convince all those concerned, not only that the excavators are competent, but that they are capable of revealing the whole history of the town in a way quite unexpected by the laymen on the council who are impatient to add to the town's car-parking space, and that they should therefore be given time to do so. Nothing succeeds like success, and it is correspondingly much easier to convince the various interests concerned that they should delay development and even contribute funds to the excavation if the results can be seen and explained, rather than postulated on the grounds of probability.

In an ideal archaeological world all sites would be examined before they were lost or deeply damaged, but the rate of present destruction is far beyond existing resources. We are forced to choose a course lying between two extremes – to concentrate on a few of the threatened sites, digging them slowly and entirely and letting the rest go; or trying to salvage something from every site before it vanishes. There is something to

be said for both points of view. The total excavation of very large settlement sites such as Warendorf (Wincklemann 1958), Dorestad (van Es 1969) and Wijster (van Es 1967) is enormously impressive, and yields information far in excess of that given by a hundred smaller excavations. On the other hand, it can be argued that if concentration on a few sites means the abandonment of the rest, the overall picture is bound to suffer; there being no guarantee, for instance, that the sites chosen for full excavation are typical of their kind, or that those left unexcavated were not of even greater importance. Devotees of the distribution map will point out that enough small excavations should eventually provide coverage for the whole country; and that from these maps the broad patterns of invasion, settlement, trade, and social and religious groupings should emerge. The answer lies somewhere between the two extremes.

The selective preservation or long-term digging of carefully chosen sites where optimum conditions for excavation can be arranged, together with the rescue and salvage excavation of as many other sites as can be adequately dealt with, is a policy already being implemented in Britain, and may be thought to achieve the best of both worlds.

What is the relevance of this dilemma for the future of archaeological techniques and attitudes? Clearly, we must keep in mind the limitations and dangers of misinterpretation inherent in the hurried and partial excavation. Beyond the difficulties outlined above there is the much more insidious hazard, unadmitted by most excavators, that, when a site is being totally destroyed, there is an unconscious slackening in the precision with which observations are made; an attitude brought about partly by the necessity for speed, but also by the knowledge that the results can never subsequently be checked, or disputed. For this very reason rescue excavations ought, if anything, to be more rigorously directed than research excavations. They certainly do not require less skill.

Rescue excavations also suffer from the drawback that, since layers and features are often only visible for a matter of hours, it is rarely possible for them to be the subject of consultation or second opinion. Thus they represent a particular danger in that excavators may find, unconsciously, what they want to find; and, once the evidence has gone, there is no basis for argument. These excavations, therefore, demand the strictest intellectual honesty from the director. This is not to suggest that anyone deliberately falsifies the evidence, since this would be about as satisfying as cheating at Patience, but it is particularly important when digging under pressure, perhaps with the press, the landowner, television news or even one's colleagues expecting instant expositions of work in progress, not to allow subconscious patterns of thought to colour the immediate interpretation of the evidence as it appears in the ground. Attractive hypotheses suggested by the emerging evidence tend to crystallize, especially if apparently supporting evidence goes on accumulating. If at some point a crucial, contradictory piece of evidence emerges it can then become very painful to perform the *volte face* necessary to accept that one's previous theories are wrong and that everything has to be rethought and public retractions made, perhaps even broadcast.

In the face of all this destruction of our sites is there any justification at all for research excavation? So far as technique is concerned, the calmer pace and controlled strategy of research fieldwork and excavation enable us to evolve and test new techniques and, at the same time, to assess the validity of our rescue work. One discipline illuminates the other. In particular, research

excavation warns us how much is likely to be missed under the conditions in which rescue and salvage excavation has to be carried out. To use again the example of Hen Domen, Montgomery, the excavation of a length of 20m (65ft) of the bailey rampart has taken 10 seasons' work. The rampart, of boulder clay, has been taken apart entirely by trowel or small hand-pick. A machine-cut section or one dug with pick and shovel would have shown the existence of a number of post-holes but would not have detected the thirteen or so buildings on the rampart's crest and rear slope, nor would it have revealed the sequence of the earliest defences (Barker and Higham 1982). Beyond this, many features of timber buildings can only be seen under optimum weather conditions, so that it is a matter of being patient and waiting for just these conditions if they cannot be created artificially. But during a rescue excavation there may be no chance whatever of obtaining such conditions, and we have to be grateful for what can be salvaged.

The recent increases in the scale of rescue excavations, brought about by the need to excavate whole sites and even whole landscapes, have required the development of new techniques of area stripping, principally to speed up the clearance of large areas of topsoil from sand, gravel, chalk, clay and loess sites. There are, however, no obvious short cuts in the excavation of deeply stratified sites containing stony layers and/or stone buildings.

Under rescue conditions much time may be saved by first examining the site using all the known non-destructive methods. On the collated results of such surveys a reasoned plan of campaign can be based. But it should be remembered that the most important structures on the site might very well escape the various forms of geophysical examination; either because their remains are not anomalously magnetic, or because they are not founded in deep post-holes or on walls or other anomalies which can be detected by the resistivity meter or ground-probing radar. In such cases, a limited excavation based solely on geophysical evidence may be seriously misguided; and there are no certain safeguards against such an eventuality.

Under present circumstances a planned sequence of quasi-research excavations may be impossible; but the situation can nevertheless be exploited in two ways. Firstly, even if sites are fully examined in the random sequence in which they are threatened, the accumulating sum of information thus gained can eventually be synthesized. Secondly, if we accept that we cannot dig or even satisfactorily observe all the sites that are being destroyed, we can with sufficient notice select well in advance those sites which we would choose to excavate under ideal conditions; and, if these sites cannot be preserved untouched, try to arrange the most favourable circumstances for their excavation. This will involve the provision not only of much more money for longer and more complex excavations, but of more highly-trained personnel, so that an intensive field-training scheme will have to go hand in hand with any expanded rescue scheme.

The rescue excavation of cropmark sites*

By definition, most cropmark sites will have been ploughed, and in many cases all, or most, of the vertical stratigraphy of the occupation layers will have been removed, leaving a palimpsest of ditches, pits, post-holes and other features which were dug deep enough to have penetrated the subsoil.

* For a concise description of the discovery of sites by aerial photography and of methods of locating sites on the ground see Coles, 1972, 21–45

The situation may be complicated by non-archaeological features caused by erosion, ice-action, solifluxion, the filling of hollows with naturally silted material and the solution of calciferous rocks by leaching water. It is imperative that these natural features should be recognized and separated in the record from the archaeological evidence, since otherwise far-reaching mistakes may be made (Limbrey 1975, 283).

In sites without vertical stratification, separation of contemporary and related structural features depends very largely on pattern making (what van Es has called the sport of 'granary building', van Es 1967, 87) and on the intersection of ditches, pits and post-holes where a sequence can be demonstrated. Both problems are illustrated and discussed in a concise article by M.U. Jones (1974) which includes an excellent plan of the excavation of an area of gravel terrace, part of a whole ancient landscape currently being destroyed by quarrying. It is a most useful exercise, for those wishing to understand the principles of interpreting sites of this kind, to take such a plan and attempt to sort it into periods, based on the intersection of features, and into coherent structures, based on pattern making. It is particularly instructive to see how many alternative 'building plans' can be made using the same features kaleidoscoped into different (but mutually exclusive) patterns. The extensive plans included in the Wijster report (van Es 1967) are ideal for the purpose (see back endpapers). The student's interpretation can then be compared with that of the excavator and the discrepancies discussed.

One of the chief difficulties in excavating a cropmark site lies in locating the cropmarks precisely in the field in which they occur. Very often the photograph shows a field or fields without readily distinguishable landmarks and often, too, the bearing of the aircraft is not precisely recorded. The problem is increased if the photographs are oblique, though it is often only oblique photographs which reveal cropmarks clearly, since in many cases they result from the reflection or absorption of light from the leaves of growing crops, so that a vertical photograph looking, as it were, straight down the leaf, is least effective.

Two simple methods of transferring oblique aerial photographs on to maps are described by Irwin Scollar in Wilson (ed. 1975, 52). One is the paper-strip method and the other the Mobius network method. Neither requires any apparatus beyond a pencil and a ruler. The degree of accuracy depends on the size and clarity of the photograph, and the corresponding size and detail of the map. Errors are also introduced if the ground is undulating, or, worse, hilly since the method assumes the ground to be flat. If a number of oblique photographs of the site taken from different directions are available they can be plotted together on the map and the mean of errors taken. Once they are plotted on the relevant map at the largest feasible scale the best way of locating them on the ground is by geophysical survey. The use of divining rods should not be despised; on some sites remarkably consistent results have been obtained where other, more conventional methods have failed. If there are ditches of clearly-defined shapes the identification of these should be aimed at. The problem is greater if the cropmarks consist of a complex of pits and post-holes, or parallel ditches where features may well be confused one with another. If geophysical methods do not locate the features sufficiently accurately, it may be necessary to cut one or more trial trenches across the site in the hope that the features can be related unambiguously to the cropmarks, though it must be borne in mind that all sites prove, on excavation, to contain many features which do not appear on the aerial photographs, so that one must beware of being misled. Such trial trenches may also recover significant amounts of pottery, building material and so on which all help in the assessment of the character of the site.

The least damage to the site will be done if the trial trenches are cut down only as far as the uppermost surfaces of the features. In this way their pattern can be recovered without their relationship with surrounding features being destroyed unobserved. If there is any doubt about the location of the cropmarks on the ground the trial trench or trenches should be wide and sited so that they will certainly cross the cropmarks at some point, preferably where they are densest and have readily identifiable shapes. Trenches narrow enough to pass between pits or post-holes are obviously not satisfactory. Such wide but shallow trenches should pick up recognizable features without damage to the site. The whole area can then be plotted from these as datum points, and the excavation strategy planned on a proper basis.

Where formerly stratified sites have been ploughed it is possible that the latest occupation layers have been destroyed, especially if the buildings were only of timber with pebble or clay floors. In such cases the pottery used by the last occupants will still be there, churned up in the plough soil. If the field has been allowed to revert to pasture, a common occurrence, the latest pottery will drift downward due to worm action until it rests on the undestroyed archaeological layers. It may then be mistakenly considered to relate to these earlier levels instead of the later levels from which it derived.

Inevitably all fast methods of stripping large areas of topsoil involve the risk of losing not only structural detail and associated finds but also whole periods of occupation. Most, but not all, of the excavators who use these or similar methods are aware of their limitations (for instance Jones 1968,

229) but are prepared to accept them. The excavator of the Carolingian city of Dorestad has quantified the loss of coin evidence. In the earlier excavations of 1842 Janssen found 11 Carolingian coins in an area of about 400 sq.m (4300 sq.ft). In the excavations of 1967–8 only 10 coins were found in an area of about 55,000 sq.m (592,000 sq.ft) (van Es 1969). These losses must be weighed against the eventual recovery of the plan of an entire early medieval city.

Where the site has been under the plough (and the fertile nature of the soils has usually resulted in the long history of cultivation after the abandonment of settlements), it is usual to strip off the ploughsoil by machine on the assumption that the uppermost structural evidence will be found at the junction of the ploughsoil or humus and the undisturbed subsoil, into which features are cut, or, exceptionally, at some stratified levels below the ploughsoil. However, this assumption has been jolted by the discovery that on some cropmark sites features seen on aerial photographs have not been found when the site has been excavated. Peter Reynolds has suggested that the soil differences which caused the cropmarks were contained within the ploughsoil. A possible explanation of this phenomenon is that ploughing disturbs the soil, but, especially on flat ground, does not move it very far from its original position. The chemical differences that cause crop differentiation, visible in the photographs, may therefore persist in the ploughsoil, which, if the site is to be fully excavated, should be examined archaeologically. The situation is paralleled by soil marks which may be seen on newly-ploughed land. Usually these soilmarks are reflections of features and other changes in the subsoil, but it is quite possible that some of them do not reach the subsoil. Work needs to be done on this problem before we can assess the losses of this sort of evidence due to topsoil stripping.

It is normal to machine-strip topsoil down to within a few centimetres of the subsoil, or, if they exist, of the occupation layers. The subsoil is then cleaned by hand, either with trowels, or dutch hoes or with spades used horizontally. The latter method is the fastest but the crudest. On stone-free sands, clay or loess, machine-stripping can be refined to produce a surface almost as clean as necessary. However, many machine drivers are highly skilled and can remove thin layers of soil very accurately (see Beresford 1987; and Pryor 1991). An outstanding example of large-scale resuce excavation both in technique and speed of publication is provided by J.G. Wainwright's work on Durrington Walls (Wainwright 1971). The reader is urged to study it.

The planum method and horizontal section
In this method, which can only reasonably be used on sites on stone-free soil and without stone buildings, layers of arbitrary thickness are removed over a whole area. These layers have no relation to vertical stratigraphy, and the method should therefore not be used where there are any preserved occupation layers. Where all the features are cut into the subsoil it can be used more successfully and with considerable speed. As each successive thin layer of the site is removed, the plan of the area with its exposed features is drawn to an appropriate scale. Slowly the pattern of the various features builds up. Some disappear with depth, others emerge, or become clearer. At no stage are the features of one period exposed and dealt with at one time, enabling a view of one building or structure to be seen in its entirety. As small features are not emptied separately and in the order in which they are stratified there is a danger that finds from discrete features will become mixed together,

confusing the chronology and perhaps the constituent parts of structures. It is necessary, therefore to plot the finds three-dimensionally, in order that they may be related precisely to the features from which they derive. The method, together with its interpretation can be seen clearly in van Es 1969, Figs 7–11. In contrast to the usual methods, in which the subsoil is left unexcavated, this technique involves the removal of enormous quantities of soil, since slices of the subsoil are removed together with those of the features. It can nevertheless also be useful on a smaller scale, for example where the junction of a series of ditches or a complex of post-holes cannot be emptied in sequence, because the soil differentiation is not sufficiently clear. In this case, the attempt to distinguish intercutting features may easily result in overdigging and the loss of evidence, and the planum method used discreetly may be more successful.

It may also be necessary, and valuable, to use arbitrary layers, where, for example, the soil or rubble make up of a timber building is being removed. It may not be at all clear how thick the layer is, or whether it is uniform in thickness and composition. Under these circumstances rather than taking the risk of overdigging and perhaps destroying or mutilating the evidence for an earlier building, it is better to remove the layer a little at a time. In this way, its composition will be better understood, and interleaved layers less likely to be missed.

In the report of his classic excavation of the Anglo-British complex at Yeavering in Northumberland, Brian Hope-Taylor describes (Hope-Taylor 1977, p. 32 and n. 49) what he calls primary and secondary horizontal sections, the first being the surfaces of all the archaeological strata lying immediately under the ploughsoil, which had been carefully cleaned off with trowel and brush. His secondary horizontal sections consist of the horizontal dissection of the structures revealed by the first process. He admits (p. 35 *ibid*.), that if he were to investigate further buildings on the same site he would 'dispense with most of the longitudinal sections and work more directly in terms of successive horizontal sections'.

Salvage excavation and recording

In the ideal excavation every aspect of a site would be dealt with slowly and meticulously; but when only a limited time is available the techniques evolved under research conditions must be streamlined and speeded up and, where necessary, adapted. There is also a distinction to be made between rescue and salvage excavations. By rescue, in this context, I am referring to the excavation of a threatened site conducted under conditions which may approach those of a research excavation to a greater or lesser degree. By a salvage excavation I mean one where the excavator salvages what can be recovered from a site either just before or during its destruction. Salvage excavation requires the greatest skill and experience of all, if the questions posed by the site are to be recognized and solved, even if only partially, and if fundamentally disastrous mistakes are to be avoided. This is instant archaeology indeed. When one is cleaning a machine-cut section or a newly-scraped surface both likely to disappear within the hour, a considerable mastery of archaeological techniques is essential together with a flexible approach and the ability to interpret the evidence as it appears and to record it quickly and accurately.

Ultimately the value of the evidence from a salvage excavation will depend on the quality of the observations made on the site. For example, in almost all cases, only positive evidence should be used. Under the sort of circumstances which give rise to salvage work the argument from negative evidence is highly suspect.

A salvage excavation may prove conclusively from a mass of stratified pottery that a site was occupied in medieval times, but it is unlikely to be able to prove that it was just as intensively occupied in a preceding aceramic period, though total detailed excavation may have done so. It may be argued that information at this level is not worth having, but if the pottery comes from an earthwork or cropmark previously assumed to have been prehistoric or Roman, the evidence may be considered to be worth the day or two spent retrieving it.

The loss of information due to the rushed and partial nature of the work is not so easy to assess, simply because we have not seen it. The excavator should qualify all the recorded observations with estimates of their reliability on a scale which ranges from certain to only possible. The dating of structures by means of stratified pottery, coins and other artefacts is particularly difficult under these circumstances, and the excavator must be certain that the datable material really was derived from the significant layer or structure and not introduced by machinery or the soles of boots. The bucket of a drag-line, cutting a section of a ditch, can embed material from the upper layers deep into the primary silting, and cover it with a smear of the same material. When the ditch section is cleaned back it is disconcerting to find a half-brick stratified in the bottom of what is quite certainly a Roman ditch of the first century. The half-brick can be discarded as contamination and the section cleaned back further until uncontaminated layers are reached, but if instead of a brick a sherd of late Roman pottery or a fourth-century coin had found its way similarly into the early ditch, it would not have been discarded so promptly, thus causing real confusion. For the same reasons, the provenance of finds

handed in by workmen or unskilled volunteers must be treated with the greatest reserve unless they can be checked on the spot.

The minimum equipment for a salvage recorder should be two good cameras, one for colour and one for black-and-white photography with two robust tripods; a quick-set level and staff, if necessary with tripod attachment for single-handed use; a large clipboard mounted with squared polyester film overlaid and drawing film to a predetermined standard size, such as A4, A3 or a square format if this is preferred; coloured pencils to an agreed area (or preferably regional) colour code; record cards, as fully printed as possible, for site contexts, finds and photographs. Thus armed, a salvage recorder or a team of two or three working together can clean features and sections, draw them in outline and photograph them in black-and-white and colour film. The key drawings of both sections and plans must have spot heights inserted, so that they can be related to previous or further work in the area. If the work is in a town or city it should be possible to get the colour negatives processed and printed within the hour. If prints (of a section for example) are made to a predetermined scale, they can be pasted together and annotated on the site. This obviates all but the most skeletal drawing. It is also cost-effective. A section 45m (150ft) long and 3m (10ft) high would take a week to draw and colour in detail; photographically it can be recorded, printed and fully annotated in a day or so, the cost of the prints being offset by the saving of time.

Such recording should be carried out by an archaeologist with considerable experience in research and long-term rescue excavation, experience against which the significance of features that may only be visible for an hour or two, or even a few minutes, can be assessed. It is not a job for an inexperienced enthusiast. Nevertheless, it is here that local volunteers can be trained and used effectively. A group of eight or ten unskilled but energetic volunteers can enormously increase the amount of information retrieved, by cleaning surfaces, sections and walls, assisting with measuring, surveying and photography, and dealing with pottery and finds on a simple basis. Usually among such a group one or two will rapidly develop skills enabling them to draw plans and sections under supervision, and to adapt previously acquired photographic techniques and so forth.

In the post-excavation work such a group is of immense value, washing, marking and sorting pottery and other stable finds, assisting with the redrawing of plans and sections, and often going on to more specialized work. In Worcester, between 1965 and 1970, some extremely skilled drawing of finds and pottery, the stabilization of leather shoes and their reconstruction, and the reconstruction of highly-decorated pottery were carried out by local volunteers, none of whom had had previous experience. This can, no doubt, be paralleled in very many rescue and salvage excavations. It has the added benefit of drawing local people into the archaeology of the town or area, and is a powerful educational stimulus as well as an intensely satisfying recreation for those who take part. Not only that, it also extends and enhances the limited funds available for rescue archaeology since most part-time local volunteers are happy to work on their own town, or on a local site, for nothing, except perhaps help with expenses such as petrol. The director of a salvage excavation, however competent and experienced, can increase its potential output tenfold by the recruiting of local volunteers. The maximum number which one person can direct is probably 10 or 15. Beyond this, a hierarchy of assistant directors or site supervisors will be needed in the proportion of about one to ten.

Needless to say, such local groups should be organized in such a way that they are fully insured (in a scheme such as that offered by the Council for British Archaeology in Britain) and, while they may come and go on site at odd times or days according to their other commitments, they must be prepared to accept all the normal site disciplines, and be subject to the same safety precautions as a full-time team. For this reason it is advisable to enrol members by name before they are allowed to take part. The director cannot and must not accept responsibility for casual visitors and small boys who may join the work uninvited.

Another constraint on excavation techniques is the sheer size of some sites, either in area or in depth. As already mentioned, unstratified sites of many acres can be stripped progressively by machine and then hand-dug, and in theory, if the money and skilled manpower are available, a site of almost any extent could be dug simply by multiplying the numbers of workers at all levels. This is not the case, however, on sites with very deep deposits where the number of people who can be deployed on the ground is limited by the surface area. If there is a multiplicity of thin but significant layers there will be a maximum speed at which they can be individually stripped and recorded. If, on the other hand, the situation is made more awkward by deep layers of sticky clay or heavy rubble the niceties of sensitive area excavation may be hard to achieve. Here one simply has to excavate with as much precision as is possible. Remembering that canals and railways were once all dug by hand, it should be possible to recruit workmen who could deal with such a situation, and there is no doubt that hand-labour has great flexibility and is less potentially destructive than machinery, although it is far more expensive.

The aim of the director of either a rescue or a salvage excavation must be maximum time and cost-effectiveness; in other words the maximum amount of reliable evidence for the time and money available. Any method of digging and recording that accelerates the excavation process with minimal loss of evidence or accuracy must be tried and exploited.

The deployment of a large number of people on a site requires clear thinking and careful co-ordination if there is not to be chaos. If the work could proceed across the site from one end to another it would be easier for the excavators to be followed by finds-recorders, draughtsmen, surveyors, photographers and so on. In such an excavation the bulk of the recording would be photographic, using polaroid film in large format, and vertical and oblique stereoscopy in colour (see Chapter 8). Nevertheless, a minimum of surveying and drawing would still be needed. If it were intended to draw the site photogrammetrically by machine, an accurate prior survey of each run or area would be necessary. If the photographs were intended to supplement the plans, outline drawings to the necessary degree of detail, rendering the photographs intelligible when related to the skeletal plan, would be necessary.

The removal of spoil is often a slow and laborious process. Conveyor belts, either with or without buckets, considerably speed up the process, and experiments should be made with the vacuum removal of the finer spoil. In either case, it should be possible, with care, to remove the spoil from discrete features or layers separately, so that sieving, either wet or dry, flotation or other sampling could take place outside the excavation area and finds assigned to the contexts from which they came.

Hand in hand with the swift recording of the visual evidence must go streamlined methods of finds recording. Here index cards, bags, boxes, labels and so forth should be printed beforehand, so far as possible, so that the minimum amount of writing is needed. Automatic consecutive numbering and lettering stamps and other such devices would save valuable time.

The thought of such a high-pressure excavation, with its non-stop activity and continuous noise, will seem a nightmare to many, especially to those of us who have experienced excavation in sylvan surroundings where the silence is broken only by the music of a dozen trowels.

It must be remembered that, whatever accelerating techniques are invented, there is a point beyond which it is impossible, for sheer logistical reasons, to speed up excavation. No technical aids, no amount of money or number of people can strip an acre of thinly stratified deposits in a day. Furthermore, high-speed excavation loses that most essential quality of the slower excavation, the opportunity to think quietly, to contemplate the evidence, to go back to it on the ground, and if necessary, to reassess it drastically. It is useless to achieve speed without understanding.

The sort of intensive excavation outlined here would, it is hoped, only be used as a last resort. We must, therefore, work towards making such extreme measures unnecessary, by means of forward planning coupled with legislation which will permit sufficient time for thorough, less hurried, investigation.

A great many of the examples of excavation cited in this book are 'rescue' excavations, necessarily so, because the continuing destruction of sites has priority on the funds and expertise available. However, as long ago as the early 1970s Martin Biddle urged that rescue excavations should be turned, where possible, into research excavations; that the aims of archaeological research should be borne in mind, however small and rushed a rescue excavation may be forced to be. There is no doubt that in archaeology, two plus two tends to equal five, so that, for instance, the accumulating excavations and examination of repairs in and around a cathedral throw light on one another, and therefore on the development of the building. The writer is responsible for the archaeology of the cathedral at Worcester and two out of many pieces of work there are illustrated here and the cumulative information has enabled us to produce a reconstruction drawing of St Wulstan's Cathedral, begun in 1084 (see Fig. 27 and Fig. 84). Equally, rescue excavations of all kinds in a town gradually accumulate evidence for the development of the town and point out the way for future research

The Wroxeter Hinterland Project

Archaeological work carried out between 1988 and 1990 by the Birmingham University Field Archaeology Unit on the line of the proposed A5 Shrewsbury bypass and the A49 link road, involved the evaluation of threatened sites on the routes of the roads, and led to four large-scale rescue excavations together with small-scale salvage excavations and watching briefs. Despite the rescue nature of the work, the whole programme was considered from the outset within the wider context of the Shropshire Upper Severn Valley in the Iron Age and Roman

40a The Wroxeter Hinterland Project – the area through which the new roads were to be constructed. (40–5 are courtesy of BUFAU and Shropshire County Council.)

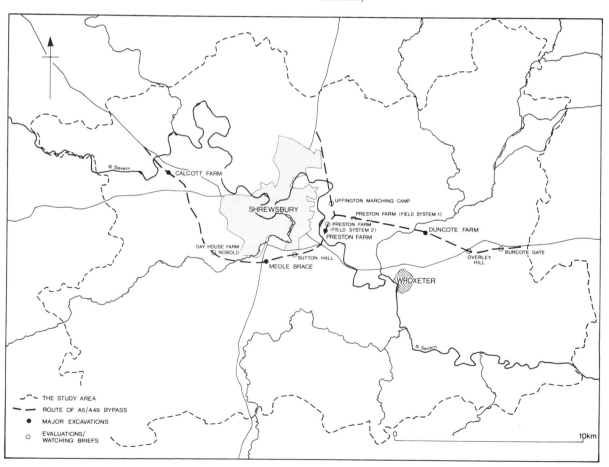

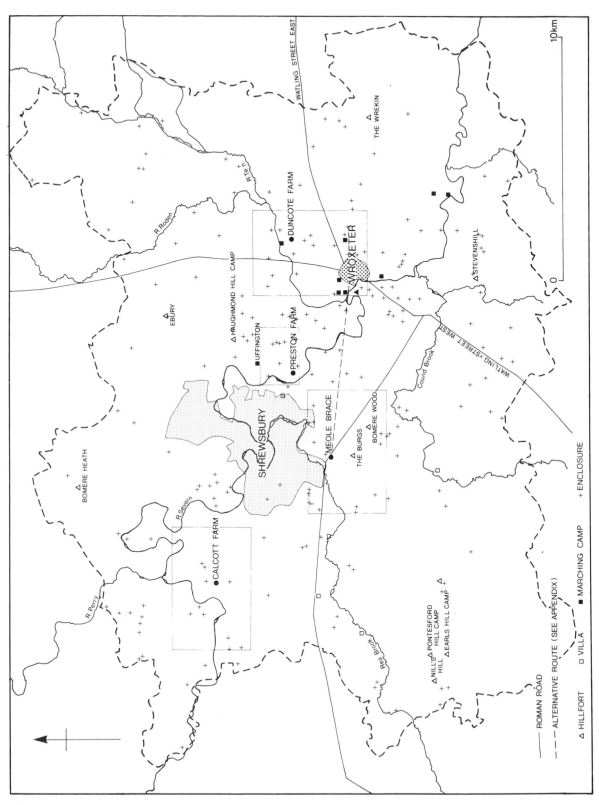

40b The distribution of archaeological sites in the region affected by the new road building.

periods – the 'Wroxeter Hinterland' – and the intention was, therefore, to carry out the excavations within a research framework and to allow the results to be presented within a set of explicit rather than implicit models.

The excavation results contributed to the question of the date and function of the numerous enclosures known from aerial photographs in the area, and gave an insight into the impact of the foundation of the *civitas* centre of Wroxeter on the surrounding countryside. As a consequence of the project the number of excavated enclosures in the study area has been doubled, and the results from the Roman period can be added to the existing excavation data which is heavily biased towards the important urban centre at Wroxeter. Inevitably the work also raises many new questions, particularly concerning the influence of Romanization in the later centuries of the Roman period (Ellis *et al*. 1992). Fig. 40a shows the Shrewsbury/ Wroxeter area through which the roads were to be constructed. Fig. 40b shows the distribution of archaeological sites in the region, with the four areas chosen for study outlined. Fig. 41 shows one of these areas between Wroxeter and Duncote with the cropmarks plotted on it. Figs 42 and 44 show one of the sites at Duncote which was crossed by the line of the road and results of the excavation of that part of the site. The excavation revealed a Romano-British enclosure constructed over a layout of first- and second-century fields. These used Roman units of measurement and were possibly market gardens and, significantly, the fields and the enclosure were on the same align-

ment as elements of the early landscape surrounding Wroxeter (illustrated by Steven Bassett in Barker (ed.) 1990 Fig. 18).

Figs 43 and 45 illustrate the excavation of a site south of Shrewsbury on the line of the Roman road from Wroxeter to Forden Goer in Montgomeryshire. The roadside settlement, which was only partially examined, was established in the second century and consisted of a number of probably successive rectangular timber-framed buildings. There was some evidence to suggest that it initially played an official role, perhaps controlling goods destined for Wroxeter, or perhaps was an in-transit overnight stop. These are only two examples of the ongoing work in the Wroxeter area.

The landscape of the Wroxeter Hinterland is a unique archaeological resource, but a fragile one. To avoid some of the shortcomings of a rescue approach developed in response to a specific threat, a strategy needs to be developed which integrates practical policies for monument protection and exploitation with academic research aims (Buteux and Gaffney 1992).

The first element of such a strategy would be the development of a data base capable of integrating archaeological information derived from a wide variety of sources – the sites and monuments record, aerial photography, geophysical and geochemical prospection, environmental sampling, fieldwalking, field and place names, excavation – with topographic, geological and soils data for the study area. In the past the creation of such a data base has been hindered by the lack of affordable technologies capable of dealing with the highly complex data sets involved. This problem, however, has now been largely overcome with the introduction of computer based Geographical Information Systems (GIS) which can store and interactively analyse most spatially referenced data (Gaffney and Stancic 1991 and see pp. 247–9.

153

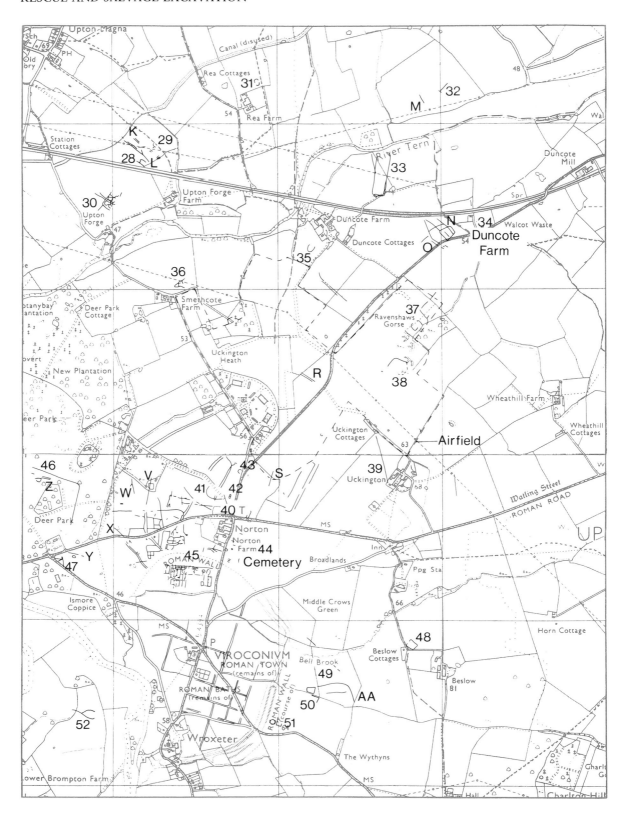

41 (*Left*) Wroxeter and Duncote (with permission of the controller HMSO, © Crown Copyright).

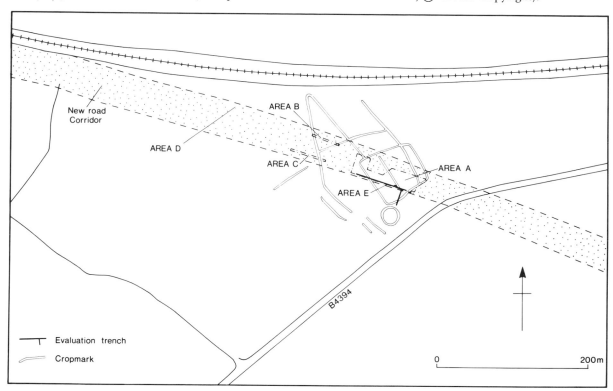

42 (*Above*) The site at Duncote

43 (*Below*) The site south of Shrewsbury on the line of the Roman road.

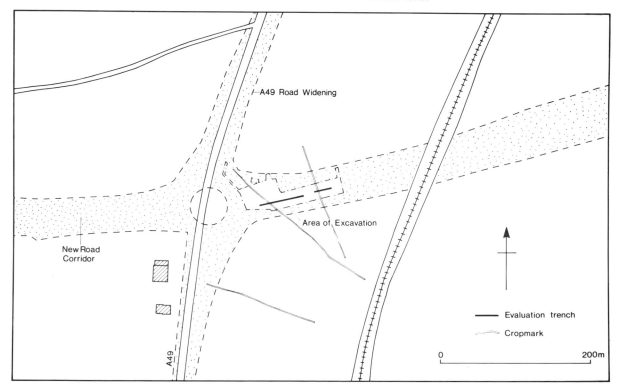

44 Phase diagrams of the site at Duncote.

45 Phase diagrams of the site south of Shrewsbury.

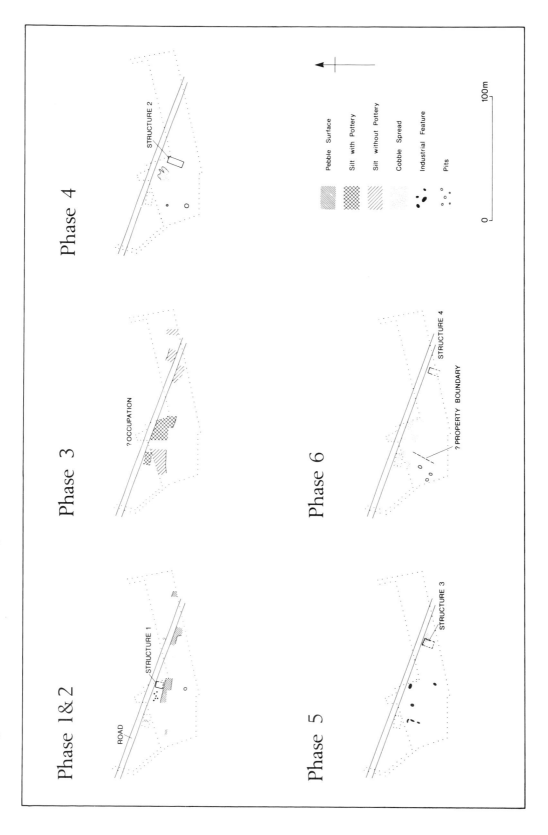

A Geographical Information System would enable the relationship between, for example, aerial photographic, geophysical and fieldwalking data on the one hand, and topography, geology and soils on the other hand, to be systematically analysed, allowing predictive models of the preservation and quality of the archaeology to be developed.

However, the full potential of a GIS database would lie not in the 'passive' marshalling and analysis of existing data, but in the provision of a framework for carefully targeted future fieldwork as part of an active strategy of research into management of archaeological resources, such as found in the Wroxeter Hinterland.

8
Recognizing and Recording the Evidence

Archaeological sites are almost infinite in their variety, from Minoan palaces to palaeolithic windbreaks. So also is the variety of evidence which is found in the ground. This may range from unmissable masonry foundations of massive size to the almost undetectable traces of a wattle-and-daub hut. To this must be added the immense variety of finds of all kinds – pottery, metalwork, preserved timber and leather, bones (both human and animal) and the macroscopic environmental evidence provided by seeds, twigs, leaves, snails and so on, together with the microscopic evidence of pollen, the remains of parasites etc.

In the face of all this, the excavator must, after the lifting of the first sod, be prepared for anything. The structural evidence may present itself in one or more of a great number of ways. The known site of a large building, say a medieval manor house, may prove to have well-preserved stone foundations, or may, if it was built in the great half-timber tradition, only survive as a level area, bounded by a few pebbles. A few small post-holes and a pattern of wear on the floor of a large Roman building may be the only indication of a later structure, built when the earlier building had gone out of use.

Too often in the past, excavators had preconceived ideas about the structures they were looking for, and so ignored other evidence which, even if it did not stare them in the face, gave them a significant glance. Excavators have, therefore, to be aware of all the varieties of evidence which might be encountered, and be very careful not to ignore evidence which inconveniently does not fit their expectations. It is difficult to be totally objective, to have a completely neutral approach to the site and its evidence — instant interpretations obtrude constantly as the site is uncovered and these have to be turned to good advantage, so that they constantly modify the questions which prompted the excavation in the first place. Nevertheless, having said this, the recording of the evidence must be as objective as possible, so that it can be looked at long after the site has been destroyed, with a fresh and unbiased eye.

Only what is observed can be recorded and observation is not an automatic process. It depends entirely on the particular knowledge of the observer. Hanson (1967) deals with just this point:

There is more to seeing than meets the eyeball, and there is more to scientific observation than merely standing alert with sense organs at the ready . . . The visitor [to the laboratory] must learn physics before he can see what the physicist observes. Only then will the context throw into relief those features in the phenomena which the physicist observes indicating (e.g.) resistance. This obtains in all cases of observation. It is all *interest-directed*

159

and context-dependent. Attention is rarely directed to the space betwen the leaves of a tree. Still, consider what was involved in Robinson Crusoe's seeing a vacant space in the sand as a footprint. Our attention rests on objects and events which because of our selective interests dominate the visual field. What a blooming, buzzing, undifferentiated confusion visual life would be if we all arose tomorrow morning with our attention capable of dwelling only on what has heretofore been completely overlooked. Indeed our mental institutions are full of poor souls, who despite having normal vision, can observe nothing. Their's is a rhapsodic, kaleidoscopic, senseless barrage of sense signals answering to nothing and signifying naught.

However, in scientific investigation there remains a basic and necessary duality of approach. On the one hand the selection of criteria of significance is crucial to the outcome of any investigation. As Alan Gregg, Director of Medical Sciences for the Rockefeller Foundation has said (Medawar 1969)

Most of the knowledge and much of the genius of the research worker lie behind the selection of what is worth observing. It is a crucial choice, often determining the success or failure of months of work, often differentiating the brilliant discoverer from the plodder.

On the other hand it is often the unsuspected fact that turns out to be crucial to understanding. Beveridge (1950) warns:

If when we are experimenting we confine our attention to only those things which we expect to see, we shall probably miss the unexpected occurrences and these, even though they may at first be disturbing and troublesome, are the most likely to lead to the explanation of the usual. When an irregularity is noticed, look for something with which it might be associated. In order to make original observations the best attitude is not to concentrate exclusively on the main point but to try and keep a lookout for the unexpected, remembering that observation is not passively watching but is an active mental process.

He also adds this corollary:

Effective scientific observation also requires a good background for only by being familiar with the usual can we notice something as being unusual or unexplained.

As Binford (1972) says:

Excavation must be conducted in terms of a running analysis and against a backdrop of the widest possible set of questions to which the data are potentially relevant. This is no technician's job. This is the job of an anthropologist specialized in the collection and analysis (and, I would add, synthesis) of data concerning extinct cultural systems.

All writers of excavation reports will know how difficult it is to keep the excavated evidence separate from its interpretation and this dilemma starts during the excavation itself. It is very easy to slip into the habit of calling dark circular soil marks 'post-holes' before they have been excavated. This not only prejudges the evidence, but can become that habit of mind which is capable of finding what it wants to find. Once a dark area had been presumed to be a post-hole it requires considerable mental discipline to accept, when it is emptied, that it is a root-hole or some other non-structural disturbance, especially if it is in just the place where a post-hole is expected (or even needed) to complete a structure. On the sites of timber buildings the opportunities for the creative imagination are immense. In the same way, 'timber slots' may turn out to be drainage gullies, or grooves worn by eaves' drip or intermittent plough furrows, and what at first sight seems to be a dump of broken tile may turn out to be a floor, or vice versa.

Also, there is the subtle but real pressure from colleagues to provide instant interpretations of phenomena as they appear. It is necessary to steer a course between a neutral, non-interpretative approach which will quickly deflate the enthusiasm that buoys an excavation along, and flights of fancy which the evidence finally cannot support. Occasionally the fossilized remains of fancies of this kind can be seen embedded in excavation reports. In many ways, the secret of good excavation lies in intense observation, in seeing as much as possible in the excavated surfaces or sections, and in the relationships between them, both while the excavation is proceeding and afterwards as the records are being analysed.

The excavation of the latest occupation of the Baths Basilica at Wroxeter Roman City, provides a good example of the necessity for immediate observation, and also of the difficulty of recording and publishing or demonstrating all that can be observed on the spot. The layers immediately below the topsoil consisted of spreads of rubble. These were clearly different in composition and were not random. As the excavation proceeded it was realized that the rubble spreads had been laid in rectangular areas, and there was every reason to believe that these were the foundations of timber-framed buildings, one of them of great size, whose ground sills simply lay on the rubble platforms. There was no doubt in the minds of those of us who saw these platforms that this is what they were, and they were drawn in great detail and with as much objectivity as possible. They were also photographed vertically and stereoscopically (though in black and white, when colour would undoubtedly have been better if it had been available). The shape and character of the platforms was seen particularly clearly when walking round the site, thus viewing them not only stereoscopically, which is our normal way of looking, but adding to this the extra dimension of movement. If we watch the passing landscape from a train the relative movement of the trees and hedgerows against one another enhances our three-dimensional understanding of the landscape. If the train stops in open country, we still see the landscape three dimensionally, but much less clearly. The difficulty of demonstrating the subtleties of the rubble platforms at Wroxeter, which could be clearly seen when we walked round them, but which were very difficult to photograph led to the suggestion that the video-camera might be the best way of demonstrating their undoubted existence.

It is difficult to separate in our minds the excavated evidence from its interpretation, which inevitably begins as features are seen, dissected and removed. There are some aspects of the interpretation of features (the word used in its widest sense) that are at their optimum when they are first revealed, since the site can never again be in that pristine, freshly cleaned state. Time and weather will immediately begin to alter it. Sometimes weathering produces new information, and sometimes it destroys the uppermost surface entirely; and although subsequent cleaning may reveal new detail, much of the original detail will have disappeared. In addition, however meticulous and accurate the recording, it is impossible to draw every texture of the exposed soil, and record all the nuances of colour in layers which may merge imperceptibly with one another. Also aspects of the site which cannot be seen or felt are likely to go unnoticed. Differences of chemical composition, for example, may not be visible but may exist and be of considerable significance in the understanding of the site. Some soil colour changes may only be made visible by ultra-violet or infra-red light or when enhanced by chemical treatment; some important differences of level may only show up under conditions of glancing light; other features may only appear as dry or wet areas, invisible on ordinary days and disappearing when dissected. To take a wider view there is the necessary contemplation of the excavated area (preferably when work on the site has temporarily stopped, so that there are no distractions), when relationships, unseen before, will become apparent, and when the overall pattern of the evidence will begin to emerge.

Thus at present the adequate and total recording of the evidence is beyond us. It follows that our responsibility for the immediate interpretation, made soon after the structures are uncovered, together with subsequent modifications, made in the light of all the observed evidence, is very great since the interpretative element in the recording can never be completely isolated, nor can drawings, photographs and written records ever be a substitute for the observations which are possible when one is present on the site. In other words, no mechanical process of recording even the nuances of the excavated surfaces will ever replace acute and sensitive observation by minds alive to all the possibilities presented by the evidence.

'Only connect' said E.M. Forster, and I believe that the most important need in archaeological excavation is to establish relationships, to interconnect structural layers and features, to relate them to finds of all kinds, from sculpture to pollen, embedded in them, and to relate the excavated site to its surroundings and to other comparable sites. Contiguous areas of excavation are almost always more illuminating than those separated from one another even by a metre or so, and interrelationships, established across and through large sites by a feature matrix are essential if the site is to be fully understood.

Data retrieval

The object of all excavation recording is data retrieval. At the end of the excavation all that remains are the site records, the drawings and photographs, and the finds. Any information which is not contained in one of these is lost for good. If it is there somewhere, but is difficult to find, its retrieval may be as laborious as the excavation itself. All aspects of the site recording system – visual, in the form of drawings, sections, contour surveys, together with photographs, vertical and oblique, in colour and black and white; or written, in the form of record cards, notebooks, punched cards, or tape – should be devised so that they make interpretation, publication and storage as easy as possible. It is not simply a question of data retrieval, but of producing from the data interpretive drawings of the site's phases and periods, buildings and structures; of wresting meaning from thousands of contexts, hundredweights of pottery and bone, and hundreds of finds, photographs and drawings. All this has ultimately to be distilled into readable prose, museum displays, popular books and reconstructions. Anything, therefore, that shortens this daunting process ought to be considered. What this means in practice is that the end product of the excavation should be borne in mind before the work begins.

There can be no hard and fast rules for excavation recording systems suitable for all types of excavation since sites vary so much in the nature of their structural evidence, and the types and quantities of finds. However, any system must satisfy the following criteria.

1 It must be simple and logical to use and understand.

2 It must be capable of indefinite extension, since the excavation itself may be extended

beyond the original intentions or the quantities of finds may be very much greater than anticipated.

3 It must be flexible. For this reason index cards or computerized records are better than books since they can be sorted into any order, and later interpolations can be inserted in place quickly and comprehensively.

4 The information must be readily retrievable.

5 The information should be presented in a form that makes the writing of the report as easy as possible.

It is maintained by some that none of the data from an excavation is objective; that an excavation produces no facts. Nevertheless, a block of sandstone is a fact; mortar is a fact (demonstrable if necessary by chemical and physical analysis); and it is only a slight shift towards subjectivity to call a hundred blocks of sandstone, coursed and mortared together in a line, a wall. Beyond this, however, we become increasingly subjective. The wall's possible or probable function and date, and its relation to other structures must be considered; and ultimately the discussion may, properly, enter the realms of speculation. What is important is that all these stages should be clearly distinguishable one from another.

For this reason, immediate on-site recording, the first stage in the process, should be as objective as it can be. It helps towards objectivity if the written recording is formalized on cards or sheets, with spaces for answering specific questions and the provision of required categories of information. This is preferable to notebooks which contain paragraphs (sometimes essays) of descriptive prose whose loose format invites the writer to confuse the stages of recording, deduction, interpretation and speculation.

The minimum information required on the index card is:

1 The abbreviated name of the site.

2 The area and grid numbers.

3 The context number.

4 The position of the context (as a grid reference).

5 Its relation to contexts above, around and, eventually, below it.

6 A description of the context including its composition or filling.

7 Finds directly associated with the context.

8 A sketch, if this would be helpful, and/or a photograph.

9 Cross reference to the measured drawings, sections and photographs.

10 Subsequent interpretive notes, e.g. 'posthole, part of structure XIII, kitchen, phase 2'.

11 The considered reliability of this interpretation.

46 a–b (overleaf) are of the record card developed by the Hereford and Worcester County Council Archaeology Section, which differs in a number of respects from that used at Wroxeter (see Fig. 47) while essentially meeting the criteria outlined above. c is a special form devised for the recording of skeletons.

HWCM 3899.	Sub-div 2	Grid ref 145/210	Type Fill	Context 16091

Sheet	Of	ORIGINAL/AMENDMENT

Mats

Type	Texture	Consistence	Colour	Shape section
Soil	Silty Loam	Mod/Com.	DK. to Med. grey-green WET/DRY	Horiz.

Layers/fills — Inclusions

Material	Frequency	Size	Shape	Comments
Charcoal	Abundant	Flecks	Sub-ang.	Small pebbles
Stone	Moderate	Small	Rounded	
Tile.	Occasional	Large	Sub-ang.	Occasional lenses of pure silty med-brown loam present.

Contamination (NONE) LOW HIGH	Reasons

Sieving	%	WET / DRY	Mesh size

Negative

Shape plan			Base	

Break from surface	N	E	S	W
Sides	N	E	S	W
Break to base	N	E	S	W

Positive

Materials	Condition	Colour WET/DRY
Matrix	Condition	Colour WET/DRY

Length 1.40 m	Width 0.90 m	Height/depth 0.72 m	Diameter –	Method of excavation SHT/LHT.

Earlier than

Below	
Sealed by	
Filled by	
Cut by	(15332) 16075
Butted by	

Matrix

```
16075
  |
16091
  |
16092
```

Contemporary

Within	
Contains	
Equivalent to	
Same as	
Bonded with	

Later than

Above	
Seals	
Fill of	16092
Cuts	
Butts	

Sketches

Description

Charcoal-flecked fine soil fill
& heavily truncated cut.

Interpretation

Silty loam suggests high proportion of cess or
liquid material. Backfill of cut 16092.

Plans	Sections	Photos	B + W		Archive	
			Trans		Archive	
Samples 5182	Recorded finds	Finds	Pot ✓	Bone ✓	B+T ✓	Iron	Glass		

Provisional period	Matrix sheet	Group	Phase	Period

Excavator HB	Recorder HB	Date 15/3/89	Checked by JT RW	Copy

46b

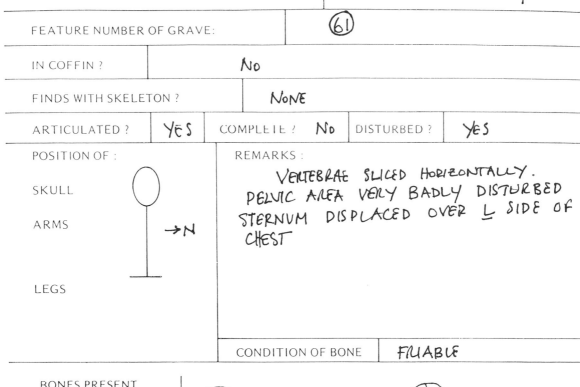

WORC. CATH. SACY 1992

SKELETON FORM   **4**

FEATURE NUMBER OF GRAVE:	⑥1

IN COFFIN ?	No

FINDS WITH SKELETON ?	NONE

ARTICULATED ?	YES	COMPLETE ?	No	DISTURBED ?	YES

POSITION OF :

SKULL

ARMS   →N

LEGS

REMARKS :

VERTEBRAE SLICED HORIZONTALLY.
PELVIC AREA VERY BADLY DISTURBED
STERNUM DISPLACED OVER L SIDE OF
CHEST

CONDITION OF BONE	FRIABLE

BONES PRESENT

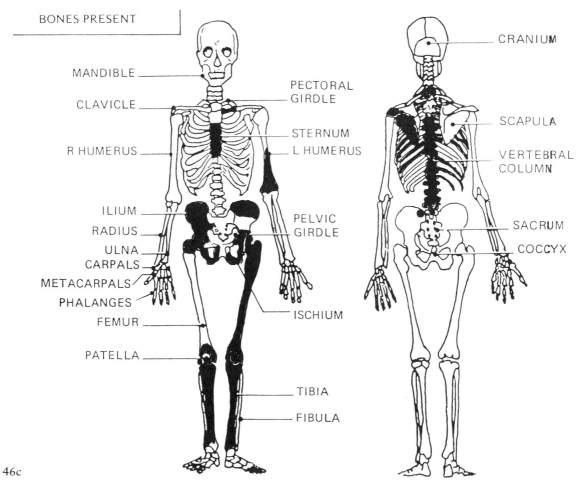

MANDIBLE

CLAVICLE

R HUMERUS

ILIUM
RADIUS
ULNA
CARPALS
METACARPALS
PHALANGES
FEMUR

PATELLA

PECTORAL GIRDLE

STERNUM
L HUMERUS

PELVIC GIRDLE

ISCHIUM

TIBIA

FIBULA

CRANIUM

SCAPULA

VERTEBRAL COLUMN

SACRUM

COCCYX

46c

Left card (context/feature record sheet):

| Site | Area | | Feature | Date Found | |
| | | | | Date Dug | |

GRID REFERENCE   GENERAL LOCATION

DESCRIPTION

INTERPRETATION

POST-EXCAVATION RELIABILITY

METHOD OF EXCAVATION
METHOD OF COLLECTION OF FINDS
TYPES OF FINDS PRESENT BUT NOT COLLECTED
RISK OF CONTAMINATION   LOW   AVERAGE   HIGH

SAMPLES
SPECIAL FINDS

PLAN NOS.

SECTION NOS.   OTHER DRAWINGS

PHOTOGRAPHS: B. W NEGS.   B. W PRINTS

COLOUR SLIDES   PRINTS   VERTICAL

Right card:

STRATIFICATION   LOCALISED MATRIX
                        SHEET NO

UNDERLIES
OVERLIES
CUTS
CUT BY
ABUTS
EQUALS
OTHER

PHOTOGRAPHS AND/OR CONTINUATION

Bottom card (pottery fabric record):

| Publication Ref. | Fabric Code |
| E.R. No. of Type Sherd | Common Name |

COLOUR   ext. margin   ext. surface
                int. margin   int. surface

HARDNESS   FRACTURE

FEEL

INCLUSIONS   1   2   3

Frequency
Sorting
Size
Rounding

SURFACE TREATMENT(S): ext.   int.

MANUFACTURE:

SLIP: extent   colour(s)

GLAZE ext.   extent   colour(s)   finish
       int.   extent   colour(s)   finish

47 Example of a feature card used at Wroxeter and Hen Domen.

Suggested layouts of cards for recording features and layers are illustrated in Figs 46–47. These written records are complementary to the visual records which consist of the site plans and sections and the drawings of individual contexts, pottery and other finds, together with both vertical and oblique photographs. The written records and the drawings and photographs must be cross indexed so that the complete information about a context, feature or layer can readily be found. The information relating to an individual context for instance, should consist of a completed context card; a set of drawings, including plans and sections; photographs; cards for small finds, and pottery found within the filling or structure of the context; and finally, the drawing of the context on the main site plan, which relates it to the structures around it.

On a site which produces hundreds, perhaps thousands, of contexts this may seem unnecessarily laborious, but there is no short cut if the excavation is to be properly recorded.

A number of larger archaeological units are producing their own handbooks on site recording, which lay out the procedures and conventions to be adopted on their sites. A good example is *The Archaeological Site Manual* (2nd ed.) 1990 published by the Department of Urban Archaeology of the Museum of London and obtainable from them.

Site notebooks

For reasons mentioned above (p. 163) index cards are preferable to site notebooks for the recording of features. However, site notebooks should be kept for recording information not to be found on the record cards; a brief day-to-day account of work in progress, observations on areas or clusters of features, speculations and hypotheses.

Where a site is full of evidence for buildings and other structures it may be helpful to have a separate card index for buildings, each card drawing together the evidence such as post-holes, walls, floors, hearths, finds and so on for the existence, form and function of the building. Such a card index will be of great help when the report comes to be written.

Single context recording

One of the most important recent developments in the last twenty years has been the introduction of 'single context recording', that is, the drawing of each site context on a separate sheet of drawing film (thus paralleling the completion of a record card for each context) as distinct from drawing a number of related contexts, or sometimes a whole phase of the site's development on a single sheet. The system evolved in urban archaeology where often the stratification is in discrete islands which cannot be related together on site and where large numbers of workers are employed to dig these islands simultaneously.

It is argued that single context recording is logical and objective and does not confuse the evidence with its interpretation. This is true. It also has the advantage that it allows delegation of a simple and routine task to comparatively inexperienced excavators rather than holding up the work while specialist planners draw the site, which has often been the case. Each of the separate plans, together with its record card, are subsequently used to create the site matrix and composite phase plans – a three-dimensional jigsaw. The clearest exposition of the method will be found in Spence, C. (ed.) *The Archaeological Site Manual*, 1990, published by the Museum of London.

While the method has the virtue of clarity, logic and the possibility of wide delegation, it seems to set its face against any on-site, immediate interpretation as being subjective and potentially misleading, preferring to reserve interpretation for post-excavation analysis. This, it seems to me, is to deny the potential of intensive on-site observation, and the attempt to understand relationships while they are visible, at a time when no recording, however subtle, will recapture every three-dimensional nuance, seen in varying light and from all angles.

As described in the London *Manual* the details and the character of the context nowhere appear to be drawn but are merely outlined. The differences between pebble or rubble surfaces, which might be crucial to their understanding, do not seem to be recorded and slopes are drawn with hachures which are somewhat simplistic ways of recording undulating surfaces. In addition, every context is drawn with a hard line round its edge – for examples, see Harris (1988), Figs 39–40 and 61. However, archaeological sites are never, in my experience, as clear cut as that and many contexts, seen in plan, merge imperceptibly into one another, or pebble surfaces peter out in all directions. Soil discolorations, such as those recorded by Bersu at Vowlan, for instance (see Figs. 13–14) have very indistinct edges and they were recorded as such.

Harris himself reproduces my drawing of the uppermost layers of part of the Baths Basilica site at Wroxeter, a site which, I believe, would have defied digging in separately definable single contexts, and he adds the comment 'If an excavation cannot define the limits of a unit of stratification, how is it possible for stratigraphic excavation to take place?' The answer to this is, with great difficulty.

The exposure, achieved by removing the topsoil, of the uppermost archaeological contexts and, in fact of all the latest occupation layers at Wroxeter and at Hen Domen (Barker *et al.* forthcoming, 1994, and Barker and Higham 1982) was straightforward. The dissection of these uppermost layers was another matter altogether and posed many difficulties of distinguishing not only one context from another horizontally, but also of determining the thickness of layers/contexts, since they often merged imperceptibly into the layer/context below, leading inevitably to a greater or lesser degree of overdigging.

It is necessary, of course, if a site matrix is to be constructed, to give each discernible context its own identity and its own number. This is easier to do in the written record, using cards, because ambiguities can be expressed in words, and also relationships, where they too are ambiguous, can be described as such, in a way which hard-edged drawings exclude.

As in so many cases, I believe that a compromise approach to recording is possible and valid. The method ultimately developed at Wroxeter, which we hoped combined the best aspects of the methods here described, consisted of a written record of individual cards, single context drawing, where this was appropriate, together with a drawn record which combined contexts which did not lend themselves to simple context recording, being diffuse and ill defined, or which seemed to be part of a coherent phase or structure. It may be objected that the last were subjective decisions, and this is true, but they were rigorously examined not only in the next stage of the excavation, when the contexts were dissected, but also in the post-excavation processes.

The other important element in the recording of the site was the use not only of oblique photographs, often taken in glancing light which could record aspects not possible either in words or plans, but of vertical colour stereoscopic photography, which meant that the excavated surfaces could be examined three dimensionally in very accurate colour long after the site had been destroyed (see pp. 181–6 below).

Now that the excavation at Wroxeter and its post-excavation analysis is finished and its more than 4000 contexts have been ordered by means of matrices and dated by all available techniques it is possible to say that comparatively very few changes have had to be made to the on-site interpretation. One hitherto unsuspected building was discovered during the post-excavation process, and one (out of 74) was discarded as having evidence that was too ambiguous. In one phase the function of a large spread of tiles had been, it must be said, misunderstood, due in part to rather summary digging, and another area of the site proved to have more permutations and combinations than had originally been suspected. But the overall interpretation stood the test of a very rigorous examination, so that I believe that a judicious combination of all the recording methods available, if sceptically and critically reviewed at all stages, will give the best opportunity of understanding the site as fully as possible.

Terminology

A number of confusing and potentially ambiguous terms have come into use to define the elements which make up archaeological sites. The earliest and most obvious was the term 'layer' (though sometimes 'strata' and, incorrectly, 'level' were used). Since the word 'layer' was inappropriate as a term for such things as post-holes, wall foundations, hearths or graves, the word 'feature' came to be used for these, and sometimes one set of numbers was used for recording 'layers' and another for 'features'. This was generally the situation in Britain in the 1950s and 1960s.

With the application of more logical thinking and the gradual development of standardized recording forms, one term applicable to all the elements of stratification which were, or could be, encountered was made necessary, and in Britain the term 'context' was preferred. It seems to me to be poor English, since although finds may be said to have a context, it is an abstract expression, in that it is difficult to lower a context by a few centimetres, or to section it. Nevertheless, in default of a better term, it has been widely adopted.

It is notable, however, that Edward Harris in his essential *Principles of Archaeological Stratigraphy* (2nd ed.) 1989 does not mention it, preferring terms such as 'layer' or 'units of stratigraphy', 'feature', 'feature interface' or 'layer interface'.

In the recording system developed by the Museum of London all these terms are subsumed in the term 'context' which is defined as 'any single action, whether it leaves a positive or negative record within the (stratified) sequence. (Spence (ed.) 1990).

Interfaces
There is another important addition to what might be called the repertory of recording terms which has been stressed by Harris and others – this is the 'interface', the junction between two contexts.

The clearest example is the surface of a floor – objects dropped on to the floor are neither within the floor make-up, nor in the layers above it, but from the interface between the two and should be recorded as such. All buried surfaces therefore have interfaces.

The other important category of interfaces might be termed 'negative' being the result of cuts into pre-existing contexts – pits of all kinds, ditches, gullies, graves, post-holes, construction trenches and robber trenches, old excavations, etc all have interfaces between the cut and the contexts which fill the hole, ditch or whatever. In the case of a post set in a post-pit, for example, the hole 'cut' for the pit, the packing for the post and the eventual post-hole filling all have interfaces which should be distinguished from their fillings. In the past, there has been a tendency to call the post-hole filling the post-hole, and the post-pit filling the post-pit when it is obvious, on stopping and thinking about it, that the post-hole filling may be many decades later in date than the post-hole with its post, so that they should logically have separate context numbers. Figs 3, 1–7 and 4, 1–7 illustrate this simple example, which is expanded in Harris's Figs 27–29 (*ibid.*). However, here Harris has defined the *feature* interfaces and not the *layer* interfaces as well.

All these examples are important and legitimate uses of the 'interface', but the fact is that every single context has two interfaces, one above and one below. The recording of each of these, regardless of the context's function, for example, in a thick series of dumping layers where there might be hundreds of contexts caused by each shovelful or barrow load, or the dozens of layers filling a large pit, would increase the recorder's work enormously and, it seems to me, with limited effect, having little or no impact on the eventual understanding of the site. On a very large site it might double the number of recordable contexts and bring the excavation to a virtual standstill.

The use of the 'interface' is, therefore, often in practice subjective, being confined to two recognizable categories – floors, paths, roads and other used surfaces on the one hand, and cuts for post-holes, post-pits, graves, ditches and their recuts and so on on the other hand, all of which have to be recognized as the work proceeds.

The site grid

The skeleton of any recording system must be the site grid. Under all but emergency conditions this should be laid out before the excavation begins; and it is essential to relate the excavation and its grid to permanent features in the landscape. With the advent of ever larger areas of development in towns, and the wholesale removal of hedgerows and other landmarks in the country, this is becoming increasingly difficult, and the excavator, in these circumstances, may become disorientated and literally may not know where the excavation is. In urban areas it is necessary to obtain the co-operation of the engineers and surveyors concerned with the development in order to locate precisely the excavation areas in the old and new townscapes. In the country, in the middle of a large gravel pit or an area of 'prairie' farming, the situation may not be so easy; rather like fixing one's position in the desert, it may be necessary to do some very accurate surveying. Anticipating the chapter on publication below, it is necessary where an excavation is taking place in a radically altered landscape, to publish its relationship to the old landscape as well as to locate it in the new.

On any but the briefest excavation a base or datum line should be chosen and its terminal pegs concreted into place at each end. A hooked metal rod is perhaps the most convenient type of peg, so that the ring of a tape will not slip off it when under tension. Needless to say this base line must be measured with great accuracy and in the horizontal plane. A third peg, on an axis at right angles to the base, should be concreted at a convenient point outside the proposed area of the excavation. From these two lines a co-ordinate or grid system in the horizontal plane can be established. Other subsidiary pegs should then be fixed on or outside the excavation to form an accurate basis for the rest of the grid. Wherever possible, the intersections of the grid lines should be marked by thin steel rods driven into the ground, thus reducing the inconvenience often caused when nails are used to mark the grid intersections since they are easily displaced and have to be realigned – a tedious and time-wasting job.

Metric units are now standard on archaeological sites. Whether the co-ordinate system or a system of numbered or lettered grids is used, the corners of the squares should be pegged with accurately placed metal pegs, and it is an advantage to paint these corner pegs a bright colour so that they can be easily seen. The grid can then be subdivided into as many smaller squares as the site demands, and the corners of these smaller squares pegged.

The problems of planning excavated areas have been dealt with by Atkinson (1953, 229), Fryer (1971), Biddle and Biddle (1969), and Coles (1972). The Biddles' paper, which

the reader is urged to study, advocates the use of a co-ordinate system based on the metric grid, rather like the National Grid Reference system. This has the advantage that any point on the site can be referred to by a single unique reference given by two co-ordinates (Fig. 48). It is usually convenient to lay out the whole site in a grid of ten-metre squares marked out with string (coloured plastic coated varieties are not only easily seen but have the necessary elasticity) so that the excavators can easily orientate themselves on the site. Plastic letters or numbers in the centre or at one corner of each major grid enable workers to see at a glance which square they are working in.

Site planning

The most usual way of recording contexts visually is to draw the plan of the surface at a scale large enough for the smallest context to be accommodated: 20:1 is usually sufficient. Since contexts will often merge almost

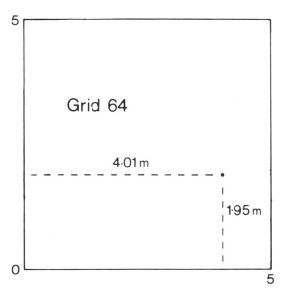
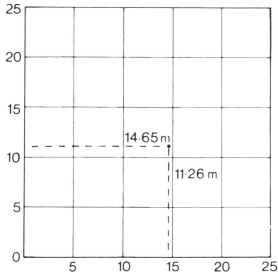

48 Using a grid. *Left* The position would be recorded as G64. 401 195; *right* as 1465.1126.

imperceptibly into one another, or are distinguishable only by changes of texture rather than of colour, it is sometimes impossible to draw hard lines round the limits of each context, in which case the drawing should depict the character of the context as closely as possible, even though it may be necessary in the interpretation to distinguish the junction more clearly. However, see above for a discussion of single context recording. In fact the principle of separating the evidence from the interpretation should be adhered to as far as possible, though, inevitably, the field drawing will include elements of interpretation, at least in part due to the limited flexibility of drawing techniques. The range of colours and symbols used cannot be as infinite as the variations in composition of the features and layers, and the completely pictorial representation of plans (and sections), especially if in colour, is apt to be overloaded with detail, and 'unreadable'. Some of Professor Bersu's 'impressionist' drawings, attempting to include everything, err in this direction. Simplification involves selection and is therefore subjective and this is the strongest argument for photographic recording.

If more than one draughtsman is used on a site the work should be co-ordinated. For instance three different draughtsmen drawing the same stony surface will in all probability produce different results because they will include stones of different minimum sizes. Many surfaces consist of stones of all sizes down to 1mm across and therefore a minimum drawn stone size has to be chosen. At 1:20 a 2cm stone will appear like this:

Stones smaller than this will be dots the size of a pencil point. With further reduction for publication they will all disappear, or will have to be drawn at an artificially enlarged scale. In cases of doubt the director should make a ruling, but usually stones of 1cm are the smallest that can reasonably be drawn at 1:20 scale. As far as possible all the draughtsmen on the site should draw in the same style; and they must certainly all use the same conventions and methods otherwise the resulting mosaic of drawings will be incoherent.

A considerable problem is posed by hollows and scarps on the excavated surface. Ideally each small hollow, each scarp, each post-hole should be contour surveyed, but lack of time usually prevents this. A compromise which may be used is to contour survey the whole site separately on a transparent overlay on a 20cm grid for small sites or a 50cm or 1m grid for large sites, dependent on the degree of detail required. Minor undulations, small scarps, etc are then put on the site drawings as form lines with an arrow indicating the downward slope. Other conventions such as hachures or 'tadpoles' can be used; but on complex sites they tend both to be more confusing than form lines and to obscure detail.

In special cases, where it is required to demonstrate the existence of slight but significant undulations, the contour survey can be made tighter and the contour lines drawn at very close intervals. A fine 'gravel' street was discovered at Wroxeter. On this street differential wear had left very slight humps and platforms like miniature earthworks. Since these were considered to be the sole evidence for a second phase of use of the street, with facades or booths of some sort encroaching on it, the survey was made at 20cm horizontal intervals, and the resultant contours plotted at 2cm vertical intervals in order to bring out the subtleties of shape of these undulations, which would have been missed in a survey on a coarser grid plotted at a greater vertical interval (see Barker *et al.* forthcoming, 1994). For detailed levelling of very uneven surfaces, or rows of post- or stake-holes, structures of rock or rubble and so on, a thin staff may be made by attaching a 3m tape to a metal or wooden rod. If necessary, the rod can be fitted with a long spike for precise positioning in holes or crevices. A more easily read staff of this kind could be made by accurately painting the divisions and lettering them with Letraset or similar stencils which should then be varnished.

50 The illustration shows a method of drawing on a steep undulating surface. The string grid joins nails located accurately in the horizontal plane by means of a level and plumb-bob. The draughtsman then draws each square as a mosaic to scale (in this case 1:20).

Any method of drawing that shortens the steps between the original field drawings made on the site and those eventually published should be tried and developed. If the field drawings are clear and accurate, and are directly and precisely relatable to the site grid it should be possible to trace the final drawings straight from them so that there are only two drawings of the evidence, one made in the field, the other the published figures. To these may be added separate interpretive plans, sections and so on, which will demonstrate the site clearly to the reader who has had no previous experience of it.

If plans on translucent plastic film are made of each stage of the excavation, together with subsidiary plans of intermediate stages they can be superimposed on one another so that their relationship can be understood visually. At the same time the interrelationship between all the features on

the site should be recorded and demon-strated schematically by means of a matrix such as that developed by Edward Harris (Harris, 1989); see pp. 233.

There are four or five principal ways in which the site plan may be drawn.

This can be done by propping the corners with stones or wooden blocks and levelling with a builder's level, but more efficiently by making some form of adjustable leg. A tried and successful method is to make a clamp for each corner of the frame with a butterfly

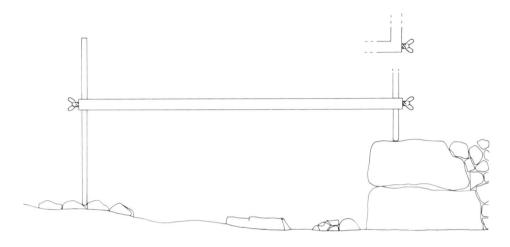

51

The drawing frame

One method is to use a frame the size of the grid unit, say a metre square, divided into smaller units, such as 20cm, and laid on the excavated surface. Through this the features and details of the surface can be directly related to sectional drawing film on the drawing board, and drawn to the desired scale. The bulk of the drawing can then be made by eye without further measuring. A frame of slotted metal or braced wooden slats is divided either by plastic or nylon string which has sufficient elasticity to stay taut, by wire, or by expanding plastic covered curtain wires. Frames 2m square may be found to be rather large and unwieldy and a 1m square is often prefer-able. Snags with the use of a frame arise when the ground is not reasonably level, or more particularly when large stones or other obstructions prevent the frame from being laid horizontally. It is of course important that the frame should be levelled, and not simply laid on the ground if there is a slope.

nut for quick release (Fig. 51). The legs can terminate in small flat plates or rubber balls so that the site is not damaged.

Offsets

An alternative method of plotting when a grid is not available is by means of co-ordinates set-off from a tape stretched across the area to be drawn. In this method a 3m metal tape or measuring rod is used to measure the distances of features at right angles from the datum tape.

The accuracy of this method depends on the ability of the draughtsman's assistant to judge a right angle. One of the easiest ways of doing this is to swing the tape with the centre at the point to be plotted until the shortest distance is read off against the datum tape (Fig. 52b).

However, since the angle of cut between the arc of the swing tape and the datum tape is minimal at the correct point on the datum tape, it may be thought that this involves an

52 Plotting: four methods
  (a) Traverse method of plotting an area.
  (b) Determining a right angle by swinging the tape until the minimum reading is obtained.
  (c) Triangulation.
  (d) Triangulation where an obstruction necessitates the use of a false datum.

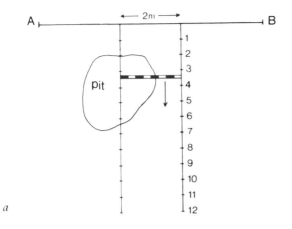

a

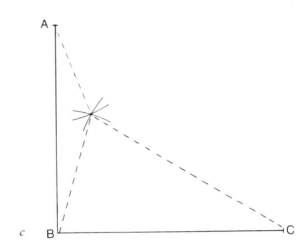

c

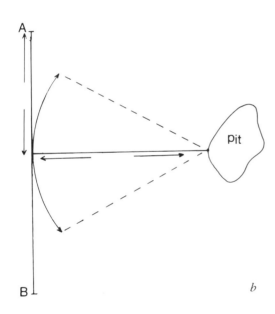

b

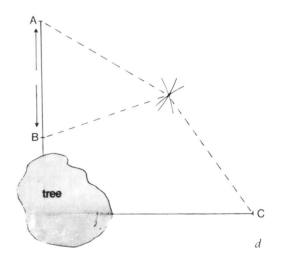

d

unacceptable degree of inaccuracy and a more accurate method of measuring a right angle such as a wooden or metal frame is to be preferred.

Two parallel tapes
A somewhat similar but more accurate method is to lay two parallel tapes across the site a short distance apart. A 3m metal tape or a measuring rod is then laid across the point to be plotted so that the lengths along the datum tapes are equal, and therefore the cross tape is at right angles, and the distance from the datum 'AB' is read off (Fig. 52a).

Co-ordinates

A fourth method is to plot co-ordinates from two axes of the grid. This method, using as it does two offsets is, of course, more accurate than the single offset method described above. A most accurate variant of this method is triangulation, preferably from two or three corners of the grid (Fig. 52c–d).

In order to plot the distances on the site plan, if it is large, it will be necessary to use a trammel and it must be remembered that three measurements will be more accurate than two. If only two are taken a good angle of cut between the arcs must be assured by choosing suitable points of origin on the grid. It is possible to plan single-handed in this way if the tapes are secured to the datum pegs, though able to rotate. The planner can then hold the two tapes in one hand at their junction, using a plumb-bob if necessary with the other hand.

Plastic film

Plastic film should be used for all drawing. Tracing paper, linen and other similar materials expand and contract under varying conditions of moisture sufficiently to move features as much as half a metre (to scale) according to the weather; and this is clearly unacceptable. In addition, with the use of plastic film, drawing in pencil can continue in wet weather, which may be a crucial factor at the end of an excavation when recording in any other medium may be impossible.

It is suggested that a comparatively soft pencil, HB or F, should be used; partly because these softer varieties give a more flexible line, but also because it is much easier to trace the drawing through the overlay if the field drawings are black in line rather than pale grey. Softer pencils must, of course, be sharpened more often if the line is not to become diffuse, though clutch pencils using thin leads do not require sharpening. The problem of smudging can be overcome by working from the top of the drawing downwards, by masking the completed part of the drawing, and by the use of aerosol fixatives such as those used for pastel drawings (though these render the surface unsuitable for subsequent colouring with crayon). Better still, the drawing may be made directly in ink using Rapidograph or similar pens, though this precludes drawing in wet weather.

Although costs prohibit the publication of archaeological plans and sections in colour except in the most lavish productions, colour should nevertheless be used on the field drawings, since it considerably extends the range of variety of the recording.

The range of colours to be used throughout the excavation must be decided on at the beginning and a sufficient stock of pencils obtained to avoid unnecessary variations in tint, especially during the course of a long excavation. A number of paler colours, particularly pink, fade within a few days of exposure to light – even during the time taken in colouring the plan! It is therefore advisable to test crayons and coloured pencils for fastness before the excavation begins. Mars-Lumochrom pencils have been tested on site for permanence and can be recommended. Almost all other pinks fade within a week. Colour codes for the varieties of stones, tile, clay, mortar and other building materials anticipated must be decided upon, and adhered to. Other colours may then be used for the plotting of nails, coins, small finds of different sorts and the many other categories of information which may be desired on the plan. In the case of complex sites it is better to avoid confusion by plotting finds and other non-structural information on separate transparent overlays.

Inevitably an element of interpretation will always enter the drawing. It is therefore

177

essential that not only the interpretation of the site, but also the drawing (which incorporates, however subtly, some of this interpretation) should be subject to constant discussion and criticism and not merely left to a lone draughtsman. There is a tendency for some draughtsmen to simplify, and worse, to stylize the features seen on the ground. Post-holes become more circular on the drawing than they really are; pebble surfaces become more uniform in the size and shape of their pebbles; and courses of stones become stereotyped. Checks on the accuracy and fidelity of the drawing must therefore be frequent, especially towards the end of the day. As an aid to accuracy of the draughtsmanship, it is very useful to have vertical stereoscopic photographs of each sector of the site printed at the same scale as the field drawings and made available to the draughtsmen while they are drawing in the field. This is not very difficult to achieve if a hut can be made into a dark room or if a local professional photographer can produce results quickly on demand, and the benefits are considerable. Drawings can then be checked immediately against the photograph and the two used to form an amalgam which is perhaps as near to an accurate record, combining objectivity with a degree of interpretation, as can be achieved at present.

For reasons discussed below (pp. 181ff.) there will inevitably be radial distortions in the scale of features recorded by the vertical camera so that features and detail cannot be traced directly on to the plan from the photographs, except close to the centre of each photograph. However, for practical purposes and taking into account the eventual scale at which the drawings will be published, errors even towards the edges of photographs carefully enlarged are not totally unacceptable. They can be eliminated by a radial line plotter if such a machine is available.

Even when a grid, frame and photographs are being used it is advisable to cross-check the accuracy of the whole plan by triangulating the main features such as walls, major post-holes or timber-slots from the principal fixed datum points since it is possible for gross errors to occur unnoticed in a mass of detail.

The drawing of sections has been dealt with exhaustively in a number of text books, notably in Wheeler (1954), Webster (1963 and 1970), Kenyon (1964), Alexander (1970) and Atkinson (1953). Essentially section drawing is drawing the plan of a vertical surface: indeed, in Britain such mystique became attached to the importance of the section during the period between the two world wars and for some years after, that it might have been wished that the opposite truth had been realized – that drawing the plan of a site is merely drawing a horizontal section – and that the plan had been given the same precise attention to detail as the highly complicated section drawings which filled excavation reports for many years. The drawing of a straightforward ditch section need not be described here, as the references given above are more than adequate.

However, as Limbrey (1975, 273–5), points out, sections are often drawn in a stylized way, by joining the dots made on the paper by someone receiving vertical and horizontal co-ordinates and not observing the layers closely while drawing them. Such a section will be meaningless to the soil

53 New Fresh Wharf, London, 1975. View along the Roman waterfront structure dated AD 155 ± 5 years. This photograph is a model of descriptive clarity. The carefully selected viewpoint gives maximum information about and three-dimensionality to the structure, and the use of an exceptional lens combined with a very small stop gives great depth of focus. (Photo: Trevor Hurst.)

scientist asked to discuss it later. It is important therefore that generally understood symbols should be used to describe the layers in pedological terms, rather than, or at least as well as, archaeological terms, such as 'destruction layer', 'build-up of foundations' and so on, which, anyway, are prematurely interpretive.

Photography

A number of good textbooks on archaeological photography are available dealing with techniques of both site photography and the photography of portable finds. Among the best are, Cookson (1954), Matthews (1968), Simmons (1969), Bracegirdle (1970) and Conlon (1973).

In addition there is a multiplicity of books on photography in general both in black and white and in colour, together with textbooks on individual cameras with their related accessories. There is no need therefore to go into the technicalities of photography here,

54 Medieval female skeleton with unborn foetus, from GPO Newgate Street, London, 1975. The recording of this long-forgotten tragic incident required very skilful cleaning (in the wind and rain of a winter excavation) which demonstrated the existence of the foetus yet left each bone in place for photography. (Photo: Trevor Hurst.)

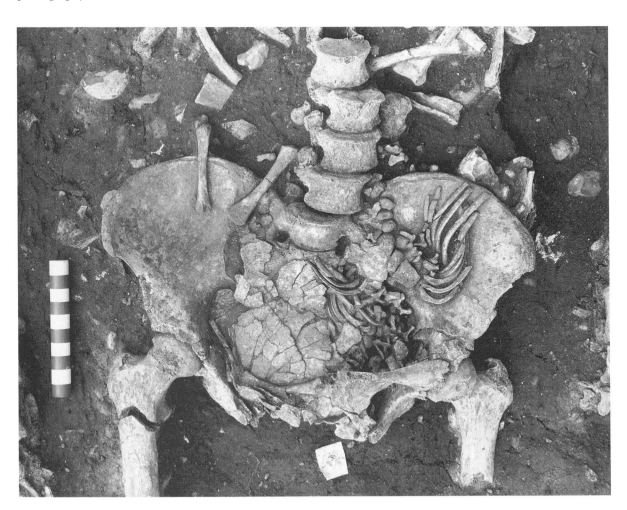

but merely to outline and comment on those aspects which are particularly relevant to the recording of excavations.

Without doubt the larger the negative used the sharper the detail on the photography. For this reason 5 × 4in (or 2¼ × 2¼in) cameras are best for photographs which are to be used for publication, or for museum displays, but such cameras can be very expensive. In practice, 35mm cameras properly handled are capable of producing results that are more than adequate for any archaeological photograph. In these days of relatively cheap 35mm camera systems with built-in exposure meters, automatic focusing and zoom lenses there is no excuse for poor pictures. Superb ones are a little more difficult, depending more on the photographer than the camera.

The three chief categories of photograph that are required on most excavations are the record photographs, vertical and oblique, both in black and white and in colour, which are specifically taken to supplement the plan and section drawings; colour transparencies designed for lectures and talks; and photographs, both of the site and of finds, which are taken specifically to illustrate the eventual publication of the excavation.

Vertical photographs

Many methods, from ladders to balloons, have been used to suspend a camera vertically over a desired point on the excavation. A number of ordinary folding tripods have a reversible section to which the camera can be attached pointing vertically downward. This method is most useful for photographs of small features, or finds *in situ*, but some large tripods have legs long enough to enable whole graves to be included on one negative. A ladder firmly lashed to two scaffold poles is a cheap and easy way of achieving a tripod up to 4–5m (12–16ft) above the ground. Above this height a scaffolding tower is recommended, though mobility then becomes a problem and the weight of such a tower may damage the excavated surface. Mobile towers which extend up to some 10m (30ft) can be moved easily about the site but are not very rigid at full height. Any apparatus that lifts the photographer safely above the site may be used, ranging from the bucket of a bulldozer to a fire escape. Such aids are of course equally valuable for high-level oblique photographs.

Kites and tethered meteorological balloons fitted with a cradle from which the camera hangs have been tried, and experiments have also been made with radio-controlled model aircraft. The chief difficulty with all these methods is that of sway due to turbulence of the air which, even if slight, will give considerable angular movement of the lens. But on a perfectly calm day a captive balloon carrying a camera triggered by radio has much to recommend it.

It is more difficult to devise a method for making an overlapping mosaic of vertical photographs. Whatever apparatus is used must be easily transportable across the site, and not so heavy that it destroys the excavated surface. Ideally, it ought not to cast shadows over the area being photographed, and it must be as quick and simple as possible to operate if large numbers of photographs are to be taken during the comparatively short time during which the site is at its best, and when the weather, in a country like Britain, is co-operative; and it must support the camera as rigidly as possible. The critical factors are the height to which the camera can conveniently be raised coupled with the focal length of the lens. The greater the height of the apparatus, the heavier it will be, the more unwieldy to move and the more affected by the wind. The longer the focal length of the lens the less radial distortion there will be on the photograph, but the smaller the area covered by each photograph. A compromise between these two factors has to be devised.

An apparatus which does eliminate the problem of shadows is the tripod with a boom extension which projects out over the area to be photographed (Nylen 1964). This method is satisfactory, but the boom is more susceptible to wind vibration and the apparatus, which has to be built of heavier section tubing, is less easy to transport across the site and its weight might damage delicate surfaces. On the whole, I have preferred a lighter and more stable support than the facility of taking pictures in sunlight.

The apparatus which we devised for recording the excavation of the Baths Basilica at Wroxeter has been fully described in IFA Pamphlet No. 2, *Vertical Archaeological Photography* by Sidney Renow, 1985. (And was used for several of the photographs here.) It proved its worth over many seasons and thousands of photographs has particularly in cutting down the amount of time spent by draughtsmen in the field while at the same time providing a startlingly accurate series of stereoscopic views of the site.

Vertical photographs are taken with a 60 per cent overlap along the length of the run and 15 per cent overlap between the runs. This gives adequate stereoscopy, although for accurate contoured photogrammetry of the site the camera would have to be at a constant height above datum, not a constant height above the ground. There is no reason why a line overlap of mosaic of a large excavation should not be taken from an aircraft, though this is an entirely different matter from the highly detailed mosaic required by the site record, in which the smallest stones can be seen in detail. Obviously it is most important that the photographer keeps an accurate plan of the photographs that make up the vertical grid, and that they are labelled so that their precise position on the grid can be quickly found. On many excavations it is unlikely that single photographs will be recognizable from the features in them, so that if the cross indexing fails a great deal of time will be wasted in identification.

Bipod for vertical and oblique photography
Another method of raising the camera above the ground is a bipod made of wood or tubular metal, which carries a cradle at its apex. The bipod is raised and held in position with the aid of two ropes attached to the cradle, one on each side. In this way heights of up to 10m (30ft) have been achieved. The method has considerable advantages on rough or sloping ground or where there are walls or deep rooms. The additional height not only gives greater coverage but also greater depth of field, necessary if the surface is undulating or if it contains deep holes. Another advantage claimed for this method is that the camera can be tilted relative to the legs to take oblique high level views.

Oblique photography
Oblique photographs of the whole site or large parts of it are very valuable for record as well as publication. In addition oblique photographs should be taken of all but minor features. In many cases groups of small features can be photographed together. All evidence for buildings should be photographed from a variety of angles and with a variety of lighting, as sometimes the details of a building will show best in a photograph taken against the light or in sunshine. Normally the best light is strong but diffused, up to pale sunshine. Structures and features can be given more solidity and detail by arranging a large white board or sheet to reflect light into shadows, or by using flash to fill them in.

A clear but unobtrusive scale should always be used, together with a readable label in the case of features. Plastic numbers and letters in slotted holders are available which are much to be preferred to hand-written labels, (see Figs 31c, 55a, 67). The scale should be placed in a position which does not distract the eye from the features to be illustrated, and it should not cover or cut across them. Often one or more ranging rods can be placed so that they define the edges of a surface, though they should not be placed on the edge but rather parallel to

it so that its character is not obscured. A small but clear north point should always be included.

Oblique photographs will be needed not only for the site record but also for the eventual publication. In many cases one photograph will serve both purposes, but if possible some extensive photographs should be taken, from a neighbouring building or a fire escape or aircraft, showing the site as a whole as well as its surroundings. Some

55 *Lighting*. In *a* the photograph has deliberately been taken against the light to show the worn stone surface leading to the threshold stone of the basilica. Such a surface is very difficult to draw convincingly.

In *b* side-lighting emphasizes the relief and shows clearly the stone drain or conduit which ran the length of the portico. Both examples from Wroxeter. (Photos: Sidney Renow.)

features or structural details of buildings can be better illustrated by oblique 'three-quarter' views than by plans and sections.

It is very helpful to imagine the caption to an illustration while the subject is in the view-finder. In this way the most comprehensive view will be taken. Without this sort of planning it may be found that two views of a vital part of the site have to be published where one would have been adequate.

On most sites a wide-angle lens (35mm or 28mm focal length) will be the most generally useful, though it must be remembered that the wider the angle the greater the distortion, since a larger field of view has to be compressed into the same size of negative. With very wide-angle lenses, straight lines become curves, verticals slope and relative sizes are wildly distorted. When taking close up photographs of features stretching back into the middle distance remember the snaps of father feet-first on the beach, and use a long focal length lens so that distortion is minimized. Rising- and cross-fronts or perspective-correcting (PC) lenses will eliminate distortion due to perspective and are especially useful where architecture is involved, or where a section has to be photographed from within the trench.

Unless it is unavoidable the camera should never be hand-held. The most solid and stable tripod obtainable and a cable release or self-timer should always be used. These, in addition to eliminating camera shake, will enable the lens to be stopped down to give greater depth of field when photographing features or structures which stretch from the foreground into the middle distance.

Experiments should be made with filters to find out which give the best results on the type of soil or other material being excavated. A green filter, for instance, will give more contrast to a hearth or reddened clay surrounded by yellow clay, a yellow filter will enhance dark features in sand and so on.

When the excavation is within range of electrical power, floodlights can be used to give ideal lighting, glancing across textured surfaces or modelling features such as hearths. Two floodlights will give great flexibility so that reflected lights can be used in the shadows to give the maximum detail. Floodlights or car headlights can be used at night to photograph faint ridge and furrow or other slight earthworks, or subtle undulation of the excavated surface.

Since archaeological photography is rarely concerned with movement, a slow, fine-grain panchromatic films such as Ilford Pan F (50 ASA, 18 DIN) will give maximum definition. Under poor lighting conditions, or if a tripod is not available, Ilford FP4 (125 ASA, 22DIN) or the very much faster HP4 (400–600 ASA 27–29 DIN) will give satisfactory results if properly developed and printed. However, two new films Ilford XP1 and Agfa Varia, combine high speed (400 ASA, 27 DIN) with very fine grain and have great exposure latitude (from 200 ASA to 1600 ASA) and this may eventually prove the ideal material for black-and-white photographs taken under difficult conditions, but still producing prints suitable for publication or exhibitions. Meanwhile under normal lighting conditions, orthodox films, such as those recommended, remain preferable. Perhaps the ideal solution is a true-colour stereoscopic mosaic of photographs of the whole site at each stage of the excavation backed up by interpretive overlay drawings. Vericolour II (VPS) or Fuji Reala films give very accurate colour rendering. Vertical overlapping colour prints enlarged to a scale of 1:20 and printed on glossy paper have proved to show a high degree of detail; for example, pea grits or 'dried peas' at the bottom of stakeholes are clearly visible as are the divisions and numbers on the 30m tape included in the print. The colour rendering is exceptional, though dependent, of course, on the colour temperature of the light, which changes according to the altitude of the sun, the amount of blue sky or cloud and the reflection of surrounding trees or buildings. The effect of this is to alter subtle colours continually. Reds become redder towards sunset and purpler or bluer at midday without cloud and the colour of the ground itself changes with the changing light. Moreover this effect is enhanced and exaggerated by colour film. In crucial cases Munsell colour chart numbers should be used. It may be that it will eventually be possible to build an apparatus which will take all photographs by flash, when the colour rendering will be constant and relatively comparable. There is no reason why sections should not similarly be photographed stereoscopically in colour (if necessary obliquely) when their textures could be viewed in detail.

There is no doubt that such a series of stereoscopic colour photographs is a very adequate, sometimes startlingly naturalistic, record of the site. The centre parts of further prints from the same negatives can be pasted together to form a mosaic photograph of all or part of the site at any desired scale. The publication of such photographs with their overlays would, at present, be prohibitively expensive, though not perhaps very much more expensive than a series of highly detailed colour drawings. The distillation of publishable plans and sections from field drawings has been discussed in detail elsewhere. Meanwhile, so far as the primary record of the site is concerned, colour stereoscopic cover is highly desirable since it is comparatively inexpensive. Complete coverage of an area some 200sq.m (2150 sq.ft) with a group of draughtsmen drawing the same area in comparable detail, takes about a week, whereas the photography takes only a few hours. The application of

colour photographic recording to rescue and salvage excavations is therefore obvious.

It may be argued that vertical stereoscopic photography is only practicable on more or less level sites, but I believe that its value is, if anything, greater on sites where, for archaeological reasons, a number of surfaces at different depths need to be recorded or the layers slope steeply, or where, under waterlogged conditions, timbers project in all directions from the layers in which they are embedded. Under all these circumstances, drawing itself is difficult, sometimes near impossible. What is needed is an accurate record of the excavated surfaces, features and structures. If photography can provide this record, in colour and three dimensions, it is arguable that detailed site drawing, in the accepted sense, is superfluous, and that the drawing can be confined to outline overlays, which include all the context numbers. Such a system would enormously speed up the recording of all kinds of site, but in particular those where the layers consist of stones, tile, tesserae, rubble, pebbles, boulders and so on, where it has become customary to draw the surface in great detail and then to colour each element. Such drawings are often very beautiful, but they cannot as a rule, ever be published. They simply form part of an archive from which the published drawings are distilled. It may be that we are no longer justified in the expense, in skilled time particularly, of such elaborate drawing but should rely, for the primary record, on photography – which can be equally beautiful.

There is a danger however that the excavator will unconsciously let photography take the place of intensive observation. The very act of drawing a plan or section on the ground necessitates close contemplation of the evidence and dependence on photography can weaken this concentrated observation. This is a problem not confined to rescue or salvage work since on any large-scale excavation it is impossible for the director or site-supervisors to do all the drawing. It is important therefore that where detailed drawing is being done by others the supervisors should check the drawings carefully against the ground and discuss them and their meaning with the draughtsmen.

Photogrammetry

If stereoscopic photographs, either vertical or oblique, are taken of the site the plans or sections can be drawn at a later date. While not ideal, this does provide insurance for loss of drawings or checks on disputed planning. A number of text-books on photogrammetry are available, for instance Williams (1969) so that there is not need to enlarge on the subject here.

Oblique photogrammetry using two cameras on a sub-tense bar is used by German traffic police for the rapid recording of plans of traffic accidents. Stereoscopic photographs are taken from a number of points of view round the accident and the plan plotted later. This is very quick and obviates the need for policemen to walk about in the road with tape measures (see *Instruments of Photogrammetry and Photo Interpretation*, Zeiss 1967, U7 and references on U4). Both the speed of the method and the fact that it enables planners to work outside the required area make it ideal for rescue and salvage excavation, as well as situations where the excavated surface is too vulnerable to be walked on. An example of this use is in the planning of the Skuldelev Ships, five Viking ships sunk in Roskilde Fjord. The wood of the ships and the soft matrix in which they lay was planned by photogrammetry without risk of damaging or losing the evidence (Olsen and Crumlin-Pederson 1967). A small bar with a sliding camera mounting equipped with a tripod bush is a simple piece of apparatus which enables

56 Vertical stereoscopic view of a group of stake-holes (at top), a vertically standing stone and part of an archaeological trench in the northern portico of the Baths Basilica at Wroxeter. This pair of photographs can be viewed stereoscopically with a simple hand-viewer. (Photo: Sidney Renow.)

oblique stereoscopic photographs to be taken with any available camera. Needless to say the same methods can be used for the recording of architecture.

Polaroid film

Polaroid photographs, whch have the advantage of instant development, have proved to be invaluable as a supplement to the feature record cards. The photographs can be fixed (with drafting tape rather than paste) to the back of the card and annotated, or may have an explanatory sketch added.

Partially excavated features can be recorded in this way without delaying the work and the excavation of a fragile or fragmentary find can be recorded in a rapid series of photographs which may be of great help in any eventual reconstruction. The method has the advantage of comparative cheapness, since it has been found that the simpler, less expensive polaroid cameras are perfectly adequate for the purpose. However, the film itself is still fairly costly.

Computerized recording

As in every other field, computers are being used increasingly in archaeology, particularly for the analysis of large quantities of data, such as pottery, bone and flint, and for the plotting of a mass of readings as in contour surveys. The increased miniaturization of computers has meant that they can now conveniently be taken on site. Dominic Powlesland, of the Heslerton Parish Survey, which is studying the evolution of the Yorkshire landscape, has pioneered the use of micro-processors in the field. Figs 57–61 illustrate the system which he has devised and some of the results. It will be clear that the potential of these small machines is very considerable, speeding up recording, storing large quantities of data in a rapidly accessible form, and enabling a great variety of analyses to be carried out swiftly and efficiently. In addition, plans and sections can be drawn on the machine using data which has been digitized.

Computing at West Heslerton
The Heslerton Parish Project was established in 1980 to provide an academic framework for a series of very large-scale rescue excavations being undertaken ahead of mineral extraction and plough damage. The project has earned an international reputation for its use of computers, particularly in relation to

the on-site recording systems. The project was among the first to introduce the use of the hand-held computer and the Electronic Distance Meter as standard excavation equipment. Since the early 1980s the recording system has evolved such that it now more closely resembles a Geographic Information Systems (see also p. 158) providing easy access not only to conventional excavation records but also to the plans, geophysical data and the photographic record through a single computer program.

The scale of the excavations has been such that without a high degree of computerization the publication process would have been well nigh impossible. Since the early 1980s hand-held computers have been used on site, both for recording context information and that concerning the objects recovered. In addition to the hand-held computer each excavation supervisor also keeps a notebook of conventional type for writing additional comments, drawing sketch plans and sections, recording the matrix and keeping any Polaroid photographs taken to assist in the presentation of the record. The introduction of the EDM and treatment of each find as an individual item which is individually recorded led to a fundamental change in the methods used in the field. In the past large and apparently uniform contexts had to be subdivided into small units so that the spatial distribution of the artefacts contained could be more readily understood. Now by maintaining a fully three-dimensional record of all artefacts and ecofacts the potential for detailed spatial analysis is possible. The excavation of an Early Anglo-Saxon Settlement currently in progress at West Heslerton has included the examination of more then 10ha (25 acres) of ground, more than 200 structures from which over 250,000 finds have been recovered, about 80 per cent of which were given an individual 3D reference. The

Heslerton Parish Project: Excavation Recording Procedures

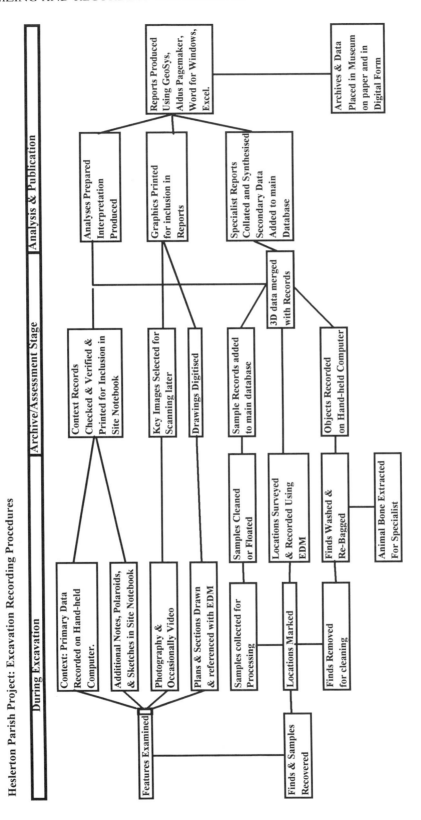

57 Heslerton Parish Project: excavation recording procedures (Dominic Powlesland).

58 Isometric views of part of the finds distribution at West Heslerton. Note the very high concentrations which represent major features (Dominic Powlesland).

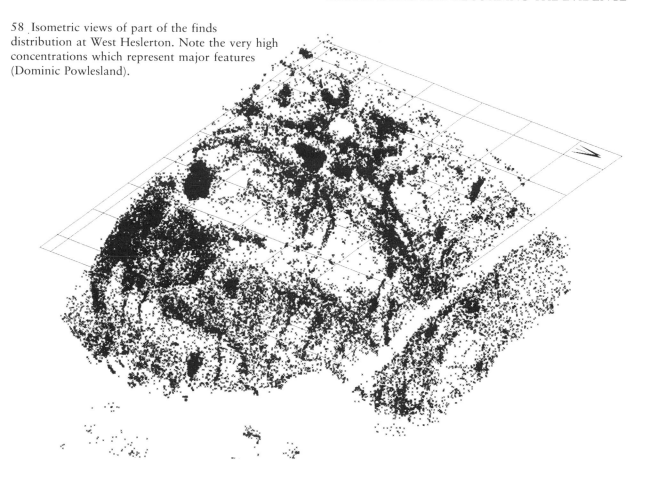

excavation has demonstrated a completely unanticipated level of sophistication in a settlement of this date, c.AD 450–850. Although the work of publishing this excavation is at an early stage the instant availability of data concerning the finds distribution has enabled the excavation the strategy to be constantly refined as the excavation progressed.

During the 1992 excavation season an experimental magnetometer survey was carried out following removal of the topsoil; a large-scale survey by English Heritage had already shown the suitability of this site for magnetic prospection. The results of the survey, carried out at 25cm resolution, were quite outstanding. Using the project's GeoSys software the results of the geophysical survey were viewed together with the plans and the object distributions allowing the excavation team to isolate a number of features that might otherwise have been missed given that the soils in the area were exceptionally difficult to read and considering the limited time and resources available.

GeoSys, the software used for managing the data right the way through from excavation to publication, uses standard data formats so that data can easily be exchanged with others and utilized with standard off-the-shelf computer packages. The power of the software lies in the way it handles a broad range of data types with an easy-to-use user interface. Once a data set is loaded it may be viewed in plan, section or isometrically; by simply pointing at a marker on the

59 Distribution of all finds and contexts, West Heslerton Anglian settlement (Dominic Powlesland).

60a (*Top right*) 1:200 plan of part of the Anglian settlement at West Heslerton produced from the computerized site plans (Dominic Powlesland).

60b (*Bottom right*) Detail of the same plot as 60a, this time with the distribution of all finds marked by dots (Dominic Powlesland).

screen the full details of a context or the objects it contains can be displayed and associated photographs viewed if they are stored on the system.

Because all data types are linked together analysis can be performed using a variety of different packages and the results then used to generate new views of the data. For example, all the grave plans produced for the report on the Anglian Cemetery were digitized from field drawings and vertical photographs. Each drawing contains labelling information which can be linked to any database. Therefore, to produce a plan of

graves shaded according to age or sex of the skeleton a database containing these details can be created and then applied to the master plans to produce a new drawing at any scale, which displays, for instance, the grave statistics. The printouts from this analysis can then be incorporated directly into the excavation report without any need for further drawing.

At West Heslerton the field drawings are

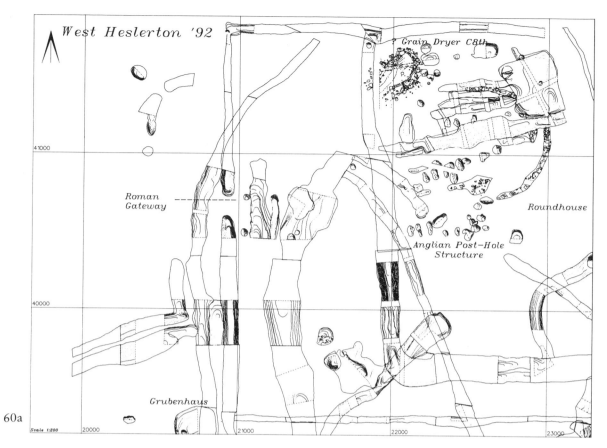

West Heslerton '92

? Grain Dryer C8th

41000

Roman
Gateway

Roundhouse

40000

Anglian Post-Hole
Structure

Grubenhaus

60a

Scale 1:200

20000   21000   22000   23000

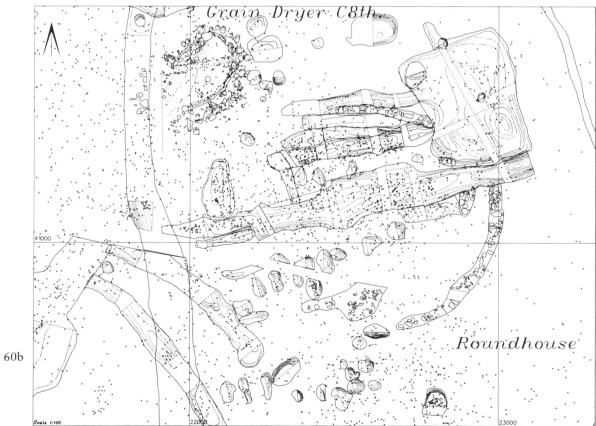

? Grain Dryer C8th

41000

Roundhouse

60b

Scale 1:100

22000   23000

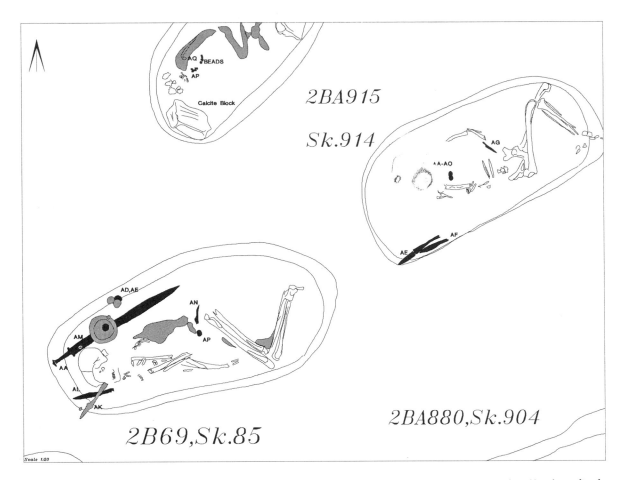

61 Grave plan at a scale of 1:20 from the West Heslerton Anglian Cemetry excavation report. The drawing was digitized by tracing the details from a series of vertical photographs printed at a scale of about 1:5 (Dominic Powlesland).

produced using conventional techniques, following this each feature is digitized and stored on computer. The computerized drawings can then be overlaid on the results of geophysical surveys and all the finds distributions added. This data can then be interrogated simply by pointing at the feature of interest using a mouse and any linked data is then shown on the screen. This might be a photograph, or a list of all contexts and associated finds. Drawings once digitized can be printed at any scale ready for publication without the lengthy redrawing process frequently needed when drawings at many different scales are required.

9

The Recording of Pottery and Small Finds

Rare and exotic finds from excavations inevitably attract most attention in the press, and on radio and television and, more significantly, in archaeological exhibitions. This high-lighting gives such pieces an exaggerated importance compared with the mass of dull body sherds, animal bones or fragments of wall plaster. Yet, as Pitt Rivers pointed out almost a century ago: '. . . the value of relics, viewed as evidence, may . . . be said to be in an inverse ratio to their instrinsic value' (Cranborne Chase, Vol. III, 1892, ix).

The collection, recording, cleaning, marking and storage of every sherd of pottery, every fragment of bone, every nail, every scrap of painted plaster is tedious, and time- and labour-consuming. But only by the study of large quantities of everyday evidence can we approach an understanding of the site and its occupants as a whole and not simply the more immediately attractive aspects, such as those which lie on the fringes of art or architectural history. An understanding of English medieval life cannot be gained wholly from the study of church architecture, painted missals and objets d'art – it is necessary to dig complete villages, including the barns and pigsties, and collect the whole mass of unaesthetic evidence if we are going to penetrate deeper than the aristocratic crust of medieval society. If this is true of medieval times, where we have considerable documentation to add to the rest of the evidence, how

much more true it is of earlier, less literate societies.

The horizontal distribution of pottery and finds is as important as their vertical distribution. It is for this reason that all finds, of whatever material, must be recorded in plan with sufficient precision to make analysis possible. Plots of the distribution of various classes of finds on transparent overlays make it easy to relate the finds to buildings, fences, enclosures and other structures. This distribution may be the only evidence for the use of a building or area. Lines of building nails may give the only clue to the former presence of a building and the quality of the finds from different buildings or areas may be a pointer to the wealth or social position of the occupants.

The study of pottery as archaeological material deserves a book to itself. Because it has a high survival rate, pottery has often been given more evidential weight than it can justifiably carry. The origins, dating and distribution of much pottery are still uncertain. New discoveries change the state of knowledge annually, making it unwise to date sites or phases of sites on the evidence of pottery alone.

The study of prehistoric pottery has had to be drastically revised in the light of recent radiocarbon and dendrochronological dates and the dating of Roman and medieval pottery is undergoing similar, though less radical, revision, as more groups, dated by evidence external to the pottery itself, are excavated. In view of these considerations alone, all earlier excavation reports should be revised, where possible, in line with current theories on pottery dating. More than this, they should be kept up to date as present theories themselves are modified. This is a daunting task, especially when the incomplete and ambiguous nature of many pottery reports is considered.

The uses and limitations of pottery as archaeological evidence

Sherds of pottery are by far the most common finds on the majority of excavated Roman and medieval sites. The reason is obvious. Pottery was quickly made and often as quickly broken. The expectation of life of a pot is difficult to assess but it seems likely that jugs, bowls, jars, etc would have lasted longer than cooking pots, which, by their nature, had to undergo the stresses set up by differential heating, especially if, as is probable, they were embedded in the embers of a hot fire. A pot was virtually useless once it was broken or even cracked since it was very difficult to mend satisfactorily, though riveted repairs and holes plugged with lead are occasionally found on particularly valuable vessels. Its scrap value, unlike that of a metal object, was small unless it was crushed and used as grog in the making of other pots. Since the sherds which remain were virtually indestructible there was little to do with them except bury them in a convenient pit. Here the majority of large sherds and nearly complete pots are found, fragments small enough to be ignored becoming scattered over the site, embedded and eventually stratified or incorporated in manure and spread on the fields. Complete pots are rarely found except in graves, wells and in abandoned kilns, or occasionally as the containers for hoards or other material. The discontinuance of grave goods with the coming of Christianity, though doubtless a spiritual advance, robbed the archaeologist of his chief source of supply of whole pots, and for each complete or nearly complete vessel the majority of sites yield many hundreds of sherds.

Pottery has the archaeological advantage over most other materials that it is affected comparatively little by most soil conditions. Only if it is grossly underfired will it be soft enough to be weathered away; many prehistoric and most Roman and medieval wares are hard enough to remain unaltered indefinitely under most conditions. Metal objects, on the other hand, with the exception of those made of gold, are subject to corrosion in varying degrees, the corrosion tending to obliterate just those decorative features which are likely to be datable.

Factors other than that of mere survival must, however, be taken into account. The objects most susceptible to the close dating so desirable archaeologically are those whose characteristics, whether of form or decoration or both, change most rapidly, and such developments are most likely when details of form and ornament are not dictated by function but by fashion. The design of knives, shears, nails and other common objects, having reached their optimum shape, changed slowly if at all. Some objects, sheepshears, cleavers and hand axes for example, have scarcely altered from medieval times up to the present day (see the London Museum Medieval Catalogue, 1954 ed. 153–7). The writer has recovered from the castle site at Hen Domen two figure-of-eight hasps from the thirteenth-century levels which are virtually identical with a hasp found during excavation of the Roman fort at *Segontium* and now in the site museum there. All these, though interesting from their social and economic points of view, are useless for dating purposes. More personal objects such as brooches, daggers and spurs were not only more highly decorated but changed their forms with changes of fashion and can thus often be grouped typologically and given a relative chronology on the basis of form alone. Coins, on the other hand, whose basic disc shape remains constant, had inscriptions and decorations which were changed frequently and it is from these that they can be dated precisely.

A discussion of the complexities of typological developments in pottery would be out of place here, but it is important for the excavator to be highly sceptical of simplistic schemes which place sherds of pottery in plausible sequences based on appearance alone. As J.G. Hurst has pointed out, in eastern England Anglo-Saxon pottery is finer and more accomplished than that of the twelfth century, though the reverse is true elsewhere, and 'rim forms in some areas become more developed and complicated, while in others they become more simple' (*Med. Arch.*, vi-viii, 148). In some regions (the West Midlands for example) there seems to have been a tendency for cooking pots to have been made increasingly large during the course of the twelfth century, but in other regions this is not apparent. Coarseness of fabric is by itself no criterion of date, nor is the presence or absence of glaze. Some forms of simple decoration persisted throughout the medieval period, while others reappeared after a temporary eclipse. The thumb-pressed base, for example, so common on thirteenth-century jugs, reappears on otherwise quite different jugs of the fifteenth century. It is clear, therefore, in a way which was not fully realized a few years ago, that medieval pottery will only be closely datable on the basis of intensive regional study, and on the study of composition of fabrics, the shapes of rims, the details of decoration and character of glazes rather than on the general development of types.

The same is true of Roman coarse pottery, which is as regional in character as its medieval counterpart. However, other forms of Roman pottery, in particular samian wares and stamped mortaria, are more closely datable, and, if found stratified in quantity, probably provide the most reliable *terminus post* and *ante quem* given by any pottery before the industrial revolution. The absolute dates of prehistoric pottery have been dependent in recent years on the revised radio-carbon and dendrochronological dates for the main periods in British prehistory, but there is a very strong regional element also which means that local typologies must be established for most areas.

Any establishment of typology, even for a restricted area, will have to be based on the study of the more rapidly evolving details of pottery forms rather than their basic shapes and fabrics, though these may in some cases also show a steady development. Ultimately every characteristic — fabric, shape, size, the treatment of rims, handles, lips and spouts as well as decoration itself — will have to be considered before a pot or sherd can be placed correctly in its local typological sequence. (See Gardin (1966), for an attempt to categorize all the characteristics of French medieval pottery.) It does not follow that sherds of obviously similar style and superficial characteristics are not by the same potter merely because the composition of fabric or glaze proves to be different. The difference may be due to circumstances: clay from a different bed, or a deliberate change of glaze; but even if the sherds or pots prove to be from different hands, the similarity of style carries its own significance of co-operation or influence between potters. Every scientific aid available should be enlisted to provide as much information as possible on which to base judgements. The composition of fabrics and thus their probable source, the composition of glazes and the temperature to which they have been fired and, with the development of thermoluminescent and remanent magnetic methods, the possibility of accurate dating independent of both stratification and typology, are all clearly of major importance for determining the relationships of groups of pottery.

It is already apparent that developing typological sequences, in which shapes and decoration proceed logically one from another in the manner relied on by historians of art and architecture, may never be established. At Adderley, in Shropshire, for instance, a number of associated thumb-pressed bases seem to exhibit every stage in the development of this form of decoration, yet there is every reason to believe that they are close together in date, and it may well be that all these variations were made at the same time (cf. *Med. Arch.*, vi-viii, 148). Their value as a dating series would therefore be nil. In the face of such difficulties any attempt to establish a precise chronology might seem doomed to failure, but the attempt must be made if we are to date more accurately the sites in which we are interested.

It seems most unlikely that it will ever be possible to date a pottery group more closely than within a bracket of 25 years. Even if we were able to date our pottery closely by archaeometric methods it would still have limitations as dating material. It must be stressed that pottery, like all other dating material, provides only a *terminus post quem* for the layer in which it was found (see below p. 224). Even a coin, whose date of manufacture may be precisely known, gives no more information about its find-layer than this. Too often, coins are said to 'date' a layer or building, and a superstructure of dated periods is erected on the basis without regard to the strict logic of the evidence. An example, so extreme that the wrong conclusions could not possibly have been drawn, is provided by the finding in 1774 at the Roman villa at Acton Scott, Shropshire, of Greek coins of the fourth century BC (V.C.H. Shrops., i, 1908, 260–1). These must have been collectors pieces or souvenirs (or were, perhaps, 'planted'), but if they had been Roman souvenirs only 50 years old, might they not have been used, even today, to give a closer date to the structures than would be justified? The danger is as great or greater in the case of pottery. P.A. Rahtz has shown at Cheddar that 185sq.m (2000sq.ft) of levels dated firmly to the ninth century or later by coins, contained no pottery but Roman. If a smaller area had been excavated and no coins found, these layers might have been considered to be Roman, whereas within the strict logic of the evidence they should have been dated to the Roman period or later. It may be wondered how many small excavations producing only Roman pottery have in fact been on post-Roman sites.

These are extreme cases; the danger is more subtle and therefore more likely to mislead when the time-lag is shorter, or when conclusions are drawn from too small a sample, either of the site or of the finds. There is no need to reiterate the misconceptions which may arise from one or two cuttings made into a complex site – examples of the pitfalls which may be encountered are mentioned in Chapter 5. A small sample of pottery may be equally misleading. One or two sherds found in a critical position may be given a significance out of proportion to their real value, unless it can be shown that they were positively sealed and could not have arrived in their position by the action of burrowing animals, rainwash or other misleading effects. The opposite also holds. A single sherd, positively stratified, which gives us an inconveniently late *terminus post quem* for its layer or structure, must not be discarded because we cannot bring ourselves to face the fact that our preconceived theories were wrong. Similarly, among a number of sherds from a sealed layer, it is the latest which gives the *terminus post quem* to the layer, so that a single late sherd among a mass of earlier material must not be discarded – it is the rest of the sherds that must be treated as residual.

By the same reasoning, pottery cannot be dated simply by association, however close, with other datable objects in the same layer. A friend of the writer recently found, on a Roman site, a coin of Edward I of *c.*1300 positively sealed with a sherd of hard green glazed pot. It is tempting, under these circumstances, to date the pottery, with the layer, to a period after 1300 but, had it not been possible to date the sherd independently, on the evidence of its appearance, it could have been prehistoric, Roman, Saxon, medieval or modern. In other words, the association of coin and sherd tells us nothing whatever about the date of the sherd, only that it arrived *in the layer* after *c.*1300.

This simple but inexorable logic has so often been ignored or not applied rigorously enough in the past that it is necessary to re-examine critically many excavation reports in which far-reaching conclusions regarding the dating of pottery have been based. Too often, also, the tentative conclusions of the original report have hardened into accepted fact in subsequent references.

Considerations of this kind demand the most careful excavation in separate contexts and the most accurate recording. Without these, pottery can be made to prove anything. In addition, the larger the quantity of pottery discovered from each period of a site's occupation, the more valid will be the conclusions which can be drawn. Similarly there is no doubt that the greater the number of sites from which pottery is obtained and the more representative their distribution, the more accurate will be the deductions regarding the pottery's development and economic distribution.

Residuality

This problem is seen in an acute form on deeply stratified Roman, medieval or post-medieval sites where pits, wells and foundations have brought earlier pottery up to later surfaces. The last period layers of such sites may contain a very high proportion of residual pot. Indeed, it is probable that in many Roman towns in Britain, whose occupation enters an aceramic period, the latest 'Roman' layers will contain nothing but residual pottery.

As one removes the layers of occupation, one by one, the problem will tend to resolve itself.

The situation can be shown diagrammatically thus:

Structural Periods	Pottery Types
Z	g + f + e + d + c + b + a
	g + f + e + d + c + b + a
	g + f + e + d + c + b + a
Y (ACERAMIC)	f + e + d + c + b + a
X	f + e + d + c + b + a
	e + d + c + b + a
W	e + d + c + b + a
	d + c + b + a
	d + c + b + a
V	c + b + a
	b + a
U	b + a
T	a
	a

When the pottery eventually comes to be studied as a whole, the points of entry of types b, c, d, e, etc., can be seen. Other types are then shown to be either residual or to go on being used and/or manufactured in parallel with the later types. Resolution of this problem will depend on the relative quantities of the earlier pottery surviving and on its condition, for instance whether the sherds are large and unabraded or small and weather-worn.

Some highly regarded pottery, such as samian wares in Roman times and fine jugs in medieval times, may have had a longer life because they were more carefully looked after, and it is common to find examples of the finer Roman wares mended with rivets in order to prolong their life. The date of deposition in an archaeological layer of sherds of one of these more highly prized pots could therefore be a century or two later than its manufacture. It is much less likely that ordinary cooking pots or dishes would have a long life. Once again, the greater the quantity of data, in this case the amounts of pottery, the more reliable will be the conclusions that can be drawn from it.

Because pottery looms so large in the archaeological record of many excavated sites it is easy to overestimate its importance in the lives of the people in whom we are interested. It is always salutary to keep in mind that there have been long aceramic periods in British history, particularly in the highland zones, or periods during which pottery was scarce and could not have been regarded as an everyday necessity. As far as it is possible to tell, the whole Welsh nation managed without pottery from the fifth century until the twelfth, except for small quantities of exotica imported from Gaul and the Mediterranean. But no one would dare suggest that this represents cultural poverty in pre-Norman Wales. And on the other side of Britain, it is illuminating to look at the ugly, badly made flask that is the only pot included in the Sutton Hoo ship burial. If the splendid objects buried with, or in honour of, this Anglian king had been perishable whatever conclusions should we have drawn about him simply from this pot? Care must be taken not to give too much weight to any surviving evidence as against the evidence which has not survived, but which can reasonably be assumed to have existed.

The recording of pottery and animal bones

Where little pottery is found, its importance is likely to be very great and each sherd should be treated as a small find. Where pottery (and animal bones) are recovered in quantity they must be treated in bulk, to some extent, or the system will be overwhelmed. It is perhaps most convenient to divide the major grids into quarters or sixteenths dependent on the degree of precision required for the subsequent analysis. Each site's pottery and bones recording will have to be assessed on its merits and it may be necessary to modify the system if the quantities recovered are much greater or much less than expected.

Pottery should be stored in polythene bags or boxes, or cardboard boxes. Paper bags are unsuitable as most types disintegrate after a few years. The life of some kinds of polythene bags is uncertain and the storage of pottery, bones and other finds should be checked annually, and the material repacked if the containers are deteriorating. In a number of important cases the reassessment of excavations carried out only 20 to 30 years ago has been made impossible because of the complete disintegration of the paper bags in which the pottery was stored. For this reason also, each sherd of pot should be marked individually with Indian ink. If the fabric of the pottery is friable the marking should be protected with a coating of varnish. The marking of each individual sherd, however tedious on a large site, means that the sherds

62 a–b Examples of recording cards for pottery and small finds, from Hereford and Worcester County Archaeology Service. (See also 47.)

HEREFORD AND WORCESTER COUNTY COUNCIL
ARCHAEOLOGY SECTION   AS10   11/88

HWCM	CONTEXT GROUP		FEATURE	SHEET 1 OF 1	CONTEXT
2809	PERIOD/PHASE		CERAMIC TPQ		1609(1)

FABRIC	DESCRIP	FORM	TYPE	QTY.	WT. (g)	DIAM. (mm)	%	DECORATION	No.	Dwg.No./Pub.No.	T.S. No.	COMMENTS	DATING
SS		R	408	1	22								
69		C		1	22								
78		C		1	6								
TOTALS				3	60								

RECORDED BY [signature]   DATE 02.03.91

DATA ENTERED BY [signature]   DATE 10.03.91

62a

199

CONTEXT FINDS RECORD

HWCM 3899	Sub-div 2	Phase / Period	Group 2514	Context 16091

	Type	Quantity	Comments
Pottery	Prehistoric		
	Roman		
	Saxon	3	
	Medieval		
	Post-medieval		
C/pipe	Stems		
	Bowls		
	Stamps		
Building Materials	Tile	4	Roof
	Brick		
	Fired clay		
	Stone		
	Mortar		
	Plaster		
	Other		
Metals	Iron		
	Copper alloy		
	Other		
	Slag		
Glass	Vessel		
	Window		
	Other		
Environ	Bone	14	
	Shell		
	Leather		
	Wood		
Misc.			

No	Recorded finds	No	Recorded finds	No	Samples	No	Samples

Site contamination NONE LOW HIGH	Processing contamination NONE LOW HIGH

Recorder N	Date 22·11·89	Checked by	Date

Hereford and Worcester County Council
Archaeology Section AS8 02/88

62b

can be re-sorted into fabrics or shapes without losing a record of the context from which they were derived.

Just as with portable finds, there are three entirely different questions asked of the pottery assemblage. The first is related to the groups of pottery from within a context, a building or phase of the site. The second is concerned with the development of the pottery itself, its earliest and latest occurrence, its group or fabric or glaze or form, or its relationships with the pottery of the region or the country as a whole. The third is the function of the various types of pottery found – cooking pots, jugs, dishes, lamps and so forth. It is important therefore to label and store the pottery in a way which makes retrieval as simple as possible; otherwise its subsequent study could become exceedingly laborious, if not impossible.

The quantitative analysis of large groups of potsherds presents a number of difficulties. Counting the numbers of sherds of each recognizable type is not very satisfactory since its validity depends on the sizes of both the original pots and the fragments into which they have been smashed – any number of sherds can be doubled simply by breaking them in half. Similarly, weighing the sherds of each type has its limitations since the results will vary according to the sizes of the original pots and the thickness and density of the fabrics used. A more valid method is to attempt to estimate the number of pots represented by reconstructing each type on paper and estimating the minimum numbers of each type in the assemblage. Orton (1980, 15ff.) describes very lucidly the problems of the analysis of a mass of potsherds and concludes that the idea of estimated vessel equivalents (*ibid.* pp. 164–6), though it has practical difficulties, is at present the most fruitful line of study. The validity of an analysis of pottery (or any other finds including, in particular, animal bones) depends upon the percentage of the total original deposit on the site which is recovered. Clarke (ed., 1972, 26ff.), has demonstrated graphically the considerable distortions in a 60 per cent sample of a series of assemblages (*ibid.*, fig 1:8). As in every other sphere of excavation, therefore, the nearer we approach the total recovery of any category of evidence the more closely our analysis will approach the truth. A sample must be as large as possible and from all parts of a multi-purpose site, where there may be kitchens, stables, halls, workshops and many other buildings and areas from which sherds may come not only in varying quantities but in types related to the function of the buildings – glazed jugs from a medieval hall, cooking pots from the kitchen area and so on. Add to this the cleanliness of many communities who swept their floors and disposed of large sherds in rubbish pits often well outside the settlement site, and it will be seen that typological analysis is liable to a series of vagaries not all of which can be quantified or even predicted. It may simply not be worth analysing small groups of pottery (or anything else). However, the cumulative assemblages from large long-term excavations or from a series of related excavations, for example within towns, will provide enough material to set up a flexible analytical framework which will produce increasingly refined and well-founded results.

The division of an assemblage of pottery into types will depend on a qualitative analysis of its fabrics, glazes and forms. Usually this has been macroscopic and intuitive depending on a more or less subjective assessment of the colour and texture of the fabrics – 'buff', 'orange', 'red with grey core', 'coarse', 'fine' or 'sandy' – without any clear definition of what these terms mean, together with similar descriptions of glazes as 'apple-green', 'yellowish-brown' or perhaps 'brownish-yellow'. In an attempt to standardize the description of colours, a Pottery Colour Chart has been published by RESCUE (Webster 1970). This is a simplified version of the sort of charts (e.g. Munsell charts) used for the descriptions of soils, and should remove some of the subjectivity from pottery publication. The standardization of fabric descriptions is a great deal more difficult.

The Medieval Pottery Research Group has produced a suggested *Key to Identification of Inclusions in Pottery*, which is 'designed to facilitate visual identification of the principal inclusions found in pottery in Britain'. This has not yet been accepted, but something of the kind is urgently needed.

The only really adequate description of fabrics would be based on thin sectioning, when the geology of the fabric can be identified and the origins of inclusions examined by heavy mineral analysis. This would be a formidable, if not impossible, task for all the pottery excavated in Britain every year but anything less must be recognized as being inadequate and potentially misleading.

The comparative study of forms both of whole pots and of their parts, such as rims and bases, and of their decorative treatment is immensely complicated since the total repertory of forms and decoration is so wide. Any system must include every form from the smaller globular cooking pot to the most elaborately decorated jug, and since almost all the pottery from excavations is hand-made (as distinct from moulded or machine turned) the forms tend to vary slightly from pot to pot. Thus, although broad divisions can and must be made, there will always be a number of examples which shade off into one or another type.

The study of glazes also needs to be more systematized with analysis of their composition and added colouring agents. By determining the nature and quantities of trace elements in the glazes it may be possible to sort an assemblage of potsherds into groups distinct from those determined by form and fabric. Since behind the pottery sits the potter, a man or woman making more or less aesthetically pleasing objects for a market, whether local or continental, in the study of pottery we enter the realm of art history and aesthetics, and must assess the degree of influence which one potter or group of potters has had on another, and whether a potter has moved about the country making characteristic wares from the available local clays. An example of potters moving across the country is postulated by P. Webster (1975), where the production of Iron Age and Roman tankards is shown to move from the Durotrigian region on the south coast up into the Severn valley. This is a more or less clear-cut example spanning two centuries. Other movements were undoubtedly more complex, and on much shorter timescales. It will obviously not be sufficient to sort pottery simply by fabric, or by decoration or by form, but by a combination of all these characteristics. Pots of a similar form but differing fabrics may well be found to overlap in their distribution with pots of one fabric but differing forms according to whether the potters were influenced by style or by the availability or desirability of local clays and tempering materials. A well-known example of an apparently alien style being imposed on an already well-established technique is the so-called Romano-Saxon pottery found chiefly in eastern England. This combines the hard, usually grey fabrics of wheel-turned Roman pottery with the forms and decorative slashes and dimples of pagan Saxon pots – a combination which was perhaps an attempt by Roman potters to capture the Saxon market, to make their wares attractive to recent immigrants with different tastes in pottery shapes and decoration.

Very large quantities of pottery must be studied before any generalized observations can be made with confidence about places of origin, distribution and stylistic affinities. The discovery of kilns with their accompanying mass of wasters is of great help, but much pottery was fired above ground in clamps or kilns which have now been destroyed without trace, so that the study of such wares is correspondingly more difficult. The analysis of a very large group of Roman sherds from Wroxeter will be found in Barker *et. al* (forthcoming, 1994), and the reader is invited to study it.

The recording of small finds

Recording systems for small finds must aim primarily to record the find positions sufficiently accurately in three dimensions that they can be 'put back' into the excavation long after it is over. For this purpose two-dimensional grid co-ordinates for each find are essential. However, it is not necessarily helpful to record the absolute height of the find above Ordnance Datum or its depth below the ground surface or some other site datum except in special cases. What is needed for the reconstruction of the site is to know from which context (however thin, or discontinuous) the find came; its absolute depth may be misleading unless at the same time the find is tied into the context from which it derives. A clear example of this mistake is seen in the practice, advocated particularly in the digging of ditch and rampart sections, of projecting find-spots horizontally on to the section. If all layers within the ditch and rampart were themselves horizontal the method might be valid, but they seldom are. More often the situation will be that shown in Fig. 63, where a ditch cutting is shown in transverse section, the removed layers being indicated by dotted lines.

If the positions of the four finds are projected on to either of the drawn sections they will be transferred to a layer above or below the one to which they really belong, with the

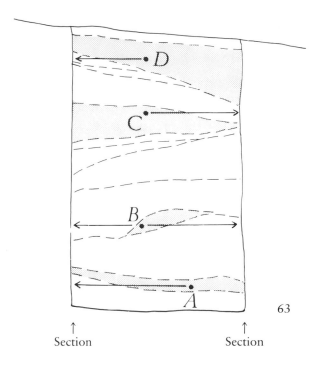

63

Section   Section

consequent distortion of the interpretation. This is a simple example, but it is not difficult to visualize its extension into more complicated situations. Only if the find comes from a thick layer will a vertical measurement be necessary. This should be taken as a spot height which can be plotted on the site plan so that it is directly related to the contour survey of the layers. Since the upper surfaces of all layers should be levelled (and ideally contour surveyed), the absolute depth of the find-spot can, if necessary, be recovered. However, the really important information is the position of the find relative not only to its own layer or feature but to those above and below it. If the procedures advocated in Chapter 8 are followed, the position and dimensions of each context are recorded on its layer record card and visually on the series of site plans and ultimately on the stratigraphic matrix. All that is necessary therefore is to refer to its context without further elaboration on its vertical position.

The essence of a finds recording system should be simplicity. The position of the find must be marked in the ground, so that it can be recorded three-dimensionally, and the point plotted on the site plan or overlay, to ensure that, subsequently, the find can be married to its find-spot, long after the site has gone. Each find should be given a serial number, which is attached both to the find and the recorded spot on the plan and it should have its own record card on which the grid reference, context number and, if necessary, depth or spot height, are recorded. On large sites, when finds are pouring out, the system should be streamlined as far as possible to avoid time-wasting recording. A system of double numbering is useful, in which cards, each with a serial number printed twice, or ordinary raffle or cloakroom tickets, are used. One of the pair is pinned to the ground at the find-spot while the other is put in the bag with the find to identify it with its find-spot. As a double check a finds book should be kept with the finds listed serially by date and by the signature of the finder. The find-spots can then be plotted by the triangulation or the use of grids on to the plans or overlays at a convenient time, such as the end of each day. If both horseshoe and building nails are to be plotted, each ancient nail can be replaced by a modern large-headed nail, if necessary with a head painted to distinguish one type from another. These are plotted in the same way on the plans and overlays and each find should be given a record card, conveniently printed as a *pro forma*.

A description of the find when it was first discovered is required and this description will be expanded when further details are revealed by cleaning, X-rays, or other scientific examination. Details of cleaning and conservation treatment should be added to the card as work proceeds so that the history of the find as it passes through the excavation and post-excavation processes is recorded. Only in this way can either specialists in the type of object, or laboratory technicians, properly assess degrees of wear, corrosion and loss due to chemical action (either before or after discovery!). Preliminary identifications may have to be modified in the light of subsequent treatment. In cases of doubt the first attribution may be pencilled in or given a question mark so that second thoughts are not inhibited. See also the Finds section in the *Archaeological Site Manual* of the Museum of London (2nd ed. 1990).

Ultimately, there are three principal ways in which the data regarding the finds will need to be retrieved. One is the relationship of the finds to structures and to important structural, occupation or dating contexts. The second is the classification of finds into types or into groups according to their function and the third is according to the material from which they are made.

The first category will throw light on the evolving occupation of the site; the uses to which buildings or area have been put; the changing economy of occupants; the extent and nature of imports and so forth. The second will be used to demonstrate the development of particular categories of object, both in relation to the site and in relation to comparable objects from other excavations and museum collections. The third will demonstrate the ways in which particular materials such as bronze, shale or ivory have been worked and the types of object which have been made from them.

On excavations producing large quantities of finds, computer storage is the most efficient means of handling them, since the computer is not only able to produce lists of required categories but can also provide distribution plots either printed or on visual display. Where the quantities of finds do not justify the use of a computer, edge-punched or light-hole cards are perfectly adequate.

Sophisticated techniques of statistical analysis are being developed to deal with artefacts of all kinds recovered from excavations. These techniques and their origins are described in Binford and Binford (1968), Binford (1972), Clarke (1968) and Orton (1980). No statistical analysis, however, can be better than the quality of its raw data, the true reflection of the nature and distribution of the samples used in the analysis. This is not the place to discuss analyses based on such disparate data as the location of Roman towns or the chance finds of a distinctive type of medieval pottery. But so far as evidence from excavations is concerned it will be obvious that only securely stratified, correctly identified and closely recorded evidence, whether of portable artefacts or of bones or other environmental material, will give a basis secure enough to justify conclusions founded on an analysis which otherwise may be far more sophisticated than the digging on which it is based. Statistical analysis of material derived from partial and inadequately recorded excavations will inevitably be misleading, though unprovably so. It is, therefore, incumbent on those of us who dig to provide the most reliable data possible and this can only be done, on the one hand, by strictly controlled excavations, and, on the other, by the adoption of agreed scales of reliability for those excavations such as salvage digs, which by their nature, cannot provide the necessary degree of precision.

The value of coins as archaeological evidence

Coins, together with seals, tokens and specifically datable inscriptions, are probably the most closely datable of all archaeological finds. As a result, they are welcomed in excavations as providing positive dating evidence. But it must never be forgotten that they provide only a *terminus post quem* for the deposit in which they are found (see p. 224 below). Nevertheless, it is helpful to try to estimate the date at which the coin was lost as distinct from the date at which it was minted, by considering its condition, that is, how much wear it seems to have suffered during circulation, and to translate this into years. Before the introduction of decimal currency in Britain it was highly instructive to look at a handful of coins taken from a pocket at random and to see how different were the amounts of wear on coins of similar date. Pennies dating from the beginning of this century would range in wear from crisply readable to almost smooth discs. The writer was with Philip Rahtz one day when he took from his pocket four old pennies in order to make a telephone call from a pre-STD phone box. This was in the early 1960s. None of these pennies was later than 1914. If Rahtz had been buried at that time in the clothes he stood up in, his interment would almost certainly have been dated half a century too early. One could only hope that his excavator would apply the *terminus post quem* rule as rigorously as he does himself.

Another factor affecting the estimates of wear on coins is the nature of the soil in which they have lain, so that it is important to attempt to distinguish between wear and corrosion, and to record the nature of the surrounding soil. For this reason, it is especially important not to overclean coins, and in fact they should, ideally, be cleaned by a trained conservator. However, sometimes it is desirable to know the date of a coin immediately (though whatever the date the coins proves to be, the *strategy* of the excavation should not be altered, since the relative chronologies will remain unchanged, the coin merely providing a *terminus post quem*). If light cleaning with a stiff brush or glass bristle brush (not a metal bristle brush) does not render the inscription legible under a magnifying glass or binocular microscope, a scalpel can be used for careful mechanical cleaning. Harder corrosion products can be removed by vibratool. Careful mechanical cleaning is to be preferred to chemical stripping but is comparatively time-consuming.

The assessment of the archaeological and historical significance of coins depends on factors other than mere dating, especially where whole coin series are discovered. An understanding of the economic conditions in which the coins were issued is of vital importance if gross errors in interpretation are not be be made, since the recovery rate of coins from sites will have to be measured against the known profusion or paucity of the issues. The subject has been concisely dealt with by Casey (1974). His paper deals with Romano-British coins but the principles apply to all coin finds.

10

The Interpretation of the Evidence

The detailed dissection of a site and the elaborate recording of all its observable phenomena are simply the preludes to an attempt to give meaning to the evidence: to decide how contexts were formed, to recognize and interpret patterns in excavated surfaces which show the former presence of buildings, fences, ditches, ramparts, fields and all the other traces which human occupation leaves in the ground; to explain, as far as possible, the complete sequence of events on the site. This mass of evidence must then be set into a pair of chronological frames, one relative, one absolute.

The relative framework is based on the study of the superimposition of layers and features, or the intersection of walls, postholes, slots, ditches, gullies and other similar features. Such a framework gives only a 'floating chronology' which can be moved up and down, or extended or contracted according to datable finds securely stratified within the sequence. Such finds may be coins, seals or tokens, datable pottery or other artefacts, or architectural or sculptural fragments; or they may be samples taken from the layers and dated by scientific methods.

The relative chronology of a site is likely to be more certain than the absolutely dated chronology, since there is usually little doubt about the broad sequence of events, even if the details are not unequivocal, or the horizontal relationships cannot be demonstrated.

However, the absolute, or calendar, dating may be subject to considerable fluctuations, as the evidence of coins is supplemented by that, say, of dendrochronology (for instance Novgorod – Thompson, 1967) or radiocarbon dating; or if the dating of a pottery group is reassessed in the light of research elsewhere; or the excavation as it proceeds uncovers further dating evidence which modifies that already used.

The establishment of structural patterns and chronological frameworks is itself only the first stage towards the economic, cultural and, in the widest sense, historical interpretation which should follow. Obviously, if the earlier stages of the interpretation are mistaken, the subsequent stages will be further removed from the truth about the site as it was in the period under investigation. If to this is added Coles's reminder of the law of diminishing returns: that the evidence which we understand from an excavation is less than we record, which, even in the best excavations is less than has survived, which in turn is less than the total evidence once existing on the site, we shall see that our understanding of an ancient site or settlement or landscape will, at best, be severely limited. We must strive, therefore, to minimize these limitations. For example, there is little doubt that the larger and more complete the excavation, the more valid will be the interpretations which we can draw from it. Though

64 This photograph shows the very worn threshold stone of the west doorway of the Baths Basilica at Wroxeter. Earlier excavations have destroyed the stratification above and beside the threshold and the considerable area in the background of the photograph has also been dug in earlier times. However, the rubble beyond the threshold in the centre of the picture can be seen to be of two sorts — a light coloured area of worn stone, bounded by an area of darker, unworn stone within which there are post-holes for a fence. The area of light worn stone leads diagonally towards the site of the door of the basilica, and is clearly a path leading into the interior of the former basilican area long after the threshold was buried by rubble (removed by the earlier excavators). It follows that the west wall of the building was still standing to an effective height at this time, otherwise there would have been no need to have entered at this point. It can be further deduced therefore that robbing of the end wall took place after this. Since the worn rubble surface is of the last period occupation, the robbing is likely to have taken place after the site was deserted.

This contrasts with the robbing of many of the other walls of the building which can be shown to have been robbed as early as perhaps the third century. (Photo: Sidney Renow; see Barker *et al.* forthcoming, 1994.)

this is particularly the case with the excavation of timber buildings, even stone structures are more certainly and completely understood in large areas.

It is not possible to give detailed advice on all the problems of the interpretation of evidence that will occur in a complex excavation. The best general advice that can be given is to keep an open mind, expect the unexpected, and then, when a provisional interpretation has been made, stop, and take the opposite view or views of its meaning. By thus initiating a dialectic, false assumptions are not so likely to be perpetuated and built upon by the addition of subsequent plausible, though mistaken, evidence. For example, if a pebble surface, bordered by stake-holes is assumed to be an internal floor, it is likely that further emerging evidence will be adduced to support this theory. But if someone then says 'Let us assume it is an outside yard', the matter can be debated in detail, and either resolved on the balance of the evidence, or, if no positive conclusion can be reached, alternative explanations published. This is a simple, perhaps simplistic, example, but it should be extended to cover everything found on the excavation.

It follows that it is a great advantage to have supervisors or assistants on the site who are capable of taking and expressing a constructively critical view of every stage of the work. Conversely, the interpretation of an excavation by a forceful individual with inexperienced volunteers or labourers can easily go awry.

It is often valuable to think 'laterally' when considering the meaning of what has been dug up. In 'lateral' thinking we discard our preconceptions of the solution to a problem and look at it from a new viewpoint, perhaps one that at first sight appears ludicrous or at least highly improbable, but which ultimately be seen to fit the evidence better than any other of the postulated solutions. Lateral

thinking has been described in a number of books by E. de Bono (for instance, 1970).

A valuable aid in the interpretation of excavated evidence (and a check on flights of fancy) is to attempt to explain the origin, derivation and purpose of every recognizable context in the light of commonsense and practicability. This involves imagining the process by which a structure might have been built, the actual work of barrowing, shovelling and spreading rubble, digging postholes, laying foundations and so on. For instance, in determining whether a bank has been piled against a wall or whether the wall has been built against a vertical face cut into the bank an examination of the character of wall where it met the bank will usually show whether the joints of the wall were pointed, or whether mortar had been merely poured down behind the stones as the wall-building proceeded up the face of the cut-back bank, since it would be impossible to point the joints if the bank were there first, unless there was a construction trench wide enough to take a man. Often explanations of excavated phenomena can be tested by trial and error, or by observation of similar situations on present day demolition and construction sites. A simple example of the information which may reasonably be deduced from the observed evidence is shown in Fig. 64.

The understanding of a series of robber trenches, for example, is helped by taking the practical view and imagining a group of labourers faced with the job of digging out the walls, or perhaps only the facing stones, of a ruined building. Were the walls visible? If not, how did they find them? Trial trenching? Stone robbers will work as economically as possible, digging the narrowest possible trenches, and often though not always, backfilling them afterwards. If the walls have been completely robbed out, the unwanted stone and mortar debris thrown back will give a great deal of information about the walls as they were when they stood. Biddle and Biddle (1969) have discussed the interpretation of robber trench excavations in some detail. To their suggestions can be added the analysis of the mortars thrown back into the trench, which may differentiate walls of more than one period.

However, the commonsense, practical approach to interpretation does not always work, partly because our habits and modes of thought, and our view of what is practical, may be very different from that of the people we are digging up. Robson Bonnichsen (1972) describes an illuminating exercise in the interpretation of a recently deserted Native American camp site, Millie's Camp, where the debris, litter and other evidence of occupation were recorded as carefully as in an area excavation, and their interpretation subsequently checked by reference to the

recent occupants. The mistakes made showed the fallibility of some 'commonsense' reasoning. The behaviour patterns which produced the anomalous, misunderstood evidence were unfamiliar to the archaeologists and the reasons behind these behaviour patterns could not have been deduced from the available evidence, so that we must be careful not to project back into the past our own habits and ways of thinking except into situations

65 A photograph of the worn entrance threshold of the Baths Basilica at Wroxeter looking out into the western portico. The low-level photograph shows how the threshold, and therefore the door, or at least the opening where the door had been, was still in use after the portico had lost its original surface and been covered with pebbles and larger stones, which are clearly worn by the passage of feet along a roughly laid path.

where they can reasonably be assumed to be valid, either because we have lived and worked in comparable situations or because we know of living communities who do so now.

Another limitation of the 'practical' approach is that we may be reluctant to accept the evidence in the ground for what it is, if it seems impractical or unlikely. An example is the discovery on a number of sites of very shallow post-holes and circles of small stones which in many cases form definite structural patterns, thus implying a style of building in which posts are set on, not in, the ground. At first sight, this seems a highly impractical, if not impossible manner of construction, but as the evidence has accumulated from a number of excavations, the former presence of such buildings has become undeniable. Accordingly, instead of working from our preconceptions of what the evidence for a timber building ought to look like, we should explore methods of construction that would fit the evidence. This has resulted, among other things, in the full-scale simulation of such a structure, Building I from the Baths

66a

66 a–d These photographs show the remains of the foundation (*stylobate*) of the portico colonnade of the Baths Basilica at Wroxeter. The pecked areas W1 and W2 are the positions of the column bases; from these the distance between the columns down the whole length of the portico can be determined. However, the photographs also show very interesting patterns of wear on the surfaces of the stones. While it would be expected that there would be wear between the columns the stone at X shows wear along the edge and over the pecking which strongly suggests that there

was a lot of traffic *after* the columns had gone, implying continuing occupation of the site (on a considerable scale, since the stones are very hard) after the destruction of the public buildings of which the portico formed a part (see next page).

In addition, the two stones at Y and Z are heavily worn on each side of the gap between them, suggesting that there was here a path or passage across the portico, not necessarily, though probably, after the columns had gone.

66b

66c

66d

Basilica excavation at Wroxeter (Barker *et al.* forthcoming, 1994) which, though destroyed by a gale before completion, proved that post-built structures will stand even if their posts are not embedded in the ground.

Further instances are provided by the late or sub-Roman building at Birdoswald, illustrated in Fig. 75a–b, while a standing example is the market hall at Pembridge in Herefordshire whose uprights stand, with the minimum of bracing, on post-pads of a type often found in excavations.

67 This photograph of one of the mortar floors of the Baths Basilica at Wroxeter shows what appears to be the line of a partition dividing off part of the north aisle. The partition was almost certainly of wood, which was later replaced, on a slightly different alignment, by a rough stone wall. The photograph was taken in the early morning (the arrow points to north) in order to show the slight indentation by glancing light.

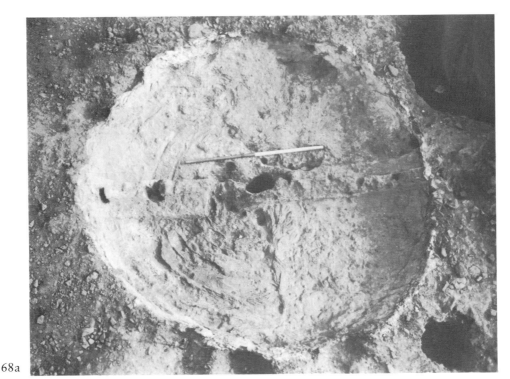

68a

68b

68 a–b During the course of excavations in Northampton in 1974 and again in 1980, five Saxon mortar mixers were found close to St Peter's Church. The mixers, circular bowls cut down into the ground or built on its surface, varied in diameter from 2 to 3m (6½ to 10ft) and all contained residues from mixing, which facilitated the interpretation of these initially enigmatic structures. All had evidence of a central post and several had traces of basket-work around their perimeter. Mixer 3 had a central ridge in which further holes were visible. On removal of the top residue from the mixer, striations could be seen in the underlying mix, which lined up with the ridge holes. These striations were almost certainly the grooves scored by rotating paddles. Presumably the earlier residue was still soft when a fresh mix was being prepared and different consistencies of the respective mixes preserved the indications of the rotary action of the mixer. Traces of grooves evidencing rotary motion were also present in the mixers excavated in 1980. (The scale is 1m long.)

b On the basis of the evidence shown in a, this reconstruction drawing has been made. (Photo and drawing courtesy of John Williams.)

WROXETER · BATHS BASILICA · Distribution of Wall Plaster

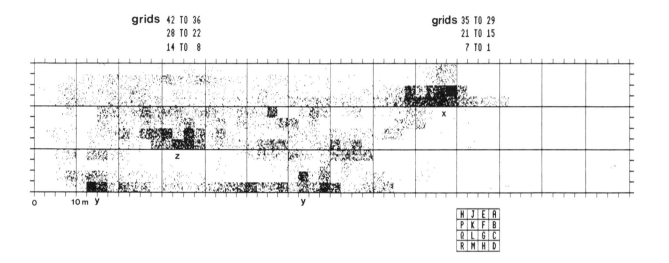

69 A computer plot of the distribution of wall plaster found in the excavation of the Baths Basilica at Wroxeter. The find spots of the wall plaster were recorded in 2½ m squares and this is how they have been plotted. The significance of the distribution has not yet been studied, though the concentrations at x and y can be accounted for, in part, by the fact that they are close to walls which still stand to a height of a metre or so. The concentration at z is not so easily explained, and must almost certainly have been brought on to the site from elsewhere. Such a plot is only the starting point for the study of the wall plaster distribution, and goes hand in hand with a study of the painted patterns on the plaster and the reconstruction of those patterns. (Plot: Georgina Shaw.)

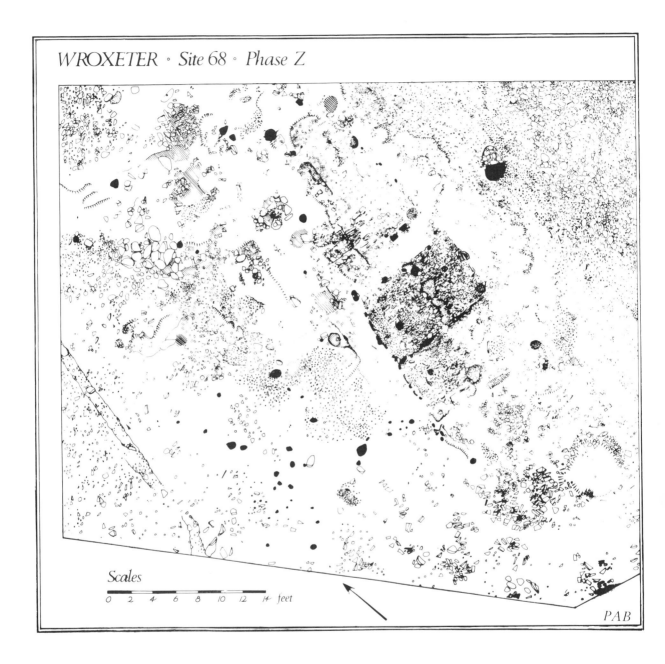

WROXETER · Site 68 · Phase Z

Scales

0 2 4 6 8 10 12 14 feet

PAB

70 Wroxeter, Baths Basilica Building I. This building was revealed when the ploughsoil was removed and the uppermost archaeological layers were cleaned simply by removing the humic soil and leaving all stones, tiles, clay etc. The maximum depth of the post-sockets was 2–3cm so that it was clear that none of the posts had been sunk into the ground and that they could not have stood independently. Some of the post- and stake-holes were packed round with tiles and pottery which projected above the floor levels. Since, if the plough had touched them, they would have been displaced, it was apparent that this was the last structure built on this part of the site before its abandonment and that, contrary to previous opinion, it had not suffered plough damage.

216

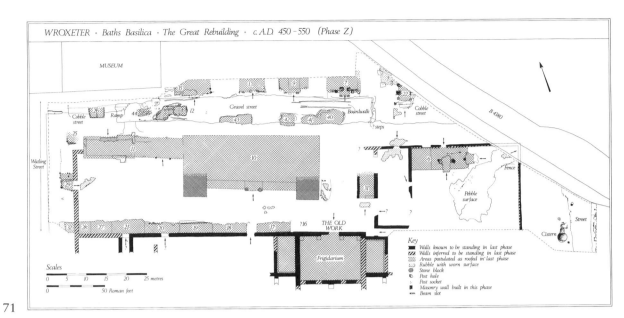

WROXETER · *Baths Basilica · The Great Rebuilding* · c. A.D. 450 - 550 (Phase Z)

MUSEUM

Gravel street

Boardwalk

? steps

Cobble street

B 4380

Cobble street

Ramp

Watling Street

THE OLD WORK

Pebble surface

Fence

Frigidarium

Cistern

Street

Key
- Walls known to be standing in last phase
- Walls inferred to be standing in last phase
- Areas postulated as roofed in last phase
- Rubble with worn surface
- Stone block
- Post hole
- Post socket
- Masonry wall built in this phase
- Beam slot

Scales

0   5   10   15   20   25 metres

0   50 Roman feet

71

72

71–72 (previous page) 72 is an attempt to show what the buildings of the final occupation of the city centre at Wroxeter may have looked like. The drawing is based on what might be considered the flimsiest of evidence – platforms of rubble laid horizontally over the remains of the basilica 71. There are, however, convincing reasons to believe that the platforms were deliberately laid, and that the plan of the largest building, in the centre of the picture, was symmetrical about two large fragments of masonry, which had been placed as foundations for the columns of a portico. Elsewhere also there was evidence of symmetrical facades of buildings constructed along one of the east-west streets (Barker *et al.* forthcoming, 1994).

One problem which arises from the publication of such a drawing is that it is seized on by authors who want to illustrate their books on late Roman Britain, often without the very strong reservations which ought to accompany a piece of kite-flying like this.

73–74 *a* (below) and *b* (right) are two drawings of a building from the excavation of the Baths Basilica at Wroxeter. *a* is a redrawing of the evidence as it was recorded in the field. The drawing includes all the evidence as seen. *b* extracts from this drawing what we believe to be significant structurally, and attempts to interpret it.

73a

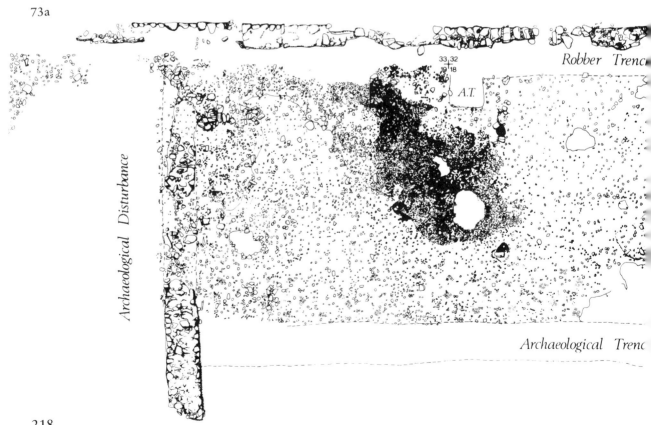

Archaeological Disturbance

33,32
19 18

A.T.

Robber Trench

Archaeological Trench

218

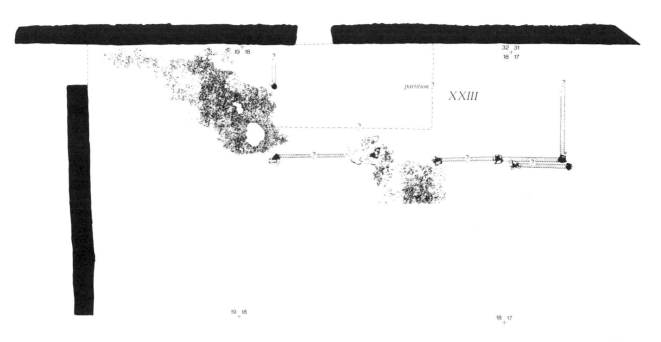

73b

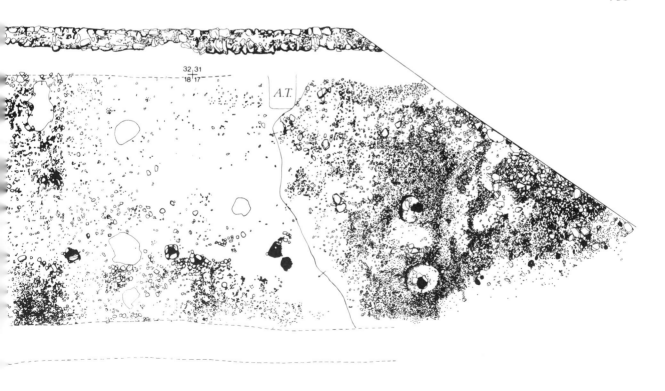

The next stage is to envisage and draw the building in three dimensions (74). Needless to say, the further we go upwards, away from the evidence on the ground, the less certain the reconstruction will be, so that the roof covering is almost complete conjecture – though not quite, since, as there was no trace of roof tiles or slates, it is very probable that the roof covering was of thatch or shingles, an example of the value of negative evidence.

The building is sited in the north-eastern corner of the precinct of the baths and it is bounded on the north by a wall which we believe to have been standing during the life of the building. The evidence consists of eight post-holes and a number of pebble spreads, shown in 73a. In 73b the presumed wall-lines have been indicated, together with the suggested positions of the doors, which were approached by the pebble spreads, presumed to be paths. A gap in the wall-line on the northern side is presumed to mark another entrance, this time into the portico of the baths insula. It will be seen that in *a* the pebble spreads appear to have straight boundaries; these perhaps mark the positions of partitions, shown with a dotted line on *b*. It is presumed that the building leant-to against the northern wall, though any evidence there may have been has been lost in a robber trench and in two small earlier archaeological trenches marked AT.

The building is thought to have been a barn or storeroom, as was its successor (see Barker *et al.* forthcoming, 1994). In these two drawings the evidence as recorded in the field has been kept separate from the suggested interpretation, so that the reader is not presented simply with a *fait accompli*, but can make up his/her own mind.

74

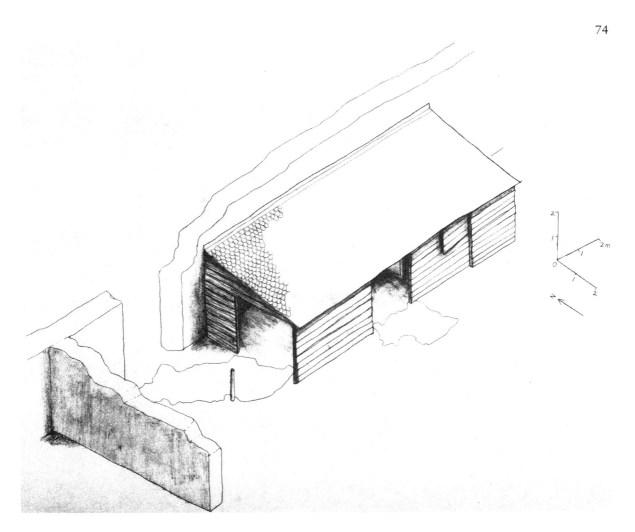

75a

75a and b During area excavation in 1987–8, a timber building measuring 23 × 8.6m (75 × 28ft) was found to overlay the north granary and part of the main street of the Hadrian's Wall fort of Birdoswald. The evidence for the building was very vestigial, consisting of stone pads laid on the road surface, and very slight indentations in the bottom of a shallow trench running along the length of the former granary. In the photograph members of the excavation team are shown standing on the principal post positions. The wall lines, interior and exterior surfaces were defined by patterns visible in the broad expanse of exposed rubble surfaces. These too are visible in the photograph, but only become apparent with reference to the figures. Without the emphasis provided by the figures an overall photograph of the building would be virtually impossible. On the plan the features of the building have been emphasized in black, with the spread of which they form a part rendered as a grey background. The recognition of the building was the result of observation by the site draughtsmen. All saw anomalies emerging from their drawings, but the way in which these anomalies linked together was not fully appreciated until viewed from above, in this case from the top of the three-storey tower of the adjacent farmhouse. The building, together with others associated with it, could only have been recovered by their total excavation, as their recognition was entirely reliant on the complete stripping and careful examination of a wide area of unpromising looking rubble and metalling.

The building is one of three which form the second of two settlement phases, the first of which post-dates the latest Roman pottery and coins on the site. They represent continuation of occupation for an unknown period beyond the early fifth century. Layers associated with the buildings were eventually sealed by deposits containing thirteenth–fourteenth century pottery.

(With acknowledgments to Tony Wilmott; photo by Greg McDonnell, English Heritage; drawn by Alan Rae, English Heritage.)

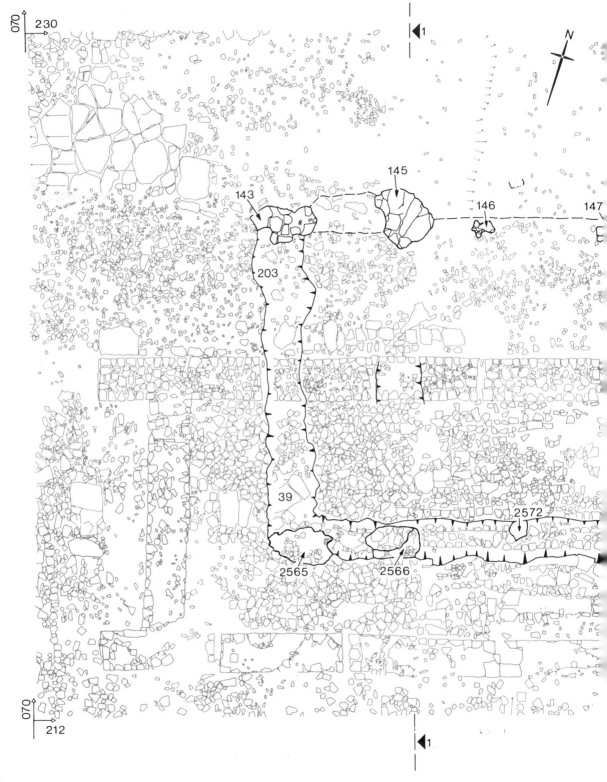

75b

0 1 5m

Dating

The understanding and strict application of the concepts of the *terminus post quem* and *terminus ante quem* are of fundamental importance in the relative dating of layers and features. Unless these concepts are applied in all cases with the most rigorous logic, far-reaching mistakes in dating and interpretation will be made. The rules can be set out simply as follows:

The terminus post quem

A datable object, such as a coin, or other datable find, such as a radiocarbon sample from a layer or feature, only gives the date on or after which the layer or feature was deposited, that is, the so-called *terminus post quem*. It follows that any continuous sealed layer in which there is a number of finds of varying date, the find of latest date is the one which provides the *terminus post quem*. It must be established that the object is not intrusive, that it has not been taken down an animal hole, or slipped down the interstices between the stones of a wall. If there is any doubt about this the object should be rejected for dating purposes. The argument is most easily demonstrated graphically (Figs 76–7).

The terminus ante quem

The *terminus ante quem* argument arises when features or layers are sealed by or are cut through by later, datable features. The later features give a *terminus ante quem* (that is a date *before* which the earlier features must have been deposited) to all those features which can be demonstrated to be earlier. For example, if a series of layers is sealed by a mosaic floor of unquestioned fourth-century date then all the layers below will be fourth century or earlier. Similarly, if a wall itself can be dated, say by architectural features, then the layers which are cut by its foundations are given a *terminus ante quem* by the

76a A clay floor is bounded by post-holes. The floor contains three coins of the second century AD. Coin D is of the first century. The floor was therefore laid during or after the second century AD.

On the basis of this evidence alone, the floor could be twentieth century. It certainly might be late Roman or Anglo-Saxon. However, if coin D was third century, coins A, B and C are all negated as dating evidence, and the floor which seals coin D must be third century or later.

76b Coin D is first century AD, Coin C second century; coin B third century and coin A fourth century. Here in a fairly common situation, somewhat simplified, in which we have a superficially plausible sequence of dating evidence which suggests that the four layers span the whole Roman period in sequence. However, if we apply the *terminus post quem* rule strictly, as we must, the whole lot could be post-Roman, even modern. Other dating factors would have to be discovered and assessed before a Roman sequence could be maintained.

76c In this figure there is increased probability that the layers above A were laid down in the second–third century and the third–fourth century, but no certainty. Again A is crucial. If it is a ninth-century coin or thirteenth-century pot, all of the material above it must be considered residual.

76d In this similarly plausible sequence, if A is an otherwise undatable sherd or object one must be careful not to use false *terminus ante quem* reasoning and maintain that A must be earlier than first–second century. It may ultimately prove to be, say, fourth century, in which case the two layers above take their *terminus post quem* from it.

76e The two objects A and B, though found together in a pit, tell us nothing about each other except that they were buried in the pit together at some time at, or later, than the date of the later of the two objects. However, if object C can be shown to be of later date than either A or B then the whole sequence takes its *terminus post quem* from C.

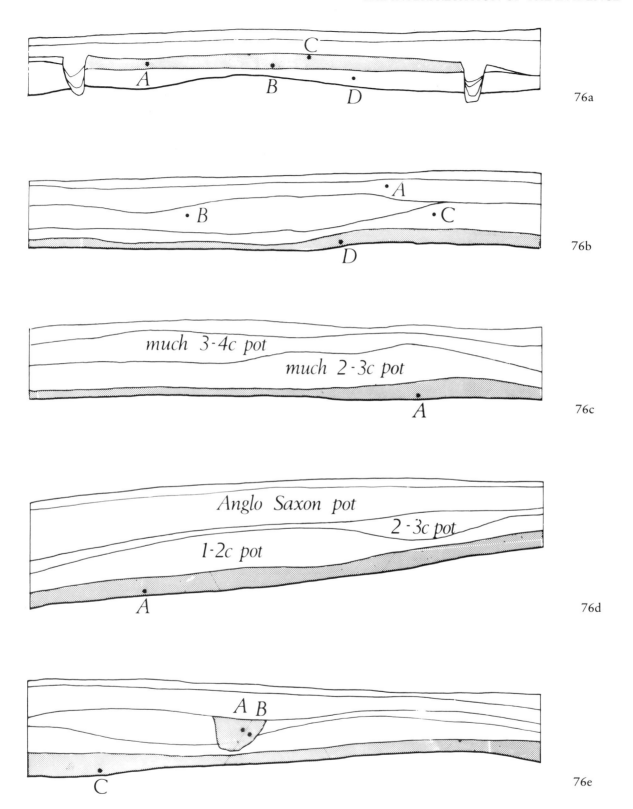

76a

76b

76c

76d

76e

77a A is a Roman coin or sherd, B is a medieval spur. It is tempting to see this as a Roman road still in use in medieval times. However, the road could be of any date, from the Roman period onward (it cannot be prehistoric if the sherd is thoroughly sealed). It is even possible that the spur was an antique dropped recently.

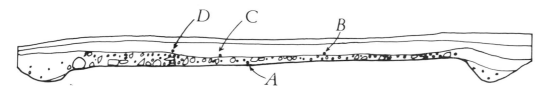

77b This illustration is based on an actual example (at Quatford in Shropshire, see Mason and Barker, 1961)

F – nineteenth-century sherd
E – medieval sherd
D – medieval bronze object
C – Roman sherd
B – neolithic flint
A – 1881 halfpenny

The presumed medieval rampart was shown to be dated to 1881 or later by the presence of the Victorian halfpenny.

The possibility for error here is that the halfpenny might not have been dropped, or that it would not have been found if the cutting had been made elsewhere along the 'rampart'.

In fact, the bank was formed by ploughing during the 1939–45 war, so that the 1881 coin actually gives a *terminus post quem* some 60 years too early.

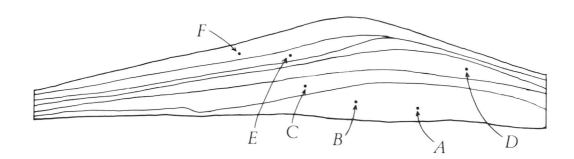

wall. Thus, if the wall can be shown to be Norman, the cut layers are Norman or earlier. They may be Saxon – or Palaeolithic.

However, we must be careful not to be led into a circular argument. A *terminus ante quem* cannot be given by a layer which is dated by an object embedded in it which merely gives it a *terminus post quem*. For example, if a floor in a house contains a coin of AD 267 firmly stratified in it, the floor must have been laid in 267 or after. If does not follow that the layers below the floor were deposited in 267 or earlier. Subsequent excavation of another floor many layers below the first might produce a stratified coin of say, AD 370. In that case all the layers above take a new *terminus post quem* of 370 or later. The whole complex might ultimately turn out to be tenth century. Unless the limitations of stratified datable objects are fully appreciated there is a danger that serious dating errors will occur in interpretation, to be perpetuated in the literature.

Inevitably, the larger the excavation and the greater the volume of deposits examined the more secure will be the dating of the sequences of contexts, especially on sites where finds are comparatively sparse, where

78 a and b. A clear example of the *terminus ante quem*. A small excavation was carried out under the floor of the splendid crypt of Worcester Cathedral, begun by Bishop Wulstan in 1084. The floor itself rested on loose earth and small rubble which lay over a concrete raft, A, some 15cm (6in) below the floor. The free-standing columns were founded not on the concrete raft, but on large fragments of rubble used to pack them to reach the desired floor level. Among these lumps of rubble was a fragment of carved stone (B and *b*). Its position under the column provides it with a firm *terminus ante quem* of 1084; in other words, since the rubble packing is earlier than the column, whose date is known, the carving must also be earlier than the column, i.e. 1084. In fact, the carving is typical of Anglo-Saxon sculpture of the ninth or tenth centuries. Furthermore, the concrete raft, by the same argument, must also be earlier than 1084. Since it appears not to be of the same build as the columns (since, unless the masons had made a gross error in laying out, the columns would hardly have needed to be packed with rubble), it seems to belong to an earlier building, perhaps the crypt of one of the Anglo-Saxon minsters which are known to have preceded the Norman cathedral. Paradoxically, the same example can be used to illustrate the *terminus post quem* argument. If it is imagined that the cathedral had long ago been destroyed, and was being excavated without prior knowledge of what it was, the fragment of sculpture would give a *terminus post quem* to the column base. If the date of the sculpture was known on general grounds, it would be clear that the column base must be later than the ninth–tenth centuries – in other words, it could *not* be Roman, but it could be medieval, or of any date between the late Saxon period and the present day.

227

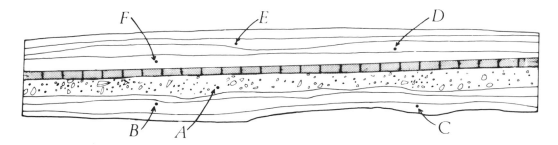

79 *Above* All the layers under the tiled floor including finds A, B and C in the illustration are given a *terminus ante quem* by the floor. If the floor is made, of say, fourteenth-century tiles then all the layers beneath must be fourteenth century or earlier. They could be prehistoric. Be sure that the floor has not been taken up and relaid in later times, perhaps in a nineteenth-century restoration.

79 *Below* This again is a diagrammatic representation of an actual situation. The walls are those of an early Norman passage leading to the cloisters in Worcester Cathedral. The steps lead down into a Norman undercroft.

Both these buildings are firmly datable by their styles of architecture. The two graves a and b are therefore clearly given a *terminus ante quem* by the early Norman passage since they must have been dug from the contemporary ground level. They are therefore late Saxon or earlier. Similarly the underlying pit c is given a *terminus ante quem* by the graves. The pit produced a large sherd of pottery of a type not readily paralleled in the region. However, it must be late Saxon or earlier. It is very possibly Iron Age.

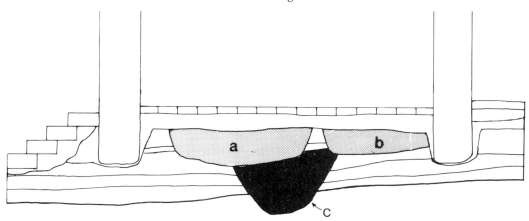

crucial *termini* depend on the recovery of perhaps only one or two sherds, coins or other datable objects.

It must also be re-emphasized that a number of objects retrieved from one context are 'associated' only in the sense that they have a common context in the excavation. Their 'association' implies nothing about their relative or absolute dates, or ultimate prov-

enance. In the past, a great deal of weight has been placed on the argument that objects are 'associated' and quite unjustifiable conclusions drawn from this. (See the example cited on p. 197 above.) Pottery cannot be dated by 'association' with a coin. It is only too easy for a stray Roman coin to get into a medieval rubbish pit. No one would redate a group of glazed jugs to the Roman period on that evidence alone. But how many times have we seen objects and pottery that have been dated by association with coins when the dates look more plausible?

Nevertheless, under some circumstances the association of objects can be accepted as of considerable importance. Objects found together in a grave, for instance, though they may not all be of one date or even of one style or culture, are associated in the sense that they were deposited either on or with the body for specific reasons – as heirlooms, trophies, equipment for the after-life or perhaps even as sentimental keepsakes. Similarly, objects found strewn on the floor of a house, particularly one that has been burnt down, when it can be supposed that the occupants fled without stopping to collect all their belongings, may be assumed to have been used by, or at least in the possession of, the occupants when the house was abandoned. The greater the quantities of material in association the more reliance can be placed on conclusions drawn from them. The objects in a single grave may be a unique assemblage. If similar objects are found in a majority of graves in a large cemetery, it can reasonably be assumed that the finds were a normal part of the belongings or equipment of the people interred. Similarly, if great quantities of pottery and coins are found in a stratified sequence, as they are on many Roman sites, it strengthens the argument for assigning in broad terms the assemblages of pottery in the layers to the dates of the coins in those layers. For example, if there is a military presence on the site which is followed by a civil development, clearly marked off in the stratification, and the earliest civil phase is followed by a period of demolition and rebuilding, the associated groups of sealed pottery, coins and finds can reasonably be assumed to be broadly contemporary, though increasingly contaminated by residual material.

Relative chronology

The principle of stratification is fundamental to archaeological excavation. This principle states that if one layer can be shown to lie upon another, the lower layer must have been deposited before the upper. The interval between the deposition of the two layers may be a millennium or the time it takes to tip two separate barrow loads of rubble, but the relative chronology remains the same. On a simply stratified site, the layers may be stripped off one at a time in the reverse order to that in which they were deposited, and the result shown as a straightforward table – which amounts to a diagrammatic section of the site.

A decisive step forward in the understanding and ordering of stratigraphy was made by Ed. Harris and the general adoption of the stratigraphic matrix which he devised (Harris 1979 and 2nd ed. 1989). This second edition is required reading for all excavators but the principles are illustrated here in Fig. 80a–c.

While the stratigraphic matrix is now an essential tool, it must be borne in mind that it is abstract, in that all contexts in the diagram are given equal size and status. While this ensures that no component of the site is ignored, it is far removed from the real relationships of these components – the worn pebble suface compared with the casual dump of gravel; the slot for a timber compared, or confused with, a plough furrow – so that the post-excavation analysis moves from the site itself towards pure abstraction, when its elements are put in order, and must then be translated back into the reality of the site.

80a The compilation of a stratigraphic sequence. In (A) all the superpositional relationships are shown in the section and in the Harris Matrix form. (B) A matrix rendition of a section, which is clarified into a stratigraphic sequence in (C) according to the law of stratigraphical succession.

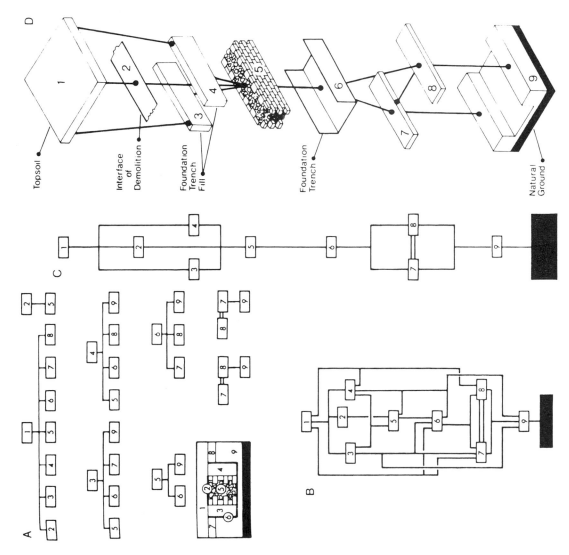

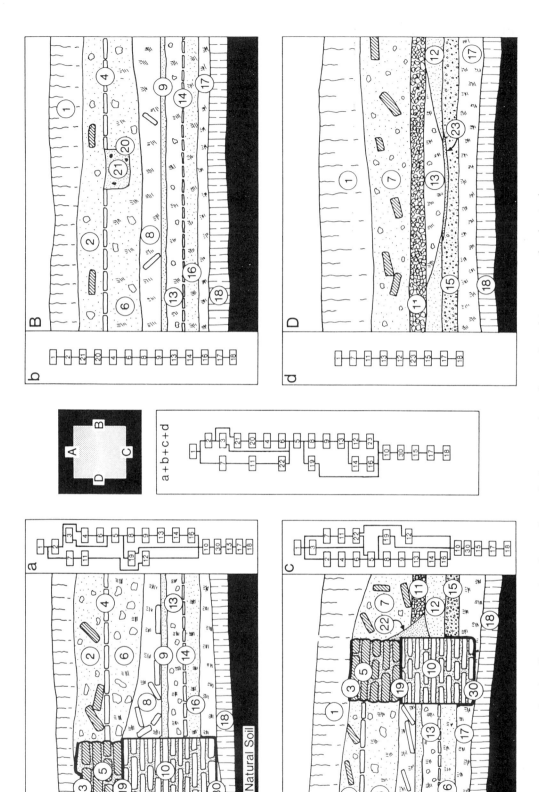

80b This illustration (and c) shows the gradual construction of a stratigraphic sequence for the single section represented by profiles A to D. By the law of stratigraphical succession, the four profiles are merged into a single sequence (a + b + c + d) and superfluous relationships are deleted.

231

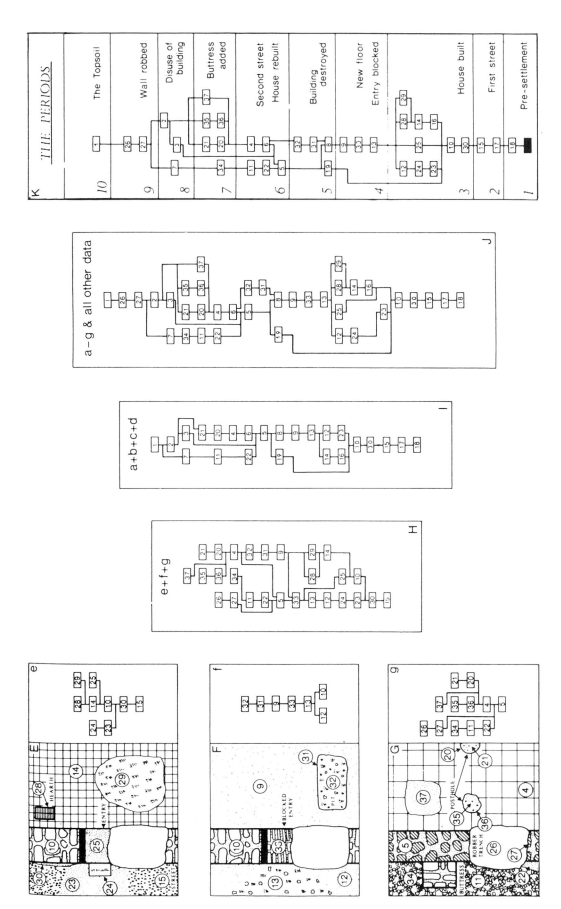

80c In e + f + g, the sequences of plans (E–G) are merged and then combined with the data from the profiles in b. The final stratigraphic sequence for this site is a-g, which is divided into periods (K).

The danger which has to be avoided is that of interpreting the record rather than the site itself. In my view, the adoption of the stratigraphic matrix does not preclude on-site, immediate interpretation, when relationships can be directly observed, but enhances and amends it.

The understanding of stratigraphy is the subject of continuous debate, as a recent series of conference papers (Steane 1992) illustrates. The difficulty for most excavators is to keep up with the ferment of ideas now being generated, not only about stratigraphy, but about all aspects of the discipline.

An extension of the use of the stratification diagram or matrix is in pottery or other artefact seriation, where quantities of pottery types (the x-axis) are plotted against the order of context deposition (the y-axis), the latter derived from the stratification diagram. Where the *typological sequence* is relatively well known, the diagram offers information on the sequence of deposition. Where the *stratified sequence* is relatively secure, the chronology of the artefact types can be improved. Clearly, a long stratigraphic sequence and a large body of pottery types give the most reliable and informative results. In practice, neither the artefact typology nor the stratification are ever completely known, and the seriation diagram becomes a model of the relationship between them. It can, therefore, also be a graphic way of proving and illustrating residuality, one of the more difficult aspects of some heavily occupied sites. (See p. 199 below and Pretty, K., in Barker *et al.* 1994, where she discusses residuality on the Baths Basilica site at Wroxeter, where the bulk of the pottery was residual.)

The reader is urged to read Martin Carver's paper 'Theory and Practice in Urban Pottery Seriation' (Carver 1985) from which this summary is derived, and an actual example of the method from Worcester in Carver (ed.) 1980 (p. 155 ff.).

A bread oven at Wroxeter

Figure 81a is an extract from one of the 10 site matrices for the Baths Basilica site at Wroxeter comprising 48 contexts out of a site total of over 4000. It shows part of the west portico matrix, concentrating on the construction and disuse of a large bread oven which was sited just to the north of the main doorway into the basilica. This was, in its turn, inside a large post-hole building (63) whose contexts lie outside the area covered by this extract. The oven was built of clay, sandstone, and broken terracotta tiles and had a large hearth made of tiles on clay at its west end. When first uncovered, the oven lay in the base of a large archaeological disturbance which had destroyed much of the evidence for the superstructure. However, as the excavation progressed, more of the oven was revealed until it, in its turn, was completely removed, context by context (Fig. 81b). Comparison of the sequence of plans, which was prepared for the final publication, with the matrix make it clear that not all the contexts are shown. This is either because some contexts were obscured during planning, or it was decided not to include them in the published plans as they did not appear to be of significance. However, all contexts were recorded on the total of 34 field drawings made, from which the publication plans were drawn.

The detailed dissection of the oven in this way revealed aspects of its construction which might not otherwise have been noticed. For example, the way that the southern wall of the oven projects further west than the north wall so that the hearth could be tucked inside the mouth of the flue, allowing an efficient transfer of the embers inside. Less obvious was the fact that the tiles of the flue (D1250) butted up to the already built south wall (D1228). The north wall (D1227, etc) was then built over the northern half of the flue

233

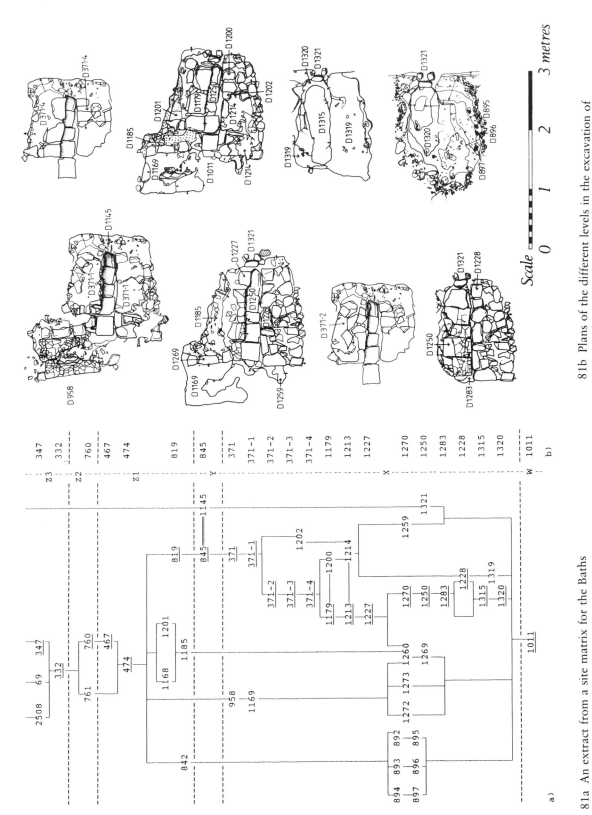

81b Plans of the different levels in the excavation of an oven, Baths Basilica Site, Wroxeter.

81a An extract from a site matrix for the Baths Basilica Site, Wroxeter.

A bread oven at Wroxeter

Context listing for Fig. 81 a–b

Context number	Description	Context number	Description
D69	post hole	D1168	ash deposit
D332	rubble spread	D1169	hearth bedding
D347	beam slot	D1179	construction layer
D371	1st layer of oven	D1185	mortar layer
D371–1	2nd layer of oven	D1200	construction layer
D371–2	3rd layer of oven	D1201	loam patch
D371–3	4th layer of oven	D1202	tile foundation
D371–4	5th layer of oven	D1213	clay foundation
D467	oven levelling	D1214	clay foundation
D474	oven debris	D1227	tile foundation
D760	oven debris	D1228	sandstone layer
D761	oven debris	D1250	flue tiles
D819	oven debris	D1259	debris from use of oven
D842	mortar layer	D1260	layer under oven
D845	fill of flue	D1269	sandstone layer
D892	stake hole fill	D1270	clay bedding layer
D893	stake hole fill	D1272	bedding layer
D894	stake hole fill	D1273	layer under oven
D895	stake hole cut	D1283	clay bedding
D896	stake hole cut	D1315	bedding layer
D897	stake hole cut	D1319	bedding layer
D958	tile hearth	D1320	bedding layer
D1011	pebble floor	D1321	post hole
D1145	fill of flue	D2508	fence line

tiles. This meant that, should the flue tiles need replacing, only one half of the oven had to be dismantled. The identification of three stake-holes on the south side (D895–7) allows us to suggest that the upper part of the oven was probably made of a frame of withies woven together and then plastered with mud.

Environmental sampling of the debris and the surrounding soil revealed many charred bread-wheat grains indicating that the oven had been used to bake bread. Its size further suggested that it was not a domestic oven but was large enough to cater for passing trade (Building 63 fronted on to the main road running through the town centre). The only dating evidence recovered from the construction layers of the oven was a coin of the Emperor Valens dated AD 367–75. Of course, this only provides an earliest possible date of construction (AD 367) and it may have been built much later than this. A more potentially useful date was provided by a thermoluminescence determination on the clay in the oven which yielded a date of AD 400 ±100. Since the coin rules out the earlier end of this date range, the oven was built, and used, between about AD 367 and 500. On other grounds (its relative stratigraphic position, its relationship to other contexts which have been put in the same phase and have been dated using other evidence) we think that the oven operated between about AD 410 and 420.

The matrix can only be fully understood

Phased context listing for Figure 81 a–b.

Context no.	Description	Phase
D1011	pebble floor	W
D371	1st layer of oven	X
D371–1	2nd layer of oven	X
D371–2	3rd layer of oven	X
D371–3	4th layer of oven	X
D271–4	5th layer of oven	X
D892	stake hole fill	X
D893	stake hole fill	X
D894	stake hole fill	X
D895	stake hole cut	X
D896	stake hole cut	X
D897	stake hole cut	X
D1169	hearth bedding	X
D1179	construction layer	X
D1200	construction layer	X
D1202	tile foundation	X
D1213	clay foundation	X
D1214	clay foundation	X
D1227	tile foundation	X
D1228	sandstone layer	X
D1250	flue tiles	X
D1259	debris from use of oven	X
D1260	layer under oven	X
D1270	clay bedding layer	X
D1272	bedding layer	X
D1273	layer under oven	X
D1283	clay bedding	X
D1315	bedding layer	X
D1319	bedding layer	X
D1320	bedding layer	X
D1321	post hole	X
D958	tile hearth	X
D845	fill of flue	Y
D1145	fill of flue	Y
D467	oven levelling	Z1
D474	oven debris	Z1
D819	oven debris	Z1
D842	mortar layer	Z1
D1168	ash deposit	Z1
D1185	mortar layer	Z1
D1201	loam patch	Z1
D760	oven debris	Z2
D761	oven debris	Z2
D69	post hole	Z3
D332	rubble spread	Z3
D347	beam slot	Z3
D2508	fence line	Z3

when used with the context listing which tells us what each number means. Only direct stratigraphic relationships are recorded on the matrix. For example, in physical terms, areas of the extensive rubble spread D332 came down directly on to the pebble floor D1011. This, and other such relationships, are not shown on the matrix as the numbers of lines would so proliferate that it would be incomprehensible. Instead, such relationships may be taken for granted *via* the intervening contexts: it is understood that such physical relationships may have occurred on site, but it is unnecessary to express them on the matrix. This process simplifies the construction of the matrix enormously, without compromising its accuracy.

Drawing up a matrix is not easy and several drafts may be gone through to get a good copy. It is not just a matter of piling up the cards and drawing out the relationships expressed on them: they have to be checked against the plans to make sure that what is written is true. In addition, it is quite common for people to forget to fill in the cards, or to have filled them in incorrectly (e.g. recording physical rather than stratigraphic relationships). Again, careful checking should sort these problems out, although if you have to change a relationship, you must record why you have done so and leave the original relationship available for others to see and judge for themselves. From this, it is clear that, as with all archaeology, subjective decisions must be made, but so long as the thought processes are clear to others, this is acceptable.

Once happy with the actual sequence of contexts, the next step is to phase the matrix. Again, this is subjective process but a useful criterion to use is to define a phase as a change in activity as physically represented on site. In this example, the earliest phase, W, is a pebble floor (D1011). The second phase, X, is characterized by the construction of the oven. Phase Y is the disuse of the oven, represented in this case by the debris in the flue (D845/D1145). By phase Z, the oven was largely buried but the superstructure was demolished to make way for a series of buildings. This phase has been divided into three sub-phases (Z1–Z3). A sub-phase may be defined as a distinct change within an overall phase. In this case there was evidence for the construction of three successive buildings of similar type but in different locations. The lack of any distinct archaeological horizon between them suggested that, rather than representing three separate phases, they merely indicated different uses of the same area in the same general phase. It is also important when considering the phasing of a site to take into account any scientific or artefactual dating evidence that is available.

One way a relatively simple matrix can be phased is shown in the table opposite. Here, a *primary path* of key contexts has been identified (these have been underlined in Fig.81a). The route taken by the path should be the most comprehensive, including contexts from all levels. This considerably simplified matrix can then be phased, the results being applied to the master matrix. Although it does not get round the problem of constructing the matrix in the first place, it at least allows the wood to be seen for the trees.

The limitations of archaeological evidence

In every excavation we must expect aspects which are beyond interpretation from the material evidence alone. A reed pipe will tell us its range of notes but not the tunes played on it.

If we can temporarily forget all that we know of the last two thousand years, we can play a salutary archaeological game. What would we make of the archaeological remains of Christianity if we knew nothing of it except what evidence could be recovered by excavation? Recurring fragments, both sculptured and painted of a crucified man, of a gentle mother and her child, of other figures, male and female, some of them being tortured and killed, others surrounded by singing winged figures; flagons and dishes included with selected male burials; temples varying in size from tiny to gigantic, many of them cruciform, perhaps significantly, perhaps not; palatial buildings set round courtyards, often in remote and beautiful settings. What reconstruction of this religion would we attempt from such remains? A cult of human sacrifice connected with worship of a mother goddess? Should we equate the child with the crucified man? Could we make the connection between the oratory of Gallerus and the ruins of Rievaulx? It is a sobering reflection that we can never excavate the upper room in which the Last Supper was held, and would not recognize it if we could, and that the site of the Crucifixion would be merely three large post-holes.

In spite of the clear limitations of excavated evidence, some deductions can be made about the spiritual aspirations, the pretensions, hopes and fears of the people whose house foundations we dissect and whose rubbish we reverently collect. Two examples must suffice here. The fact that very many burials from the earliest times onwards are furnished with grave goods or other evidence of posthumous provision suggests that man has always hoped for continuation of life after death. If the provisions which are made include the equipment, furniture, food and weapons of the dead person's everyday life, it is a reasonable assumption that the afterlife in that case was considered to be a continuation or resumption in some form of the life they had just left, and not a spiritual Nirvana, or a Dantean paradise.

Another example is furnished by the petty king (if that is what he was) who rebuilt the centre of *Viroconium* sometime in the late fourth or fifth century (Barker *et al.* forth-coming, 1994). He had pretensions to former grandeur; his buildings, though all in timber, are symmetrically planned on classical lines, with colonnaded porticoes and a private alley or arcade (*ibid.*). They are quite unlike the aisled halls of the later, so-called 'Arthurian' period or the Anglo-Saxon palaces of Yeavering or Cheddar. We can see in his mind a conscious attempt to revive (or keep alive) the rapidly fading past, the last flicker of the classical tradition in Britain until Inigo Jones and Christopher Wren.

Post-excavation work

English Heritage's Management of Archaeological Projects, quoted in Chapter 5, points out that phase 3 of its recommendations may be less familiar than the others. This phase emphasizes the necessity of selectivity when planning post-excavation work. It is, of course, extremely, if not notoriously, difficult to assess the extent of post-excavation work in advance, since the richness of the evidence and the extent and nature of the finds cannot be known before the excavation is completed. This phase, here called 'assessment', or potential for analysis, cannot therefore realistically be made before the excavation is in its later stages, which, of course, makes prior planning and costing very difficult. The example, described on pp. 98–9, of the small excavation of a cellar which might have revealed little or nothing of archaeological interest but, in the event, produced more than fifty medieval burials, is a case in point. Judgement then had to be made as to whether the skeletons should be examined in detail, or only superficially; whether radiocarbon dates were desirable and their expense justified; what environmental analysis should be sought and who should be expected to foot this bill.

This is a small example but it exemplifies the questions which must be asked and the decisions which must be taken on excavations of whatever size, since, in the past, there has been a tendency to ascribe equal importance to every aspect of the site, with consequent waste of money and effort on undirected and unco-ordinated research.

At the other end of the scale from the example just quoted, the recently completed excavation of the Baths Basilica at Wroxeter Roman City, mentioned often here, has produced a vast quantity of finds, all dug stratigraphically and three-dimensionally recorded. In many cases the quantities of stratified finds are the largest ever recovered from Roman Britain. This has placed a severe strain on the post-excavation resources available, so that with many categories of finds analysis has been curtailed or postponed indefinitely. The situation has been compounded by the fact that large proportions of the finds are residual, but this does not alter the fact that there is here a very large reservoir of information, over which hard decisions have had to be made, partly for financial reasons and because of the shortage of specialist skills, but partly also because of the assessed cost-effectiveness of the proposed analysis. Here the needs of academic research conflict with financial stringency.

However, where large groups of well-stratified finds have been meticulously recorded and carefully stored, they remain available for scholars working in the future, when funds may (we hope) be more plentiful and when the emphasis of research priorities may have shifted.

Soil micromorphology

One of the most intractable problems in site interpretation is that of understanding the origins and formation of the extensive deposits known as 'buried soils' or 'dark earth', the latter characteristically found lying between the Roman and early medieval phases of urban sites. They are often said to be 'dumps' or 'soil accumulations' and their interpretation is based on analysis of artefacts or ecofacts contained within the soil, rather than the soil structure itself. Sometimes 'dark earth' deposits have been interpreted as natural soils and therefore evidence for prolonged periods of settlement abandonment. Recent work on Roman Worcester has shown that the Roman town was, in the areas excavated, founded on an earlier, Iron Age, agricultural soil, and that the late Roman 'dark earth' resulted from the penning of stock and the dumping of silty soil, perhaps from the nearby river Severn. These deposits were eventually reworked by earthworms to produce a grassland soil, which was then sealed by the clay, earth and turf rampart that formed part of the defences of the late Saxon burh (Dalwood in Steane 1992). Clearly, micromorphology provides a firmer basis than inspired guesswork for the interpretation of these hitherto enigmatic soils. The range of current applications will be found in Courty *et al.* (1989).

11

Scientific Aids

Compared with the situation as it was only fifteen years ago, the amount of information which can be added to and deduced from excavated evidence by scientific means is enormous and increases annually. It is instructive to compare the descriptions of techniques in Brothwell and Higgs (1969) and in Sherratt (ed., 1980, 416–32) and Clarke (1990).

One of the most important advances is in the development of dating techniques. These include radiocarbon dating, which is based on the assumption that on the death of a living organism, whether animal or vegetable, carbon 14 atoms present in the organism decay at a measurable rate (Brothwell and Higgs 1969, 46ff.). While the early theories postulated by Libby in the years immediately following the Second World War have undergone modification, particularly in methods of calibration, and while tree-ring analysis of the same samples has achieved greater precision leading to the recalibration of earlier determinations, the method remains of supreme importance for the dating of organic material (Sherratt (ed.) 1980, 417; Stuiver and Pearson (1986) and Pearson and Stuiver (1986)). Another important, though less widely applicable technique, is that of thermoremanent magnetism, in which the directions of the magnetic fields induced in hearths, ovens, kilns and the like while they are being fired are compared with the earth's magnetic field at the present day (Brothwell and Higgs (1969) 76ff.). Though the method is still being developed it provides dating evidence from material not susceptible to other forms of analysis. Thermoluminescence, in which pottery is heated until visible measurable light is emitted by released electrons, is a method of dating the pottery, since for reasons explained in Brothwell and Higgs (1969, 106ff.), the greater the age of the pot, the greater the thermoluminescence. Though at present the method is liable to errors of up to ± 10–15 per cent it is a most important technique, offering for the first time a method of pottery dating independent of stylistic or typological criteria. Other scientific dating methods include the dating of obsidian artefacts based on the fact that the surface of obsidian absorbs water from its surroundings at a known rate from the moment it is chipped or flaked until the present day (Brothwell and Higgs (1969) 62ff.) and the determination of relative dating by means of the fluorine, nitrogen and uranium contents of ancient bones (Brothwell and Higgs (1969) 35ff.). These techniques are independent of the usual stylistic or typological criteria, the studies of which were tending to become bogged down due, very often, to lack of independent dating so that there had been a tendency for circular arguments to develop between excavators and finds specialists.

In the environmental field, examination of

the contents of pits, ditches, wells, cess-pits and other deposits in which organic materials are preserved has revolutionized the understanding of the ecology of our sites and their environs. The study of animal bones on a much increased scale is beginning to build up more reliable pictures of the development of domestication and of food habits, while more sophisticated examination of human bones is shedding light not only on the incidence of diseases, but on the relationships of blood groups among populations, information which, if extended, may help towards solving many problems of invasion, diffusion, immigration and integration. In addition, analysis of metals, pottery clays with their inclusions, glazes and other manufacturing materials throws light, often unexpected, on methods of manufacture and on patterns of trade.

Two indispensable conspectuses of archaeologically orientated scientific techniques will be found in Brothwell and Higgs (1969) and Sherratt (ed. 1980). To these must be added the Council for British Archaeology's *Handbook of Scientific Aids and Evidence for Archaeologists* (1970). This is a handlist in loose leaf form which deals with 'artefacts and other material providing evidence' together with 'instrumental techniques (analytical, dating and geophysical)' and which contains bibliographical references for each technique. Recent work and technical advances are described in the journal *Archaeometry* and the *Journal of Archaeological Science*. To these should be added more specialized text-books such as Dimbleby (1967), Fleming (1976) and Clark (1990).

Since these publications are readily accessible there is no need to repeat here the information given in them, but rather to urge that they, and the other more specialized text-books referred to, be studied by all directors of excavations.

There are two chief problems in the use of scientific aids. One is the necessity for the excavators to comprehend the processes involved, some of which are highly technical. Unless they understand at least the basic theory behind each process it will be impossible for them to use the results with the necessary degrees of caution and flexibility, or even to discuss the method intelligently with the scientist concerned. It is certainly not enough to accept a bare statement about the origin of pottery inclusions, or a thermo-luminescent date, and use it blindly in a report. Even if we are not capable of carrying out the techniques involved ourselves, we must appreciate their possibilities and limitations or we are likely to compound errors of all kinds. There is no doubt that the present-day excavation director is required to have an increasingly wide understanding of disciplines ranging from nuclear physics to the history of painting. He or she cannot simply be a technician who digs competently, takes samples, and then receives a mass of information from a battery of experts which has to be welded into a conglomerate of unrelated facts embedded in archaeological jargon.

The other problem facing the excavator who seeks scientific help is the cost of such help and, more particularly, the comparative rarity of scientists able and willing to provide *ad hoc* services. State-financed excavations are in the strongest position, being serviced by the Inspectorate of Ancient Monuments Laboratory which can arrange for a great variety of scientific help. In addition, some of the major units have their own, environmental and scientific staff.

For the director of non-State-aided excavations scientific help may be difficult to obtain, often being dependent on local personnel and facilities in museums and universities. The larger museums may have at their disposal a comprehensive range of techniques, others will be only able to offer a minimal service with access to other facilities in urgent and important cases. Universities offer a wide but variable range of scientific aids to the excavations which they run or with which they are associated. It is, at the moment, largely up to the directors to arrange what facilities they can within the comparatively restricted network of specialists, an unsatisfactory situation, but one unlikely to be improved in the immediate future. As a result, many excavations suffer from a partial or total lack of scientific and specialist help and so the full potential of the excavated evidence is not realized. The battery of scientific information potentially available to the excavator is formidable, but, if it is to be fully exploited, requires greater understanding of and sympathy with scientific method than has often been the case in the past.

Relationships between excavators and scientific specialists have often been bedevilled by difficulties arising from the lack of mutual understanding of each other's problems, and from the essentially part-time nature of much scientific involvement in archaeology. The problems have been succinctly described by Mrs D.S. Wilson in an open letter to archaeologists (Wilson 1973) which incorporates many valuable suggestions to archaeologists on the ways in which scientists should be treated. Equally, scientists who are anxious to make the fullest contribution to an excavation should learn the scope and limitations of the techniques involved, ideally by taking part themselves. It is far more satisfactory if scientists can take their own samples, rather than receive them in a laboratory, even if they are accompanied by drawings and photographs of their contexts. The more understanding each has of the other's techniques, problems, and limitations, the greater will be the value of the joint work which they will be able to produce.

The use of scientific evidence

Excavators have tended either to seize on pieces of scientific evidence and give them undue weight in the support of their theories, or to relegate them to appendices, printed in the report beyond the acknowledgements, as if they bore little relevance to what was dug up. Pressure from the more forward looking archaeologists and from scientists themselves, who see the potential of the information they can extract, has now made it *de rigeur* to send samples of all kinds for analysis, often without great thought of the relevance of the information which is likely to come from them. For, instance, identification of a scatter of charcoal samples from the occupation layers of a medieval site is unlikely to add much to our knowledge of the aboreal flora of medieval Britain, and will only give a broad and diffuse picture of the trees growing in the vicinity and used for firewood. The information from these scraps of charcoal is, in most circumstances, not worth the considerable labour involved in identifying them. A large quantity of charcoal, clearly part of the structure of a burnt building, will be of more interest, especially if it can be shown that the sample comes from floor planking or weather-boarding, since the types of wood used for subsidiary structural elements are not well known.

The identification and analysis of a scatter of unstratified or poorly stratified mollusc shells, animal bones, mortar fragments or lumps of slag may simply not be worth the time it will undoubtedly take. Under these circumstances it is wise to ask the specialist to assess the probable importance of the material in the context of the excavation, rather than to collect it and send it, regardless, for analysis.

This necessitates the specialist visiting the site, or being kept fully informed about the nature of the excavation and the contexts of any samples. This in itself would be a step forward from the situation in which the samples land on his or her desk. Only if the scientist, whether an environmentalist, a soil scientist, or an expert in mortars, slags, window glass or other materials, can discuss on the site the problems raised by the samples can he or she expect to give a full appraisal of their significance rather than a mere identification and tentative interpretation. This is asking a lot. Since there are many excavations, all bristling with problems spanning the whole spectrum of scientific expertise, and few archaeological scientists, it is imperative that excavators help scientists to give the most effective service by prior consultation and by pruning requests for identification and analysis to those subjects and samples which are most relevant to the excavation, or the regional archaeology of the region, or which the scientists want as comparative material.

It may be argued that an accumulation of small samples of apparently irrelevant material might eventually be synthesized in the manner of a large sample, but this is a decision to be made by the specialist in the discipline concerned. It is always possible, too, that a small sample may provide unequivocal evidence of something quite unexpected, the bones of an exotic animal,* a vital fragment of a wall-painting or proof of an otherwise undetectable industrial process. But, in general, it is the large well-stratified samples that are likely to be the most useful, and to yield the best results.

If scientific reports on excavated material are to be comparable with one another it is important that the same criteria are used in the assessment and measurement of the samples. This again, is ultimately a matter

* Such as the phalange of a Barbary ape found in the excavation of the baths basilica at Wroxeter.

for the specialists concerned, but archaeologists should be aware of the problems, and should perhaps initiate discussions aimed at solving them.

Excavators are as prone to simplifying scientific evidence as historians are to simplifying archaeological evidence. A prime example is in the use of radiocarbon dates, where too often the central date of what is, in fact, a bell curve stretching over maybe two centuries, is taken as the most probable date for the sample, and a historical argument built on this assumption. There is no doubt that a long series of determinations can be the basis for revolutionary reassessments of conventional dating (see Renfrew (ed.) 1974) but a single radiocarbon date is beset by too many uncertainties to justify its use as more than a suggestion of the range within which the true date falls (see Mackie *et al.* 1971). If the central radiocarbon date happens to coincide with the excavator's nascent theories, it is tempting not to point out in the report that the real date might be far from the central one.

Many other scientific dating techniques such as thermoluminescence and remanent magnetism share the same lack of precision, and they should not be made to carry a greater weight of argument than they can bear. Dendrochronology can, under optimum conditions, give a fairly precise date for the felling of a tree for timber. But it would be unwise to date a whole building on the evidence of one of its beams, which may have been reused from an earlier building. Here again, the larger the number of samples the more reliable the conclusions which can be drawn from them.

The arts and sciences which converge in an excavation are all imprecise in varying degrees. The wider the areas from which we draw our evidence, the more detailed our digging and recording, the more samples we take, the more techniques we deploy, the nearer we shall get to the truth about the site in the periods which concern us.

Excavation and the environment

In the past the study of the evironment relating to archaeological sites has often been peripheral to the excavation of structures, the recovery of a dating sequence or a series of pottery types. In many cases the environment in which the site developed was completely ignored. These attitudes are now changing and with techniques for recovering and interpreting environmental evidence being rapidly developed and multiplied, ancient environments are seen to be crucial for the full understanding of the siting, the food economy, the exploitation of the surrounding countryside and in some cases the uses to which the site has been put.

Most excavated sites contain a wealth of biological evidence which, properly interpreted, can add another dimension to the understanding of the site and its region by producing otherwise unobtainable information about the contemporary flora and fauna, pests, diseases, climate and weather. Seeds, mollusca, insects and the elusive bones of the smaller mammals, birds and fishes are not so easily recovered as potsherds and food bones, but techniques of sieving, both wet and dry, can produce significant quantities of material from the majority of sites. The extraction of pollen is a more specialized technique which supplements the information given by seeds and other preserved plant remains.

A number of wet-sieving and froth flotation methods for the recovery of organic remains have been developed recently. Some are quite simple; others, for use on large-scale excavations, are designed for the continual processing of large quantities of soil. The simplest method is the use of sieves of various meshes through which the soil, made into slurry, is passed. An even more basic method of recovering the larger fragments is to agitate a sieve full of the deposit in a barrow filled with water. Various more sophisticated mechanical flotation and sieving machines have been developed. Their chief attribute is cheapness achieved by the ingenious use of scrap machinery. A number of plans have been published, among them the machine used by David Williams at Siraf (Williams 1973), a mechanical sieve developed in Italy (Guerreschi 1973) and the machine developed by the Marc 3 Unit in Hampshire (Lapinskas 1975). To these must be added the Ankara and Cambridge machines described in Renfrew, Monk and Murphy (1976).

Some environmentalists believe that flotation machines should be used with reservation since they are apt to distort the sample due to some of the specimens floating while others of the same species do not. Tiny snail shells full of silt, for example, may sink, while those that happen to be empty float. There is a case for recovering the complete evidence from some large samples of the material by washing and sieving everything, including the sediments in which the organic remains are embedded. Only in this way will control samples be recovered, samples which will monitor the recovery rate from the flotation of very large quantities of deposits.

As in all other sampling techniques the larger and more representative the samples the more valid the results are likely to be. If possible, the samples should be taken by the specialist himself. They should not simply be derived from the pits, ditches, floors or other structures in which we are particularly interested but from a wide variety of contexts (if not the whole site), in order to provide controls and comparanda.

The nature of the soil, as well as its degree of waterlogging will affect the survival of bones, seeds or pollen. Any assessment of evironmental evidence must take this into account, and the specialist consulted will do so, no doubt, but it is important that the precise nature of the soil and the conditions under which samples were taken should be made clear so that valid comparisons can be made with other sites.

The analysis of preserved organic materials, of pollen, seeds, insects, snails and the microscopic remains of plants has implications which are only just beginning to be realized. As an example, work on the silt from a Roman sewer system in York has provided a spectacular demonstration of the information to be inferred from microscopic remains. The presence of sewerage flies, human intestinal parasites and sponge spicules (derived from toilet sponges imported from the Mediterranean) in some of the channels contrasted with entirely different assemblages from other channels. One of the other systems contained grain beetles and grain weevils, derived in all probability from a grain storage building, while another series contained mollusca, water beetles, pollen and other evidence which suggests that it drained a closed, artificially-heated baths building. Thus the presence of long destroyed buildings can be postulated on the microscopic evidence alone (Buckland 1974).

Recent work on past climates has shown that there is now sufficient evidence from glaciology, evironmental archaeology and historical records to justify postulating climatic reasons for some of the major changes in agriculture and population movements over the last 10–15,000 years (Lamb 1972, esp. 170–95). For example, the well-attested increase in ploughland in the twelfth–thirteenth centuries AD with its corresponding increase in population and the expansion and creation of villages and towns, followed by the contraction of the fourteenth and fifteenth centuries, can be attributed, at least

in part, to slight but significant shifts in the levels of temperature and rainfall. An earlier and more dramatic dissimilarity from our present climate is well attested in the Bronze Age between the sixth millennium BC, and the third millennium BC, when average land temperatures were 2°–3°C higher than today's figures' and the sea was 2°C warmer. As a result oak, elm and lime trees were growing in Britain up to 300m (1000ft) higher than the present limit. (The drop in the average temperature is about 3°C per 300m (1000ft) of height.) Clearly such considerations are vital in the interpretation of our excavated sites and the understanding of their economy, the character of housing and the recreation of life on and around the site.

The changes in the flora and particularly in woodland species may record the clearance of forest and the expansion of agriculture, changes which may be reflected in the composition of the buried soils of the site. Such changes may be paralleled and supported by an increase in domesticated animal bones, a corresponding decrease in the bones of wild species and the first appearance of querns on the site. Conversely, an increase in woodland or scrub species in the pollen spectrum may indicate a reversion to forest, paralleling shrinkage or temporary abandonment of the settlement.

An introduction to pollen analysis will be found in Brothwell and Higgs (1969, Chapter 14) and RESCUE has published a booklet *First Aid for Seeds* (Renfrew, Monk and Murphy 1976) which concisely describes the preservation of seeds in archaeological deposits, sampling, flotation and the storage for specialist analysis. It is essential reading for excavators.

Analysis of the animal bones from a site will, of course, give information about the meat eaten by the inhabitants, but it may go further and throw an unexpected light on the marketing of the meat, and also, by implication, the comparative poverty of the consumers. For instance, if all the meat bones are from butcher's joints it is probable that the animals were slaughtered elsewhere as is the practice today; but if the remains include horns, skulls, hooves and so on, the animals probably came into the settlement or town 'on the hoof'. Sometimes a change in the practice can be observed. For example, the meat sold in the centre of a Roman town in its heyday may all be butchered, with the horns going elsewhere in the town to be made into handles, the hooves to be made into glue, the hides into leather and so forth. Later, in the town's decline, contracted and with a changed economy, live animals may well be sold, perhaps bartered, in the market. The poorer a community, the more it will exploit every scrap of the animal, just as in more recent times, no part of the family pig was wasted, and the evidence will appear in the rubbish pits. Sometimes variations of the animal contents of rubbish pits within communities can point to differing social strata. On the site of the Blackfriars in Worcester three pits, all datable by pottery to the period 1480–1560, showed marked variations in their bone content, one of them containing bones from older animals, whose meat would be tougher and less palatable, together with less variety of species. Though the deductions cannot be certain, the implications are that the households using this pit were poorer or had, at least, less attractive meat, than the families using the other two pits (Chaplin in Barker *et al.* 1970). Such analysis and reasoning can of course be extended into much wider fields.

The character of animal diseases detectable in surviving bone is also of great interest, though here again, the more samples which can be examined from the region the sounder will be the conclusions drawn from them – one could not reasonably postulate a disastrous murrain from two individuals.

In a long and well-stratified sample the introduction of new strains of animals may be detected. Does this reflect an immigrant community, or simply good husbandry? Here, other varieties of evidence would have to be brought to bear. If the introduction of the new variety coincided with the introduction of a new type of pottery the case for immigrants would be strengthened, and so on. Clearly once again, the larger and more carefully dug and recorded the sample, the more valid and illuminating will be the deductions which can be drawn from it.

Many of these scientific disciplines are still in the data-collecting stages, since it is only recently that their potential has been realized by archaeologists. It is incumbent on those of us who dig to help develop and refine these techniques through the closest possible co-operation with their practitioners.

The study of building materials

Many archaeological sites, particularly, though not exclusively, in towns, consist of, or contain, large areas of hard core foundations, pebble surfaces, rubble spreads, clay floors, post-sockets and other remnants of former structures. The study of these layers and features from the structural point of view is an unexploited source of information supplementing that obtained from the study of the soils formed naturally in and around the site. For example, it may be very difficult to determine the length of time that a pebble floor was in use, especially in aceramic periods. Exhaustive tests on the wearing capacity of surfaces of all kinds made in the course of research into road construction may enable close estimates to be made of the length of time taken to wear facets on pebbles of varying hardness. Equally, long term experiments on the wear of paving stones, stone stair treads and thresholds make close estimates of wear time on these features available. While there will always, in archaeological terms, be imponderables, such as the estimated number of persons using a surface per day, any experimentally proven figures are better than guess-work as a basis for argument. (For a discussion of this problem at Wroxeter, see Barker *et al.* forthcoming, 1994.) Similarly an analysis of the load-bearing capacity of the various surfaces assumed to be foundations may avoid interpretations which are impractical or even ludicrous.

On the other hand a half-metre thick layer of make-up on one of the sites at Wroxeter was shown by the materials engineer who was consulted to have been laid wet, as slurry rather like pre-mixed concrete. In this form, once it had dried, its load-bearing capacity would be considerably increased, so that it can be assumed that it was laid as a deliberate foundation for the timber structure subsequently built on it, and not as an accumulation of soil and debris fortuitously used (Barker *et al.* forthcoming, 1994).

When a post or sill-beam supporting a building rests on the ground, the area under and round the timber becomes permanently compacted. This compaction can be measured by simple methods dependent upon the differential penetration of the surface by a probe. In this way the existence of former buildings may be demonstrated (*ibid.*).

Another example of the sort of information which may be sought from the study of the behaviour of materials is one from the same excavation at Wroxeter, where a large fragment of masonry, apparently part of a window embrasure, had fallen from one of the walls of the baths basilica, apparently that of the clerestory, and embedded itself in a sequence of sandy and pebble floors. By measuring the degree of compaction at a number of points under and around the

fallen masonry, and then by weighing the fragment, it is hoped to be able to calculate the height from which it fell. As it is part of a window this should give the approximate height of the clerestory windows above the ground.

Though the information supplied by the study of the materials used on our sites may not always be very precise, this approach, coupled with that of the natural soil scientist (exemplified in Limbrey 1975), should add considerably to our understanding of their stratigraphic development and the intentions of past builders.

GIS and archaeology

Richard Selby of Remote Sensing Services has kindly supplied the following note:

Geographical Information Systems, commonly and collectively referred to as GIS, provide a computer-based means of capturing, manipulating and displaying information that has a spatial content. GIS can play two major roles within archaeology. The first involves assisting in the location of sites of interest and the second concerns the recording and visualization of the site in digital form once it has been excavated. The use of GIS in the search for archaeological sites has been well documented for a relatively new technology (Allen K.M.S. *et al.*, 1990). GIS can aid in site location by combining data layers that each in some way help determine a site's location. These data layers can themselves be interrogated and modified in such a way that their entry into the model combining the data layers enhances its value. It is also important that the model is iteratively developed in order to claim the best advantage from those available data layers.

GIS have become an important technology because they attach non-geographical

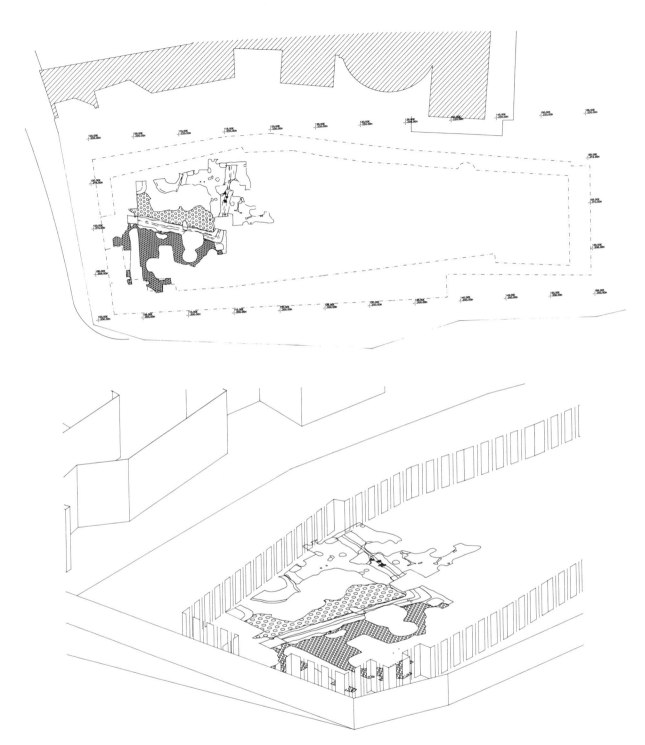

82a and b These are two plots from AUTOCAD drawings of part of the Deansway, Worcester, excavations of 1988–90.

a shows a conventional site plan of a Roman ditch and adjacent pebble surfaces.

b is an isometric view of the same surfaces but the plan has been tilted and rotated using standard AUTOCAD routines. This, by combining plans and elevations, gives a three-dimensional view of the excavation and its surroundings, enabling it to be more easily visualized. (Illustrations by courtesy of Laura Templeton and Hereford and Worcester County Council Archaeology Section.)

information to geographic locations. These geographic data can then be manipulated on the basis of this additional or attribute information. Data layers can therefore be built up for an area that define archaeological regions of interest rather than physical ones. It is the combination of the data layers describing physical information (land slope, height, etc) and archaeological information that makes GIS work for archaeologist. The ability to enter satellite scenes or aerial photographs into a GIS as a data layer can be a great advantage providing detailed and *current* land-use information. Areas identified through results of GIS analysis as being potential archaeological sites can be found easily on the ground because GIS will describe their position in a user-defined co-ordinate system. Valuable use can also be made of handheld Global Positioning Systems (GPSs) that describe your position in real time expressed in degrees of latitude and longitude – these are extremely useful where maps are old or non-existent for a region of interest. Well known and widespread GISs that can incorporate satellite data include ERDAS, Intergraph and Arc/Info.

More specialist systems found within the GIS family can be used to great effect for the logging and visualization of artefacts and structures found within an excavation site. These products are known as Computer Aided Design or CAD instruments.

As with GIS, CAD systems attach non-geographical information to geographic co-ordinates such as those describing an object found within a site and its position within the site as a whole. CAD systems are better adept at visualizing elements in three dimensions and from various viewpoints than their GIS relatives. However, they lack some of the latter system's broad-scale analysis and modelling features. CAD products can therefore be used to recreate the site in three dimensions once it has been excavated and recorded. Once objects found within a site have been logged into a CAD system additional measurements can be made that were not made at the time of the excavation; a valuable aid when on-site time is limited. The most widespread CAD system in use is known as AUTOCAD (Fig. 82a–b).

GIS is currently the most active development area in the Information Technology arena and so one can be assured that as it continues to advance, archaeologists will find new ways of adapting it to their needs.

12

Synthesis: the History of the Site

The ultimate aim of an excavation is to draw together the very varied strands of evidence into a coherent whole: the sequence of natural and structural events which has taken place on the site from the earliest occupation (or before) up to the present day. To this structural framework is added all the converging cultural, economic, domestic and environmental evidence which can be detected and assessed.

It has been suggested in Chapter 5 that the truth about the site may be more closely approached if we attempt to identify and explain the origin of every observable feature. In doing so we impose on ourselves a discipline that prevents us from ignoring awkward or inconvenient features. Similarly the use of a formal matrix or graph, such as that described on pp. 229–37, compels us to consider the relative positions of all layers and features and not simply to take a broad view of the more important or extensive.

Another exercise, which helps to clarify thinking at the later, synthetic stage of the excavation, is to take at random, or at 50- to 100-year intervals, a number of dates which fall within the known period of occupation of the site and to write descriptions or, better, make sketches of the whole site at those times. This ensures that every part of the site will be considered as part of the continuum of occupation and not just those structures which can be given relatively firm dates. There will, inevitably, be a good deal of uncertainty about the nature of the open spaces round buildings, and more particularly, the survival of old buildings when new ones are erected. Usually we tend to simplify and rationalize the periods of occupation of our sites, partly because it is easier to describe and particularly to illustrate these periods as a series of complete rebuildings across the site. However, as an almost cursory glance at a group of farm buildings, a small village or an area in a town centre, will show, the situation is in reality kaleidoscopic, with single buildings being replaced while older buildings on each side remain, and with the infilling of gardens or vacant plots, the demolition of old buildings and their sites left open, to say nothing of repairs and extensions, such as kitchens or garages, to existing buildings, and more ephemeral structures, like garden sheds, coming and going at even shorter intervals.

Such a kaleidoscopic, one might almost say contrapuntal, interpretation of an excavation is not easy to achieve, mainly due to the limitations of our ability to date precisely the building and demolition of structures. Another major cause of difficulty in phasing is the impossibility of demonstrating horizontal relationships unambiguously across the site. For example it may be possible to say that Buildings 4 and 5 are earlier than 3 and demonstrate this by means of a feature matrix, but it may not be possible to demonstrate the chronological relationship of 4 and 5 to each other, if they have no common horizontal stratigraphy beyond their mutual relationship to 3. Under these circumstances, alternative phase diagrams and plans would be necessary. However, if the site contains dozens of buildings, the permutations and combinations, all possible but none demonstrable, might be endless, and difficult to describe and illustrate without an unwieldy proliferation of phases and sub-phases. This detailed illustration would not only be tedious and potentially confusing, but also exceedingly costly. Yet what is the alternative? Certainly not simplification in the name of tidiness or economy. If we are to approach a true description of the site (and this must be the first aim of any excavation) we must interpret and present the evidence as fully as we can, even if this means the loss of a strong story line such as the celebrated narrative introduction to the Maiden Castle report (Wheeler 1943).

Archaeological evidence and historical documents

The relationship between archaeology and documented history has been the subject of a good deal of heart-searching in recent years. Perhaps the two most thoughtful and cogent discussions of the subject are Wainwright's (1962) and Dymonds's (1974). There is no room here to summarize their arguments and the reader is referred to the books as a whole.

The establishment of the relationships between the archaeological evidence from an excavated site and historical documents relating to that site is full of pitfalls and must be approached with caution. It is only too easy to equate drastic changes in the archaeological evidence, such as rebuildings

after burning, or abandonment of the site, with well-documented historical incidents. However, not every fire in south-eastern Britain in the mid-first century was due to Boudica nor every fourteenth-century village abandonment to the Black Death. On many sites, it would be very difficult indeed to detect the date and impact of the Norman Conquest. Building techniques, house styles and pottery types remain the same, or change progressively throughout the period. Perhaps only on defensive sites such as Sulgrave (Davison 1969) where a ring-work is imposed on an apparently undefended domestic complex, could a sudden and radical political change be postulated, though the cumulative evidence from fieldwork and excavation of castles would undoubtedly point to a new intensity in fortification and a change in military structures. However, as Davison has pointed out, it cannot be shown that the new types of fortification (motte and bailey castles) were introduced from elsewhere, so that on purely archaeological grounds one could postulate an English conquest of Normandy (or a conquest of England and Normandy by a third party) (see Higham and Barker 1992)

Perhaps the most thoroughly integrated study of a settlement by excavation and by examination of the documentary sources is that of Store Valby (Steensberg 1975) where a mass of evidence relating not only to the excavated farms, their buildings and their furniture has been adduced, but where, by a close study of the registers of births, marriages and deaths, ownership, tenancies and the relationships and social standing of generations of farmers have been correlated with the buildings they lived in and worked from. In this case, as in that of so many deserted village sites, the archaeological evidence was often tenuous and ambiguous, and here the documentary descriptions of the farms at various periods illuminated the fieldwork and enabled more well-founded interpretations to be made than could have emerged with either form of evidence alone. The weakness of the excavation, as the author admits, was the paucity of environmental evidence and the summary treatment of the animal bones, of which there were insufficient for a full statistical analysis. The work remains a model of its kind, however, as yet unequalled by any British excavation.

A model interpretation

Another most illuminating interpretive study of a settlement site is that of the Glastonbury Lake Village by D.L. Clarke (1972). In this reconsideration of Bulleid and Gray's excavations carried out between 1892 and 1907 (published 1911 and 1917) the objective was 'simply to explore the old data in new ways' (*ibid*. 802). The method used was 'the erection of a set of alternative models, explicitly justified and derived from many sources, embodying alternative reasonable assumptions and then the explicit testing between the alternatives of their consequences for predictive accuracy and goodness of fit, by using skilfully devised experiments in the field or upon the recorded observations' (*ibid*. 801).

It is significant that the excavation chosen by Clarke is not only one of the few of a complete settlement available, but that in addition, being waterlogged, the retrieval of organic material and objects was very high, supplementing by many whole factors the information which would have been achieved if the site had been dry. The same study carried out on a partial excavation of a much eroded or otherwise damaged site would have started with so much less information that the potential results would have been a good deal less trustworthy. As Clarke himself said: 'No archaeological study can

be any better than the reliability of the observations upon which it is based and the assumptions that frame the development of its analysis and interpretation.' To my mind, the reliability of evidence from settlement sites depends on the quantity and the size of the sample as well as on the accuracy of the observations made on the spot.

Another distinct advantage that the Glastonbury site has for analysis and study of this kind is that the settlement was a multiple of structures which were repeatedly reproduced. There were none of the more or less violent changes of occupation and use which characterize many sites or parts of sites.

On the one hand, we have the type of site which, by reason of the comparative homogeneity of its development, allows the stages of that development to be more easily compared one with another, and its relationships with its economic and cultural territory to be more confidently predicted. Such sites include some deserted medieval villages (Wharram Percy will, eventually, no doubt, provide a classic example for the Glastonbury type of analysis); extensively excavated Saxon settlement sites, such as Chalton (Addyman, Leigh and Hughes 1972) and Mucking (Jones 1974), and prehistoric sites such as hillforts where one of the most pressing problems is the relationship of defended settlements to their contemporary valley counterparts. In a slightly varied way cemeteries excavated on a large scale also lend themselves to statistical analysis and model building.

On the other hand, towns, whether Roman or later, are more difficult, because of the multiplicity of structural types, the constant destruction of earlier deposits by later building and the consequent losses of artefacts as well as structural evidence. One notable exception is the Russian town of Novgorod, constructed entirely of timber, the earliest phases of which have been preserved by waterlogging, together with an extraordinary assemblage of finds.

Clarkes's Glastonbury paper, which is more concerned with the direct results of excavations than many of the other applications of analytical archaeology, is essential reading for would-be directors.

The convergence of varying kinds of evidence: an example

This example, again taken from the motte and bailey castle site at Hen Domen, Montgomery, demonstrates in a microcosm how a number of different techniques can be made to converge on one problem, each, in its own way, reinforcing the others.

It had been noticed that the outer ditches and ramparts of the castle bailey apparently overlay (and were therefore later than) slight traces of ridge and furrow in the field north of the site (A on Fig. 16a). Since even relatively datable early ridge and furrow is rare, especially on the Welsh border, the possibility that this field system was pre-Norman was of great interest. When trowelling of a small area under the rampart revealed a buried soil which itself covered plough furrows cut into the undisturbed boulder clay, it was decided to contour survey the adjacent field and to examine the evidence buried under the rampart. At the same time, the documentary evidence was re-examined.

The various techniques used are here listed for convenience:

Fieldwork: the field adjacent to the site was photographed in various lights, including car headlights, in order to observe the slight undulations of the ground in the greatest detail. It was then contour surveyed on a grid with 1m intervals and the contours were drawn at 20cm vertical intervals. The visible ridges and furrows were plotted by interpolation.

Computer print-out: the grid of readings was fed into a computer which was programmed to draw the resulting contours in a three-dimensional print-out. This was more objective than drawing by eye, and necessary because there was some scepticism about the existence of the field system.

Excavation: a 20m length of the rampart was trowelled down to the buried soil and its surface contour surveyed at 2cm vertical intervals. This demonstrated the existence of ridge and furrow buried under the rampart. The buried soil was removed and the visible plough furrows plotted. Amorphous holes dug through the buried soil and into the underlying subsoil were interpreted as places where bushes or small trees had been removed before the construction of the rampart.

Pollen analysis: samples of the soil buried under the rampart were sent for pollen analysis. The botanist concerned was not told at the time the implications of what he might find. As a result of the analysis he deduced that the pollen indicated that the area in which the rampart was built was open land, which had been used for arable agriculture, perhaps for cereals. The abandonment had been of several years' duration and the area had perhaps been used for rough grazing.

Radiocarbon dating: a sample of charcoal from the buried soil was dated by the laboratory at Birmingham to AD 980 $\pm$ 290 (uncalibrated).

Finds: the only find from the buried soil was a fragment of Roman pottery carved into an amulet(?) and incised with what appears to be a letter A. As pottery was virtually unknown on the Welsh border between

253

c. AD 400 and *c.* AD 1100, the Roman sherd would have been an object of considerable curiosity, worthy, in an aceramic period, of being carved into an amulet.

Documentary evidence: Domesday Book (fol. 254, a, 1) is explicit that Roger, Earl of Shrewsbury, built a castle, which he called Montgomery, in an area of waste which had formerly contained 22 vills but which, in the time of Edward the Confessor, had been a hunting ground for three Saxon thegns. Roger was made Earl of Shrewsbury in 1070 or 1071 so that the castle (which can be shown to be Hen Domen) was built then or shortly afterwards.

It will be seen that any one or two facets of this evidence, taken independently, would be suggestive but not conclusive, whereas together they provide incontrovertible proof of a ridged field system, probably belonging to a Saxon vill, and abandoned before the Norman Conquest. The evidence is published in full in Barker and Lawson (1971).

The more varied the forms of evidence which can be adduced in our investigations the richer and more unequivocal will be the results. There is now an enormous variety of aids at our disposal. By understanding their potential through discussion with the specialists who use them and by prior planning we must learn to deploy these techniques to the greatest advantage.

A much more intensive, and perhaps the best, example of integrated landscape archaeology is C.C. Taylor's study of Whiteparish in Wiltshire (Taylor 1967), which the reader is urged to study. Another excellent example is Austin, Gerard and Greeves (1989).

All excavations are local history

However widespread the ramifications of an excavation may ultimately prove to be,

initially it is a piece of local history, embedded in the immediate landscape, and relating to the area around it. Even sites of the remoter prehistoric periods were settled by men influenced by at least some, and perhaps many, of the factors which influenced Anglo-Saxon farmers and medieval traders. The gulf which separates so many local historians from archaeologists (and archaeologists from local historians) is regrettable and unhelpful to both. The undocumented and the documented history of a parish or a district must be seen as a continuum from geological times to the present, and though we may be interested in one period more than others, we shall stultify our work if we do not see it in the broadest context. The excavator has therefore to see the site from two points of view, one vertically though time as part of the development of settlement, agriculture, industry, religion or architecture – the cultural pattern of the area; and the other horizontally through space, when the site is seen as one of a contemporary group or series of related groups, which may cover the whole of a continent. The legionary fortresses at Gloucester or Lincoln are facets of the local histories of those cities – they are also examples of a type of fortification which once covered most of the known world. These are obvious examples, and the excavators of these cities see their fortresses in both contexts. But how many pagan Saxon cemeteries or open Iron Age settlements are related by their excavators to the siting of the nearby medieval village or its Saxon predecessor, or the expansion and contraction of settlement in the periods before and after those being dug?

Another element of landscape study often neglected by archaeologists is the geographical development of the area, whether natural or influenced by man. For example, the rise or fall of the water table due to deforestation or afforestation, to a programme of land drainage or the development of bog may be crucial in the siting of villages with their wells and springs, or in the pattern or character of their agriculture. Similarly, the study of the courses of rivers and streams may be of the utmost importance to the archaeologist. Until comparatively recently, the Roman city of Wroxeter was thought to have lost as much as a quarter of its area through erosion by the river Severn. A geographer, David Pannett, working independently of archaeology, has shown that the river has hardly changed its course in the last 5000 years, so that the remains of the city are intact. Recent excavation on the eastern defences overlooking the river strongly supports this view, which has revolutionary implications for the siting of the legionary fortresses which underlie the civil settlement, for the siting of the Roman river crossing, the ultimate size of the city, and many other problems.

There is little doubt that consultation with local historians and geographers could add yet another dimension to the understanding of an excavation.

Works of art as archaeological evidence

From the sculpture and cave-paintings of palaeolithic times onwards, works of art can be of great assistance in the interpretation of contemporary archaeological evidence. There is little need to stress the value of Egyptian tomb-painting, Greek sculpture or Roman wall-painting in the understanding of the material remains of these civilizations. There are fewer survivals of art from very early times in north-western Europe, but medieval and later drawings and paintings of towns with their defences, individual buildings, markets, workshops, fields, animals and implements can all be helpful in the understanding of excavated remains, while

figure paintings and carvings, in particular those on tombs, can elucidate problems of dress ornament and detail.

The chief difficulty in the use of works of art as interpretative evidence is to determine whether or not the depiction is contemporary with the incident depicted, or makes use of traditional forms, or alternatively, whether the work sets a traditional scene in dress and surroundings contemporary with the artist. Many Anglo-Saxon illuminated manuscripts use architectural backgrounds which can be traced back to Byzantine or Roman models, so that it would be unwise to use them as evidence for Anglo-Saxon building styles. Conversely it was common practice for later painters from Masaccio onward to set Biblical scenes in their own landscapes, towns and buildings so that the soldiers guarding Christ's tomb in a painting by Mantegna are a better guide to fifteenth-century Italian uniform than to first-century Roman, and the dresses in a Nottingham alabaster, the altar vases shown in a fifteenth-century altarpiece or the farming practices in a book of hours or on a misericord are likely to be up-to-date rather than an attempt at historical reconstruction.

On the other hand, tomb effigies may be added much later than the burials of the persons they commemorate. The effigy in Shrewsbury Abbey of Roger de Montgomery, who died in 1094, is dressed in the armour of a thirteenth-century knight. If we did not know this from the external evidence of many other thirteenth-century carvings we might well take this sculpture as evidence of Roger's dress.

In the later Renaissance and in the seventeenth and eighteenth centuries painting became increasingly naturalistic, culminating in Canaletto's use of the *camera obscura*. As a result, the paintings and drawings of these centuries are a very rich source of

83 Giulio Campagnola (1485–c. 1515), *The Old Shepherd* (Ashmolean Museum, Oxford).

information on contemporary buildings, dress, furniture and pottery.

As an example Fig. 83 is a remarkable sixteenth-century engraving which seems to show a timber castle standing on a motte or natural mound surrounded by a ditch. If this is so, it is one of the few realistic contemporary representations of a timber castle. The Bayeux Tapestry castles straddle the dividing line between the descriptive and the decorative, while most other illustrations of castles, such as the magnificent series in *Les Tres Riches Heures du Duc de Berry*, are of stone buildings (see also, Higham and Barker 1992, Chapter 5, *The Pictorial Evidence*).

The engraving shows a somewhat ramshackle, perhaps roofed, bridge leading from a gate-tower over the ditch to a complex of buildings which includes a great hall (?); two towers (the second just appearing over the roof of the hall) and other roofed buildings, one with a louvred smoke outlet, perhaps surrounding an inner courtyard. The construction throughout is of vertical timbers which appear to have rotted characteristically at their lower ends. The buildings are of two storeys, with the upper storeys jettied. There is a suggestion of a postern towards the right-hand side of the nearest building and perhaps a garde-robe structure at the opposite end. The hall has two chimneys. On the extreme right is a complicated jettied structure apparently built out over a valley.

The question is, of course, how fanciful is this drawing, and how far can it be used as a guide in the interpretation of a timber castle excavation? On the one hand, the careful realism of the shepherd, dressed in contemporary clothes, inspires confidence in the castle's authenticity. On the other hand, some of the structural details are dubious and impractical. The impression given is that the castle is not imaginary or derived from a long line of other background drawings but is of a building known to the artist, though drawn, as buildings often are, without an understanding of structural principles, so that it does not stand up too well to architectural scrutiny. Nevertheless, since we have so little to guide us it should not be discarded altogether. The general layout, with its piling of buildings together on the mound, is borne out by surviving stone castles and the excavated evidence, so far as it goes, of timber castles. (For example, the bailey at Hen Domen was crowded with buildings, some of them of two storeys.)

Such a drawing may suggest solutions to otherwise intractable interpretive problems, though the dangers of arguing from one individual example to another are obvious, and it may be contended that a timber castle in Italy is minimally relevant to one in England or Wales. Used critically, however, contemporary illustrations can be another and otherwise unparalleled form of evidence, especially helpful in areas where the written evidence fails. A recent and most interesting example of the use of sculpture and painting in the interpretation of excavated evidence will be found in Schmidt 1973.

Experiments and reconstructions

The most valid, and sometimes the most dramatic, way of assessing our interpretative assumptions is to simulate the conditions which we believe produced the excavated evidence and to test the results against our observations. Such experiments can range from small-scale work on techniques of working metal to large-scale agricultural or house-construction projects. The subject has recently been dealt with at length by Coles (1973, revised edition 1979) so that there is no need to expand on it here. In addition, there is a new journal, the *Bulletin of*

Experimental Archaeology, whose first issue appeared in 1980, produced by the Department of Adult Education of the University of Southampton, which summarizes recent experimental research, together with details of where further information can be obtained.

It is worth adding, however, that intense observation of the effects of natural agencies on a site currently being excavated will often throw light on problems encountered only a short while before. This applies particularly to long-term excavations, where continuous monitoring of changes on the site due to exposure should be routine.

The scope for archaeological experiment is almost unlimited, though it is, at present, inadequately financed and receives little official encouragement, even though it promises to make more valid the results of excavations costing thousands of pounds.

The publication of the outlines of walls or the patterns of post-holes which appear to be the plans of buildings is the minimum duty of the excavator. But, so long as the observed evidence is kept firmly separated from the stages of interpretation, it can only be helpful and stimulating to the reader to discuss the form and construction of the buildings represented by the plans, and where feasible to illustrate the discussion with tentative elevations and sections. Such attempts are criticized by many archaeologists and architects with the argument that they tend to crystallize one out of the many possible reconstructions which might be based on the evidence as found in the ground. It is often difficult to deduce anything about the roof construction from the plan and therefore the 'reconstruction' becomes less reliable the further it rises above the ground. Nevertheless, the attempt should be made. The conscious effort to translate a pattern of timber-slots or post-holes or a fragmentary wall foundation — even a series of robber trenches, into a three-

84 Study of the fabric of the Cathedral at Worcester from the work of Robert Willis in the mid-nineteenth century down to the present day, combined with the cumulative results of excavations both inside and outside the building enable us to reconstruct the probable appearance of the church begun by St Wulstan in 1084. Though this reconstruction, like most others, may not be correct in all its details, it cannot be far from the truth, and gives the visitor a much clearer picture than a written description.

Although Wulstan's Church was almost the same size as the present building, its simple whitewashed exterior contrasted starkly with the Gothic church which ultimately replaced it, as this the drawing attempts to show.

The next step in interpreting the eleventh-century church to the public will be the construction of a scale model which should be even more immediate in its impact.

dimensional entity is a salutary one, bringing home the limitations of archaeology but also forcing one to think practically, in terms of structures that would stand up. For this reason it is of great value for the excavator to consult an architect or a structural engineer on the feasibility of the reconstruction attempted. Only thus will some of the ludicrous mistakes which have been made in the past be avoided, where a few moments with pencil and paper would have shown the suggested forms and structures to be highly unlikely if not impossible. Where two or three variant reconstructions are possible for one ground plan, all should be included, with a note indicating the degree of probability of each.

Reconstructions may be on paper only, may be scale models or full-size simulations. Elevations and sections, axonometric reconstructions or computer simulations are, of course, very valuable for stimulating discussion posing questions, such as the possible height of walls or the run-off and disposal of rain water, which might not otherwise be considered in detail, and releasing the imagination from the two-dimensional plane. Scale models go further in that they demand a fully three-dimensional appraisal of the building. But in neither of these cases is there the necessity of solving structural problems. Almost anything can be made to look viable on paper, and balsa wood and glue can by-pass many problems of weight, stress, loading and the nature of joints.

Paper reconstructions include pictorial representations such as those made famous by the late Alan Sorrell. These do not attempt to suggest solutions to structural difficulties (which they are often accused of glossing over) but are far more evocative of place and period than formal elevations and sections. They are therefore more suitable for short reports for the general public, museum displays and dioramas, text-books and the like. This does not mean that they should ever be inaccurate, mere flights of fancy. They should be capable of standing up to rigorous criticism, or should not be made at all. However, by their very nature they will be largely conjectural, and the accompanying text should make this clear. The difficulty is that drawings of this kind, if well done, are convincing even if wrong, and may perpetuate errors for generations. How many reconstruction drawings of timber castles have only a tool shed or two in the bailey? Yet it is clear from almost every excavation carried out on a castle bailey that they were packed with buildings.

Where an excavation has revealed evidence for timber-framed buildings resting on ground-sills the structure can assume any of the forms known from existing or postulated framed buildings. In such cases, the evidence is usually minimal, and the scope for creativity maximal. However, where post-hole buildings are discovered any reconstruction or simulation must fit the evidence without distortion, and too often only one of a number of possible reconstructions is described

and illustrated and often also non-existent post-holes are adduced to support the chosen argument, while other, awkwardly placed but existing ones, are discarded.

Recently published perspective or axonometric drawings include a series of Anglo-Saxon houses at Maxey (Addyman 1964), the Arthurian period hall at South Cadbury (Alcock 1972), Anglo-Saxon houses at Chalton (Addyman, Leigh and Hughes 1972), Hen Domen (Higham and Barker 1992) and Goltho (Beresford 1987).

At South Mimms, Dr John Kent demonstrated that the timber tower of the motte was, contrary to expectations based on other excavated examples, a massive tapered framed tower (not unlike the twelfth-century tower of the church at Pembridge, Herefordshire; Higham and Barker 1992, Figs 8.9–11) which had had the motte piled round its base. This mound was itself revetted by a circular palisade, so that in fact no earth was visible, the tower rising from the centre of what must have appeared from the outside to be a solid wall of wood (see Higham and Barker 1992, Fig. 8.39).

On the other hand, at Lismahon, Dr Dudley Waterman showed that the motte there carried a small bipartite hall not unlike one of the houses of a medieval village, to which was attached a small four-post look-out tower (Waterman 1959). No two timber castles could have been more different. Their paper reconstructions, though perhaps not accurate in every detail, bring home the point in a way that ground plans never do.

In none of the drawings of eleventh-century town houses in Antwerp (van der Walle 1961) is there any attempt to illustrate more than one of a number of possible roof constructions. For example, the cantilevered aisled roof structure of the Antwerp house, may, on German parallels have had the cantilevers as a continuation of the tie-beam and not as separate lower projections. But

259

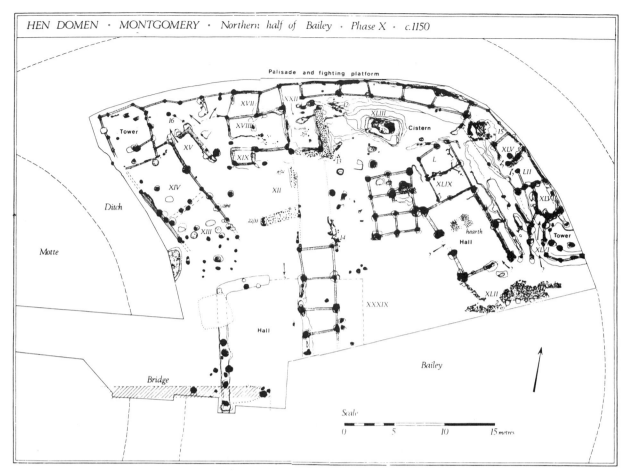

Palisade and fighting platform

Tower

XVII XXII

XVIII

XV

XIX

16

XLIII

Cistern

15

XLV

L

LII

XLIX

XLVI

XIV

XII

Ditch

XIII

Hall

hearth

Tower

XLVI

Motte

XLII

14

XXXIX

Hall

Bridge

Bailey

Scale

0   5   10   15 metres

the important thing is that these drawings should be published and discussed.

At Goltho, however, Beresford (1975) has made a suggestion regarding roof-jointing which is based strictly on the excavated evidence. As in so many cases in which buildings are founded on post-holes or post-pads, the wall posts were clearly not in a straight line and therefore the posts could not have been mortised into a straight wall-plate. Beresford has postulated that 'reversed assembly' was used in which a tie-beam was mortised on to paired studs with a post-head mortise tenon joint; '(the wall plate) would then have been dowelled on to the upper sides of the tie beams' (*ibid*.).

Precisely this problem had to be faced in the full scale simulation of the Wroxeter house built at Avoncroft Museum of Buildings, Bromsgrove, where a similar conclusion was reached purely empirically.

Because roof construction is one of the chief diagnostic features used by students of vernacular architecture, the almost complete lack in excavations of all but ground plans makes it difficult to bridge the gap between the excavator and the architectural historian.

85 a–c Hen Domen, Montgomery. *a* is the plan of the northern half of the bailey in phase X, *c*.1150. On the basis of the excavation plan the reconstruction drawing of this sector was made, *b*, which in turn was transformed into a three-dimensional model, a detail of which is seen photographed here, *c*. (Drawing and model: Peter Scholefield.)

A number of fundamental premises are nevertheless beginning to emerge as a result of the experiments in reconstruction now being made and the discussions and disputes which these experiments have generated. One is that it must be remembered and assumed that the buildings whose plans are recovered by excavation were, almost without exception, constructed by men with great experience, building within a long tradition, and that therefore the styles of buildings and the forms of their structures were the most efficient, and most convenient and the most closely adapted to their builders' needs. Whether we are dealing with a wattle-and-daub hut or Saxon palace it is highly unlikely that the building being excavated is the first of its kind to have been built. It is more likely to be an example taken from a very long sequence. Since no one, except under extreme circumstances, builds inefficiently, risking the whole structure collapsing, which at best is a waste of valuable time and work, or at worst fatal, it must be assumed that the buildings recovered were, by and large, the best that could be built at that time, and the most fitted for their purpose. The Native American tepee and the Bedouin tent leave little archaeological trace but are marvellously adapted to the way of life of their inhabitants – these are the portable houses of nomads. At the other extreme, it would be no use building an inefficient, carelessly thatched roof on a house in the Hebrides – the first strong breeze would remove it. Almost without exception the builders of the structures we excavate were working within traditions which embodied thousands of years' experience. We should therefore be wary of dismissing as inefficient or 'jerry built' structural evidence which, at first sight, does not seem to be explicable in terms of buildings with which we are familiar. We should rather take the opposite view, that all the evidence

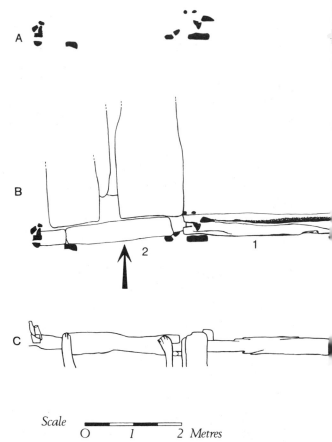

Scale

0 1 2 Metres

86 a–d Part of a waterlogged timber structure excavated by the York Archaeological Trust. The remains consist of three sill-beams pinned to the ground by short vertical pegs or posts. B and C are the plan and section respectively of the timbers shown in the photograph. A is a plan of the pegs and posts which were driven into the ground, and which would have formed post-holes if all the wood had rotted. The upper surface of sill-beam 1 is slotted, presumably to take horizontal weather-boarding or a wattle wall. Beam 2 forms a threshold leading to a heavily-planked floor, perhaps of a passage. It happens that these remains were preserved by waterlogging, but this is of course exceptional. On the majority of sites only the post-holes would remain.

A shows what would be found of this structure on a non-waterlogged site, and is a dramatic illustration not only of what is lost when timbers rot, but of the amount we may be justified in restoring to sites where post-holes are all that are found.

we find is to be explained in terms of efficiency, or practicability for the particular structure, given the materials available to the builder. This is not to say that all excavated structures are architectural masterpieces, but only a small minority are likely to have been dangerously ramshackle when they were put up even though the plan of post- or stake-holes may look incoherent.

There is little doubt too, that the buildings whose traces are excavated were often more elaborate, more highly finished, and more structurally sound than the excavation implies. This is evident if we look at examples where, through waterlogging, above-ground timbers which would normally have rotted, are preserved. A good example is shown in Fig. 86 a–c and d, from recent excavations in York, where it would be highly unlikely that we should postulate so massive and well-founded a structure from the evidence of a few small post-holes alone, if they were all that had survived. Another good example comes from Der

263

Hüsterknupp, a defensive site in Germany in which a motte-like mound buried the remains of an earlier building at ground level. It was highly significant that the posts of this earlier building were unworked tree-trunks below ground, whereas above ground, the visible posts were squared and chamfered. If only the post-holes, full of earth, had been found, as would be the case on the great majority of sites, the building would almost certainly have been reconstructed as having walls of unworked timber — no one would have been likely to have drawn the walls as they are known to have been, but for which there would have been no evidence (Higham and Barker, 1992, pp. 268–71). Similarly if no stave churches survived in Norway, who would dare, on the basis of a cross-shaped plan alone, to erect a great pagoda-like structure bristling with dragons at every corner? They would be laughed out of court.

As a result, therefore, of the inevitable paucity of excavated evidence we are likely to under-interpret, to err on the safe side, and to produce 'reconstructions' which are simpler and less sophisticated than were the actual buildings.

Paper reconstructions of stone buildings are usually based on more than a ground plan or a series of robber trenches. Where the structures are preserved for a significant height above the original ground level, reconstructions will naturally be more reliable, though, again, roof structures will be largely conjectural or based on other known examples. A recent carefully argued pair of reconstructions are those of the amphitheatres at Chester where evidence survived for both a timber and a stone phase (N.J. Sunter in Thompson 1976). A famous surviving fragment of wall, the Old Work, at Wroxeter has been carefully examined by Paul Woodfield and the suggested reconstruction published (Webster and Woodfield 1966). On a small scale the successive stone and timber-framed buildings which stood on the Town Wall of Shrewsbury in Pride Hill have been conjecturally restored and published by Philip Clarke and the successive phases of the pre-Conquest Church at Deerhurst are being recovered and drawn isometrically in very great detail.

In recent years an increasing number of full-scale simulations of timber buildings have been attempted. These range from Iron Age houses at Avoncroft, and the prehistoric experimental farm at Little Butser, Hampshire (Reynolds 1979), Saxon *Grubenhauser* at the Open Air Museum, Singleton, Sussex and at West Stow in Suffolk, to the most ambitious, the rampart and gateway and the granary at The Lunt Roman Fort, Coventry (Hobley 1973). Though none of these simulations is demonstrably accurate, their undertaking is of the greatest importance. Initiators of such projects lay themselves open to criticism, but by doing so raise questions which would not otherwise get off the ground either metaphorically or literally. While questions of detail will always be disputed some of the disputes generated have been fundamental. One of the most important is that of the gatehouse at The Lunt where the controversy centres on whether it is ever feasible or sensible to raise post-hole structures.

Deep post-holes imply that the posts were ground-fast, that is that they were meant to stand on their own, otherwise there would be little point in digging such deep holes. On the other hand, an increasing number of sites produce post-holes which are not and could never have been deep enough to support their posts. This implies that the posts merely stood in these sockets (or alternatively, on stone post-pads) and were framed in some way to the horizontals, whether wall-plates, ground-sills or tie-beams, which made up the rest of the structural skeleton.

(See Higham and Barker 1992, and Barker *et al.* forthcoming, 1994.)

Other notable reconstructions or simulations are those at Lejre in Demark where a group of Iron Age houses has stood for some years, and been used for short experiments in living under quasi-Iron Age conditions. A most interesting experiment was carried out at Lejre when one of the houses was deliberately burnt down. The whole episode was filmed and the temperatures which were reached in various parts of the house were recorded. The fire lasted a frighteningly short time and was a vivid reminder of the climax of *Njal's Saga*, when the hero is burnt alive in his house by his enemies.

Six months after the fire the site was excavated and the plan of the remains drawn (see Coles 1973, Figs 9–11). As Coles says 'The correlation of the plans was quite remarkable . . . door frames, partitions and flooring could be recognized, if with difficulty.' Experiments such as this give us greater confidence in the interpretations of slight and ephemeral traces of structures, interpretations which we should otherwise have to make almost solely on intuition.

The building of a variety of full-scale models, and their observed destruction either by fire or demolition, or by the much longer processes of natural decay, is very laborious, but will in the future be one of the most important ways in which we shall deepen our understanding of the excavated evidence.

Excavation and the public

Until comparatively recently, excavations were either private, being carried out by amateurs from Pitt Rivers and Schliemann onward, or were funded by museums (anxious for the finds) or universities. It is only within the last fifteen to twenty years that, chiefly in response to the realization of

the extent of destruction of archaeological sites of all kinds, a great deal of public money has been put into excavation. This is not the place, however, in which to chronicle the rise of rescue archaeology; this has been done by Philip Rahtz in *Rescue Archaeology* (1974), and by Barri Jones in *Past Imperfect: the story of rescue archaeology* (1984). Now, government agencies, such as English Heritage, Historic Scotland and Cadw, together with the newly privatized industries, such as gas and water, and also most local authorities subsidize or support rescue excavation to the tune of millions of pounds. To this must be added funds or help in kind given by developers in advance of the destruction which they cause. Excavators have a duty, therefore, to show the public how this money is being spent, to show that we, taxpayers all, are getting value for money in terms of new and reliable information about our past. This information must be presented in as lively and accessible a way as possible. It is not easy to conjure buildings from holes in the ground, or from pebble surfaces with straight edges, or the robber trenches of a long vanished building. Even the massive fragments of stone buildings require elucidation, especially if they are of many periods. To do this requires all the imagination and technical expertise in presentation that can be mustered. The methods which can be used effectively range from architectural reconstruction drawings through imaginative representations of inhabited buildings, towns and cities, scale models and full size furnished interiors, to the detailed recreation, as at the Jorvik Viking Centre in York, of an inhabited village, based strictly on the excavated evidence, plus the likely sounds and smells. The discreet labels and shaven grass of English Heritage monuments will never be the same again.

The lively and imaginative presentation of

excavations and excavated sites will help to convince the public and industry that archaeology is not just the private pursuit of intellectuals, but describes the past for all of us. In spite of the increase of public and private money spent on excavation, archaeologists have conspicuously failed to capture the imagination and the sympathy of the mass of people in the way that, for example, the bird and animal conservation societies have.

Sites of the greatest interest and importance, in some cases whole landscapes, are being destroyed almost unnoticed; only public outcry will strengthen the law and cause it to be vigorously enforced. At the moment it is too often flouted or evaded; and the majority of all archaeological sites are not protected in any way by law. Their only hope of survival into the twenty-first century and beyond is either by a ten-fold increase in statutory protection or a vastly enhanced understanding by all concerned of the destruction that is caused by ploughing, afforestation, quarrying, road-building and rural and urban development. At the root of all this is, of course, money – the money to be made by levelling the earthworks of a deserted village, or quarrying away a hillfort, or redeveloping a historic town centre. Archaeologists can so easily be cast in the role of backward-looking fuddy duddies, opposed to progress, wishing to fossilize the countryside and turn it into a museum. That we are not. On the contrary, in spite of our preoccupation with the past, we see further ahead than most, to a time when our historic roots will no longer be visible on the ground, or even under it.

Excavation in the future

All excavation, as we have said, is destruction, and the number of archaeological sites, not only in Britain, but in the world, is diminishing daily for a wide variety of reasons. It is increasingly necessary, then, to conserve this rapidly diminishing resource and as a result it is likely that the number of excavations, other than those carried out in advance of destruction, will decrease. As a corollary, those that are undertaken will have to be more sensitive and more efficient, extracting more reliable evidence than the best of our present excavations and subjecting that evidence to more rigorous analysis. How will this be done?

The first necessity is a rapid development of all kinds of non-destructive methods of site examination: magnetic, radar, sonar, infra-red, ultra-violet methods, some now in their infancy, some not even yet imagined, which will enable site potential to be assessed in more reliable ways than at present. This will enable unthreatened sites to be chosen for excavation on sounder bases than at present and better choices to be made between those sites which are threatened.

Excavation, when it takes place, will be made much more subtle by methods of enhancement of otherwise invisible soil differences – by chemical means, by the use of lighting of different wavelengths and, again, by means not yet considered. The analysis of the results will, no doubt, depend more and more on computer programs of increasing power, and on electronic methods of which holography is only the first.

Though I suspect that our chief tool, the trowel, will not be superseded for a long time, I guess that those of us digging now will be looked on as the primitives of excavation, the proto-diggers, earnest, but lacking refinement. Nevertheless, I cannot improve on Martin Carver's prediction, given to a conference on *Excavation in the 21st century*, that '. . . archaeological excavation will remain what it is now, the most creative, challenging and exhilarating activity that the practioners of any discipline are privileged to enjoy'.

Epilogue

Most of us dig out of insatiable curiosity coupled with the perhaps arrogant conviction that by dissecting ancient sites we can understand them. The subtle flanks of an ancient earthwork, embedded in the landscape like a half-submerged sculpture by Henry Moore, or the dark green contrapuntal tracery of a cropmark seen from the air, give us a powerful *frisson* of discovery and recognition and an overwhelming desire to know what it means.

Man is, after all, the only animal which realizes that it has a past, and that it can consciously study it. And one of the principal ways in which we can get back into that past is by excavation, the first-hand study of the material evidence.

While we all acknowledge Wheeler's dictum that we should dig up people, not things, archaeologically we can only get at the people of the past through the things that they left, chiefly the debris of their buildings, their domestic rubbish, and, sometimes more closely, their own skeletal remains. So we spend weeks cleaning cobbled surfaces which were always deep in mud when they were in use, or conscientiously collect and record scraps of pottery which were discarded by their owners without a second thought. And what Roger de Montgomery would think if he saw us at Hen Domen lovingly dissecting his soldiers' sewage and packing it into little polythene bags we can barely guess.

Yet the sum total of all this apparently ludicrous activity, integrated by means of all the converging skills and techniques of analysis and synthesis we can muster, gives us, so long as we keep our heads, and do not get bogged down in mathematical or linguistic abstractions, a panoramic view of the past obtainable in no other way. More than that, it enables us individually to put down deep roots in our landscape – or townscape – to realize our place in the continuum of history, and, by sympathetic direction, teaching and example, to help others to do the same.

Glossary

aceramic – without pottery; used of periods, both historic and prehistoric, in which pottery was not used, usually in contrast with other preceding or succeeding periods or neighbouring contemporary cultures, in which pottery was used.

anaerobic – without air; used to describe conditions, such as waterlogging, where there is insufficient oxygen for bacterial or fungal growth, so that organic materials reach a state of equilibrium beyond which they do not decay.

balk (baulk) – a strip of an archaeological site left undug to form a barrow-run, or to provide *vertical sections (q.v.)*.

contexts – an omnibus term for all the stratigraphic units (layers, features, strata, etc) found in an excavation.

froth flotation – by adding a detergent to the water in which the soil samples are agitated, light-weight materials such as seeds and charcoal fragments can be more easily separated from the *matrix (q.v.)*.

hachure – a tapering line (tadpole) used to indicate the direction of a slope on the survey of an earthwork. The hachure points downhill and its length is related to the steepness of the slope. See Taylor (1974), for excellent examples of hachured survey.

isometric and axonometric projections (see Figs 29 and 82b) – in these projections the plan and elevations are combined to give a 'three-dimensional' view on which correct measurements can be taken either in any direction (isometric) or along two or three axes (axonometric).

levelling – in the context of this book, levelling means to establish the height above site datum of a number of points (spot heights) which will either record the level of the surface of a feature or layer, or enable a contour survey to be constructed.

magnetometer – an instrument for the measurement of changes in the magnetism of the earth's surface. By picking up anomalies in the earth's magnetism it can detect the presence of kilns, hearths, pits, ditches, etc (see p. 61).

matrix – 1 the mass of material such as mud, enclosing waterlogged vegetable remains, clay containing flints etc;

2 by extension, the word is used to describe a pro-forma of rectangles used to construct a table of the relationship of contexts one to another (see pp. 229–37).

micro-climate – the specifically local climate brought about by hills, slopes, woodland, lakes or other features of the landscape which modify the general climate of a region.

micro-podsol – the podsol is formed when water leaches dissolved chemicals through the uppermost layers of the soil, changing their appearance and often precipitating salts at lower level, where they may, for instance form an iron-pan. The effect has often misled excavators into believing that they have found floors, etc though the process is entirely natural. See Limbrey (1975), pp. 137–45.

mortice – a hole, usually rectangular, cut into a beam or plank, to take a tenon, which is a projection cut on the end of another beam and inserted into the mortice so that the beams can be joined together.

motte – a motte is a castle mound, usually of earth, but sometimes of stone. Attached to it may be one or more baileys, which are enclosures surrounded by ramparts or stone walls.

Munsell Colour Chart – a book of colour samples each perforated with a hole through which the colour of the soil or other material can be compared with the standard sample which has a code denoting its hue and tone.

photogrammetry – the use of an overlapping stereoscopic mosaic of photographs to produce (usually with the aid of a mechanical plotter) a contour survey, or an elevation of a building etc.

planum – a method of digging in which horizontal slices are removed either from the whole site, or from specific features, in order to reveal a succession of plans.

pollen spectrum – the diagram resulting from the analysis of the pollen from a column of peat or other soil.

post-hole; post-pipe; post-pit – in this book the term post-hole is used to mean the void or soil-filled mould where a post has stood. Some archaeologists use the term post-pipe to mean the same thing. Post-pit is used here to mean the pit dug to take a post. The pit is usually, though not always, bigger than its associated post-hole.

protohistoric – the earliest historic periods, that is, those early periods which have documentary evidence, often minimal, relating to them.

resistivity meter – a machine which measures the electrical resistivity of the earth between two probes. Since the resistivity of the soil changes with humidity, humus content, etc the machine can detect pits, ditches, roads, floors etc (see p. 60).

robber trench – the trench left (usually backfilled) by the labourers who have 'robbed' out a wall either completely or of its facing stone.

section – as here used, means the stratification revealed by the cutting of a trench or other vertical face through an archaeological site.

sleeper-beam; sill-beam; cill-beam; ground-sill – a horizontal foundation beam of wood, either lying directly on the ground or in a *timber slot* (q.v.).

solifluction – the downhill movement of saturated soil.

stratification – the successive layers, either natural or man-made, which make up the surface of the earth, and which, in this context, are revealed by an excavation.

stratigraphy – the scientific description of stratification.

timber-slot – a trench dug to contain a horizontal beam. See *sleeper-beam*.

vivianite – ferrosoferric phosphate, a white powder which forms in some buried soils and on iron objects. It turns a characteristic blue on contact with air.

Bibliography

It would be quite impossible to list all the important or useful papers and books which have appeared in the ten years since the publication of the second edition of this book, but a selection is included here in order to point the reader in their direction.

In addition, many of the publications cited in the earlier editions have been retained, either because they were seminal at the time, or because they are still relevant, or because they are of interest in the development of excavation techniques.

Addyman, P. (1964), 'Dark Age Settlements at Maxey, Northants', *Medieval Archaeology*, VIII

Addyman, P., Leigh, D., and Hughes, M.J. (1972), *Anglo-Saxon Houses at Chalton, Hampshire*, *Medieval Archaeology*, XVI, 13–32

Adkins, L. and Adkins, R.A. (1989), *Archaeological Illustration*, Cambridge

Aitken, M. (1990), *Science-based Dating in Archaeology*, London

Alcock, L. (1972), *By South Cadbury is that Camelot*, London

Alexander, J. (1970), *The Directing of Archaeological Excavations*, London

Allen, K.M.S., Green, S.W. and Zubrow, E.B.W. (eds) (1990) *Interpreting Space: GIS and Archaeology*
— A collection of papers on geographic information systems, their theory and methodology; hardware and software and practical applications.

Aston, M. and Rowley, R.T. (1974), *Landscape Archaeology*, London

Atkinson, R.J.C. (1953), *Field Archaeology*, 2nd edition, London

Atkinson, R.J.C. (1957), 'Worms and Weathering', *Antiquity*, 31

Austin, D., Gerard G.A.M., and Greeves, T.A.P. (1989), 'Tin and Agriculture in the Middle Ages and beyond: landscape archaeology in St Neot Parish Cornwall', *Cornish Archaeology*, 28

Barker, P.A. (1958), 'Moated enclosure at Watling Street Grange, Oakengates, emergency excavations, 1958' *Shrops. Archaeol. Trans.* LVI, Part I, 21–5

Barker, P.A. (1961), 'A pottery sequence from Brockhurst Castle, Church Stretton, 1959' *Shrops. Archaeol. Trans.* LVII, Part I, 63–80

Barker, P.A. (1964), 'Excavations on the moated site at Shifnal', *Shrops. Archaeol. Trans.* LVII, Part III, 194–205

Barker, P.A. (1966), 'The Deserted Medieval Hamlet at Braggington', *Shrops. Archaeol. Trans.* LVIII, Part II, 122–39

Barker, P.A. (1969), 'Some aspects of the excavation of timber buildings', *World Archaeol.* I, No. 2, 220–35

Barker, P.A. *et al.* (1970), 'The Origins of Worcester', *Trans. Worcestershire Archaeol. Soc.*, 3rd Series, 2, 1968–9

Barker, P.A. (1970), *The medieval pottery of Shropshire from the Conquest to 1400*, Shropshire Archaeological Society

Barker, P.A. *et al.* (forthcoming, 1994), *Excavations on the Baths Basilica at Wroxeter*, English Heritage

Barker P.A. and Higham, R.A. (1982), *Hen Domen, Montgomery: A Timber Castle on the English-Welsh Border*, R.A.I. Monograph

Barker, P.A. and Lawson, J. (1971), 'A pre-Norman field system at Hen Domen, Montgomery', *Medieval Archaeology*, XV, 58–72

Barrett, John, Bradley, Richard and Green, Martin (1991) *Landscape, Monuments and Society : the Prehistory of Cranborne Chase*

Benson, D. and Miles, D. (1974), *The Upper Thames Valley: an archaeological survey of the river gravels*, Oxford
— A model of fieldwork publication combining the results of aerial photography, excavation and surface finds.

Beresford, M. and Hurst, J.G. (1971), *Deserted Medieval Villages*

Beresford, G. (1987), *Goltho*, English Heritage

Bersu, G. (1940), 'Excavations at Little Woodbury', *Proc. Prehist. Soc.* VI, 30–111

Bersu, G. (1949), 'A Promontory Fort on the Shore of Ramsey Bay, Isle of Man', *Antiquaries Journal*, Vol. XXIX, January-April, 62–79

Bersu, G. (1977), edited by C.A. Ralegh Radford, *Three Iron Age Round Houses in the Isle of Man*, The Manx Museum and the National Trust.
— The report on a remarkable series of excavations carried out under armed guard while Bersu, with other 'enemy aliens', was interned in the Isle of Man during the Second World War.

Beutiner-Jannaech, J. (1954), 'Use of Infrared Photography in Archaeological Work', *American Antiquity*, 20, 84, Salt Lake City

Beveridge, W.I.B. (1950), *The Art of Scientific Investigation*, London

Biddle, M. and B. Kjolbye Biddle (1969), 'Metres, areas and robbing', *World Archaeology* I (2), 208–19

Biddle, M. (Winchester Interim Reports), *Arch. Journ.* CXIX, (1962), 150–94; XLIV (1964), 188–219; XLV (1965), 230–64; XLVI (1966), 308–22; XLVII (1967), 251–79; XLVIII (1968), 250–84; XLIX (1969), 295–329; L (1970), 277–326; LII (1972), 93–131; LV (1975) 96–126

Biek, L. (1963), *Archaeology and the Microscope*, London

Binford, L.R. (1983), *In Pursuit of the Past*, London

Binford, S.R. and L.R. (eds.) (1968), *New Perspectives in Archaeology*, Chicago
— A symposium of essays by one of the founders of the 'New Archaeology' linked by slightly embarrassing autobiographical passages.

Bonnichsen, Robson (1972), 'Millie's Camp: an experiment in archaeology', *World Archaeology*, 4, 277–91
— An illuminating exercise in the interpretation of a deserted Native American camp site, checked by subsequent reference to the recent occupants, and demonstrating the fallibility of some of our 'commonsense' reasoning. A useful biliography of similar analogies is appended.

Bowen, H.C. (1970), *Ancient Fields*, London

Bracegirdle, B. (1970), *Photography for Books and Reports*, London

Bradley, R. (1970), 'The Excavation of a Beaker Settlement at Belle Tout, East Sussex, England', *Proc. Prehist. Soc*, XXXVI, 312–79

Bradley, R. (1976), 'Maumbury Rings, Dorchester: The Excavations of 1908–1913' *Archaeologia*, CV, 1–98

Brisbane, M.A. (ed.) and Judleson, K. (trans.) (1992), *The Archaeology of Novgorod, Russia, Society for Medieval Archaeology, Monograph Series*, No. 13

Brooke, C.J. (1989) *Ground Based Remote Sensing*, IFA Technical Papers No. 7

Brothwell, D. (1963), *Digging up Bones*, London

Brothwell, D. and Brothwell, P. (1969), *Food in Antiquity*, London

Brothwell, D. and Higgs, E. (eds) (1969), *Science in Archaeology*, London

Bruce-Mitford, R.L.S. (ed.) (1956), *Recent Archaeological Excavations in Britain*, London
– Contains the first published account of the development of the techniques of excavations used at Wharram Percy.

Bruce-Mitford, R.L.S. (1974), *Recent Archaeological Excavations in Europe*, London

Buckland, P.C. (1974), 'Archaeology and Environment in York', *Journal of Archaeological Science*, 1974, 1, 303–16

Budd, P. (ed.) (1989), *Archaeological Sciences*, Oxbow

Burl, A. (ed.) (1988) *From Roman Town to Norman Castle*, Birmingham
– Essays in honour of Philip Barker

Bushe-Fox, R. (1913, 1914, 1916), *Excavations on the Site of the Roman Town at Wroxeter, Shropshire in 1912; Second Report on the Excavations of the Site of the Roman Town at Wroxeter Shropshire in 1913; Third Report on the Excavations on the Site of the Roman Town at Wroxeter, Shropshire in 1916* Society of Antiquaries

Buteux, S. and Gaffney, V. (1992), *The Wroxeter Hinterland*, Birmingham University Field Archaeology Unit

Carver, M.O.H. (1981), 'Sampling Towns: an optimistic strategy' in Clack and Haselgrove (eds), *Approaches to the Urban Past*, Durham.
– Contains a useful bibliography.

Carver, M.O.H. (1983), 'Theory and Practice in Urban Pottery Seriation' *Journal of Archaeological Science*, 12, 353–66

Carver, M.O.H. (ed.) (1980) 'Medieval Worcester. An archaeological framework' *Trans. Worcestershire Archaeol. Soc. 3rd series*, vol. 7

Carver, M.O.H. *et al.* (1992) *Archaeological Publication, Archives and Collections; towards a national policy*, Society of Antiquaries, London

Case, H. (1952), 'The Excavation of Two Round Barrows at Poole, Dorset', *Proc. of the Prehist. Soc.*, N.S. XVIII, 148–59

Casey, J. (1974), 'The Interpretation of Romano-British Site Finds', *Coins and the Archaeologist*, British Archaeological Reports, 4, 37–51
– A salutary article on the misuse of coin evidence due to misunderstanding of the historic and economic background.

Cherry, J.F., Gamble, C. and Shennan, S. (1978), *Sampling in Contemporary British Archaeology*, Oxford
– Papers stemming from a conference held at Southampton in 1977. Many of the papers take a fundamentally different stance on excavation from that taken in this book and it is therefore required reading for those wishing to achieve a balanced view.

Clack, P. and Haselgrove, S. (eds) (1981), *Approaches to the Urban Past*, Durham

Clark, A. (1990), *Seeing Beneath the Soil*, London
– A comprehensive introduction into prospecting methods.

Clark, G. (1957), *Archaeology and Society*, 3rd edition, London

Clark, T. (1987), *Scientific Dating Techniques*, IFA Technical Paper No. 5

Clarke, D.L. (1968), *Analytical Archaeology*, London
— The best introduction to statistical methods of archaeological analysis.

Clarke, D.L. (ed.) (1972), *Models in Archaeology*, London

Coles, J. (1972), *Field Archaeology in Britain*, London

Coles, J. (1973), *Archaeology by Experiment*, London

Coles, J. (1979), *Experimental Archaeology*, London

Coles, B.J. and J.M. (1986), *Sweet Track to Glastonbury*, London

Collingwood, R.G. (1939), *An Autobiography*, Oxford

Computer Applications in Archaeology (1991), British Archaeological Reports

Conlon, V.M. (1973), *Camera Techniques in Archaeology*, London

Cook, S.F. and Heizer, R.F. (1965), *Studies on the Chemical Analysis of Archaeological Sites*, Berkeley

Cooke, F.B.M. and Wacher, J.S. 'Photogrammetric Surveying at Wanborough, Wilts' *Antiquity*, 44
— A description of vertical photography on a fourth-century AD excavation using a turret similar to that described in Nylen 1964

Cookson, M.B. (1954), *Photography for Archaeologists*, London

Cornwall, I. (1956), *Bones for the Archaeologist*, London

Cornwall, I. (1958), *Soils for the Archaeologist*, London

Council for British Archaeology (1970) *Handbook of Scientific Aids and Evidence for Archaeologists*, London
— With bibliographies for each subject.

Courty, M.A., Goldberg, P. and MacPhail, R.I. (1989), *Soils and Micromorphology in Archaeology*, Cambridge

Crawford, O.G.S. (1953), *Archaeology in the Field*, London

Crummy, P. (1987), *Reducing Publication Costs*, IFA Technical Paper No. 6

Cunliffe, B. (1973), 'Chalton, Hants, The Evolution of a Landscape', *Antiq. Journal* LIII, Part II, 173–90

Cunliffe, B.W. (1983) *The Publication of Archaeological Excavations*, Dept. of the Environment

Daniel, G. (1950), *A Hundred Years of Archaeology*, London

Daniel, G. (1967), *The Origins and Growth of Archaeology*, Harmondsworth

Daniel, G. (1976), *A Hundred and Fifty years of Archaeology*, Cambridge

Darwin, C. (1881), *The Formation of Vegetable Mould Through the Action of Worms with Observations on their Habits* (republished by Faber and Faber London, 1945, under the title *Darwin on Humus and the Earthworm*, with an introduction by Sir Albert Howard)

Darvill, T. and Atkins, M (1991), *Regulating Archaeological Work by Contract* IFA Technical Report No. 8

Davison, B.K. (1969), 'Early Earthwork Castles: A New Model', *Château Gaillard* III, Chichester, 37ff.

de Bono, E. (1970), *Lateral Thinking: a textbook of creativity*, London

de Bouard, M. (1975), *Manuel d'archéologie médievale*, Paris
— A study of medieval archaeology in France by one of her late and most respected elder statesmen.

Department of the Environment (1975), *Principles of Publication in Rescue Archaeology*, London

Dimbleby, G. (1967), *Plants and Archaeology*, London

Dimbleby, G. (1978), *The Scientific Treatment of Material from Rescue Excavations*, Department of the Environment

– Although principally concerned (through its terms of reference) with rescue archaeology, the recommendations of the report apply equally to all excavated material, however recovered.

Doran, J. (1970), 'Systems theory, computer simulations and archaeology', *World Archaeology*, I, No. 3, February, 289–98

Dorrell, P. (1989) *Photography in Archaeology and Conservation*, Cambridge

Dowman, E.A. (1970), *Conservation in Field Archaeology*, London

Dymond, D.P. (1974), *Archaeology and History – a plea for reconciliation*, London

Eckstein, E., Baillie, M.G. and Eggar, H, *Dendrochronological Dating*, European Science Foundation

Ellison, A. (1981), *A Policy for Archaeological Investigation in Wessex*, Salisbury
– A clear and logical analysis of the massive destruction of the Wessex landscape together with proposals for period-based projects designed to examine those problems which are deemed to be the most urgent or which have, in the past, received least attention.

English Heritage (1991) *Management of Archaeological Projects*

Eogan, G. (1992), *The Discovery Programme*, Dublin

Es, W.A. van, (1967), 'Wijster: a Native Village beyond the Imperial Frontier 150–425 AD', *Palaeohistoria* XI
– An exemplary report on the excavation of a village of timber buildings.

Es, W.A. van, (1969), 'Excavations at Dorestad, a Pre-preliminary Report: 1967–68', *Berichten van de Rijksdienst Voor het Oudheidkundig Bodemonderzoek*

Farrugia, J.P., Duper, R., Luning, J., Stehli, P. (1973), 'Untersuchunger zur Neolithischen Besiedlung der Aldenhovener Platte', *Bonner Jahrbucher*, 226–56

– Describes and illustrates the large-scale machine stripping of a linear pottery settlement with examples of feature and find recording cards.

Fasham, P.J., Schadla-Hall, R.T., Shennan, S.J. and Bates, P.J. (1980), *Fieldwalking for Archaeologists*, Andover, Hampshire
– A clear and concise guide

Fleming, S. (1976), *Dating in Archaeology: A Guide to Scientific Techniques*, Oxford

Flond, R. (1973), *An Introduction to Quantitative Methods for Historians*, London

Fowler, E. (ed.) (1972), *Field Survey in British Archaeology*, London

Fowler, P.J. (ed.) (1972) *Archaeology and the Landscape*, London

Fowler, P.J. (ed.) (1972), *Responsibility and Safeguards in Archaeology Excavation*, Council for British Archaeology

Fowler, P.J. (1977), *Approaches to Archaeology*, London
– A successor to Piggott's *Approach to Archaeology* (1959) which reviews the changes in British archaeology in the last 18 years, and looks forward to the next decade.

Fox, C. and Hope (1891), Fox (1892), Fox and Hope (1893), *Excavations on the site of the Roman City of Silchester, Hants*, (in 1890, 1891, 1892) London

Fox, Aileen and Cyril (1960), 'Wansdyke Reconsidered', *Archaeological Journal* CXV, 1–48
– A reassessment of a famous linear earthwork based on intensive observation and a study of the historical evidence.

Fox, Sir Cyril (1952), *The Personality of Britain: Its influence on inhabitant and invader in prehistoric and early historic times*, Cardiff
– Though written before the full impact of aerial photography on settlement patterns was realized this is still a classic archaeological geography and one of the

few monuments to the work of Miss Lily Chitty.

Fox, Sir Cyril (1955), *Offa's Dyke*
— A classic field study of a linear earthwork. Though some questions remain unanswered (and some unasked) it is probable that little more can be discovered about the dyke without excavation (though see Hill (1974) and Noble (1983)).

Fox, C. and Hope C., (1891), Fox (1892) Fox and Hope (1893), *Excavations at Silchester, Hants 1890, 1891, 1892*, Society of Antiquaries

Frere, S.S. (1959), 'Excavations at Verulamium, 1958', *Antiq. Journal* XXXIX, 1–18

Frere, S.S., (1971), *Verulamium Excavations I*, Oxford

Fryer, D.H. (1971), *Surveying for Archaeologists*, 4th edition, Durham

Gaffney, C., Gater, J. and Ovenden, S. (1991), *The Use of Geophysical Techniques in Archaeological Evaluations*, IFA Technical Report No. 9

Gaffney, V. and Sancvvicvv, Z. (1991), *GIS Approaches to Regional Analysis: a case study of the Island of Hvar*, Ljubljana

Gardin, J.G. (1966), *Code pour l'analyse des poteries médievales*, Université de Caen
— An attempt to codify all possible characteristics of medieval pottery, so that a punch-card system (and subsequently computer storage) can be developed. The publication demonstrates the vast range of characteristics for which entries are required if all variants are to be recorded.

Garratt-Frost, S. (1992), *The Law and Burial Archaeology*, IFA Technical Report No. 11

Giffen, van (1958), 'Prehistorische Hausformen auf Sandboden in den Niederlanden', *Germania*, Jaargang 36, 36–7

Gillam, J.P. (1957, 2nd ed. 1968), *Types of Roman Coarse Pottery Vessels in Northern Britain*

Gillespie, R. (1986), *The Radio-carbon Users' Handbook*, Oxford

Green, A. and Zubron (eds) (1991), *Interpreting Space: GIS in Archaeology*, London

Greig, T. (1987), *Archaeobotany*, European Science Foundation

Griffiths, Jenner and Wilson, (1990), *Drawing Archaeological Finds: A Handbook*, London

Grimes, W.F. (1960), *Excavations on Defence Sites, 1939–1945*, I, London

Grimes, W.F. (1968), *The Excavation of Roman and Medieval London*, London

Grinsell, L., Rahtz, P. and Price Williams D. (1974), *The Preparation of Archaeological Reports*, Revised edition, London
— This revised and enlarged edition replaces that of 1966

Guerreschi, A. (1973), 'A mechanical sieve for archaeological excavations', *Antiquity*, XLVII, 187, September

Haggett, P. (1965), *Location Analysis in Human Geography*, London

Hamilton, J.R.C. (1956), *Excavations at Jarlshof, Shetland*, London
— A multi-period site excavation published in exemplary style.

Hanson, N.R. (1967), 'Observation and Interpretation' in ed. S. Morgenbesser Philosophy of Science Today, New York

Harris, E.C. (1975), 'The Stratigraphic Sequence: a question of time', *World Archaeology*, Vol. 7, No. 1 June, 109–21

Harris, E.C. (2nd ed. 1989), *Principles of Archaeological Stratigraphy*, London
— A fundamental statement of the laws of stratigraphy and the ways in which they may be applied and understood.

Hassall, T.G. (1971), 'Excavations at Oxford', *Oxoniensia*, 36

Hatt, G. (1957), 'Nørre Fjand, an Early Iron Age Village in West Jutland', *Arkaeol.*

Kunsthist Skr. Dan. Vid. Selsk. 2, No. 2, Copenhagen

Hawkes, C.F.C. (1948), 'Britons, Romans and Saxons in and around Salisbury and Cranbourne Chase', *Archaeol. Journal*, CIV, 27–81

Hayfield, C. (1980), *Fieldwalking as a Method of Archaeological Research*, Department of the Environment
 – A collection of highly suggestive papers from a conference held in 1976.

Hayward, J.A. (1968), 'Unshored Excavations are Killers', *The British Journal of Occupational Safety*, Vol. 7, No. 85, Autumn
 – A very useful survey with check list of safety questions.

Heizer, R.F. and Graham, J.A. (1967), *A Guide to Field Methods in Archaeology*, California
 – A comprehensive exposition of American methods with a very extensive but unclassified and uncritical bibliography.

Higham, R. and Barker, P.A. (1992), *Timber Castles*, London

Hill, D. (1974), 'The inter-relation of Offa's and Wat's Dykes', *Antiquity*, XLVIII, 192, 309–12

Hirst, S. (1976), *Recording on Excavations I, the Written Record*, RESCUE publication No. 7, Hertford

Hobley, B. (1973), 'Excavations at "The Lunt" Roman Military Site, Baginton Warwickshire 1968–71, Second Interim Report', *Trans. Birmingham and Warwickshire, Archaeol. Soc.* Vol 85, 1972

Hodges, H. (1970), *Technology in the Ancient World*, Harmondsworth

Hodson, Kendall and Tautu (eds) (1971), *Mathematics in the Archaeological and Historical Sciences*, Edinburgh

Hogg, A.H.A. (1981), *Surveying for Archaeologists and other Fieldworkers*, London

 – A highly detailed handbook supplementing instruction in the field (which it or any other manual cannot replace).

Hope-Taylor, B. (1966), 'Archaeological Draughtsmanship, II', *Antiquity*, XL

Hope-Taylor, B. (1966), 'Archaeological Draughtsmanship, III', *Antiquity*, XLI

Hope-Taylor, B. (1977), *Yeavering, An Anglo-British centre of early Northumbria*, London

Howell, C. and Blanc, W. (1992), *A Practical Guide to Archaeological Photography*, London

Hurst, J.G. (1956), 'Deserted Medieval Villages and the Excavation at Wharram Percy, Yorkshire', in Bruce-Mitford, R.L.S. (ed.), *Recent Archaeological Excavations in Great Britain*, London

Hurst, J.G., (1969), 'Medieval Britain in 1968', *Med.Archaeol*, XIII, 252–3

Hurst, J.G. (ed.) (1974), *Medieval Pottery from Excavations*, London

Hurst, J.G. (ed.) (1979), *Wharram, A Study of Settlement on the Yorkshire Wolds* Society for Medieval Archaeology Monography No 8

Institute of Field Archaeologists (1991), *Guidelines for Finds Work*

Jankuhn, H (1969), 'Vor-und Fruh- geschichte vom Neolithikum bis der Volkerwanderingszeit', *Deutsche Agrargeschichte*, I, Verlag Eugen Ulmer
 – Contains many plans of settlement sites.

Jeffries, J.S. (1977), *Excavation Techniques in Use by the Central Excavation Unit*, Department of the Environment

Jones, M.U. *et al.* (1968), 'Crop-mark Sites at Mucking, Essex', *Antiquaries Journal*, XLVIII, Part II 210–30

Jones, M.U. (1974), 'Excavations at Mucking, Essex: A second interim report' *Antiquaries Journal*, LIV, Pt. II 183–99

Joukowsky, M. (1980), *A Complete Manual of Field Archaeology*, New Jersey

– Contains an exhaustive and very useful bibliography. However, the text has a number of fundamental weaknesses which invalidate much of its advice.

Kenrick, P. (1971), 'Aids to the drawing of finds', *Antiquity*, XLV

Kenyon, K.M. (1964), *Beginning in Archaeology*, London

Kjolbye-Biddle, B. (1975), 'A Cathedral Cemetery: problems in excavation and interpretation' *World Archaeology*, Vol. 7, No 1

Laflin, S., Roper, A., Symonds, R.P., and White, R.H. Analysis of Pottery from Wroxeter Roman City in Torsten Madsen, Jens Andressen and Irwin Schollar (eds) *Computer Applications and Quantitative Methods in Archaeology* 1992 in press

Lamb, H.H. (1971), 'Britain's Worsening Winters', *The Times*, 30 January, London

Lamb, H.H. (1972), *Climate, Present, Past and Future*, London

Lapinskas, P. (1975), 'Flotation Machine' *M3 Archaeology 1974*, ed. Fasham, Winchester

Leigh, D. *et al.* (1972), *First Aid for Finds*, Worcester

Limbrey, S. (1975), *Soil Science and Archaeology*, London

Lock, G. and Moffett, T. (forthcoming 1995), *Using Information Technology in Archaeology*, London

Lyman, R. Lee (1992), *Pre-history of the Oregon Coast. The Effects of Excavation Strategies and Assemblage Size on Archaeological Enquiry*

Mackie, E. *et al.* (1971), 'Thoughts on radio-carbon dating', *Antiquity*, XLV, No. 179, 197–204

Macphail, R.I. (1992), *Soil Micromorphology in Excavations in Deansway, Worcester, 1988–89*, in Mundy C.F. and Dalwood, C.H. (eds) C.B.A. Res. Rep.

Mason, J.F.A. and Barker, P.A. (1961), 'The Norman Castle at Quatford', *Trans Shrops. Archaeol, Soc.* LVII. Pt.I, 362

Medawar, P.B. (1969), *Induction and Intuition in Scientific Thought*, London

Megaw, J.V.S. (ed.) (1979), *Signposts for Archaeological Publication*, C.B.A., London

Mook, W.G. and Waterbolk, H.T. (1988), *Radio-carbon Dating*, European Science Foundation

Morgan, J.W.W. (1975), 'The Preservation of Timber', *Timber Grower*, 55

Musson, C.R. (1971), in *Durrington Walls, Excavations 1966–1968*. Report of the Research Committee, Society of Antiquaries of London XXIX, 363–77 London

Noble, F. (1983), *Offa's Dyke Reviewed*, Oxford

Norlund, P. (1948), *Trelleborg*, Copenhagen

Nylen, E. (1964), 'A Turret for Vertical Photography', *Antikvariskt Arkiv*, XXIV
– Describes the techniques, including those for enhancing soil colour differences, used to re-excavate post-holes at the Viking fortresses of Trelleborg and Fyrkat.

Olsen, O.S. and Crumlin-Pedersen, O. (1968), *The Skuldelev Ships*, Copenhagen
– Demonstrates methods of excavating and particularly of recording (photogrammetrically) surfaces on which it is impossible or undesirable to walk.

Orton, C. (1980) *Mathematics in Archeology*, London
– A splendidly lucid exposition for the semi-numerate of the uses of mathematics in archaeology.

Panton, *et al.* (1958), 'The Clarendon Hotel, Oxford', *Oxoniensia*, XXIII, 1.129

Pearson, G.W. and Stuiver, M. (1986) 'High Precision Calibration of the Radio-carbon

Time-scale 500BC–2500BC' *Radio-carbon*, Vol. 28, No. 2B, 1986

Petch, D.F. (1971), 'Earthmoving machines and their employment on archaeological excavations' *Journal of the Chester Archaeological Society*

Petrie, W.M.F. (1904), *Methods and Aims in Archaeology*, London

Philip, C. and Swann, A. (1992), *Preparation of Artwork for Publication*, IFA Technical Paper No. 10

Piggott, S. (1959), *Approach to Archaeology*, London

Piggott, S. and Hope-Taylor, B. (1965), 'Archaeological Draughtsmanship: Principles and Practice', *Antiquity*, XXXIX, 5–8

Pitt-Rivers, A.H.L.F. (1887–98), *Excavations in Cranborne Chase*, 4 vols. London

Pryor, F. (1974), *Earthmoving on Open Archaeological Sites*, Nene Valley Archaeol. Handbook I

Pryor, Francis, (1991), *Flag Fen*, Batsford/English Heritage, London

Rahtz P.A. (1969) *Excavations at King John's Hunting Lodge*, Writtle Essex. 1955–57, Society for Medieval Archaeology Monograph Series 3, London
– An exemplary report on a rescue excavation of a complex moated site with only tenuous evidence of some of the major buildings.

Rahtz, P.A. (ed.) (1974), *Rescue Archaeology*, Harmondsworth

Rahtz, P.A. (1975), 'How Likely is Likely?', *Antiquity*, XLIX, 59–61. Required reading.

Rahtz, P.A. (1979), *The Saxon and Medieval Palaces at Cheddar*, B.A.R. British Series 65, Oxford

Rahtz, P.A. and Hirst S. (1975), *Bordesley Abbey*, Oxford

Raikes, R. (1911), *Water, Weather and Prehistory*, London

Renfrew, C. (ed.) (1974), *British Prehistory, A New Outline*, London

Renfrew, C. and Bahn. P. (1991), *Archaeology: theory, methods and practice*, London

Renfrew, T.M., Monk, M. and Murphy, R. (1976), *First Aid for Seeds*, Hertford

Reynolds, P. (1979), *Iron Age Farm*, London

Richards, J.D. and Ryan, N.S. (1985) *Data Processing in Archaeology*, Cambridge Manuals in Archaeology

Rodwell, W. and K. (1973), 'Rivenhall (Church)', *Current Archaeol*. 36

Rodwell, K. (1976), 'The Archaeological Investigation of Hadstock Church, Essex, An Interim Report', *Antiq. Journal*, LVI, Part I, 55–71

Rodwell, W. (1989), *Church Archaeology*, London

Royal Society (1965), *The Preparation of Scientific Papers*, London

Ryder, M.L. (1969), *Animal Bones in Archaeology*, Oxford

St Joseph, J.K.S. (ed.) (1966), *The Uses of Air Photography*, London

SCAUM (1986), *Health and Safety in Field Archaeology*

Schmidt, H. (1973), 'The Trelleborg House reconsidered', *Med. Archaeol. XVII*, 52–77

Schofield, J. (ed.) (1991), *Interpreting Artefact Scatters*, Oxbow

Simmons, H.C. (1969), *Archaeological Photography*, London

Slosson, E.E. (1928), 'The Science of the City Dump' *Snapshots of Science* in Raport and Wright, 1963, *Archaeology*, New York
– A very early example of the view that archaeology began yesterday.

Society of Antiquaries (1992), *Archaeological Publication Archives and Collections – Towards a National Policy*

Sorrell, A. (1977), 'The Artist and Reconstruction', *Current Archaeology*, 41 November, 177–81
— A valuable statement by the late Alan Sorrell on the aims and methods of the archaeological artist.

Spence, C. (1990), *Archaeological Site Manual*, Museum of London

Steane, K. (1992), *Interpretation of Stratigraphy; a Review of the Art*, Lincoln

Steensberg, A. (1968), *Atlas over Borups Agre*, Copenhagen
— The record of an astounding piece of fieldwork in which the positions of about a million stones and boulders were plotted to demonstrate the pattern of field systems over an area of some 72ha.

Steensberg, A. (1952), *Farms and Water Mills in Denmark during 2000 Years* Copenhagen
— Contains reports of the excavations of three major sites. Bolle, Pebringe and Asa and a smaller site, Nodskovlede. These excavations, made between 1938 and 1940 mark a turning point in the development of medieval archaeology.

Steensberg, A. (1975), *Store Valby*, Copenhagen

Stuiver, M. and Pearson, G.W. (1986), 'High Precision Calibration of the Radiocarbon Time-scale AD1950–500 BC', *Radiocarbon, Vol. 28*, No 2B, 1986

Szmanski, J.E. (1991), *Archaeological Sciences, 1991: Abstracts from the Third National Conference on Archaeological Sciences*, Univ. of York

Taylor, C.C. (1967), 'Whiteparish', *Wilts. Archaeol. Magazine*, 63, 79–102

Taylor, C.C. (1974), *Fieldwork in Medieval Archaeology*, London

Taylor, C.C. (1975), *Fields in the English Landscape*, London

Taylor, R.E. (1987), *Radio-carbon dating: An Archaeological Perspective*, London

Terrell, J. (9171), 'Potsherd rim angles: a simple device', *Antiquity*, XLV

Thompson, F.H. (1976), 'The Excavation of the Roman Amphitheatre at Chester' *Archaeologia*, MCMLXXVI

Thompson, M.W. (1967), *Novgorod the Great, Excavations at the Medieval City*, 1951–62

Trump, D.H. (1971), 'Aids to drawing: sherd radii', *Antiquity*, XLV

Tylecote, R.F. (1962), *Metallurgy in Archaeology*, London

Ucko, P.J. and Dimbleby, G.W. (eds) (1969), *The demonstration and exploitation of plants and animals*, London

Wade, K. (1974), 'Whither Anglo-Saxon Archaeology?' in Rowley, ed., *Anglo-Saxon Settlement and Landscape*, Oxford

Wagner, G.A. (ed.) (1983), *Thermoluminescence Dating*, European Science Foundation

Wainwright, G. (1971), *Durrington Walls, Excavations, 1966–1968*, Report of the Research Committee, Society of Antiquaries of London, XXIX

Wainwright, F.T. (1962) *Archaeology and Place Names and History*, London

Walker, K. (1990), *Guidelines for the Preparation of Excavation Archives for Long Term Storage*, UK. Arch. Soc.

Walle, A. van de, (1961), 'Excavations in the Ancient Centre of Antwerp', *Med. Archaeol.*, V 123–136, Fig. 36
— These important excavations show how slight traces of town houses may be and how walls may simply be built of wattling without corner posts.

Waterman, D.M. (1959), 'Excavations at Lismahon, Co. Down', *Med. Archaeol.* III, 139–76

Watkinson, D (ed.) (1987), *First Aid for Finds* 3rd edition, RESCUE, United Kingdom Institute for Conservation

Webster, G. (1970), *Pottery and Colour Chart*, RESCUE, Worcester

Webster, G. (1974), *Practical Archaeology*, 2nd edition, London

Webster, G. (ed.) (1976), *Romano-British Coarse Pottery. A Student's Guide*, 3rd edition, London

Webster, G. and Woodfield, P. (1966), 'The Old Work at the Public Baths at Wroxeter', *Antiq. Journal*, XLVI, 234–7

Webster, P. (1975), 'Roman and Iron-Age Tankards in Western Britain', *Bulletin of the Board of Celtic Studies*, XXVI, 231–6

Wells, C. (1964), *Bones, Bodies and Disease*, London

Wheeler, R.E.M. (Sir), (1943), 'Maiden Castle, Dorset', *Society of Antiquaries*, London
— A classic excavation report. The first part of the report, in particular is a model of exposition.

Wheeler, R.E.M. (Sir), 1954, *Archaeology from the Earth*, Oxford Reprints in Pelican Books, 1956 and 1961

Williams, D. (1973), 'Flotation at Siraf' *Antiquity*, XLVII, 188, December

Williams, J.C.C. (1969), *Simple Photogrammetry*, London
— A useful introduction to photogrammetry.

Wilson, D. Gay (1973), 'An open letter to archaeologists', *Antiquity*, 47, No. 188, December, 264–8
— A plea for archaeologists to understand the limitations and difficulties of scientific techniques.

Wilson, D.R. (ed.) (1975), *Aerial Reconnaissance for Archaeology*, CBA Research Report No. 12

Wilson, D.R. (1982), *Air Photo Interpretation for Archaeologists*, London

Wincklemann, W. (1958), 'Die Ausgrabungen in der frühmittelalterlichen Siedlung bei Warendorf, *Neue Ausgrabungen in Deutschland*, 492–517

Woolley, L. (1930), *Digging up the Past*, London, Penguin ed. 1954

Young, C.J. (ed.) (1980), *Guidelines for the Processing and Publication of Roman Pottery from Excavations*, Department of the Environment
— An attempt by the DoE and the Study Group for Roman-British Pottery to create and bring into use common standards for examining and recording the masses of pottery commonly found on Romano-British sites.

Index